T0350386

Implementation of Machine Learning Algorithms Using Control–Flow and Dataflow Paradigms

Veljko Milutinović
Indiana University, Bloomington, USA

Nenad Mitić
University of Belgrade, Serbia

Aleksandar Kartelj
University of Belgrade, Serbia

Miloš Kotlar
University of Belgrade, Serbia

A volume in the Advances in
Systems Analysis, Software
Engineering, and High Performance
Computing (ASASEHPC) Book Series

Published in the United States of America by
  IGI Global
  Engineering Science Reference (an imprint of IGI Global)
  701 E. Chocolate Avenue
  Hershey PA, USA 17033
  Tel: 717-533-8845
  Fax: 717-533-8661
  E-mail: cust@igi-global.com
  Web site: http://www.igi-global.com

Library of Congress Cataloging-in-Publication Data

Names: Milutinović, Veljko, author.
Title: Implementation of machine learning algorithms using control-flow and
  dataflow paradigms / by Veljko Milutinovic, Nenad S. Mitic, Aleksandar
  Aleksej Kartelj, and Milos Kotlar.
Description: Hershey, PA : Engineering Science Reference, [2022] | Includes
  bibliographical references and index. | Summary: "This is a reference
  book for experienced professionals, that treats four widely used
  data-mining algorithms in a novel way, offering a basic introduction
  with issues of importance, advantages and disadvantages of these
  algorithms"-- Provided by publisher.
Identifiers: LCCN 2021050298 (print) | LCCN 2021050299 (ebook) | ISBN
  9781799883500 (hardcover) | ISBN 9781799883517 (paperback) | ISBN
  9781799883524 (ebook)
Subjects: LCSH: Data mining. | Algorithms. | Machine learning. | Data flow
  computing.
Classification: LCC QA76.9.D343 M485 2022 (print) | LCC QA76.9.D343
  (ebook) | DDC 006.3/12--dc23/eng/20211206
LC record available at https://lccn.loc.gov/2021050298
LC ebook record available at https://lccn.loc.gov/2021050299

This book is published in the IGI Global book series Advances in Systems Analysis, Software Engineering, and High Performance Computing (ASASEHPC) (ISSN: 2327-3453; eISSN: 2327-3461)

British Cataloguing in Publication Data
A Cataloguing in Publication record for this book is available from the British Library.

All work contributed to this book is new, previously-unpublished material.
The views expressed in this book are those of the authors, but not necessarily of the publisher.

For electronic access to this publication, please contact: eresources@igi-global.com.

Advances in Systems Analysis, Software Engineering, and High Performance Computing (ASASEHPC) Book Series

ISSN:2327-3453
EISSN:2327-3461

Editor-in-Chief: Vijayan Sugumaran Oakland University, USA

MISSION

The theory and practice of computing applications and distributed systems has emerged as one of the key areas of research driving innovations in business, engineering, and science. The fields of software engineering, systems analysis, and high performance computing offer a wide range of applications and solutions in solving computational problems for any modern organization.

The **Advances in Systems Analysis, Software Engineering, and High Performance Computing (ASASEHPC) Book Series** brings together research in the areas of distributed computing, systems and software engineering, high performance computing, and service science. This collection of publications is useful for academics, researchers, and practitioners seeking the latest practices and knowledge in this field.

COVERAGE

- Storage Systems
- Enterprise Information Systems
- Computer System Analysis
- Virtual Data Systems
- Computer Networking
- Performance Modelling
- Metadata and Semantic Web
- Human-Computer Interaction
- Software Engineering
- Parallel Architectures

IGI Global is currently accepting manuscripts for publication within this series. To submit a proposal for a volume in this series, please contact our Acquisition Editors at Acquisitions@igi-global.com or visit: http://www.igi-global.com/publish/.

Titles in this Series

For a list of additional titles in this series, please visit:
www.igi-global.com/book-series/advances-systems-analysis-software-engineering/73689

Technology Road Mapping for Quantum Computing and Engineering
Brojo Kishore Mishra (GIET University, India)
Engineering Science Reference • © 2022 • 305pp • H/C (ISBN: 9781799891833) • US $225.00

Advancing Smarter and More Secure Industrial Applications Using AI, IoT, and Blockchain Technology
Kavita Saini (Galgotias University, India) and Pethuru Raj (Reliance Jio Platforms Ltd., Bangalore, India)
Engineering Science Reference • © 2022 • 309pp • H/C (ISBN: 9781799883678) • US $245.00

Deep Learning Applications for Cyber-Physical Systems
Monica R. Mundada (M.S. Ramaiah Institute of Technology, India) S. Seema (M.S. Ramaiah Institute of Technology, India) Srinivasa K.G. (National Institute of Technical Teachers Training and Research, Chandigarh, India) and M. Shilpa (M.S. Ramaiah Institute of Technology, India)
Engineering Science Reference • © 2022 • 293pp • H/C (ISBN: 9781799881612) • US $245.00

Design, Applications, and Maintenance of Cyber-Physical Systems
Pierluigi Rea (University of Cagliari, Italy) Erika Ottaviano (University of Cassino and Southern Lazio, Italy) José Machado (University of Minho, Portugal) and Katarzyna Antosz (Rzeszow University of Technology, Poland)
Engineering Science Reference • © 2021 • 314pp • H/C (ISBN: 9781799867210) • US $225.00

Methodologies and Applications of Computational Statistics for Machine Intelligence
Debabrata Samanta (Christ University (Deemed), India) Raghavendra Rao Althar (QMS, First American India, Bangalore, India) Sabyasachi Pramanik (Haldia Institute of Technology, India) and Soumi Dutta (Institute of Engineering and Management, Kolkata, India)
Engineering Science Reference • © 2021 • 277pp • H/C (ISBN: 9781799877011) • US $245.00

701 East Chocolate Avenue, Hershey, PA 17033, USA
Tel: 717-533-8845 x100 • Fax: 717-533-8661
E-Mail: cust@igi-global.com • www.igi-global.com

Table of Contents

Preface

This book presents four widely used data mining algorithms with their variations and treats four different general aspects thereof: (a) A basic introduction with issues of importance, advantages and disadvantages, (b) A part on relevant algorithmic details related to the mathematical treatment of the selected four algorithms, (c) A part on possible applications of selected algorithms, with special attention dedicated to machine learning, and (d) A part on fast and energy efficient implementations using a dataflow technology, comparatively with control flow technology; this part shows how to implement these four algorithms on a selected Controlflow machine and on a selected Dataflow machine.

The four basic algorithms presented in this book are: Neural Network, Rule Induction, Tree Algorithm, and Density-Based Algorithm. These four algorithms were selected based on the frequency of their appearance at Google Scholar and similar search engines. Many other related algorithms were derived from these four ones. Consequently, these four represent an excellent starting point for studies of DataMining. Mastering these four algorithms and their implementation in the new DataFlow paradigm enables easy mastering of a plethora of other DataMining algorithms, as well as their usage in new application domains, which were unreachable before, due to prohibitively high data volumes, or due to a prohibitively high power dissipation. This book could be used by practitioners, teachers, students, and all those interested to do implementations in the new and promising technology: DataFlow. Specific implementations are based on the Maxeler technology, for the following reasons: It proves to be both fast and energy-efficient, it is available via Amazon AWS, it is/was used by giants in the business of finances, like J. P. Morgan, CME (Chicago Mercantile Exchange), Hitachi, and CitiBank, and finally, it is/was used in a large number of other applications, in Science, GeoPhysics, Security, and Machine Learning.

Introduction and conclusion provide insight about the main topics covered in this book. Chapter 1 introduces data mining and provides definition of algorithms used for extraction of hidden knowledge from data. Also, it provides overview of relevant references in data mining field according to the open literature. Chapter 2 introduces controlflow paradigm, presents key aspects of the paradigm and relevant applications in the classification domain. Chapter 3 introduces dataflow paradigm, presents key aspects of the paradigm compared to the controlflow paradigm, and presents relevant applications in the classification domain. Chapter 4 presents scientific applications of data mining with overview of the relevant literature. Chapter 5 presents industry-based applications of data mining with overview of the relevant literature. Chapter 6 to 9 present essential optimization mechanisms on the dataflow paradigm for four selected algorithms: Neural Network, Rule Induction, Tree Algorithm, and Density-Based Algorithm. Also, they discuss implementational details of the presented algorithms, and discuss optimizations that could been achieved by using introduced constructs. Chapter 10 presents general optimization techniques for the ultimate dataflow paradigm using systolic arrays and suboptimal operations.

Veljko Milutinović
Indiana University, Bloomington, USA

Introduction

This book presents data mining in general, its algorithms, and applications. Data mining presents the key mechanism for extracting hidden knowledge from data. Depending on the environment and deployment location, the hidden knowledge could be extracted in the cloud environment with unlimited resources, or on edge devices with minimal resources. Proliferation of data in diverse industries presents suitable environment for extracting valuable data from unstructured repositories. By using data mining, patterns and hidden knowledge could be extracted. By using statistical and probabilistic machine learning algorithms, it is possible to extract behavior patterns from data. According to the open literature, the following four machine learning algorithms are the most common ones for data mining: Neural Network, Rule Induction, Tree Algorithm, and Density-Based Algorithm. The algorithms are analyzed through two computing paradigms. Machine learning presents broad field that is used besides data mining for image processing, natural language processing, and many others.

Applications of data mining are present in different environments and deployment locations. Recently, size of data publicly available has rapidly increased which led to utilization of alternative paradigms for processing such amounts of data. Control-flow paradigm presents conventional paradigm for processing that is suitable for general purposes. Dataflow paradigm presents a novel paradigm that relies on execution graphs and reconfigurable hardware that could achieve acceleration.

The main goal of this book is to introduce data mining techniques based on machine learning algorithms, and to present an alternative computing paradigm for processing large amounts of data, such as dataflow paradigm. Advanced optimization constructs presented in this book could be applied in machine learning to mitigate general application problems, such as matrix tailing, complex tensor operations.

Chapter 1
Introduction to Data Mining

ABSTRACT

This chapter presents four widely used data mining algorithms and treats their four aspects: essence, applications, advantages, and disadvantages. The algorithms are neural networks, rule induction, tree algorithms, and neighborhood-based reasoning. This chapter is a basic introduction with an overview of important issues. It includes links to relevant algorithmic details related to the mathematical treatment of the selected four algorithms explained in Chapter 2, links to issues on fast and energy-efficient implementations using the dataflow technology of Maxeler, which is explained in Chapter 3, and links to the part on possible applications of selected algorithms treated in Chapter 4.

INTRODUCTION

An important question to answer at the very beginning of this chapter is to explain the major differences between datamining and semantic web. In both cases, the goal is the same: Efficient retrieval of knowledge from large databases or from the Internet (in this context, knowledge is defined as a synergistic interaction of data and links between data). The major difference is in the placement of complexity.

In the case of datamining, data and knowledge are represented using relatively simple mechanisms (typically, HTML, or derivatives thereof) and no metadata (data about data) are included. Consequently, during the retrieval process, relatively com- plex algorithms have to be used. This means that the

DOI: 10.4018/978-1-7998-8350-0.ch001

complexity is placed into the retrieval request time, and that the complexity related to the system design time is relatively low - only the code of the algorithm has to be injected into the system.

In the case of semantic web, data and knowledge are represented using relatively complex mechanisms (like XML or derivatives thereof) with lots of metadata included (a byte of data could be accompanied with megabytes of metadata); with the help of quality metadata, even the simplest algorithm could do the retrieval success- fully. Consequently, at the knowledge retrieval time, relatively simple algorithms could be used, meaning that the complexity of the retrieval request time is relatively low. This means that the complexity is placed into the system design time, when the metadata structures get formed; the larger the metadata, the more work at the system design time (Agrawal, 2000) (Halbwachs, Caspi, Raymond, & Pilaud, 1991).

The above tells clearly about the stress in textbooks that cover the two tangential subjects: When teaching datamining, the stress should be on algorithms and the related math, as demonstrated in the second part of this book. When teaching se- mantic web, the stress should be on tools for creation and treatment of metadata. Consequently, this book concentrates on algorithms, while the tools are outside the scope of this book. The selection of algorithms presented here is based on their popularity, using the Google Scholar as the criterion of popularity. The popularity of a particular datamining algorithm is highly correlated with possible application domains of that algorithm, as discussed in the third part of this book.

The major issues in datamining are discussed in the papers (Berry & Linoff, Berry, M. J., & Linoff, G. S.) (Tan, Chawla, Ho, & Bailey, 2012) (Hand, 2007) (Hall, et al., 2009) (Fayyad, Piatetsky-Shapiro, & Smyth, 1996) (Tan, Steinbach, & Kumar, Introduction to data mining, 2006) (Witten & Frank, 2002) (Berson & Thearling, 1999). They are: (a) Effective uncovering of the hidden knowledge, in conditions when the search space is n-p complete, and (b) Effective development of a multidimensional interface that enables easy comprehension of the obtained results. These two major goals are achieved through the interaction of several system software layers: (a) A database at the bottom, followed by (b) layers responsible for artificial intelligence and automated presentation.

The important issues are presented using appropriate figures (Jovanovic, Milutinovic, 2002).

The history of datamining did not start in recent years; it started long ago. For example, the researchers that deciphered the ancient alphabets portrayed in Figure 1, did use the same datamining algorithms as those described in

2

Figure 1. Selected ancient alphabets data mined by human brain.

this book; only, for the processing, they did not use modern computers, but their brains. As indicated in Figure 2, this means that Galileo Galilei and Heinrich Schwabe, who discovered the periodicities related to sun rotation and sun spots, would not had become famous, had they been born at the time after the introduction of datamining tools; that same knowledge for which they became famous, could be uncovered even with the simplest datamining software working on the top of data obtained from a telescope directed to sun.

One has to keep in mind the differences between data mining on one side, and techniques like Data Warehousing, AdHoc Query, OnLine Analytical Processing (OLAP), or Data Visualization, on the other side. In theory, datamining is all that plus much more, as it will be shown in the rest of this book.

In its essence, datamining represents automated extraction of predictive information from various data sources. In its most sophisticated form, datamining is not working on the top of data randomly accessed from memory, but on the top of data streamed through communication lines. This is why the dataflow paradigm is well suited for datamining, since it allows effective analysis of data streams, which will be demonstrated in the last part of this book, comparatively with the control flow paradigm.

Overall, for any algorithm, the energy saving ratio is basically equal to the clock frequency ratio, which is typically about 20x, for a number of different implementations (for example, in a number of compared systems, the control flow clock was 4GHz, while the dataflow clock was 200MHz). The

Figure 2. Repetitive solar activities that could be effectively uncovered using modern datamining software.

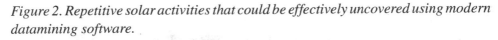
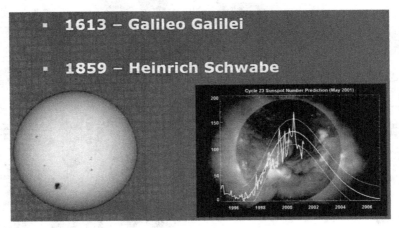

computational complexity is related to the programming model used. Over the few past years, the programming models of the two paradigms are steadily converging to each other. As far as space saving, across most applications, the space ratio is based on the thing that the ALU part of control flow engines is a lot smaller than the ALU part of dataflow engines.

Generally, there are six major application areas for datamining: (a) Data Description and Summarization, (b) Data Segmentation, (c) Data Classification, (d) Concept Description, (e) Prediction or Regression, and (f) Dependency Analysis.

Data Description and Summarization aims at concise description of data characteristics. It provides the user with an overview of the data structure. It is considered to be at a lower end of scale of problem types, and is typically a sub-goal.

Data Segmentation separates the data into meaningful sub-groups or classes. It could be a problem for itself or just a step in solving a larger problem. It can be automatic, semi-automatic, or manual, because in a number of problems the best results are obtained if the level of automatization is minimized.

Data Classification always starts from the assumption that objects do exist with characteristics that belong to different classes. Segmentation can provide labels that characterize data or even restrict access to selected data, as indicated by the associated labels.

Concept Description defines an understandable essence of concepts or classes. According to some researchers, this is the most sophisticated application of datamining. It could enable search by concept match, rather than search my semantic match. Prediction finds the numerical value of the target attribute for unseen objects. In some way, it is similar to classification, except that discrete becomes continuous. In other words, discrete points are interpolated into a continuous curve, which is used for extrapolation, to reach a future value of interest.

Dependency Analysis creates a model that describes significant dependencies between data items and related events. A special case of dependency analysis is creating associations. In other words, if two events happen, sometimes the question is if they are correlated or not.

NEURAL NETWORKS

Neural Networks characterize the processed data with a single numeric value. They enable efficient modeling of large and complex problems. Neural Networks are a mathematical concept based on the analogy with biological neurons that are grouped in layers.

One mathematical neuron is presented in Figure 3. A vector of inputs (I) is applied to a set of input links (W), the input values are multiplied with the weights of the links, a weighted sum is formed, it gets applied to the transfer function in the body of the neuron, and the output value is created.

The major issue of Neural Networks is the training process. During that process, computer time is spent and no results are obtained, as far as the user problem is concerned; only the Neural Network is trained and tuned to the problem. In the set of Figures 3-5, steps of the iterative training process are presented, indicating that lots of time elapses before we can stamp the system TRAINED!

In conclusion, the advantage is that we can solve even the problems for which we do not know a closed-form algorithm, and the disadvantage is that the training process takes time. This determines the typical application areas for Neural Networks: Ideal for new and unknown problems that are not latency sensitive.

TREE ALGORITHMS

Decision Trees are based on a series of rules that lead to a value that determines a decision. In essence, the algorithm does iterative splitting of data into

Figure 3. Training process in Neural Networks: Step 1 (forming the difference between the trained and an untrained Neural Network).

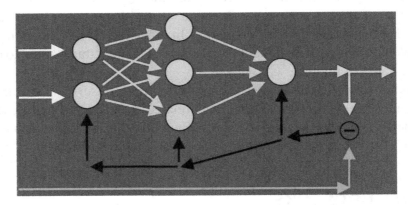

discrete groups, maximizing the distance between possible decision options at each split. The splits could be univariate (IF-THEN-ELSE) of multivariate (CASE). Since, in theory, the process could continue indefinitely, stopping rules are required.

An example is given in Figure 6. The example is related to banking and the decision making related to approving a loan to a customer. The bottom-line of the example is that the married persons are more likely to obtain a loan, since they are more to be trusted:)

Algorithms of this type are difficult to develop, since they are useful only when the tree is large enough for the given problem. This means that

Figure 4. Training process in Neural Networks: Step 2 (updating the function in the neuron body and/or the weights in the neuron synapses).

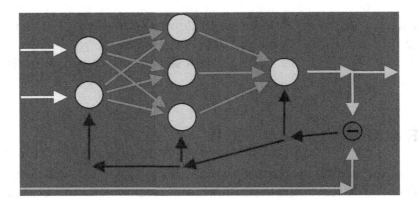

Figure 5. Training process in Neural Networks: Step 3 (reaching the end of training condition).

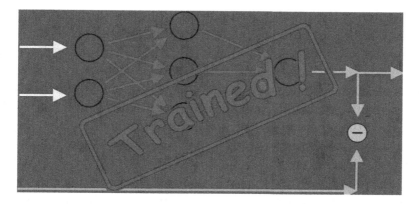

the development process is time-consuming and implies the interaction with colleagues from many other disciplines.

Algorithm of this type potentially have an important advantage: If the decision tree is properly developed, the traversing of the tree goes fast, conditionally speaking, in LOG N steps, meaning that a relatively sophisticated problem could be solved relatively quickly.

In conclusion, the advantage is the speed (which in many applications translates into a low system latency). The disadvantage is that only large enough trees could be useful. Consequently, the applications should be limited to domains in which the listed advantages are important and the listed disadvantages do not matter.

Figure 6. An Example of Decision Tree: Decision making in a banking application.

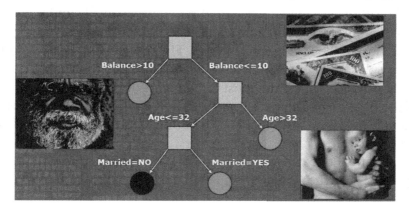

RULE INDUCTION

Rule Induction is a method of deriving a set of rules to classify data. This algorithm builds a set of independent rules that are unlikely to form a tree. Rules may not cover all possible situations, and rules are allowed to conflict with each other, in which case the rules definitely cannot form a tree. The fact that rules could be opposing each other, brings this approach closer to reality. In reality, especially in issues related to social domains, different people have different opinions; yet, at the end of the day, they typically come to a conclusion and derive a decision (they select parliament members, the best song of a festival, etc.).

An example of Rule Induction that includes two opposing rules is given in Figure 1.7. The first and the last rule are opposed to each other. The same figure also points to an important issue of algorithms of this type: Some events may have a high impact, but a relatively low probability. For example: Given the scenario in the lower left corner of Figure 7, the question is what is the next possible scenario in the logical sequence of a decision making process. The point is that events of an extremely low probability sometimes do happen, as indicated in the lower right corner of Figure 7.

An advantage of this algorithm and the related ones is that one could mimic the reality more effectively, while a disadvantage is that some high-impact events may be overseen, if the rules do not recognize their importance, and the probability of their happening is relatively small. These two facts determine the major application domains of Rule Induction.

NEIGHBORHOOD ALGORITHMS

These algorithms use the knowledge of previously solved similar problems, when attempting to solve a new problem. They assign a class to a group, based on where most of the K neighbors belong. The first step is to find the suitable measure for distance between attributes of the data, since that helps determine the neighborhood. This is the most critical part of the algorithm, since the size of the final results could be very sensitive to the size of neighborhood. An example is given in Figure 8, where the size of the neighborhood is marked with circles.

From Figure 8 one can see the following: (a) In three circles with events of only one color, the decision is easy to derive; (b) In the fourth circle in

Figure 7. An Example of Rule Induction: The first and the third rule are contradictory and the events with an extremely low probability sometimes do happen.

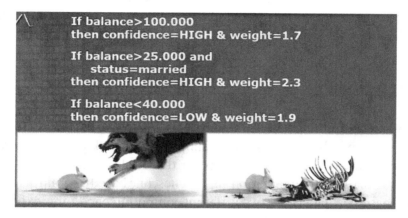

which the balls are only black or white, the decision is very sensitive to the size of the neighborhood; for the given neighborhood, white balls represent the majority; for a smaller or a bigger neighborhood, black balls represent the majority; (c) In the fifth circle, we have three balls of three different colors, meaning that this algorithm is not able to derive a solid decision in that particular case.

An advantage of this algorithm is that it can be used to reduce the problem, by eliminating quickly the obvious cases, so much less data have

Figure 8. An Example of a Neighborhood Algorithm: It is obvious that the neighborhood size is the most sensitive issue.

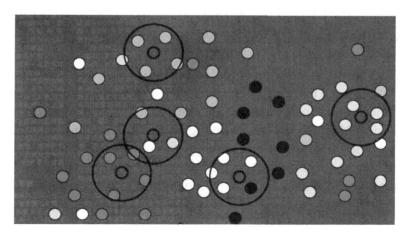

to be forwarded to a more sophisticated algorithm. A disadvantage is that it is very sensitive to the size of the neighborhood, as indicated in the fourth circle above. These two facts (one advantage and disadvantage) determine the applications for which this algorithm is suitable.

CONCLUSION

Many other datamining algorithms do exist, and the interested reader is referred to many other sources on the subject. This book puts stress on only four algorithms, because the stress is on the implementation, and on the comparison of two implementation approaches, one based on control flow and the other based on data flow (two different computing paradigms expected to synergize a lot in the future). The implementations presented later in this book imply that the CRISP model is used on higher software levels, as indicated in Figure 9, which is self-explanatory, and will not be further elaborated here.

If the implementation needs not only speedup, but also power saving and size saving, then dataflow implementations are preferred (Lee & Messerschmitt) (Lee & Messerschmitt, Static scheduling of synchronous data flow programs for digital signal processing, 1987) (Rapps & Weyuker, 1985). If flexibility is an issue, then FPGA-based implementations are preferred over the implementations based on systolic arrays (Buck & Lee, 1993) (Dennis, 1974) (Dennis, Data flow supercomputers, 1980) (Dennis & Gao, Multithreaded architectures: principles, projects, and issues, 1994) (Frankl & Weyuker, 1988) (Kam & Ullman, 1977).

SELECTED REFERENCES ON DATAMINING AND DATAFLOW

For a further study on the subject of dataflow, for convenience of the reader, in the first reference part of this chapter, we list the 10 most referenced texts (articles and books), using the number of Google Scholar citations at the time of writing this text. In the second reference part of this chapter, we list 10 texts (articles and books) on the dataflow subject (these include also the early research by professors Jack Dennis and Arvind of MIT). In order to present the most relevant papers in the open literature, we conducted search

Figure 9. The CRISP Model with its six stages.

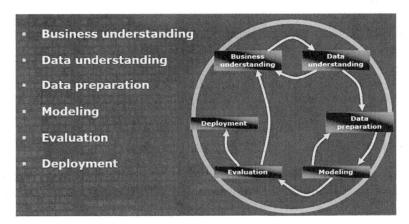

- **Business understanding**
- **Data understanding**
- **Data preparation**
- **Modeling**
- **Evaluation**
- **Deployment**

using Google Scholar database, where we focused on keywords related to machine learning, data mining, dataflow, acceleration.

REVIEW QUESTIONS

This section provides questions for better understanding of the key aspects of the chapter.

1. What is data mining?
2. List 3 use cases of data mining?
3. What are common techniques used for data mining based on machine learning algorithms?
4. What is the main difference between controlflow and dataflow paradigms?

ACKNOWLEDGMENT

The authors are thankful to Nemanja Jovanovic and Valentina Milenkovic for their creative approach to the generation of self explanatory figures along the lines of the principle "one figure is worth one thousand words" (the first presentation of these figures and the related tutorial dates back to the year 2000 and the NATO summer school in L'Aquila, Abruzzo, Italy).

REFERENCES

Agrawal, R. (2000). Privacy-preserving data mining. In *ACM SIGMOD International Conference on Management of Data* (pp. 439-450). ACM.

Berry, M. J., & Linoff, G. S. (n.d.). *Data mining techniques: for marketing, sales, and customer relationship management*. John Wiley & Sons.

Berson, A., & Thearling, K. (1999). *Building data mining applications for CRM*. McGraw-Hill.

Buck, J. T., & Lee, E. A. (1993). Scheduling dynamic dataflow graphs with bounded memory using the token flow model. *IEEE International Conference on Acoustics, Speech, and Signal Processing*, 429-432.

Dennis, J. B. (1974). First version of a data flow procedure language. In *Programming Symposium*. Springer.

Dennis, J. B. (1980). Data flow supercomputers. *Computer*, 48–56.

Dennis, J. B., & Gao, G. R. (1994). Multithreaded architectures: principles, projects, and issues. *Multithreaded Computer Architecture*, 1-72.

Fayyad, U., Piatetsky-Shapiro, G., & Smyth, P. (1996). From data mining to knowledge discovery in databases. *AI Magazine*, 37–37.

Frankl, P. G., & Weyuker, E. J. (1988). An applicable family of data flow testing criteria. *IEEE Transactions on Software Engineering*, 1483–1498.

Halbwachs, N., Caspi, P., Raymond, P., & Pilaud, D. (1991). The synchronous data flow programming language LUSTRE. *Proceedings of the IEEE*, 1305-1320.

Hall, M., Frank, E., Holmes, G., Pfahringer, B., Reutemann, P., & Witten, I. H. (2009). The WEKA data mining software: An update. *ACM SIGKDD Explorations Newsletter*.

Hand, D. J. (2007). Principles of data mining. *Drug Safety*, *30*(7), 621–622. doi:10.2165/00002018-200730070-00010 PMID:17604416

Jovanovic, N., Milutinovic, V., & Obradovic, Z. (2002, September). Foundations of predictive data mining. In 6th Seminar on Neural Network Applications in Electrical Engineering (pp. 53-58). IEEE.

Kam, J. B., & Ullman, J. D. (1977). Monotone data flow analysis frameworks. *Acta Informatica*, 305–317.

Lee, E. A., & Messerschmitt, D. G. (1987). Static scheduling of synchronous data flow programs for digital signal processing. *IEEE Transactions on Computers*, 24–35.

Lee, E. A., & Messerschmitt, D. G. (n.d.). Synchronous data flow. *Proceedings of the IEEE*, 1235-1245.

Rapps, S., & Weyuker, E. J. (1985). Selecting software test data using data flow information. *IEEE Transactions on Software Engineering*, 367–375.

Tan, P. N., Chawla, S., Ho, C. K., & Bailey, J. (2012). Advances in Knowledge Discovery and Data Mining, Part II. In *16th Pacific-Asia Conference, PAKDD 2012*. Springer.

Tan, P. N., Steinbach, M., & Kumar, V. (2006). *Introduction to data mining*. Pearson education.

Witten, I. H., & Frank, E. (2002). Data mining: Practical machine learning tools and techniques with Java implementations. *SIGMOD Record*, *31*(1), 76–77. doi:10.1145/507338.507355

KEY TERMS AND DEFINITIONS

ALU: Arithmetic logic unit in processor.

Data Mining: Technique for extracting hidden knowledge from data.

Hidden Knowledge: Output of data mining techniques where valuable data are extracted from unstructured data.

Layer: One layer in neural network consisted of many neurons.

Neuron: Neuron in one layer of neural network.

Chapter 2
Classification Algorithms and Control-Flow Implementation

ABSTRACT

Supervised classification algorithms exploit many features that are tightly related to control-flow architecture. This reduces the possibility of applying these algorithms to dataflow architecture. This chapter makes an overview of some features characteristic to various classification algorithms that cannot be implemented on dataflow architecture. The chapter provides examples of applying various classification algorithms to three datasets with different types of material.

INTRODUCTION

Supervised classification (in further text only classification) is the most commonly used method among all the methods developed in the area of data mining and machine learning, with a large number of developed classification algorithms used to solve problems in various fields. The emergence of new areas in which the application of data classification is required relatively quickly leads to the development of new algorithms suitable for application, as it is the case with big data or data streaming, for example. All these algorithms are based on the control-flow paradigm, with the idea that the implementation is performed on computers with von Neumann architecture.

The development of computers with dataflow architecture began thirty years after the emergence of computers with control-flow architecture. Due

DOI: 10.4018/978-1-7998-8350-0.ch002

to low use (as the space for application had already been occupied by control-flow computers, especially for commercial purposes), lower intensity of development, and significant and well-developed competition (control-flow computers), a relatively small amount of software has been developed for dataflow computers as a target platform. This is especially visible in various (mathematically based) algorithms, even in algorithms related to the field of classification. Although some of the ideas on which the currently developed classification algorithms are based can be applied to the dataflow paradigm with minor modifications, there are a number of features and characteristics of algorithms that are essential and directly related to computer architecture and corresponding software support. If the development of dataflow computers continues at the same rate with the momentum it gained in recent years, it is possible to foresee a growth in the number of algorithms which will with minor changes be suitable for mapping to the dataflow architecture. Currently, the dataflow software support that would allow solving various problems is poor compared to the software developed for the control-flow paradigm.

A large number of applications require classification but for various reasons, even to a certain extent, cannot be implemented on a purely dataflow architecture (an architecture that does not include control-flow components such as the control-flow CPU). The reasons for the impossibility of simple implementation of algorithms can be divided into several groups. The first group is related to data types that cannot be represented on dataflow computers. The need for these types of data arises during the classification of:

- text data (text classification as part of text mining);
- multimedia data (images, sound, hybrid material, etc.);
- data based on specific data properties (e.g. working with time series);
- materials contained in databases (e.g. relational databases);
- categorical and discrete data;
- non-existent data, which causes problems during work.

The second group is related to the methods on which algorithms or their parts are based. This group includes:

- Preprocessing and preparation of input material. Preprocessing can involve different types of dimensional reductions, sampling, class balancing, normalization, discretization, and so on, as well as work with multidimensional data of different types and structures.

- The need for complex mathematical calculations. Such calculations are often performed via built-in functions from software libraries (e.g., various statistical calculations or activation functions in neural network nodes).
- The need for classification in a distributed environment.
- Use of methods that have different execution requirements, such as classification through association rules.
- Variation of different algorithm parameters and hyperparameter tuning.
- Visual classification of materials.

The third group of constraints is related to algorithms that require multiple readings of input data, the need for different data flows—reverting to previous steps, large memory requirements of the control-flow algorithm, and insufficient hardware capacity on dataflow (insufficient number of dataflow nodes to implement deep learning neural networks), etc.

Some of these features and methods will be explained below in more detail. The text itself does not contain a detailed description or overview of existing classification algorithms (a detailed description of classification algorithms can be found in (Aggarwal, 2015), but indicates the properties that are essentially related to today's widespread control-flow paradigm. These properties represent a restriction that prevents the direct mapping of most currently existing algorithms and their notation consistent with the use of the dataflow paradigm.

The general conclusion that can be drawn is that if the application of the classification method aims to solve a real problem, then the assistance of the control-flow component is necessary, with limited use (pure) dataflow components in those places where they can contribute to increased efficiency, such as parallelism or lower power consumption.

The rest of the chapter is organized as follows. Section 2.1 presents some problems related to the classification of material with different data type attributes. In Section 2.2, we briefly describe text mining and role of classification algorithms used in this process. Section 2.3 presents some requirements for the ensemble learning process, which is frequently used for increasing the quality of results. Section 2.4 includes a list of some other features that appear in the classification process. Section 2.5 includes a short overview of algorithms and section 2.6 presents the comparative results of their application to various input material.

CLASSIFICATION, CONTROL-FLOW, DATAFLOW, AND DATA TYPE ATTRIBUTES

In the process of classification, an input dataset is divided into two parts: training dataset and test dataset[1]. Each dataset consists of several *instances* (records), where each record consists of several *attributes* (variables, fields). Among them, one of the attributes stands out, and it is called the *target* attribute. This attribute is dependent on the remaining ones and this characteristic is used as the basis of the prediction process. The remaining attributes are called *predictors*. The goal of the classification process is to construct a model for predicting the value of the target attribute based on the value of predictors.

In general, the type of attributes depends on the domains of their values. The attributes whose values are numerical are called numerical (continuous) attributes, while attributes with non-numerical domains are called categorical[2]. If the target attribute is categorical, the process of prediction is called *classification*, and the target attribute is called the *class attribute*. Otherwise, when the target attribute is numerical, the process of predicting its values is called *regression*. The prediction model is constructed based on the training dataset using an algorithm. The verification of the constructed model is performed by applying the model on a set of testing records to obtain the predicting value, which is then compared to the actual value of the target attribute.

The efficiency of the chosen algorithm depends on both the amount of data and the type of predictor attributes. Some algorithms accept only discretized values of continuous variables, which is the reason why they automatically discretize continuous predictors into ordinal categories. Discretization is usually performed by division into intervals of equal length, intervals with an equal number of values (with or without using reorders weighting), by using MDLP (minimum description length principle), etc.

On the other hand, algorithms in which mathematical expressions are calculated cannot use categorical values in the original form. Instead, they are coded in the form of binary vectors. If an attribute has x different values (categories), then its value in the current record is represented using the vector of length x. Each unique value is presented as vector with 1 at exactly one position, while others are filled with zeroes. Vector $(1, 0, 0)$ represents the first unique value, $(0, 1, 0, 0)$ is the second one, etc. The obtained vectors are used in further calculations.

These prerequisites for using attributes are a major obstacle to the implementation of algorithms on dataflow computers. Even if algorithms perform a simple comparison of categorical values (which is most common in algorithms based on decision trees), records with categorical attributes (which can be of arbitrary length) require more space for storage and operation. Representation of records in the form of multidimensional vectors is also an obstacle due to the impossibility of efficient representation and processing of vectors on dataflow machines. Some of the predictor attributes that have a specific basic type (e.g., date/time data) require the existence of special date/time arithmetic (which exists in the software on control-flow computers) in order to work with them. The problem is even more pronounced if one of the predictors of the attribute is multimedia data (image, sound) that must be reprocessed and presented in the form of structured data. Unlike control-flow computers, software and hardware on (purely) dataflow computers do not have mechanisms for storing and processing different types of data and transforming them into a form suitable for use in classification algorithms. For these reasons, there are still few classification algorithms on dataflow computers and cases in which they can effectively process data to the same extent as in the control-flow paradigm.

TEXT CLASSIFICATION

Text classification is just one of the steps in the field of text mining. One of the informal definitions of text mining is obtaining useful information from large collections of texts. In order to better understand the place of text classification in the text mining process, as well as the reasons why text classification algorithms are executed exclusively on computers based on the control-flow paradigm, the following text will briefly present some characteristics of the text mining process itself.

Throughout history, communication and information exchange have been conducted in natural language. Information written in this way formed the basis of the development of civilization and described various human activities. Thanks to the development of technology and the exchange of data over the internet, there has been an enormous increase in the amount of available information in the last twenty years. A significant part of this data are written (completely or partially) in natural language. Data on social networks and web pages are also written in one of the natural languages. Considering the importance of the information contained in such material, there is a need to develop methods (text mining) that would allow their efficient processing and analysis. Text mining is applied in various fields: artificial intelligence, medicine, biology, data science, banking, network traffic analysis (e-mail, spam detection, military affairs), marketing (especially electronic advertising), etc. A notable example are the large search engines on the internet that provide answers to various types of queries that mostly relate to the terms found in the texts.

Text mining is a multidisciplinary field that involves different techniques related to different aspects of data. Typical text mining tasks are (Hudík, 2015; Liu, Shang, & Han. 2017; Miner et al, 2012):

- Information retrieval—retrieving documents that include information needed from a large collection of documents. Information extraction—extracting structured information or relations from unstructured texts.
- Text categorization and classification—categorizing/classifying a document or its part to one or more predefined categories.
- Text summarization—finding the synopsis of a long section of a text to generate a significantly shorter summary of the document(s).
- Extracting the semantic meaning of documents—identifying hidden topics, concepts, analyzing sentiments, emotions, and opinions.
- Clustering—grouping documents according to their similarity.
- Association mining—finding associations between discovered/predefined concepts or terms in texts.
- Machine translation—automatically converting a text written in one language into a text in another language.
- Bioinformatics/biomedical text mining—mining bioinformatics/biomedical information from bioinformatics material or a biomedical text.

Many of these techniques originate from data mining/machine learning. The first thing to be taken into account is the fact that classical algorithms are designed to work with structured data. As textual data are mostly unstructured, the first step is to extract structured information from unstructured text. Although classical algorithms can recognize syntactic constructions and build links between documents based on them, they are oriented exclusively to the form of raw character strings and quite often do not give good results.

In order to perform efficient analysis, it is necessary to connect information from different documents using various analytical methods for extracting information. The documents that are processed usually contain unstructured textual (categorical, non-numerical) data written in one of the natural languages. Constructions in texts carry a certain meaning (semantics), which is sometimes necessary for correct information extraction. The overview of semantic issues of text mining is discussed in (Stavrianou et al, 2007). Text mining involves the analysis of both syntax and semantics of materials using a dual approach: (1) machine learning methods applied to formalized text representation (often written using mathematical methods), and (2) natural language processing (NLP) to establish links between (formal) elements in a document. The output of the algorithms is a model that can be used to analyze, find patterns, and predict outcomes on new material.

One of the challenges in the simple application of data mining methods is that natural language (including semantics) cannot be completely correctly formalized. If we want to formalize a set of documents, one of the possible solutions is to single out all the words that appear in them, and form a vector of words ("bag of words"), while storing information about which word appears and how many times it appears in one of the documents. There are situations in which the direct application of DM techniques to such structured textual data may not lead to correct results or even produce the opposite effect (Li & Liu, 2003). The reasons for this are the following:

- Vectors formed in this way are usually very rare because one document does not have to contain all the words that appear in other documents. Also, a large number of words appear in each of the documents (which increases the dimension of the vector), but are irrelevant in the process of extracting information (for example, the conjunctions and, or, ..., numbers one, two, etc.).
- An enormous number of words appear in a large number of documents. If word combinations were also taken into account (which occurs quite often in natural languages), the number of word/combination and the size of the vector would further increase.
- Vectors can be formed only from words that exist in dictionaries. This would not result in significant savings because dictionaries often contain several hundred thousand words. Even if only words that are used effectively were included, a vector of several tens of thousands of dimensions would be obtained, which would prevent efficient processing. On the other hand, the distribution of words in texts is not uniform. Only a small number of words (which occur more than once) really determine the meaning of the text, while a larger number of

words occurs relatively rarely and usually has very little or no impact on the information contained in the document.

- Some words are ambiguous, while at the same time there are different words that have the same meaning (homonyms and synonyms). Moreover, the same word can have different meanings depending on the context. This further complicates the construction of data mining models with strictly mathematical basis.
- Texts often contain noise, i.e. words or even sentences that are unnecessary or represent a kind of allegory or sarcasm that formally has a completely opposite meaning. In addition, texts contain typographical and syntactic errors, as well as incorrect marking (e.g., incorrect text below the image).
- In some texts, when it is necessary to explicitly mark certain information, this has not been done. This is especially true when talking about sensitive topics and when the authors are afraid to label the situation in the right way. In this case, the reader is asked to draw their own conclusions ("reading between the lines").
- Sometimes in the case of formal consideration or enumeration of terms, it is difficult to get the right information. For example, hotel descriptions given by tourists on the internet or social networks are dominated by positive reviews. However, for potential readers, negative information is sometimes more relevant than a large number of positive comments, which may be produced by a large number of bots (human or machine).

Due to these issues, when preparing material for text classification, one should take into account the concepts that appear in the text, their categories, possible semantic dependencies, and possible hidden meanings. A review of text classification algorithms is given in (Kowsari et al, 2019), while a comprehensive description of the text mining process can be found in (Aggarwal, & Zhai., 2012) and (Zong, Xia, & Zhang., 2021).

Related to these conditions, text classification and the complete text mining process are supported exclusively on computer systems based on the control-flow paradigm.

ENSEMBLE LEARNING

Ensemble learning is not an algorithm but a technique that contains a set of classifiers that "perform together" to achieve a better result. In principle, there is no classifier (algorithm) that gives the best results for any input material. Different classifiers have different bases and different hypotheses used in model building. The basic idea is simple: combine different classifiers and choose the best from each. For each of the classes for which classification is performed, prediction will be taken from the model that gives the most accurate prediction for that class. A prerequisite for a combination of classifiers to be successful is their mutual independence; in addition, their accuracy should be greater than random guessing. Otherwise, if the classifiers are dependent and give similar results, their combination will not lead to an increase in the accuracy of the final result. Moreover, if basic classifiers have poor accuracy (less than 50%, or worse than random guessing), their combination cannot produce a satisfactory result.

Individual classifiers (models obtained by different classification algorithms) can be strong and weak. Strong classifiers are those that have an arbitrarily small prediction error, while weak classifiers are those whose accuracy is only a slightly higher than random guessing. A precise classifier can be obtained by the ensemble method and based on several weak classifiers if they are mutually independent and their models are not mutually correlated. In the result, the class assigned to the input record can be obtained with "voting" methods, i.e. the class label that receives the highest number of votes among classifiers. Alternatively, the class with the highest probability or highest mean probability in a set of classifiers can also be assigned as a class label. As in all other classification methods, ensemble learning contains training data for model construction and a test that is used to verify the obtained model.

Ensemble learning provides a better model for at least two reasons:

- The expected error of an ensemble model is smaller than the error of its individual component models. The reason is that we do not know in advance which classifier has the best prediction when applied to previously unseen data. Therefore, we make a model which includes many difference classifiers with the hope that at least one of them will fit future data.
- Using several classifiers in the ensemble overcomes the problem of taking wrong settings (hypotheses) on the basis of which the model is constructed. By combining several classifiers, ensemble learning is flexible and combines several possible hypotheses to get the best one, with the best hypothesis not having to match any of the initial ones.

An additional reason for an ensemble of weak classifiers is that it is easier to construct more weak classifiers than a single strong one. The classifiers used in an ensemble do not have to be of the same type. The ensemble of methods works better with unstable classifiers that are sensitive to slight changes in the training set, such as decision trees, neural networks, and classifiers based on rules.

Ensemble learning techniques can be divided into four large groups according to the activities carried out in the training phase:

- Techniques in which the set of input data is changed. Multiple training sets are formed by selecting instances from the initial dataset based on certain criteria. At the same time, the distribution and the way of choosing instances can change with each choice. The resulting classifier is formed by applying the same classification algorithm to each of the training sets. The most prominent representatives of this group of techniques are bagging and boosting.
  - *Bagging* (Bootstrap AGGregatING) is a technique that generates data for testing by repeated sampling records from an input dataset. Sampling is done with replacement and according to uniform distribution. Each of the initial (bootstrap) sets formed in this way has the same cardinality as the original set. On average, the training sample contains approximately 63% of the initial dataset of N records because each sample was selected with probability $1-(1-1/N)^N$. If N is large enough, the probability converges to $1-1/e \approx 0.632$. When such model is applied to dataset testing, class labels are assigned according to selected criteria (voting, high probability, etc.).
  - *Boosting* is an iterative technique of adaptively changing the distribution in the content of a set of training data depending on the classification error in the previous iteration. The selection of instances in the next iteration can be affected by several factors. Most often, extracting a set of records for which the prediction in the previous iteration was bad, favors increasing the weighting factor of such instances and reducing the weight of the correctly classified ones. The final results are obtained according to selected criteria. One of the most popular algorithms in this group is AdaBoost (Adaptive Boost) (Freund, & Schapire, 1997).
    - Techniques that change the set of input attributes. A subset of the input attribute set is selected for each training dataset. The

choice can be either random or based on a given criterion. These techniques produce good results even in cases where the input dataset contains redundant data. The most notable representative of this group of techniques is Random forest. Random forest is an ensemble model composed of multiple classification trees, each of which grows on a bootstrap sample with replacement and randomly selects a subset of attributes.

- Techniques in which a set of class labels is changed. This group of techniques is used when the set of classes is large enough. The initial set of classes is randomly divided into two disjoint sets: A and B. The set of current class labels in instances is mapped to classes A or B depending on the set to which the original class label belongs. In the process of classification of such modified instances, if the classifier for the current instance correctly predicts the class, then all instances belonging to that predicted class get a positive vote. The procedure is carried out iteratively, and in the end the instance receives a predicted class label according to the highest vote.

- Techniques in which different classification algorithms are applied to the same (unchanged) set of input data.

A schematic representation of the ensemble learning technique is presented in Figure 1.

More details about ensemble learning can be found in (Zhou, 2012) and (Aggarwal, 2015). A rudimentary version of the ensemble learning method could appear on dataflow computers as soon as the complete implementation of some of the basic classification algorithms and sampling methods is done. At the moment, the simplest variant seems to be the implementation of some form of the bagging technique, where the implemented algorithm would be applied on different sampling sets of the input dataset. At the moment when this text is written, such implementations still does not exist, so ensemble learning is for now very closely related to the control-flow architecture of computers.

Figure 1. Ensemble learning representation. Depending on algorithm selection and data sampling, it is possible to schematically outline classification using all four techniques.

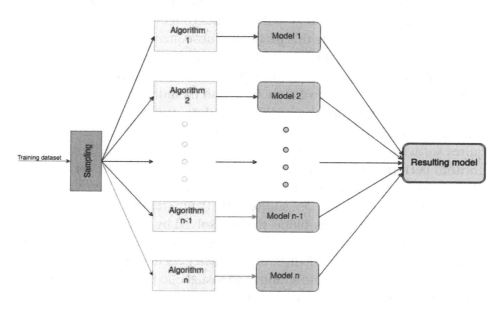

ADDITIONAL ALGORITHM FEATURES

The development of classification algorithms for control-flow architecture has also included mechanisms for successfully overcoming some potentially problematic situations. In addition, algorithms perform certain actions that are common to the control-flow architecture but are difficult to perform on native dataflow machines. Of course, all these actions are supported on hybrid dataflow architectures where they run on control-flow components, but this does not bring improvement compared to the native control-flow version. This section presents some of these mechanisms and features that dataflow architecture lacks.

Repetitive reading of input data is a very common action in programs; it is used daily and is very often required in classification algorithms. For example, depending on the content of the input material, if it is necessary to divide and forward it to the rest of the program, the usual sequence of steps is to read the complete material, count the required property, and then go through that same material and arrange material instances into target groups. When executing instructions sequentially, it may be required to read the complete set of input data multiple times within the program. According to the original dataflow concepts (Dennis, 1980), in addition to the lack of a control flow concept and a request that information is transmitted rather than stored in memory, there are no global resources (not even "global" memory) that can be used to overcome this problem. Subsequent modifications to the dataflow concepts did not bring significant changes related to this limitation, so efficient multiple readings of the input data are currently only possible with the assistance of a control-flow CPU and memory.

Classification algorithms use **different data types** depending on the input material and the classification goal. The use of each of such data types requires software and/or hardware support. For example, if the classification algorithm performed Time Series Data Classification, support for working with date/time data including date/time arithmetic must be provided (for example, if current time is 23:55, addition of 10 minutes must provide correct time 00:05, etc.). Today's problems that are solved by data mining methods often require working with strings whose length is not known in advance, as well as the ability to work with different character encodings. Representation of multimedia data (image and sound) and visual classification is supported on control-flow but not on dataflow computers.

One of the important prerequisites for the implementation of classification algorithms is the ability to **perform various mathematical operations** and use predefined functions and formulas. This use can be more or less intensive but occurs in all classification algorithms (e.g., see description of algorithms in (IBM, 2020)). The program code of predefined functions is stored in software libraries whose use is supported only on control-flow components. Additionally, efficient work with some data types requires hardware support (e.g. implementation of IEEE 754R standards and decimal floating point), which is not fully supported by computer dataflow components.

Today, most data is stored in **databases**, especially in relational ones. They represent an indispensable component in the data mining and machine learning process. Working with databases is not supported on dataflow computers, which significantly limits the possible application of data classification. Some of the data processed in real applications has **missing** (undefined or unknown) **values**. Unknown values can occur for a variety of reasons (e.g., the absence of these values—the name of the first person who walked on Mars, or a value that exists but is unknown, such as the exact population of the Aztecs before Cortes's conquest). Instances containing unknown values cannot simply be discarded as this would undermine the correctness of the resulting model. Instead, various techniques have been developed to process such instances when modeling and when later on applying the model to unknown data. More about how to process instances with non-existent data can be found in (Quinlan, 1989).

There are still a large number of properties and activities that occur with classification algorithms. We would like to mention two more—working with **unbalanced classes** and **cost-sensitive prediction**. Input material may contain different percentages of the target classes. A large imbalance in the representation of classes can affect the accuracy of the constructed model. For example, let input material include only two classes, marked A and B, whose ratio is 99% (A) to 1% (B). Then the algorithm that always assigns class A label to the instance would have an accuracy of 99%, which is almost ideal, but it would be completely useless because it could not assign class B to any instance. This problem can be solved in several ways: by sampling the material so that in the training/test material classes are represented in the desired ratio (which is different from the ratio in the complete material), by giving higher importance (higher weight) in the model to the correct prediction of instances belonging to a smaller class, or by special mechanisms as priors in CART (Breiman, Friedman, Olshen, & Stone, 1984). Assigning weight to classes with the goal of achieving a particular class is one variant of cost-sensitive learning. Another case when weights can be used is forcing the correct prediction of a particular class. The price of an operation in which another (wrong) class is predicted instead of the current one is increased in relation to the (default) price of correct prediction. The final solution is a combination in which the total sum of prices (weight) for all instances of the model is the smallest.

CONTROL-FLOW CLASSIFICATION ALGORITHMS: A SHORT OVERVIEW

The previously described properties have a significant impact on the accuracy of the obtained model. The influence of some properties on classification results will be shown in the next section. This section includes a short overview of four groups of algorithms used in the section that follows: decision trees, instance base learning, rule induction, neural networks, and the ensemble learning method.

Decision Trees

CART (Classification and Regression Trees) is one of the cornerstones of the later development of algorithms in the data mining field. Defined in 1984, when decision tree algorithms had already been developed, it is one of the first algorithms that define the decision tree method for classification on rigorous mathematical basis. In their monograph (Breiman, Friedman, Olshen, & Stone, 1984) on over 360 pages, the authors described in detail the method of constructing the decision tree and introduced many new ideas that were later used in the development of a large number of other algorithms. They also gave examples of the use of classification trees for mass spectra classification and medical diagnosis and prognosis.

Because of its rigor and comprehensiveness, CART has been applied in numerous business projects and applications, as well as science and research. The most important features of the CART algorithm defined in the monograph are:

- Depending on the type of the target attribute, CART can do classification (categorical target attribute) or regression (numeric target attribute).
- The method of constructing a tree for classification has been described in detail. The tree is binary, and the division in the node is done based on an attribute that can be either categorical or numeric and whose values have been sorted.
- The question of material division is always in the following form:

If $x \leq c$ where x is a numeric attribute and c is a constant, or

If $x \in B$ where x is a categorical attribute, $B \subset S$, and S is a set of attribute x values.

- If the answer to the question is positive, the instance is directed to the left side of the current node. This way of partitioning allows the same attribute to occur in multiple nodes (of course, without including the values that have previously been used). Initially, the division in the node is presented only on the basis of one attribute, and then in order to increase the efficiency of the method, the possibility of combining attributes is considered and introduced. Improvements include a linear combination of numeric attributes $(ax_1 + bx_2 + ... + mx_n) \leq const$, Boolean combinations of categorical attributes (Is $x_1 \in B_1$ and $x_2 \in B_2$ and ... and $x_n \in B_n$), or addition of features, which can be done as an ad hoc combination of variables (i.e. specific dimensionality reduction).

- The authors considered the following measure of impurity and criteria to find the improvement for a split during tree growth:
  - Gini index criterion. Gini index $g(t)$ at node t is defined as

$$g(t) = 1 - \sum_{i=1}^{j} [p(i \mid t)]^2$$

  where j is the number of classes and $p(i|t)$ is the fraction of records belonging to class i at node t.
  - Twoing criterion. The twoing criterion for split s at node t is defined as improvement function F

$$F(s,t) = p_L p_R \sum_{i=1}^{j} [| \, p(i \mid t_L) - p(i \mid t_R) \, |]^2$$

  where j is the number of classes, t_L and t_R are the subnodes of note t created by split s, $p(i|t_{L/R})$ is the fraction of records belonging to class i at node t_L or t_R, and p_L/p_R are the proportions of records in node t directed to the left and right side.
  - In addition, the ordered twoing criterion was mentioned as a natural choice for situations where classes are naturally ordered. As both Gini and twoing has its own advantages, the authors proposed that both Gini and twoing criteria be implemented in CART.
- Without possibility to define the stopping criterion, trees grow without restrictions. Pruning is done using the cost complexity pruning strategy. A tree is pruned upwards, calculating the estimated misclassification rate until it is finally cut back to the root node. Finally, the smallest subtree with minimal cost complexity is selected. The authors prove the existence of such tree and show that cost complexity pruning significantly lowers the number of possible subtrees that need to be inspected. The tree pruning process considers only material available

for training, not for testing. If the number of instances in the training material is small, the authors propose using cross-validation.

- It is possible to set up and use the misclassification cost between each predicted/actual class pair.
- Unbalanced classes can cause individual class misclassification rates. Class balancing (and consequently preventing misclassification rates) is automatically enabled using the prior mechanism. A prior is assigned to each class and represents probability (weight) that estimates the overall relative frequency for each class in the training dataset.
- The concept of the *surrogate split* is introduced. At any given node t, if s^* is the best split, then *surrogate split (in node t)* can be interpreted as the split on attribute[3] x_m that most accurately predicts the action of s^*. Surrogate attributes can be ranked in each node according to prediction accuracy. Surrogate splits have three major uses: handling missing data, variable importance ranking, and detection of masking.
  - To handle missing values, the authors decided to use surrogates as a more robust procedure instead of filling the missing data. The simplified version of the procedure stated as follows: let s^* denote the best split on a current node; s^* is obtained by calculation using all instances available for the split at this node, where the attributes included in s^* have known (non-missing) values. The instances with encountered missing values for the splitting attribute in the current node move left or right according to the value of surrogate attribute. If the surrogate attribute is also missing, the next surrogate according to the rank is used for splitting.
  - Variable importance ranking is the sum of all nodes of the improvement obtained by the best split on the variable at each node. In the case when a variable has a missing value, surrogate is used in the sum.
  - Detection of masking—a variable split node can in some rare cases have a large importance score. Using the importance score in such cases helps to discover a nonlinear correlation between variables and eliminate one of them from mining.

CART experienced a number of implementations and additions. Later implementations include the possibilities of earlier stopping of tree growth, entropy as a measure for the splitting rule, boosting, bagging, etc.

C5.0 is the successor of the C4.5 algorithm (Quinlan, 1993). It is developed as a commercial product by Rulequest Research, Inc. (https://www.rulequest.

com/) which includes the basic features of C4.5 (using categorical and numerical predictor attributes, multiway splitting tree, entropy and information gain for the splitting node, handling missing values, pruning trees, etc.) but also certain improvements, the most significant of which are:

- higher accuracy, greater speed, and significantly lower memory requirements than for C4.5;
- faster and smaller decision trees;
- a support boosting mechanism;
- generating a smaller set of rules whit comparable level of accuracy;
- support variable misclassification costs for each predicted/actual class pair;
- support winnowing—examination of the usefulness of predictors and elimination of irrelevant ones before starting to build the model.

C5.0 also appears as See5 for the Windows operating system. A free source code for a single-threaded version under Gnu GPL can be downloaded from the Rulequest Research website.

SPRINT (Scalable PaRallelizable INduction of decision Trees) (Shafer, Agrawal, & Mehta., 1996) is a decision tree classifier that allows for the classification of large training data. SPRINT was developed based on the SLIQ algorithm (Mehta, Agrawal, & Rissanen, 1996) but it also brought significant improvements. The basic characteristics of the SPRINT algorithm are:

- It uses both categorical and continuous attributes as predictors.
- A tree in SPRINT grows using the "breadth-first" tree growing strategy instead of "depth-first" as in CART or C4.5/C5.0.
- Gini index is used for finding split points in nodes (the formula is shown above in the description of CART).
- The tree pruning algorithm is based on the Minimum Description Length principle (Rissanen, 1989).
- The algorithm sorts the values for each attribute and creates an attribute list for each attribute in the dataset. The list includes attribute values, class labels and identifiers of the records (rids) from which these values were obtained. The list is scanned in the process of finding split points. Implementation with one list containing both values and class labels makes it easier to update and, in the case when the entire list cannot fit into main memory, store and maintain the list on a disk. This removes all memory restrictions related to the size of classification material.

- The algorithm can be easily parallelized; speed-up improves for larger datasets and it is highly scalable.

The overview of decision tree techniques and algorithms can be found in (Rokach, & Maimon, 2014), while a more detailed description of CART and C4.5 (and some other non-decision tree algorithms) is given in (Wu, & Kumar, 2009).

Instance Base Learning: K Nearest Neighbors

The basic idea of the **K Nearest Neighbors** (K-NN) classifier is simple—"Birds of a feather flock together". For each (previously unseen) instance, using a distance measure, find the K "closest" ones among training set instances, check their class labels, and assign the class by taking the majority of neighboring instance classes. The first version of this approach was defined in 1951 in (Fix, & Hodges, 1951). A detailed description with refreshed and innovated versions is shown in (Cunningham, & Delany, 2021).

Instances are represented as n-dimensional vectors where n is the number of predictor attributes. The following formula can be used as a distance measure used for determining similarity/dissimilarity of instances x and y with n attributes (referred to as Minkowski distance):

$$d(x,y) = \left(\sum_{i=1}^{n} w_i \left| x_i - y_i \right|^r \right)^{1/r}$$

where w_i is the weight of attribute i, and r is a natural number (variants: r=1 - Manhattan, r=2 - Euclidean, ..., r=∞ - supremum or Chebyshev), cosine similarity, Mahalanobis distance, correlation, Kullback-Leibler divergence, x^2, etc. The list of different measures applicable to K-NN is listed in (Cunningham, & Delany, 2021).

Some advantages and disadvantages of K-NN are as follows:

- Due to its simplicity, the algorithm is easy to implement. The presentation of results is simple to understand.
- The classifier is lazy and there is no classical model as in other classification techniques. The model in K-NN consists of all training instances that are stored and reused in processing each time when an unknown instance is classified.

- The speed of the algorithm is inversely proportional to the number of instances in the training set.
- The algorithm is very sensitive to irrelevant values (noise and outliers) or redundant features, as well as selection of appropriate similarity measure.
- K is not known in advance and the results strongly depend on selecting the value for K. If K is too small, classification is sensitive to noise; if K is too large, instances from other (non-similar) classes can be considered.
- Attributes can be scaled to prevent a single attribute from dominating in distance calculation.
- If instances have a complex structure, K-NN may often be outperformed by other classification techniques.

Rule-based Classifiers

Rule-based classifiers are those which use a set of rules in the form *if (condition) then class* for classification. The classifier consists of *n* rules in the form r_i: *(condition$_i$)* → *class$_i$* *(i = 1, ..., n)* where each rule can be a conjunction of expression of the form *variable = value*. For example, the rule for prediction "has the client subscribed a term deposit" during classification of the dataset bank-additional-full (see examples below) has the following form:

if (job = management and contact = telephone and month = may and campaign > 1,500 and pdays > 513) then no

The left side of the rule (condition) is called the **rule antecedent**, while right side of the rule (*class* identifier) is called the **rule consequent**. The rules in the classifier are placed in the rule list and examined one by one, starting from the first rule in the list.

Rules can have different characteristics:

- Can be mutually exclusive (the same instance is not covered with more than one rule).
- Can be ordered according to a different criterion.
- Rules can be exhaustive if there is a rule for each possible combination of attribute values. If not all instances are covered with at least one rule, then there can be a rule with a default predicted class. The default rule is placed at the end of the rule list.

Rule-based classification includes (1) rule induction/learning algorithms and (2) classification based on association rule mining. According to the way the rules are induced, the methods can be divided into two large groups:

- Indirect methods: rules are extracted from other classification models (classification trees, neural networks, etc.). An example of an algorithm that belongs to this group is C5.0 rules.
- Direct methods: rules are extracted directly from the training dataset. For extracting rules, direct methods often use a **sequential covering** algorithm. Sequential covering extract rules for the next class using Learn-One-Rule function. After extracting, all instances covered with extracted rules are removed. The process continues until all training instances are covered or no new rule can be learned from the remaining data. In this case, a default rule can be added to the bottom of the rule list. 1R (Holte, 1993), CN2 (Clark, & Niblett, 1989), and Ripper are algorithms that belong to this group.

Short characteristics of rule induction algorithms are:

The C5.0 rules algorithm induced rules from the classification tree formed with the C5.0 algorithm. C5.0 rules provide rule optimization by removing redundant elements from rule antecedents.

1R is a simple rule induction algorithm where for each attribute forms one rule, and then selects the rule with the highest accuracy. It works with discrete attributes.

Ripper (Cohen, 1995, 1996) uses sequential covering and induces a set of all rules ordered according to classes. During learning, a class is pre-fixed, and after rule learning for this class is completed, the learning process proceeds to the next class. Learned rules are added to the rule list. Rule ordering inside an individual class is not important, but rules in the list are ordered according to the predicted class. In the case of binary classification, rules are mined for the least frequent class, while a more frequent class is default. In the multiclass classification algorithm, rules are first mined for the least frequent class, then for the second least frequent, and so on, while the most frequent class is default.

Artificial Neural Networks

Artificial neural networks (ANN) have become very popular in recent years. They are an important technique used to solve problems in many areas. A detailed description of the techniques and possibilities of neural networks is beyond the scope of this book and can be found in (Aggarwal, 2018). Only a brief description of the basic ideas will be given below.

The idea of ANN is to simulate the work of biological nervous systems and the human brain. Analogous to the structure in the brain, ANN consists of nodes and connections between them. Nodes in ANN represent neurons or units. Perceptron (see Figure 2) is the simplest version of ANN that models a single cell. There are two types of nodes (input and output) that are connected to the central part of the perceptron by a connection with weights. Weights simulate the strength of the synaptic connection in biological neurons. The perceptron training process involves changing weight values until synchronized data input/output dependencies are established. The perceptron calculates the output value *y'* as the weight sum of input values, by subtracting the bias by checking the sign of the result. ANN is constructed as a combination of a number of perceptrons.

Mathematically, the output model of the perceptron equals:

$$y' = sign(w_d*d + w_{d-1}*d{-}1 + \cdots + w_2*2 + w_1*1 - b) = sign(\mathbf{w} \cdot \mathbf{x})$$

In training, the new value of weight $w_i^{(k+1)}$ that corresponds to input node *i* in *k+1*-th iteration is a combination of the old value $w_i^{(k)}$ from the previous iteration and the value proportional to the prediction error (y − y'). The goal of training ANN with *n* input nodes is to determine the set of weights **w**, which minimizes the total square error

$$Error(w) = \frac{1}{2}\sum_{i=1}^{n}(y - y')^2$$

Substituting y = w • x gives the error function a quadratic function so the global minimum can be determined.

There are several types of neural networks; these include:

- Networks with more than one layer of interconnected nodes (an example of such network is shown in Figure 3; multilayer neural networks are the base of deep learning neural networks and the deep learning process);
- Convolutional ANN;
- Networks with backpropagation;

Figure 2. Perceptron with four input nodes. Each node has its own weight. Bias is subtracted from weight sum before applying activation function.

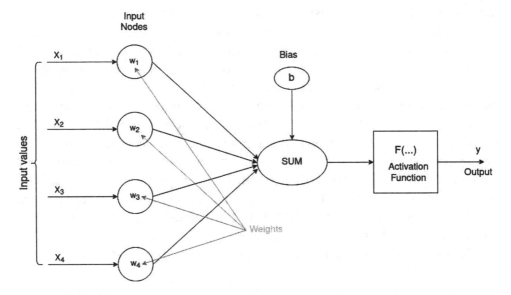

- Recurrent networks (with connections within the same or previous layer);
- RBF (Radial Basis Function);
- SOM (Self Organizing Map, Kohonen networks);
- Associative neural networks.

ANN can use different activation functions (linear, sign, sigmoid, hyperbolic tangents, etc.). The perceptron training algorithm guarantees convergence towards the optimal solution for linearly separable classification problems. If the activation function F is not linear, the output from the ANN is a nonlinear parameter function. Since the error function is nonlinear, it is possible to use gradient descent, but without the guarantee to get a global minimum, which renders poorer results in the mining process.

Ensemble Method Algorithms

There are plenty variants of algorithms that provide ensemble learning. In the example below, three different algorithms will be used:

Random trees is an ensemble model that consists of multiple CART-like trees. The random trees algorithm uses bootstrap sampling with replacement

Figure 3. ANN with two hidden layers. An example is from the classification dataset bank-additional-full (see examples below). The input layer has seven input nodes, hidden layer 1 has four neurons and hidden layer 2 has seven neurons. Each hidden layer has its own bias as well as an output node.

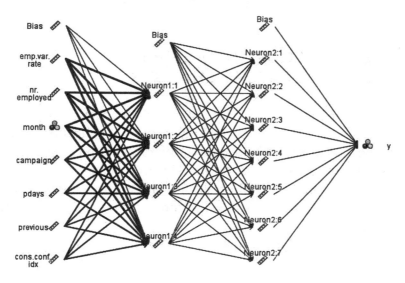

to generate an initial training set, which is used to grow a tree model. The tree grows in a specific way: for each node, a smaller number of attributes are randomly selected to find the best split attribute. Each tree is grown to the maximum possible depth. Pruning does not exist. At the end, random trees are scored by majority voting (for classification) or average (for regression). Additional features compared to CART are:

- Random trees add bagging as a feature.
- At each split of the tree, only a sampling of the input fields is considered for the impurity measure.

Random forest is an advanced implementation of a bagging algorithm with a tree model as the base model. The characteristics of the splitting process are very similar to those in Random Trees (sampling, randomly selected subset of attributes). The best split attribute is found either from a set of all attributes or from a random subset of the size specified with an input parameter. Moreover, tree size can be controlled by specifying the number of leaf nodes.

XGBoost tree algorithm is an advanced implementation of a gradient boosting algorithm with a classification tree model as the base. It provides the possibility to use hyperparameter optimization (based on Rbfopt), specify the maximum depth for trees, and the number of boosting iterations.

EXAMPLES OF ALGORITHM RESULTS DEPENDENT ON FEATURE CHANGES

Previously described properties have a significant impact on the accuracy of the obtained model. This section will illustrate the application of different algorithms on the same set of input data with some of the previously described properties. The obtained results do not aim to compare the efficiency of the algorithms, but rather to illustrate the influence (sometimes of small changes) of the previously mentioned features on the accuracy and stability of the obtained model.

Three groups of data are available at UCI Machine Learning Repository (Dua, & Graff, 2019):

1. Wine Quality dataset. Two separate datasets (red and white wine) are put together to form a dataset with 6497 instances and 11 predictor attributes. Class attribute *quality_type* is obtained as a combination of wine type (red/white) and wine quality. Instances include only numerical values in predictor attributes, without missing values.
2. Connect-4 dataset. The dataset includes 67557 instances with 42 predictor attributes, where all attributes are categorical, without missing values.
3. Bank Marketing dataset (Moro, Cortez, & Rita, 2014), dataset bank-additional-full.csv. This dataset includes 41188 instances with 20 attributes (mixed categorical and numerical) + binary class attribute with values "yes" or "no" ("Has the client subscribed a term deposit?"). The dataset includes 10700 instances where at least one attribute has a missing value and 30488 instances without missing values in attributes.

The test is provided on the following cases:

-   test on the numeric, categorical, and mixed material. All three datasets are divided in relation 70% (training): 30% (test)
-   test on influence ensemble learning on all three datasets divided in relation 70% (training): 30% (test)

- test on balancing classes on *connect-4* and *bank marketing* datasets divided in relation 70% (training, with balanced classes): 30% (test, classes not balanced)
- test on dataset *bank-additional-full.csv* divided in relation 70% (training): 30% (test) after removing the records with missing values

Although all three datasets include unbalanced classes, dataset *wine quality* is not included in the test because of large disbalance among classes, which prevent obtaining comparable results. The ratio of classes in *connect-4* dataset is 9.55(draw): 24,62 (loss): 65,83(win), while ratio of classes in *bank marketing* dataset is 88,73 (no): 11,27 (yes).

Class distribution in the *wine quality* dataset is shown in Figure 4. The largest class is 225 times frequent than the smallest one. Data balancing is done using *Balancing* node in SPSS modeler because automatic balancing is not supported within all algorithms. After balancing datasets *connect-4* and *bank marketing* frequency of classes in the training material differs at most 10%. Frequency of classes in test material remains unchanged.

Three tools are used for the test:

1. IBM SPSS Modeler V18.2.2 (https://www.ibm.com/products/spss-modeler) for algorithms CART, C5.0, K-NN, ANN, random trees, random forest, XGBoost Tree, C5.0 rules, and ensemble learning using CART, C5.0 K-NN and ANN
2. Weka 3-8-5 (https://www.cs.waikato.ac.nz/ml/weka/) for algorithms Ripper and 1R
3. IBM Intelligent Miner (https://www.ibm.com/docs/en/db2/11.1?topic=api-data-mining-intelligent-miner) for SPRINT Algorithm

All algorithms were used with default parameters and without misclassification cost. Test results are shown in Table 1—Table 4. Table 1 presents data types influence of result quality and model stability. The largest difference in accuracy can be observed in wine quality classification where all attributes are numeric. Models with large difference between training and test mode are not useful because of overfitting. Models for two other groups of material with pure categorical and mixed attribute types have differences not larger than 5%. Some models are almost completely stable with difference less than 1% in training and test. All algorithms give better (more useful) prediction if data include categorical attributes.

Figure 4. Distribution of classes in the wine quality bank-additional-full.csv dataset. Classes are unbalanced—the largest class ("6 white") has 33.83% of material while the smallest class ("3 red") has 0.15%.

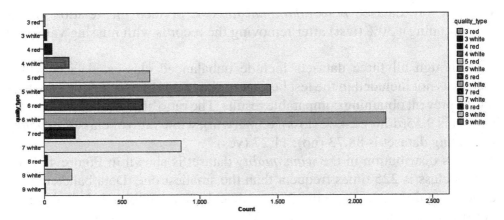

Table 2 includes results of applying ensemble-learning method to all three datasets. Ensemble learning is done with individual algorithms as well as combination of CART, C5.0 and ANN. General conclusion is that algorithms that are specially designed for ensemble learning and have embedded procedures used in processing data (XGBoost Tree, Random Forest and Random Trees) produce slightly better and more stable results than algorithms initially designed without boosting facility.

Table 3 shows influence of class balancing to model accuracy. Class balancing is done only on training data. Majority of algorithms have small changes in accuracy, while results for some of them stay almost unchanged (for example CART).

Table 4 present sensitivity of algorithms on missing values. Although percent of missing values in bank marketing dataset is small (approximately 1.5%), it make big influence on results produced with K-NN algorithm. It is expected related to conversion of categorical attributes to vectors and further distance calculation.

REVIEW QUESTIONS

This section provides questions for better understanding of the key aspects of the chapter.

Table 1. Data types influence on correct instance classification (in percent) using different algorithms. Wine quality include only numerical values, Connect-4 only categorical, and Bank marketing include combination of numerical and categorical values in predictor attributes. All datasets are divided according to ratio 70% (training): 50% (test).

	CART	C5.0	SPRINT	K-NN	ANN	C5.0 Rules	1R	Ripper
Wine quality training	53,21	87,36	62,20	69,32	56,22	85,29	47,14	61,08
Wine quality test	49,04	55,33	48,83	54,21	53,86	57,41	41,37	52,23
Connect-4 training	69,29	87,08	74,11	80,64	73,11	86,93	65,96	74,35
Connect-4 test	69,55	80,34	72,02	73,65	73,20	81,06	66,53	73,99
Bank marketing training	91,41	92,95	90,35	67,05	91,22	92,26	90,05	91,76
Bank marketing test	90,99	91,29	88,78	65,49	91,09	91,22	89,08	91,21

1. What are the key aspects of the control-flow paradigm?
2. List 3 use cases of classification algorithms.

Table 2. Ensemble learning influence on correct instance classification (in percent) using different algorithms and combination of algorithms. All datasets are divided according to ratio 70% (training): 50% (test). Combination include ensemble of CART, C5.0 and ANN

	CART Boosting	C5.0 Boosting	ANN Boosting	Random Trees	Random Forest	XGBoost Tree	C5.0 Rules Boosting	Combination
Wine quality training	53,52	99,07	58,82	65,25	98,50	75,19	99,20	93,51
Wine quality test	48,07	61,98	53,76	48,58	63,40	57,01	61,83	53,76
Connect-4 training	73,67	93,79	80,10	59,29	99,49	77,20	93,66	87,02
Connect-4 test	73,90	83,12	79,88	56,74	80,06	76,89	84,09	79,88
Bank marketing training	91,40	95,69	91,22	87,90	99,30	92,96	94,25	93,04
Bank marketing test	90,97	91,01	91,10	85,59	90,76	89,17	91,42	91,09

Table 3. Class balancing influence on correct instance classification (in percent) using different algorithms. All datasets are divided according to ratio 70% (training): 50% (test).

	CART	C5.0	SPRINT	K-NN	ANN	C5.0 Rules	1R	Ripper
Connect-4 training	69,00	87,08	74,11	80,64	73,11	86,93	65,96	77,15
Connect-4 test	69,23	80,34	72,02	73,65	73,20	81,06	66,53	75,77
Bank marketing training	86,67	97,47	93,42	75,37	85,18	96,21	75,60	94,89
Bank marketing test	79,25	88,88	86,34	61,80	86,82	88,80	74,24	86,63

3.   What is ensemble learning?
4.   List data types suitable for classification algorithms implemented using control-flow paradigm.

REFERENCES

Aggarwal, C. C. (Ed.). (2015). *Data Classification Algorithms and Applications*. CRC Press.

Aggarwal, C. C. (2018). *Neural Networks and Deep Learning: A Textbook*. Springer. doi:10.1007/978-3-319-94463-0

Table 4. Missing values influence on correct instance classification (in percent) using different algorithms. Bank marketing datasets is divided according to ratio 70% (training): 50% (test), before and after removing missing values

	CART	C5.0	SPRINT	K-NN	ANN	C5.0 Rules	1R	Ripper
training dataset with missing values	91,41	92,95	90,35	67,05	91,22	92,26	90,05	91,76
test dataset with missing values	90,99	91,29	88,78	65,49	91,09	91,22	89,08	91,21
training dataset without missing values	90,63	93,08	89,70	90,77	90,44	92,50	88,85	91,22
test dataset without missing values	89,79	89,54	88,09	88,17	89,81	89,60	87,72	89,93

Aggarwal, C. C., & Zhai, C. X. (Eds.). (2012). *Mining Text Data*. Springer. doi:10.1007/978-1-4614-3223-4

Breiman, L., Friedman, J., Olshen, R. A., & Stone, C. J. (1984). *Classification and Regression Trees*. Chapman&Hall / CRC.

Clark, P., & Niblett, T. (1989). The CN2 induction algorithm. *Machine Learning*, *3*(4), 261–283. doi:10.1007/BF00116835

Cohen, W. W. (1995). Fast effective rule induction. *Proceedings of the Twelfth International Conference on Machine Learning*, 115–123.

Cohen, W. W. (1996). Learning trees and rules with set-valued features. *Proceedings of the Thirteenth National Conference on Artificial Intelligence*, 709–716.

Cunningham, P., & Delany, S. J. (2021). k-Nearest Neighbor Classifiers - A Tutorial. *ACM Computing Surveys*, *54*(6), 1–25.

Dennis, J. B. (1980). Data Flow Supercomputers. *Computer*, *13*(11), 48–56. doi:10.1109/MC.1980.1653418

Dua, D., & Graff, C. (2019). *UCI Machine Learning Repository*. University of California, School of Information and Computer Science. http://archive.ics.uci.edu/ml

Fix, E., & Hodges, J. J. (1951). *Discriminatory analysis: Non-parametric discrimination: Consistency properties. Technical report*. USAF School of Aviation Medicine.

Freund, Y., & Schapire, R. E. (1997). A decision-theoretic generalization of on-line learning and an application to boosting. *Journal of Computer and System Sciences*, *55*(1), 119–139.

Holte, R. C. (1993). Very Simple Classification Rules Perform Well on Most Commonly Used Datasets. *Machine Learning*, *11*(1), 63–91. doi:10.1023/A:1022631118932

Hudík, T. (2015). Machine translation within commercial companies. In J. Žižka & F. Daŭena (Eds.), *Modern Computational Models of Semantic Discovery in Natural Language* (pp. 256–272). IGI Global. doi:10.4018/978-1-4666-8690-8.ch010

IBM. (2020). *IBM SPSS Modeler Algorithms Guide, V18.2.2*. IBM. Retrieved from https://www.ibm.com/support/pages/spss-modeler-1822-documentation#en

Kowsari, K., Jafari Meimandi, K., Heidarysafa, M., Mendu, S., Barnes, L., & Brown, D. (2019). Text Classification Algorithms: A Survey. *MDPI Information.*, *10*(4), 150. doi:10.3390/info10040150

Li, X., & Liu, B. (2003). Learning to classify texts using positive and unlabeled data. *IJCAI*, *3*, 587–592.

Liu, J., Shang, J., & Han, J. (2017). *Phrase Mining from Massive Text and Its Applications*. Morgan & Claypool. doi:10.2200/S00759ED1V01Y201702DMK013

Mehta, M., Agrawal, R., & Rissanen, J. (1996). SLIQ: A fast scalable classifier for data mining. In P. Apers, M. Bouzeghoub, & G. Gardarin (Eds.), Lecture Notes in Computer Science: Vol. 1057. *Advances in Database Technology — EDBT '96* (pp. 18–32). Springer. doi:10.1007/BFb0014141

Miner, G., Elder, J., Hill, T., Nisbet, R. A., Delen, D., & Fast, A. (Eds.). (2012). *Practical Text Mining and Statistical Analysis for Non-structured Text Data Applications*. Academic Press.

Moro, S., Cortez, P., & Rita, P. (2014). A Data-Driven Approach to Predict the Success of Bank Telemarketing. *Decision Support Systems*, *62*, 22–31. doi:10.1016/j.dss.2014.03.001

Quinlan, J. R. (1989). Unknown Attribute Values in Induction. Technical report, Basser Department of Computer Science, University of Sydney doi:10.1016/B978-1-55860-036-2.50048-5

Quinlan, J. R. (1993). *C4.5: Programs for Machine Learning*. Morgan Kaufmann.

Rissanen, J. (1989). *Stochastic Complexity in Statistical Inquiry*. World Scientific Publ. Co.

Rokach, L., & Maimon, O. (2014). *Data Mining With Decision Trees: Theory and Applications*. World Scientific. doi:10.1142/9097

Shafer, J., Agrawal, R., & Mehta, M. (1996). SPRINT: A Scalable Parallel Classifier for Data Mining. *Proceedings of the 22nd VLDB Conference*, 544-555.

Stavrianou, A., Andritsos, P., & Nicoloyannis, N. (2007). Overview and semantic issues of text mining. *SIGMOD Record, 36*(3), 23–34. doi:10.1145/1324185.1324190

Wu, X., & Kumar, V. (Eds.). (2009). *The Top Ten Algorithms in Data Mining.* CRC Press. doi:10.1201/9781420089653

Zhou, Z.-H. (2012). *Ensemble Methods Foundations and Algorithms.* CRC Press. doi:10.1201/b12207

Zong, C., Xia, R., & Zhang, J. (2021). *Text Data Mining.* Springer. doi:10.1007/978-981-16-0100-2

KEY TERMS AND DEFINITIONS

ANN: Artificial neural network dominant in supervised machine learning.

CART: Algorithm for classification entitled Classification and Regression Trees.

Control-flow: Convectional programming paradigm for general purpose.

Ensemble Learning: Machine learning technique that combines results of multiple algorithms for achieving better results.

KNN: Algorithm for classification entitled K nearest neighbors.

ENDNOTES

[1]   As some classification algorithms used test data to optimize the constructed model, in order to further verify the correctness of the constructed model, data are sometimes divided into three parts: for training, testing, and verification, whereby the verification set acts as previously unseen data.

[2]   These generic types can be further divided into numeric (integer, real, decimal) and categorical (categorical, nominal, date/time, etc.).

[3]   Or attributes if a linear or Boolean combination of attributes is used.

Chapter 3

Classification Algorithms and Dataflow Implementation

ABSTRACT

The implementation of data mining methods on dataflow computers enables an easy use of parallelism, but it also faces numerous obstacles. The problem underlying the impossibility of using currently developed algorithms in their existing form is their adaptation to von Neumann computer model, which assumes sequential calculations and intensive use of memory. This is one of the reasons why there are no fully developed classification algorithms on dataflow computer models in the open literature at the moment when this text is written. This chapter summarizes the characteristics that can be used as directions in the future construction of algorithms and outlines drafts for two implementations of the K-nearest neighbor algorithm.

INTRODUCTION

The dataflow paradigm has been used in an increasing number of software products (Maxeler Technologies, 2021). The characteristics of the dataflow paradigm have proven to be practical in various kinds of applications that involve processing large amounts of data (for example, in *Google's Cloud dataflow)*. On the other side, different data mining methods and analyses based on data mining are nowadays incorporated in numerous business projects and applications as well as science and research. Incorporating the possibility of using data mining methods and algorithms (especially classification

DOI: 10.4018/978-1-7998-8350-0.ch003

methods and algorithms which are most prevalent in applications) are very important for the future development of dataflow for at least two reasons: (1) in the dataflow paradigm itself, the possibility of implementing various data mining methods on dataflow machines is related to an increasing number of application areas, and (2) a wider presence on the market means a higher level of profit for manufacturers of dataflow computers. More initial steps have already been taken (for example see (Guo et al, 2016)), but due to the complexity of implementation, full use of data mining methods in the control-flow paradigm is still a long way off.

The development of dataflow systems started from the first "pure" dataflow architectures (static and dynamic), went through the introduction of new concepts during the 80's (Hurson, & Kavi, 2007; Treleaven, Hopkins, & Rautenbach, 1982), and evolved into today's dataflow computers that include hybrid architectures containing "pure" dataflow components with associated control-flow parts (Ye et al, 2020). In parallel with the development of dataflow computers, dataflow programming languages were also developed. Starting from "pure" dataflow programming languages (Whiting, & Pascoe, 1994), over a mixture in dataflow and another paradigm (for example, functional paradigm), up to contemporary specially developed variants of "ordinary" languages and their compilers used to generate a dataflow code such as the Maxeler Java/maxCompiler (Milutinović, Salom, Trifunović, & Giorgi, 2015), or the Wave tool used to compile programs into a dataflow graph (Nicol, 2017a).

As modern commercial dataflow systems include control-flow CPU (and sometimes additional GPU), all currently known data mining algorithms can consequently be implemented in a certain way. This kind of implementation can only be named as "implementation on dataflow" but does not bring any program improvement or significant advantage compared to solving an identical problem on control-flow computers.

The implementation of complete data mining methods with all corresponding options solely on dataflow computers without using control-flow components does not exist in open literature at the moment when this text is written. Only the first steps have been taken, including the implementation of Euclidean distance calculation, correlation or elementary linear regression (see (Maxeler Technologies, 2021)). Data mining methods often include very complex calculations, data preprocessing, work with different data types and value manipulation, anomaly detection, and (hardware) operations that are not always supported by available dataflow hardware. These facts are valid to methods from all three groups of data mining techniques—classification[1], clustering, and association rules.

Instead of implementing complete algorithms, it is possible to perform partial implementation on dataflow[2], while parts of the algorithms that are not suitable for dataflow implementation can be implemented in accordance with the control-flow paradigm on control-flow components on a (hybrid) dataflow computer. Emphasis will be placed on parts of algorithms whose characteristics correspond more to the dataflow paradigm and bring new quality, i.e. implementation (parts) of algorithms whose execution is potentially more efficient on data flow machines compared to the classical (von Neumann) control-flow architecture. The term "more efficient", in addition to lower energy consumption which is expected for dataflow computers, covers better program performance or easier writing of correct programs. A short description of Maxeler dataflow architecture is added at the end of this chapter in order to clarify and illustrate the basic concepts and architecture of currently available commercial systems.

As classification methods are most often used in nowadays applications, in the rest of this chapter we will concentrate on the possible directions in the implementation of classification algorithms on dataflow computers. Hereinafter, we will talk about "classical" (not big-data) classification algorithms and their parts and properties that are suitable for implementation on dataflow computers. Algorithms for big data classification, which is the next step in the development of data mining methods, are outside the scope of this article.

DATAFLOW PARADIGM AND CHARACTERISTICS OF CLASSIFICATION ALGORITHMS

Contemporary classification algorithms have been developed for several decades on bases that correspond to control-flow computers. Their theoretical foundations are adapted to using the capabilities of control-flow machines. This is why their models cannot be completely rewritten to dataflow components only. To fully use the capabilities of dataflow machines, it is necessary to make a qualitative step forward and form algorithms with completely different models that are adapted to dataflow architecture, as it was done with algorithms for quantum computers. This process is at the very beginning; increasing the use of dataflow computers for commercial purposes will enable their further development and, in the future, create conditions for the realization of these ideas.

In order to recognize and identify the characteristics of classification algorithm components that better suit the dataflow paradigm, it is necessary to list several key features of the dataflow paradigm that significant for implementation. We will first list the drawbacks for full implementation of classification algorithms on pure dataflow:

- There is no concept of *variables* and *memory updates* or *shared data storage*.
- Instructions do not interact with each other (low level of communication).
- There is a smaller set of supported data types.
- It is difficult to implement dynamic data structures.
- Executing a long sequential code degrades performance.

In relation to these characteristics, the problems that can occur when trying to write the complete code of the algorithm to the dataflow machines are the following:

- All classification algorithms strongly depend on using shared memory and some "global" variables, either parameters or threshold values. To substitute global variables with enlarging tokens (that passed among nodes) requires (a) intensive communication among nodes which is possible but not well supported in dataflow, especially if processing is organized in parallel with two or more threads, and (b) a complex instruction code in each node that is required to process such enlarged tokens with many data fields.
- Shared memory is a problem for applying ensemble methods which combine the results of two or more classification algorithms. It is not possible to efficiently organize dataflow hardware to support a different number of ensemble models based on input parameters without using shared (external) memory to store results of processed models.
- Many algorithms use dynamic data structures which are essential (for example, trees in decision tree algorithms) but which are not supported at all or have very little support in the dataflow paradigm.
- Some algorithms include specific operations (for example, class balancing and using priors in C&RT) which require multiple reading of different parts of input data. In control-flow versions of algorithms,

such operations are sometimes applied automatically, and consist of the sequential code and require (global) storage for calculated values for further use.

- Some algorithms (for example SVM) often require intensive numerical calculations that are usually performed sequentially. This also requires a lot of nodes with program codes to support mathematical operations/functions or access to the library in shared memory. Parallelization of such algorithms requires intensive communications between threads (Do, Nguyen, & Poulet, 2008).

- Manipulating with different data types can be very intensive. For example, attribute values prefer to be categorical and should be binarized, while numerical values should sometimes be discretized.

- Pruning should also be considered: each of the different techniques at some point requires access to shared memory (for example, decision tree postpruning requires access to stored decision tree).

In this chapter we will present some ideas for implementing specific parts of classification algorithms in an attempt to avoid the aforementioned problems. We use the K-Nearest Neighbor (K-NN) algorithm as a model because of its simplicity and relatively uncomplicated implementation. Concrete implementation of this abstract models (which does not exists yet) will strongly depend on underlying (dataflow) hardware characteristics and efficiency of tools used to compile model (pseudo)code to dataflow program. For that reason, it is not possible to give precise characteristics of improving in computational complexity and space savings compared to corresponding control-flow implementations of this algorithms (for examples of compare dataflow vs. control-flow implementations in other areas see section 3.6).

FUNCTIONAL PROGRAMMING AND DATAFLOW PARADIGM

As dataflow computers developed, so did dataflow programming languages (Whiting, & Pascoe, 1994; Johnston, Hanna, & Millar, 2004). The development of dataflow languages took place in several directions:

- Defining new, purely dataflow-oriented programming languages that support the architecture of dataflow computers (the most famous is VAL);
- Defining languages based on a functional paradigm (the best known are Id, Lucid (Wadge, & Ashcroft, 1985) and SISAL);
- Developing languages alongside the flavor of imperative languages (whose successor is, for example, Maxeler Java).

Most dataflow languages are based on a mixture of dataflow and functional paradigms or originate directly from functional programming languages languages (Whiting, & Pascoe, 1994; Johnston, Hanna, & Millar, 2004). This similarity is not accidental—a comparison of the features of functional programming languages and dataflow programming languages shows a large number of similarities/matches. If purely functional languages are observed, the coincidence is remarkable (Backus, 1978; Field, & Harrison, 1988).

The concepts of the first pure functional programming languages (FP, FFP (Backus, 1978), and LispKit Lisp (Henderson, 1980)) included the basic premises of the dataflow paradigm. Several languages that were developed later were at the same time functional and dataflow programming languages (Id, Lucid, SISAL, and many more). The comparison of significant features of dataflow and pure functional programming languages is shown in Table 1.

There have been various attempts to unify these two paradigms. There is a framework that combines both programming styles (Widemann, & Lepper, 2014). Moreover, it is very interesting that there is a large similarity in the way dataflow and functional programming languages are executed. This has resulted in modifying dataflow machines in order to execute functional programming languages (Giraud-Carrier, 1994) and using (functional) graph reduction machine possibility for parallel execution in order to expand dataflow modeling calculations by modifying dataflow computer architecture (Amamiya, 1988). The dataflow model does not allow for efficient processing of all types (especially structures) of data. An additional advantage related to the similarity of these two paradigms is that functional programming languages are not as rich in different types of data as imperative ones, so the types of data used in functional programs can be relatively easily adapted to the needs and possibilities of dataflow programming.

If we return to the field of classification algorithms, the question is how this similarity can help in adapting algorithms to dataflow architecture. The features of functional programming languages provide an appropriate environment for relatively simple implementation of algorithms in various

Table 1. Comparative features of dataflow languages and pure functional programming languages.

Features of Dataflow Languages	Features of (Pure) Functional Languages
Variable does not exist as a concept	*Variable* does not exist as a concept
No side effects	No side effects
All instructions are functions	Program is a function which includes other nested functions; high order functions are supported
Shared data storage does not exist	Storage does not exist—all values are passed as parameters
Support recursion/iteration	Recursion is mechanism of program execution; iteration is supported via (tail) recursion
Efficient parallel executing	Programs can be native parallelized—each function depends only on parameters and can be executed in parallel
Instructions are executed only when all arguments are available	Lazy/eager evaluation
All instructions are functions (i.e., there are no side effects)	Functions are basic program building blocks; programs are constructed by function calls
Not all data types are supported	Not all data types are supported, but the set of supported types is very similar to the dataflow type set
Executed as a data stream through a graph	Executed on functional abstract machines; one of such machines is the G-machine

data mining/machine learning techniques (Allison, 2005; Kerdprasop, N. & Kerdprasop, K., 2007; Kholod, Rodionov, Tarasov, & Malov, 2017; Kholod, Kupriyanov, & Shorov, 2016). The answer to question is simple—if some of the classification algorithms can be implemented in functional programming languages, then such algorithms can very probably be implemented in dataflow programming languages on dataflow computers. A prerequisite is the existence of dataflow nodes that implements the basic constructions of functional programming languages. The number of such nodes is not necessarily large—just a few basic constructions and built-in mathematical functions make it possible to create programs that efficiently solve complex problems (Mitic, 1994; Mitic, 1995). Different measures used for model correctness do not require complicated code and can be easily programmed/ incorporated in dataflow nodes. Since functional programs can be native parallelized, translation to dataflow does not involve any drawbacks related to dataflow parallelism and execution acceleration.

The development of Haskell in the last few decades, when it became the standard language for functional programming, coincided with more intensive development of data mining/machine learning techniques, so today almost all classification algorithms in the functional paradigm are implemented in Haskell. Different algorithms have been developed, for example:

1. Since functional programming languages are simply implemented in parallel, the number of Haskell libraries developed for deep learning classification is particularly large (https://hackage.haskell.org/package/haskell-ml); moreover, there is a large number of developed modules and libraries on the GitHub (for example, haskell-torch).
2. The Machine Learning Toolbox Haskell package (https://hackage.haskell.org/package/mltool) provides implementations of various classification algorithms, binary and multiclass classification, neural network (with different activation functions), including MultiSVM Classifier as well as various tools for data preprocessing.
3. The method of implementation, among others, is a decision tree classifier (ID3 and K-NN) that uses the Haskell package. It is presented in detail in (Shukla, 2014). The implementation covers all necessary aspects (including computing entropy/information gain as a measure when splitting up material based on an attribute value/feature) and gives good directions for implementation of complicated algorithms such as C4.5.
4. Draft versions of K-Nearest Neighbors, Random Forest, ID3, and Feedforward Neural Network (de Alarcón Gervás, 2019).

All these implementations can be used as the core for implementing listed algorithms in the dataflow. To conclude this section, one way to relatively easily write classification algorithms to a (purely) dataflow component that will take advantage of the dataflow paradigm is to implement the basic expressions of a functional programming language in dataflow nodes. If this condition is met, the next step is to "translate" the algorithm from a functional code to a dataflow code following the structure and organization of functional programs.

PARALLEL CLASSIFICATION ON DATAFLOW

The initial development of all traditional data mining algorithms (and hence classification) was adapted to von Neumann computer model. Input data were stored in memory from where they were transferred to a processor, and after processing re-stored in the memory. The increase in the amount of data to be processed created the problem of scalability of the developed methods.

One of the potential ways to solve this problem, oriented towards reducing the time required for execution, is to parallelize the algorithms. There are many different approaches to algorithm scaling and parallelization. The attempt to implement algorithms on a parallel architecture had to solve the problems of both data sharing and synchronization of the obtained results and communication between the processes by which data processing was performed on different (usually tightly coupled) processors. The execution of data mining algorithms in a distributed environment can also be considered as a specific way of parallelization, but with introducing additional problems related to process communication, role of coordinator, synchronization of the processing flow, and exchange of results.

A description of some scaled/parallelized algorithms suitable for data mining is presented in (Bekkerman, Bilenko, & Langford, 2012), while paper (Zaki, 1999) includes an introduction to parallel and distributed data mining. Although there have been attempts to define distributed dataflow architecture (Kavi, Kim, Arul, & Hurson, 1999), this has not materialized in practice. Therefore, the content of this section implies that algorithms will be designed to work on the local computer.

Historically, the algorithms underlying the classification methods were initially developed in a sequential form, and their parallelization was attempted later. Only some of the classification algorithms appear in successfully developed versions that support parallel execution. The most common among them are classification algorithms with instances (K-Nearest Neighbors), algorithms based on ANN (Artificial Neural Networks), and decision tree algorithms. K-NN has more different implementations, using either common CPUs (Aparício, Blanquer, & Hernández, 2007) or GPUs (Liang, Liu, Wang, & Jian, 2009). The general principles for formulating parallel classification algorithms using decision trees are described in (Srivastava, Han, Kumar, & Singh, 1999). The decision tree algorithms with the most successful parallel versions are SPRINT (Shafer, Agrawal, & Mehta, 1996), RainForest (Gehrke, Ramakrishnan, & Ganti, 2000), and BOAT (Gehrke et al, 2000).

A look at a simplified dataflow computation scheme with interconnected nodes imposes an association with parallel computing, where each of the nodes represents a single processor. Unfortunately, there is not much work or implementation of parallel classification algorithms on pure dataflow architecture. Some of the main reasons are the limited ability to use shared memory and problems with synchronizing parallel processes. In this context, paper (Schelter, 2016) presents the principles of scaling data mining (not only classification) in massively parallel dataflow systems.

In the case of parallel execution, K-NN will be used as an example of possible implementation of the classification algorithm on a dataflow computer. K-NN is ideal because it is the simplest one among possible candidates. The general principle of constructing and verifying classification is that initial data (which includes class labels) are divided into two parts: training and testing. The model is constructed based on training records, while the test set is used to verify the constructed model by comparing predicted and actual class labels[3].

The K-NN algorithm is lazy and does not produce a model in the true sense as other classification algorithms. The model essentially consists of of all records belonging to the test set. If the test set contains m records of the form $(\mathbf{x}, y)$, where $\mathbf{x}$ are data attributes, and y is the class label, then class label ya for previously unseen record $a = (\mathbf{x}a, ya)$ is determined as a majority of class numbers counted from K records from the test material which are closest to input record. The term "closest" is usually related to distances, usually Euclidean or cosine distance, but in some situations (some of) hybrid distance calculation can be used if records have a mixture of numerical and categorical attributes.

As all dataflow implementations differ from each other, for the computer model on which a parallel version of the K-NN classification can be

Figure 1. Model of the dataflow computer for implementation of the K-NN classification algorithm. The architecture includes several dataflow engines (DFE). Each DFE consists of several kernels, which include dataflow nodes. Traditional (control-flow) CPU is used as the host for the operating system and operations that are not efficient on dataflow.

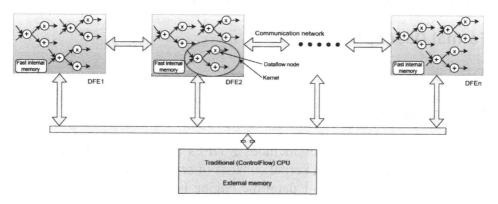

implemented, we will take the model of the (hybrid) dataflow computer system whose structure is presented in Figure 1 and which is in some parts similar to the Maxeler dataflow computer (Maxeler dataflow, 2021).

The model of the K-NN algorithm for dataflow computers is presented in two steps: the first one (informal description) presents a sketch of the basic idea, and the second one presents the idea in more detail.

Informal Description

Hypothesis: the distance of two records can be calculated in the dataflow kernel. No matter which distance is used (Euclidean, cosine, etc.), it can also be implemented in the kernel as shown in (Maxeler Technologies, 2021), where Euclidean distance for n-dimensional space is implemented as a measure for clustering (unsupervised classification).

Each of the dataflow engines (DFE) contains (in fast internal memory) a portion of the training data. DFE calculate the distance from the input record to several training data records. One dataflow kernel (denoted as F) has been especially singled out to select records that have K minimum distances and store them with their corresponding labels. The kernel is constructed in such a way that the values of these K distances are kept in an ascending order. In case the number of training records portion in DFE is greater than the number of kernels, distance calculations would be performed in several cycles by filling the next set of training data in kernels. The results of each intermediate calculation should be stored in fast memory and used by the F kernel. One of the DFEs was singled out to determine the lowest K "global" distances, and to count which labels of the class are the most numerous (the "voting" method) in those K records. This label is assigned to the input record.

Formal Description

Algorithm steps:

A. Prerequisites

- The dataflow computer includes z DFEs and each DFE includes w dataflow kernels (each kernel consists of several nodes).
- w-1 kernels in each z-1 dataflow engine is programmed to calculate required distance d of records t and a.

- One kernel (named *F*) in each *z*-1 dataflow engine is programmed to determine *K* minimal distances and corresponding class labels while keeping selected values in an ascending order.
- One dataflow engine (named DFE-*G*) is programmed to determine "global" *K* minimal distances and the determined majority class label which is assigned to input record *a*.

B. Input

- *T* is a set of *n* training records (vectors) *ti*=(*xi*,*yi*) *i*=1,..,*n*, where *yi*=class label, *xi* are attribute values, and *xi*=(xi1,xi2, …, xip), (*xi* is a set/vector of attribute values).
- *A* is a set of *m* input records (vectors) *aj*, *j*=1,..,*m* of the form aj=(aj1,aj2, …, ajp), (aj is a set/vector of attribute values; the number of attribute values is equal in records from *T* and *A*).
- *K* is the number of records from *T* with the lowest distances from the input record.

C. Preprocessing

- Divide records from set *T* into equal portions with size [*n*/(*z*-1)] and load into fast memory in each DFE.

D. Predicting the Labels of Input Records

```
for  i=1 to m
     load record a  in each of z-1 DFE with records from T
                  i
     in each of z-1 DFE
        {
         load -1 as initial value for K minimal distance in
kernel F in each DFE
         repeat
           load w-1 t records from DFE fast memory
           Calculate distance from a  to training records in
                                    i
each of w-1 kernels
           If w-1 is is less than number of records from T in
this DFE
                than
                  {
                    save intermediate result in fast memory
                    load new set of w-1 t records from DFE fast
```

```
memory
                }

        until all records from fast memory have been read
        Select K minimal distances in F and corresponding class
labels y₁,...,yₖ
        }
    Use DFE-G to determine "global" K minimal distances and
class label that will
        be assigned to record aᵢ
end for
```

Distance calculation can be fully parallelized since kernel calculations in the same DFE are mutually independent. If the dataflow system contains z DFEs, each of which contains w kernels, in this way an approximate acceleration of $(z-1)*(w-1)$ times is obtained compared to the sequential distance calculation. The value of acceleration is orientation because it depends on other factors (e.g., speed of data transfer and reading, fast memory size, number of readings per $w-1$ records, etc.)

The algorithm formulated in this way has one interesting feature. The traditional K-NN algorithm contains a set of training data in internal memory, while data records whose class labels should be predicted are loaded one by one. In the modification of the previously described K-NN algorithm, depending on the size of sets A and T, the places of training data and the data whose class is predicted can be reversed. This is the way to achieve a simultaneous prediction of class labels for input records.

DATAFLOW AND NEURAL NETWORK CLASSIFICATION ALGORITHMS

Artificial neural networks (ANN) are one of the techniques whose application has largely grown in the last decade. There are many examples of ANN implementations on control-flow computers used in various classification and clustering applications. These applications most often use multi-layer ANN ("deep learning") whose simplified appearance is presented in Figure 2. When this image is compared with the image that represents a simplified version of the dataflow model, a great structural similarity can be observed.

As the full potential of neural networks is better realized on computers that allow parallel processing, this was an additional reason for connecting neural networks with a dataflow paradigm, which, by its nature, allows

Figure 2. Multi-layer artificial neural network. The structural similarity with the dataflow model (set of connected nodes) is obvious.

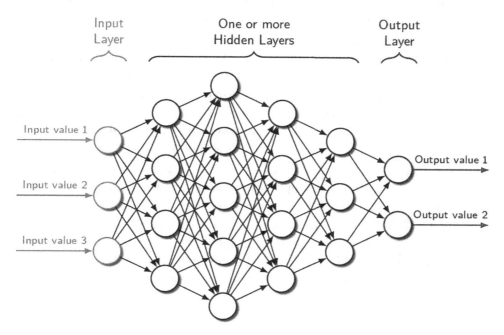

parallel execution. There are several papers (for example, see (Vokorokos, & Ádám, 2011)) that propose a new dataflow architecture with a number of reconfigurable elements that can support a neural network classification algorithm.

Neural networks have been successfully implemented on dataflow computers. The implementation of convolutional neural networks on the Maxeler MAX5 dataflow engine platform is described in (Voss, Bacis, Mencer, Gaydadjiev, & Luk, 2017). When tested on the image processing material, the implemented version showed very high performance compared to state of the art implementations. In addition to being at the very top in terms of speed, the implementation has also showed high accuracy. A dataflow computer model optimized for the execution of convolutional neural networks is presented in (Farabet et al, 2011). The authors studied different use cases and verified that the mapping of the convolutional neural network was straightforward on dataflow architecture.

There are hybrid dataflow architecture computing devices with special constructions intended for deep learning applications (Feldman, 2017; Liu et al, 2019). In addition, neural networks (with different activation functions) are implemented on the dataflow architecture developed by commercial companies (see (Maxeler Technologies, 2021)). Due to parallelism support combined with a large number of nodes, such implementations often have significantly better performance compared to implementations on control-flow machines. For example, in (Nicol, 2017b) it was reported that it was possible to accelerate deep learning training by up to 1000x.

TensorFlow can serve as a good direction for implementing classification algorithms on dataflow computers. Google TensorFlow (Abadi et al, 2016) is an open source software library for machine learning developed primarily for work with (deep) neural networks. Although Tensor Flow was initially designed for control-flow machines and GPUs, it is based on the dataflow programming concept and computation can be abstracted and represented by a directed oriented graph.

A clear parallel can be drawn between the graphs representing the set of nodes in the dataflow paradigm and the graphs representing the computational flow in Tensor Flow. Figure 3 shows the graph for calculation C^2*B + (A+B) whose form is similar to the set of dataflow nodes that calculate the same expression.

In addition, there is a similarity between the graph representing execution of functional programming programs (already connected with the dataflow paradigm), and the TensorFlow graph. The lines on the "functional" graph indicate the composition of functions in the functional program, and the lines on the TensorFlow graph indicate the flow of data between nodes. Each

Figure 3. Graph calculation for expression $C^2*B+(A+B)$. This can represent a calculation graph in TensorFlow, but also a connection among dataflow nodes in the dataflow paradigm. The elements of the TensorFlow graph represent a counterpart to the set of nodes in the computed dataflow in which multiplication and addition operations are performed.

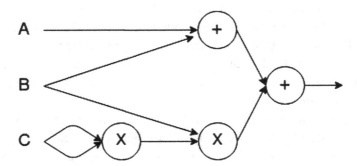

operation (or complex calculation) in the TensorFlow node represents some of the built-in functions of the functional programming language. Large graph segments in TensorFlow correspond to functions with embedded (more elementary) functions in the functional program.

TensorFlow, beside neural network/deep learning algorithms, also supports other classification algorithms like Tensor Flow Decision Forest (variant of Random Forest) and Support Vector Machines. Although the implementation of neural networks in dataflow computers with the main goal of classifying materials has not been done so far (at least not a complete algorithm with all possibilities), the above experiences, especially the relatively simple mapping of neural networks to dataflow architecture, show that no major changes will be needed for classification algorithms to be performed on dataflow architecture.

DATA STREAM CLASSIFICATION

The development of information technologies in the last twenty years, both in terms of hardware and software, resulted in the increase in the volume of data available for processing. Among them, the data that are collected or come in the form of a data stream stand out. Such data are collected or generated in a large number of areas such as astronomical data, meteorological data, data in computer networks, stock exchange data, data related to the state of nuclear power plants, etc. Their characteristics are a constant flow (arrival) of new data, possible high speed and large volume due to which they cannot be stored, multidimensionality, dynamic change of characteristics, and potential infinity in (stream) length.

The classification of such data is of great importance in applications that cover these areas in order to extract the information carried by the data. However, due to the characteristics of data streams, classical classification algorithms cannot be applied in most cases. The process of classification in data streams has the following new challenges that do not exist in traditional classification algorithms:

- Data streams are continuous, i.e. without upper size limit.
- Due to the vast number of elements, there is no memory for their storage, and after processing, records must be discarded. The consequence is that algorithms must be only single-pass on the data.

- The classification of an unknown record must be faster than the incoming record speed in the data stream to prevent accumulation of unclassified records.
- The classification model is often a part of a real-time application.
- Class labels distribution can change in time compared to the initial set used for training. This change may reduce the accuracy of the classification (concept drifting).
- In continuous incoming, the data flow might appear in some instances with new class labels that do not exist in the initial set of labels, which can lead to unclassified/misclassified instances (concept evolution).
- There are issues with rare class labels. If the distribution of class labels changes in time and/or new class labels are added to training data, class labels whose elements appear very rarely can be lost from the training data.

There are many classification algorithms especially designed for data streams. A review of data stream classification approaches is shown in (Wankhade, Dongre, & Jondhale, 2020) and (Li et al, 2019), while more details about data stream classification algorithms can be found in (Aggarwal, 2007) and (Aggarwal, 2014). As in previous cases, there are no defined or implemented algorithms for data stream classification on dataflow computers. As K-NN is the simplest one, using it as an implementation example is naturally imposed.

There are various implementations of K-NN for data streams on control-flow computers (for example see (Law, Zaniolo, 2005; Ueno, Xi, Keogh, & Lee, 2006 ; (Bahri, Maniu, Bifet, Fernandes de Mello, & Tziortziotis, 2020), but none of them can be easily mapped to dataflow architecture. Instead of mapping or modifying some of existing control-flow solutions, we will try to sketch a naive version of K-NN for the dataflow computing paradigm. This naive version tries to exploit parallelism as the natural advantage of dataflow computers with a large number of dataflow nodes.

The algorithm is based on the previously defined K-NN algorithm in section 3.3, with modifications that eliminate the possibility of rare classes being lost from training data and allow for concept drift. The algorithm does not handle the detection of novel classes (avoid semi-supervised approach, see (Aggarwal, 2007)) and it is assumed that the number of classes does not change during execution.

Informal Description

Hypothesis:

- The distance of two records can be calculated in the dataflow kernel. No matter which distance is used (Euclidean, cosine, etc.), it can also be implemented in the kernel.
- Data arrive in a stream; the number of attributes in data is unchanged in time.
- All data are prepared (categorical attributes) for distance counting and nodes in DFE are programmed for distance calculation.
- There are two special DFEs: one is used for concept drift (denote as DFE-D) and the other one used for determining the lowest K global distances (denote as DFE-G).
- Each of the remaining DFEs contains (in fast internal memory) a portion of training data.

In DFEs, the distance to several training data records is calculated for the input record. One dataflow kernel has been specially singled out to select records that have K minimum distances and store them with their corresponding labels. The kernel is constructed in such a way that the values of these K distances are kept in an ascending order. DFE-G was singled out to determine the lowest K "global" distances, and to count which labels of the class are the most numerous ("voting") in those K records. This label is assigned to the input record.

The initial action in enabling concept drift consists of counting class labels in training instances, calculating their percentage and storing labels and corresponding values in DFE-D. The instances in the training set form a virtually ordered list with counter. The counter used as a specific "pointer" to the instance which will be replaced with the next incoming instance from the stream. The current value of the counter is stored in DFE-D. When a new instance arrives, after determining its label, it replaces "the oldest" instance indicated by the current value of the counter. Before initiating the replacement, it is checked which percentage of the class corresponding to the instance to which the current value of the counter points. If the percentage is below a predefined threshold, the current value of the counter increases by 1 and checks the percentage of the class from the corresponding new "oldest" training instance. The process continues until appropriate instance is found. After the initial replacement, the counter increases by 1 to point to the next "oldest" instance. Replacement is initiated by sending the counter value, determined class, and new instance record to appropriate DFE in which the "oldest" record with the sent counter value is located.

Using predefined threshold prevents eliminating instances with rare classes and consequently eliminates the need to handle infrequently recurring classes.

Formal Description

Algorithm steps:

A. Prerequisites

- Dataflow computer includes z DFEs and each of z-2 DFEs includes w dataflow kernels (each kernel consists of several nodes).
- One kernel (named F) in each z-2 dataflow engine is programmed to determine K minimal distances and corresponding class labels and keep selected values in an ascending order.
- One kernel (named R) in each z-2 dataflow engine is programmed to replace the instance with the received counter value.
- w-2 kernels in each z-2 dataflow engine is programmed to calculate the required distance d of two records: t and a.
- DFE (named *DFE-G*) contains kernels programmed to determine the lowest K "global" distances, and to count which labels of the class are the most numerous ones in those K records.
- DFE (named *DFE-D*) contains kernels which hold class labels, its percentage in current version of the training material, counter C that holds the value of the candidate instance for replacement counter, and predefined threshold V.

B. Input

- T is a set of n training records (vectors) $ti=(\boldsymbol{xi}, yi)$ $i=1,..,n$ where yi=class labels, $\boldsymbol{xi}$ are attribute values, and $\boldsymbol{xi}=(xi1, xi2, ..., xip)$ ($\boldsymbol{xi}$ is a set/vector of attribute values).
- A is a set of input records (vectors) from stream $\boldsymbol{aj}$, $j=1,..,\infty$ of the form $aj=(aj1, aj2, ..., ajp)$, (aj is a set/vector of attribute values—the number of attribute values is equal in records from T and A).

- K is the number of records from T with minimal distances from the input record.

C. Preprocessing

- Divide records from set T into equal portions with size $[n/(z-2)]$ and load into fast memory in each of $z-2$ DFEs. Each record is extended with a counter which contains the order of arrival, with minimal value 1 and maximal n (values are global for all DFEs).
- The value of the counter C in *DFE-D*, which holds the indicator of current candidates instance for replacement, is changed by modulo n, where n is the number of training records.
- Calculate the percentage Pclass of each class in the training material and store the obtained values together with the minimal threshold V in *DFE-D*.

D. Predicting the Labels of Input Records

```
in each of z-2 DFE load w-2 t records from DFE fast memory
set C=1

repeat
    load next incoming record a in each of z-2 DFE with
records from T
    in each of z-2 DFE
        {
        load -1 as initial value for K minimal distance in
kernel F in each DFE
        Calculate distance from a to training records in each
of w-2 kernels
        Select K minimal distances in F and corresponding class
labels y₁,...,yₖ
        }
    Use DFE-G to determine "global" K minimal distances and
class label L that
    will be assigned to record a
    Use DFE-D to replace the current " oldest" instance in z-2
DFEs.
        {
        select class O of current "oldest" training instance
        while (PO ≤ V)   /* percentage for class O is less than
or equal V */
            {
            set C=mod(C+1,n) /* skip to next oldest
```

```
instance in training set */
                select class O of current "oldest" training
instance
            }
        determine DFE with "oldest" instance
            /* "oldest" - instance with counter equal with
current value of C */
        send request to selected DFE to update instance with
new record (a,L)
        set C=mod(C+1,n)
        }
until end_of_stream  /* forever */
```

This concept of the algorithm assumes that the number of available kernels in DFE is sufficient to handle training record portions. If this is not the case, the algorithm becomes more complicated because distance calculations must be performed in several cycles by filling the next set of training data in kernels, similarly as in the algorithm described in section 3.3. This implies the need for additional steps because intermediate results of at least K calculated distances must be stored for further comparisons, which will slow down performance in the case of a very fast data stream.

EXAMPLE OF DATAFLOW ARCHITECTURE

In this chapter, only a sketch of the dataflow architecture will be presented in order to provide basic information about the possible dataflow advantages over the control-flow ones. The Maxeler computer dataflow concept (Maxeler dataflow, 2021) will be used as an example. A more detailed description of the dataflow architecture goes beyond the scope of this chapter. More details on the dataflow architecture and its characteristics can be found in (Milutinović, Salom, Trifunovic, & Giorgi, 2015; Milutinovic, & Kotlar, 2019).

Simplified schemes of control-flow (von Neumann architecture) and Maxeler dataflow architecture is shown on Figure 4.

In control-flow architecture (Figure 4a) the source program is compiled into a list of instructions for a concrete processor (or processor family). Data and instructions are read from external (off-CPU chip) memory and loaded into the processor cash memory where operations are performed. Structure and relation of CPU and memory is fixed and can not be reconfigured according to the problem to be solved.

Figure 4. A comparison between a conventional control-flow (von Neumann) architecture (a) and a Maxeler Dataflow architecture (b)
Source: Maxeler - https://www.maxeler.com/technology/dataflow-computing/

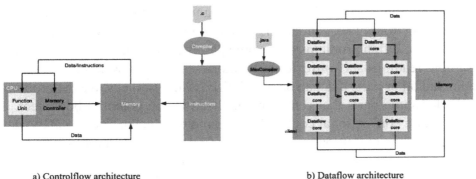

a) Controlflow architecture   b) Dataflow architecture

In dataflow architecture (Figure 4b) the source program is transformed into a Dataflow engine configuration file. Configuration file describes the operations, layout and connections of a Dataflow engine, which can be reconfigured according to the problem to be solved. Dataflow engine includes many computational units whose connections are defined in configuration file. Each computational unit ("dataflow core") can perform some operation on input data. Data can be streamed from external memory into the computational units and after applying operation result will be forwarded over connection to another connected computational units, without need for writing it to off-chip memory until computation is complete. Each Dataflow engine can hold one or more dataflow kernels that consist of dataflow nodes. Such dataflow structure provides computations entirely without instructions or accompanying control mechanisms - data flows from one functional unit directly to the next one. This computational model can be represent over a graph - functional units are graph nodes that performs only a simple operation (like addition, substraction or multiplication), and connection between graph nodes represent connection between functional units. In this model, data enter in graph and flows from one node to another, and computation inside graph (nodes) are carried out in parallel.

Presented concept enables that hundreds or thousands of operations can be perform on single chip surface, which makes dataflow computers energy efficient and highly parallel. Consequences is that dataflow computation outperforms control-flow one if problem solving process can be parallelized. Dataflow engine also include, along with many computational units, large

67

amounts of DRAM memory and a manager that is responsible for managing the connections between kernels, memory, and other external devices including control-flow CPU, if exists.

Not all problems are eligible for solving using dataflow computation. If problem is strongly sequential, than using only control-flow paradigm will be efficient. Often problems have some part that is naturally sequential (for example, reading data from external memories like hard disk drive or magnetic tape) and other parts that can be parallelized. Analyst that solve the problem looks for some parts that can be paralellized or are potential bottleneck if executed on conventional control-flow computer. Such parts are candidates for transferring execution to dataflow computers. Compiling program code that correspond to these parts are done with specific tolls that compile (or translate) code from high-level languages to dataflow configuration which include kernels to generate a hardware dataflow implementation, connection configuration and CPU application, which is used in process of read and write data among kernels and engine RAM. An example of such tool is Maxeler MaxCompiler (Maxeler dataflow, 2021; Top500, 2021).

Because application in real world often consists of both control-flow and dataflow eligible parts, modern dataflow computers systems are hybrid - they include control-flow CPUs and Dataflow part. For example, Maxeler

Figure 5. Maxeler MPC-C Series node architecture
Source: Maxeler (https://www.maxeler.com/products/mpc-cseries/)

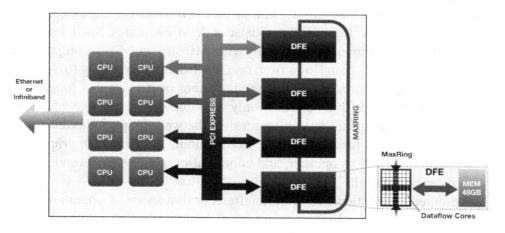

MPC-C series computer can have 4 dataflow engines, up to 192GB DFE

RAM (48GB per DFE), 12 Intel Xeon CPU cores and up to 192GB CPU memory (Figure 5).

COMPARING DATAFLOW VS. CONTROL-FLOW COMPUTERS

Due to different basis it is not easy to make simple performance comparison of Dataflow and Control-flow computers. Usable general benchmarks that suits to both paradigms does not exists. The current ranking using FLOPS (PFlops, TFlops, MFlops) and LINPACK as benchmark program for creating TOP500 supercomputer list (Top500, 2021) does not suit to dataflow computers. Flynn et al. in (Flynn et al., 2013) suggest introduction new alternative performance measures for computer ranking, possibly ones with a much wider scope.

Similar situation is when compare energy efficient. Current criteria are not adapted to dataflow. On site (Top500, 2021) exists GREEN500 list, but ranking (gigaflops/watt power-efficiency) and benchmark are strongly related to control-flow architecture. In general, due to large number of computational units dataflow computers have, in general, higher energy efficient level than control-flow ones. But, because dataflow computers are reconfigurable and adaptive to problem solving process, their energy efficient level also depends on concrete problem. An simple approach to analysis the performance, resource usage and energy consumption of reconfigurable computing systems is described in (Luk, 2015; Munday, Pell, Mencer, & Flynn, 2015). Stojanovic et al. in (Stojanovic et al., 2013) present comparison of Maxeler MAX3 with Intel Core i7-870 and Nvidia C2070, and found that MAX3 used approximately half of power consumed by Intel I7-870, and only 36% of Nvidia C2070 with declared performance (in GFlops) app. 960% higher than Intel i7-870 and 54% lower than Nvidia C2070. In test, MAX3 had smaller execution time than both competitors.

The efficiency of the dataflow approach has been demonstrated in several special applications (Koliogeorgi et al., 2019; Becker et al., 2017; Nestorov et al., 2017). In (Becker et al., 2017) authors shows that implementation of well-*known Smith-Waterman* algorithm for DNA sequence aligning and including this version in Bowtie-2 aligner gives 18x speedup over standalone components and up to 35% boosting in performance. A list of systematic transformations and optimizations targeting Maxeler dataflow systems that typically yield one to two orders of magnitude improvements in terms of both performance and energy efficiency are presented in (Becker et al., 2017). In (Nestorov et al., 2017) authors reported that implementation of Curran's approximation algorithm using dataflow oriented approach on Maxeler server-class HPC system produce speed-up of 111x and 278.3x compared to a single-threaded software implementation, and 4x and 9.2x compared to a multi-threaded software implementation running on a dual socket CPU server with 12-core Intel Xeon E5-2697 v2 CPUs.

Despite the currently small number of applications developed compared to control-flow computers, these examples show that the use of dataflow computers and dataflow approach can have significant advantages, and that their use will increase in the future.

REVIEW QUESTIONS

This section provides questions for better understanding of the key aspects of the chapter.

1. What are the key aspects of the dataflow paradigm?
2. What are the key aspects of the functional programming?
3. What is the main difference between dataflow and functional programming?
4. Describe major drawbacks in implementing data stream classification algorithm using dataflow paradigm.

REFERENCES

Abadi, M., Barham, P., Chen, J., Chen, Z., Davis, A., Dean, J., Devin, M., Ghemawat, S., Irving, G., Isard, M., Kudlur, M., Levenberg, J., Monga, R., Moore, S., Murray, D. G., Steiner, B., Tucker, P. A., Vasudevan, V., Warden, P., ... Zhang, X. (2016). TensorFlow: A system for large-scale machine learning. *12th USENIX Symposium on Operating Systems Design and Implementation (OSDI 16)*, 265-283.

Aggarwal, C. C. (Ed.). (2007). *Data Streams - Models and Algorithms*. Springer-Verlag.

Aggarwal, C. C. (2014). A Survey of Stream Classification Algorithms. In C. C. Aggarwal (Ed.), *Data Classification: Algorithms and Applications* (pp. 245–273). CRC Press. doi:10.1201/b17320

Allison, L. (2005). Models for machine learning and data mining in functional programming. *Journal of Functional Programming*, *15*(1), 15–32. doi:10.1017/S0956796804005301

Amamiya, M. (1988). Data flow computing and parallel reduction machine. *Future Generation Computer Systems*, *4*(1), 53–67. doi:10.1016/0167-739X(88)90019-2

Aparício, G., Blanquer, I., & Hernández, V. A. (2007). Parallel Implementation of the K Nearest Neighbours Classifier in Three Levels: Threads, MPI Processes and the Grid. *Proceedings of the 7th international conference on High performance computing for computational science - VECPAR 2006*, 225–235. 10.1007/978-3-540-71351-7_18

Backus, J. (1978). Can programming be liberated from the von Neumann style? A functional style and its algebra of programs. *Communications of the ACM*, *21*(8), 613–641. doi:10.1145/359576.359579

Bahri, M., Maniu, S., Bifet, A., Fernandes de Mello, R., & Tziortziotis, N. (2020). Compressed k-Nearest Neighbors Ensembles for Evolving Data Streams. In *ECAI 2020 - 24th European Conference on Artificial Intelligence*. Santiago de Compostella / Virtual. http://ecai2020.eu/papers/57_paper.pdf

Becker, T., Burovskiy, P., Nestorov, A. M., Palikareva, H., Reggiani, E., & Gaydadjiev, G. (2017). From exaflop to exaflow. 2017 Design, Automation & Test in Europe Conference & Exhibition (DATE), 404-409. doi:10.23919/DATE.2017.7927024

Bekkerman, R., Bilenko, M., & Langford, J. (Eds.). (2012). *Scaling up machine learning: parallel and distributed approaches*. Cambridge University Press.

de Alarcón Gervás, M. F. (2019). Functional Programming Paradigm for Machine Learning Algorithms in Data Mining. Degree work, Universidad autonoma de Madrid, Madrid, Spain.

Do, T.N., Nguyen, V.H., & Poulet, F. (2008). A Fast Parallel SVM Algorithm for Massive Classification Tasks. *Communications in Computer and Information Science*, *14*, 419-428.

Farabet, C., Lecun, Y., Kavukcuoglu, K., Martini, B., Akselrod, P., Talay, S., & Culurciello, E. (2011). Large-Scale FPGA-Based Convolutional Networks. In R. Bekkerman, M. Bilenko, & J. Langford (Eds.), *Scaling up Machine Learning: Parallel and Distributed Approaches* (pp. 399–419). Cambridge University Press. doi:10.1017/CBO9781139042918.020

Feldman, M. (2017). *Wave Computing Launches Machine Learning Appliance*. https://www.top500.org/news/wave-computing-launches-machine-learning-appliance/

Field, A. J., & Harrison, P. G. (1988). *Functional Programming*. Addison-Wesley.

Flynn, M., Mencer, O., Milutinovic, V., Rakocevic, G., Stenstrom, P., Trobec, R., & Valero, M. (2013). Moving from Petaflops to Petadata. *Communications of the ACM*, *56*(5), 39–42. doi:10.1145/2447976.2447989

Gehrke, J., Ganti, V., Ramakrishnan, R., & Loh, W.-Y. (2000). BOAT---Optimistic Decision Tree Construction. *SIGMOD Record*, *28*(2), 169–180. doi:10.1145/304181.304197

Gehrke, J., Ramakrishnan, R., & Ganti, V. (2000). RainForest—A Framework for Fast Decision Tree Construction of Large Datasets. *Data Mining and Knowledge Discovery*, *4*(2/3), 127–162. doi:10.1023/A:1009839829793

Giraud-Carrier, C. G. (1994). A reconfigurable dataflow machine for implementing functional programming languages. *ACM SIGPLAN Notices*, *29*(9), 22–28. doi:10.1145/185009.185014

Guo, T., Xu, J., Yan, X., Hou, J., Li, P., Li, Z., Guo, J., & Cheng, X. (2016) Ease the Process of Machine Learning with Dataflow. *CIKM '16: Proceedings of the 25th ACM International on Conference on Information and Knowledge Management*, 2437–2440. 10.1145/2983323.2983327

Henderson, P. (1980). *Functional Programming: Application and Implementation*. Prentice-Hall International.

Hurson, R. A., & Kavi, M. K. (2007). Dataflow Computers: Their History and Future. In B. W. Wah (Ed.), *Wiley Encyclopedia of Computer Science and Engineering* (pp. 1099–1111). John Wiley & Sons, Inc. doi:10.1002/9780470050118.ecse102

Johnston, M. W., Hanna, J. R. P., & Millar, J. R. (2004). Advances in Dataflow Programming Languages. *ACM Computing Surveys, 36*(1), 1–34. doi:10.1145/1013208.1013209

Kavi, K. M., Kim, H.-S., Arul, J., & Hurson, A. R. (1999). A decoupled scheduled dataflow multithreaded architecture. *Proceedings Fourth International Symposium on Parallel Architectures, Algorithms, and Networks,* 138-143. 10.1109/ISPAN.1999.778930

Kerdprasop, N., & Kerdprasop, K. (2007). Mining Frequent Patterns with Functional Programming. *International Journal of Computer, Electrical, Automation, Control and Information Engineering, 1*(1), 124–129.

Kholod, I., Kupriyanov, M., & Shorov, A. (2016). Decomposition of Data Mining Algorithms into Unified Functional Blocks. *Mathematical Problems in Engineering, 2016*(1), 1–11. doi:10.1155/2016/8197349

Kholod, I. I., Rodionov, S. V., Tarasov, K. A., & Malov, A. V. (2017). Using the features of functional programming for parallel building of decision trees. *2017 IEEE Conference of Russian Young Researchers in Electrical and Electronic Engineering (EIConRus),* 445-449. 10.1109/EIConRus.2017.7910587

Koliogeorgi, K., Voss, N., Fytraki, S., Xydis, S., Gaydadjiev, G., & Soudris, D. (2019). Dataflow acceleration of Smith-Waterman with Traceback for high throughput Next Generation Sequencing. *Proceedings of the 29th International Conference on Field Programmable Logic and Applications (FPL),* 74-80. 10.1109/FPL.2019.00021

Law, Y. N., & Zaniolo, C. (2005). An Adaptive Nearest Neighbor Classification Algorithm for Data Streams. In A. M. Jorge, L. Torgo, P. Brazdil, R. Camacho, & J. Gama (Eds.), Lecture Notes in Computer Science: Vol. 3721. *Knowledge Discovery in Databases: PKDD 2005* (pp. 108–120). Springer. doi:10.1007/11564126_15

Li, L., Sun, R., Cai, S., Zhao, K., & Zhang, Q. (2019). A review of improved extreme learning machine methods for data stream classification. *Multimedia Tools and Applications, 78*(23), 33375–33400. doi:10.100711042-019-7543-2

Liang, S., Liu, Y., Wang, C., & Jian, L. (2009). A CUDA-based parallel implementation of K-nearest neighbor algorithm. *2009 International Conference on Cyber-Enabled Distributed Computing and Knowledge Discovery,* 291-296. 10.1109/CYBERC.2009.5399145

Liu, L., Zhu, J., Li, Z., Lu, Y., Deng, Y., Han, J., Yin, S., & Wei, S. (2019, October). A Survey of Coarse-Grained Reconfigurable Architecture and Design: Taxonomy, Challenges, and Applications. *ACM Comput. Surv., 52*(6), 1–39. doi:10.1145/3357375

Luk, W. (2015). Analysing Reconfigurable Computing Systems. In Transforming reconfigurable systems: a festschrift celebrating the 60th birthday of professor Peter Cheung, (pp. 101-115). Imperial College Press. doi:10.1142/9781783266975_0006

Maxeler Dataflow Computer Products. (2021). https://www.maxeler.com/products/

Maxeler Technologies. (2021, August 15). *Maxeler Application Galery.* https://appgallery.maxeler.com

Milutinovic, V., & Kotlar, M. (Eds.). (2019). *Exploring the DataFlow Supercomputing Paradigm: Example Algorithms for Selected Applications.* Springer Nature Switzerland. doi:10.1007/978-3-030-13803-5

Milutinović, V., Salom, J., Trifunovic, N., & Giorgi, R. (2015). *Guide to DataFlow Supercomputing: Basic Concepts, Case Studies, and a Detailed Example.* Springer International Publishing. doi:10.1007/978-3-319-16229-4

Mitic, N. (1994). A solution to the parts explosion problem (LispKit) LISP/SQL language. *Matematicki Vesnik, 46*(3-4), 105–112.

Mitic, N. (1995). *Functional interface towards relational databases and its applications* [PhD thesis]. Faculty of mathematics, Belgrade, Serbia.

Munday, M., Pell, O., Mencer, O., & Flynn, M. J. (2015). Maximum Performance Computing with Dataflow Technology. In Transforming reconfigurable systems: a festschrift celebrating the 60th birthday of professor Peter Cheung, (pp. 137-150). Imperial College Press. doi:10.1142/9781783266975_0008

Nestorov, A. M., Reggiani, E., Palikareva, H., Burovskiy, P., Becker, T., & Santambrogio, M. D. (2017). A Scalable Dataflow Implementation of Curran's Approximation Algorithm. *2017 IEEE International Parallel and Distributed Processing Symposium Workshops (IPDPSW)*, 150-157. 10.1109/IPDPSW.2017.67

Nicol, C. (2017a). *A coarse grain reconfigurable array (cgra) for statically scheduled data flow computing.* Wave Computing White Paper. http://www.silicon-russia.com/public_materials/2017_10_08_msu_rountable/background/CGRA+Whitepaper.pdf

Nicol, C. (2017b). A dataflow processing chip for training deep neural networks. *Proceedings of the IEEE Hot Chips 29 Symp.*

Schelter, S. (2016). *Scaling data mining in massively parallel dataflow systems* [PhD Thesis]. Technische Universität Berlin. https://depositonce.tu-berlin.de/bitstream/11303/5294/4/schelter_sebastian.pdf

Shafer, J., Agrawal, R., & Mehta, M. (1996). SPRINT: A Scalable Parallel Classifier for Data Mining. *Proceedings of the 22nd VLDB Conference,* 544-555.

Shukla, N. (2014). *Haskell Data Analysis Cookbook.* Packt Publishing.

Srivastava, A., Han, E. H., Kumar, V., & Singh, V. (1999). Parallel Formulations of Decision-Tree Classification Algorithms. In Y. Guo & R. Grossman (Eds.), *High Performance Data Mining.* Springer. doi:10.1007/0-306-47011-X_2

Stojanovic, S., Milutinovic, V., Bojic, D., Bojovic, M., Pell, O., Flynn, M. J., & Mencer, O. (2013). *Comparing MultiCore, ManyCore, and DataFlow SuperComputers: Acceleration, Power, and Size.* http://home.etf.rs/~vm/papers/m1/IEEE_Micro_V1.pdf

Top500. (2021). *TOP500 - 500 most powerful commercially available computer systems.* https://top500.org/

Treleaven, P. C., Hopkins, R. P., & Rautenbachm, P. W. (1982). Combining data flow and control flow computing. *The Computer Journal, 25*(2), 207–217. doi:10.1093/comjnl/25.2.207

Ueno, K., Xi, X., Keogh, E., & Lee, D. (2006). Anytime Classification Using the Nearest Neighbor Algorithm with Applications to Stream Mining. *Proceedings of Sixth International Conference on Data Mining (ICDM'06),* 623-632. 10.1109/ICDM.2006.21

Vokorokos, L., & Ádám, N. (2011). An introduction to the Neural DF architecture. *2011 IEEE 9th International Symposium on Applied Machine Intelligence and Informatics (SAMI),* 33-37. 10.1109/SAMI.2011.5738906

Voss, N., Bacis, M., Mencer, O., Gaydadjiev, G., & Luk, W. (2017). Convolutional Neural Networks on Dataflow Engines. *2017 IEEE International Conference on Computer Design (ICCD)*, 435-438. 10.1109/ICCD.2017.77

Wadge, W. W., & Ashcroft, A. E. (1985). *Lucid, the Dataflow Programming Language*. Academic Press.

Wankhade, K. K., Dongre, S. S., & Jondhale, K. C. (2020). Data stream classification: A review. *Iran J Comput Sci*, *3*(4), 239–260. doi:10.100742044-020-00061-3

Whiting, P. G., & Pascoe, R. S. V. (1994). A history of data-flow languages. *IEEE Annals of the History of Computing*, *16*(4), 38–59. doi:10.1109/85.329757

Widemann, B. T., & Lepper, M. (2014). Foundations of Total Functional Data-Flow Programming. Electronic Proceedings in Theoretical Computer Science, 153, 143–167. doi:10.4204/EPTCS.153.10

Ye, X., Tan, X., Wu, M., Feng, Y., Wang, D., Zhang, H., Pei, S., & Fan, D. (2020). An efficient dataflow accelerator for scientific applications. *Future Generation Computer Systems*, *112*, 580–588. doi:10.1016/j.future.2020.03.023

Zaki, M. J. (1999). Parallel and Distributed Data Mining: An Introduction. *Lecture Notes in Computer Science*, *1759*, 1–23.

KEY TERMS AND DEFINITIONS

Dataflow: Programming paradigm based on execution graphs.

DFE: Dataflow engine which reconfigures according to the execution graph.

Execution Graph: Execution graph of the dataflow paradigm which describes the program.

Functional Programming: Programming model based on expressions and closures.

Von Neumann: Von Neumann paradigm as conventional programming paradigm.

ENDNOTES

[1]   We use the term *classification* to denote supervised classification, and *clustering* for unsupervised classification.

[2]   In the rest of the chapter we will use the term *implementation on dataflow* as a synonym for implementation using components of the dataflow computer that does not contain control-flow parts.

[3]   As some classification algorithms used test data to optimize the constructed model, data are sometimes divided into three parts: for training, testing, and verification, whereby verification acts as previously unseen data used for additional verification of the constructed model.

Chapter 4
Scientific Applications of Machine Learning Algorithms

ABSTRACT

This chapter considers several popular scientific applications of machine learning/data mining algorithms. The survey-like introductory section provides a brief overview of some relevant historical and trending applications, while the other four sections present specific details on four selected scientific applications. Each section focuses on one of the following algorithms: neural networks, rule induction, tree algorithms, and neighborhood-based algorithms.

INTRODUCTION

Machine learning (ML) has a huge impact on modern science. Its impact can even be compared to the impact that mathematics has had in a more traditional scientific context. Scientists from diverse fields either use ML methods directly or adjust them to be better suited for posed problematic. Scientific fields interested in ML are numerous and they include physics, space sciences, chemistry, biology, economy, medicine, etc. The presented overview is non-exhaustive and represents only a sample of all relevant applications of ML in science, organized by categories. The following text will first provide a more detailed insight of recent ML applications in four scientific (sub)disciplines, namely:

1.   computer vision,

DOI: 10.4018/978-1-7998-8350-0.ch004

2.   bioinformatics and computational biology,
3.   communication networks,
4.   astronomy and astrophysics.

After this, four specific scientific applications will be discussed in much more detail. More precisely, the chapter will present the application of each of the four selected ML algorithms:

1.   neural network algorithm for image classification,
2.   tree-like algorithm for protein structural class prediction,
3.   rule-induction algorithm for intrusion detection,
4.   neighborhood algorithm for the sample selection bias problem in astronomy.

APPLICATIONS IN COMPUTER VISION

Computer vision is one of the busiest areas of artificial intelligence, within which scientists of various backgrounds collaboratively solve complex tasks such as object detection, object tracking, semantic segmentation, etc. Autonomous vehicles represent a technology that is the main driver of new scientific results in computer vision. The reader is referred to (Janai et al., 2020) for a deeper understanding of problems, data sets, and state-of-the-art methods in computer vision for autonomous vehicles. Since there are hundreds of successful ML methods for computer vision, we will mention only some more recent and more relevant ones.

The object detection problem consists in locating and classifying objects visible in natural images. It is similar to the problem of image classification that will be reviewed in the following sections. But unlike image classification, where the goal is to assign a class to an input image, object detection also needs to localize one or more objects on a single image with bounding boxes, and then further classify each one. Solutions to this problem are usually modeled as software systems that are tightly coupled with underlying hardware, such as video, thermal infrared cameras, or laser scanners. It matters to have better hardware because the software system can be fed by more useful information, i.e., more features and/or better feature measurements. There is a vast number of methods for completing the object detection task by employing deep neural networks—see the recent review by Zhao et al. (2019).

Object tracking deals with a related but not identical problem: its goal is to estimate the state of one or multiple objects through time. The state can be represented in various ways, such as position, velocity, acceleration, etc. In contrast to object detection, where each image is independent, in this case, the contextual information, or the sequence of images can be useful. Moreover, the state dynamics of other objects in an image sequence can impact the state of observed objects. One of the most cited use-cases of object tracking is in the area of autonomous driving vehicles, where an automated driving system relies on various environmental information, such as other vehicles, pedestrians, cyclists, road signalization, etc. There are many approaches to solving this problem in literature and they are mostly based on a certain machine learning method. Hatwar et al. (2018) and Soleimanitaleb et al. (2019) provide critical reviews of the problem, in which they categorize approaches for solving it. For example, Soleimanitaleb et al. (2019) consider four large groups of methods: feature-based, segmentation-based, estimation-based, and learning-based. The learning-based group is the biggest and the most diverse one; it contains many ML methods, such as reinforcement learning, discriminative approaches belonging to deep and shallow learning, and generative methods. For a recent thorough review of literature, we refer the reader to (Luo et al., 2020).

The semantic segmentation task consists in assigning a semantic label to each pixel inside a natural image. This is one of the most important steps in robotic vision systems which the other automated procedures depend on. According to Yu et al. (2018), there are two essential questions to be considered regarding this task:

1. how to design efficient feature representation and predict various objects,
2. once the predictions of objects are made, how to use the contextual information to further improve consistency between object labels and pixels.

For the first subproblem, aside from some early approaches that used hand-crafted or semi-automated feature engineering, a vast amount of new and successful methods employs deep learning. For a deep learning focused review, we refer the reader to (Garcia-Garcia et al., 2017), where many kinds of deep neural networks are discussed: convolutional networks, Bayesian networks, LSTM, recurrent neural networks, etc. On the other hand, for making contextual improvements, the standard methodology is to use models such as the Markov random field, conditional random field, or recurrent neural networks.

APPLICATIONS IN BIOINFORMATICS AND COMPUTATIONAL BIOLOGY

Bioinformatics and computational biology are two disciplines gathered around the expanding fields of data science and biotechnology. Bioinformatics is mostly concerned with studying large sets of biological data, and providing statistics and conclusions on top of them. Standard applications in bioinformatics include microbial genome applications, molecular medicine, drug development, gene therapy, evolutionary studies, etc. On the other hand, computational biology is concerned with issues that occur in bioinformatics, which are some lower-level tasks such as metabolic pathway studies, cellular biology, systems biology, and genetic analysis. Both fields are heavily interdisciplinary, mostly reusing or introducing concepts from the field of artificial intelligence, mathematics, and general computer science, such as neural networks, deep learning, statistics, stochastic modeling, database management, text mining, etc.

Due to a large quantity of publications in this interdisciplinary context and high pressure from both the side of computational biology and computer science, it is expected and common to observe misconceptions regarding ML applications. In (Chicco, 2017), the author provides a list of ten quick tips for ML in computational biology. One of perhaps the most frequent errors that scientists and practitioners make is related to the usage of the test data set. Scientists sometimes knowingly or unknowingly use/observe a test data set during the training or validation phase. This overestimates the real method quality, which further disables other researchers to perform fair comparison to the presented method.

Olson et al. (2018) analyze performances of 13 state-of-the-art ML classification algorithms on a set of 165 publicly available classification problems from the field of bioinformatics. The goal of algorithm comparison was to make recommendations for future research in the process of algorithm selection, as well as its hyperparameters. The conclusion was that classifiers based on Gradient boosting offered the highest data set coverage, which was followed by random forests, SVC (support vector classifier), extra trees, and logistic regression.

Angermueller et al. (2016) provide insights of deep learning applications in the fields of bioinformatics and computational biology. The paper mostly focuses on the applications of deep learning in regulatory genomics and cellular imaging. Conventional approaches for regulatory genomics make relations between sequence variations and changes in molecular traits. The main drawback is that they cannot operate directly on the sequence since they require predefined features. On the other hand, a deep neural network can form implicit features, and it also works for large-scale data sets, which are expected in DNA and RNA sequences. Similarly, the usage of the convolutional neural network allows state-of-the-art image analysis of entire cells, cell populations and tissues, which is useful, for example, in cancer diagnosis based on tissue, analysis of bacterial colonies in agar plates, and many other. Besides application analysis, the authors of (Angermueller et al., 2016) also provide general deep learning guidelines such as training/validation/testing methodology, hyper-parameter optimization, training on GPU, overfitting, etc.

Cuperlovic-Culf (2018) provides insights into the ML-aided development of metabolic networks. Besides describing popular ML tools for different applications in the metabolic analysis, the author also presents an exhaustive review of ML methods in metabolic modeling.

Camacho et al. (2018) give a primer on ML for life scientists and discuss issues that occur in the intersection of ML and network biology, i.e., biological network. Biological networks are any networks that are obtained by observing biological systems—for example, protein-protein interaction networks, gene regulatory networks, metabolic networks, between-species interaction networks, etc. The authors focus on several trending application areas, such as disease biology, drug discovery, microbiome research, and synthetic biology.

Silva et al. (2019) provide a review of ML methods and applications in plant molecular biology. One of the discussed applications is analysis of plant promoters, where the goal is to develop disease-resistant or abiotic stress-tolerant plant varieties.

APPLICATIONS IN COMMUNICATION NETWORKS

Communication networks are a fertile area for ML applications. They offer plenty of room for introducing ML innovations. This is partially due to communication network complexity that combines multiple disciplines such as physics and electrical engineering in the lower layers, mathematics and computer science in the intermediate layers, and applicative programming at the top. There is also a variety of network types, such as classical wired networks, optical networks, wireless sensor network, wireless vehicular networks, etc.

Cote (2018) reviews general communication networks and some of the corresponding ML applications. He starts with tasks that can be performed as "read-only" operations on the network, which include regression, classification, and anomaly detection. Regarding the regression, the author points out to a problem of determining network capacity exhaust, bandwidth congestion, or device failures. This problem is modeled via time-series, so models such as recurrent neural networks can be used to solve it. In anomaly detection, the goal is to discriminate atypical events from typical. This can be performed by various ML techniques such as SVM (support vector machine), neural networks, random forests, etc. The author also discusses applications that are not considered "read-only", such as deciding when and how to act under certain circumstances. For example, reinforcement learning can be used to decide on adjustments of bandwidth profiles or re-routing traffic.

Wireless networks impose many issues, mostly because of their tradeoff in the context of availability and power usage—having higher power usage increases signal strength but reduces battery life or simply increases power costs. Therefore, novel paradigms that imply self-awareness, self-adaptiveness, and predictive behavior are being constantly introduced or improved. There is also a problem of big data, since there is a vast amount of data that needs to be processed, usually in the distributed (non-centralized) fashion. Kibria et al. (2018) point out to some ML and optimization-oriented issues. Optimized cell placement corresponds to a positioning of wireless antennas, having in mind their strength, frequency interference issues, and coverage. Advanced load balancing is also one of the issues. It occurs due to a difference in traffic patterns over distinct cells through time, so there is a need for an adaptive time-dependent load balancing among cells, meaning some cells might increase its coverage to reduce the burden of its neighboring cells. Chen et al. (2019) review artificial techniques based on neural networks used for solving a variety of tasks such as communication using unmanned aerial vehicles, Internet of Things, virtual reality over wireless networks, etc. Sun et al. (2019) survey recent applications classified per network layer. They consider resource management in the MAC layer, network (IP) layer issues such as networking and mobility management, and localization inside the application layer. Besides covering many issues, this survey also points to many different methods, ranging from the nearest neighbor methods to deep reinforcement learning. Kumar et al. (2019) focus on the wireless sensor network and its heterogenic tasks, such as anomaly and fault detection, routing, data aggregation, congestion control, to name just a few. The authors also review necessary supervised learning techniques such as decision trees, SVM, k-nearest neighbors, as well as some unsupervised ones such as k-means clustering, singular value decomposition, independent component analysis, etc. Finally, Wang et al. (2020) present the thirty-year history of ML, while the authors later expose their employment in heterogenous wireless networks applications such as cognitive radios, Internet of Things, machine-to-machine networks, etc.

The second large group of communication networks, and a subgroup of wireless networks, are vehicular networks. An obvious difference from its parenting wireless group is the dynamics *in* the emitter/receiver node movement speed. In addition, future vehicular networks are oriented towards expected intelligent vehicles, so this type of network has a special set of current and future anticipated issues. Some of the dynamics-related tasks, as pointed out by Liang and Li (2018), include vehicle trajectory prediction, traffic flow prediction, and learning-based channel estimation. The authors also consider some ML-based decision-making settings. By using learned dynamics of the vehicular network, some decision-making systems can be made to improve network performance. For example, the hidden Markov model can be applied to predict vehicle future locations, which is later used to decide which routing scheme should be used to deliver packages to those vehicles. Similar scenarios can be set for the network congestion problem or load balancing. Ye et al. (2018) present a short but informative review of applications and examples grouped by ML category. The authors review examples of classification, regression, clustering, dimension reduction, and policy learning in the context of vehicular wireless networks. Tang et al. (2019) consider challenges of future AI-based 6G vehicular networks. The authors discuss performances and intelligence, but also highlight the importance of security aspects. They mention two important categories of ML applications: ML in resource allocation and ML in network traffic control.

APPLICATIONS IN ASTRONOMY AND ASTROPHYSICS

Astronomy and astrophysics are scientific disciplines engaged in the study of celestial objects and phenomena. They use both observations and theory, so they can be viewed as inductive (data-driven) on one hand, and deductive on the other. The observational part depends on a vast amount of data, so its relations to computer science is natural and is expected to grow in the future. The theoretical part also uses computational power to validate theoretical findings, for example by using simulations.

Kremer et al. (2017) discuss the importance of large-scale data (big data) analysis in astronomy. For example, ML methods can successfully uncover the relation between galaxy images and their physical properties. One of the concerns of scientists in applying ML methods in astronomy in some cases is the lack of interpretability. There are two complementary approaches to predictive modeling in astronomy. The first one is physical modeling, in which scientists incorporate the knowledge of astronomy/astrophysics, which can later be used to simulate (Monte Carlo simulations) real processes occurring in space. This approach is interpretable and less prone to making semantic errors, but very difficult to construct. On the other hand, there is a data-driven approach in which ML models produce outputs without giving reasoning behind them; this is especially evident for the neural network approach. In a recent study, Hogg (2021) proposes which kinds of astronomy/astrophysics problems should be solved by ML. The author claims that most astronomy problems fall into the category of regression and not classification. Further, the training sets tend to be very unreliable, non-representative and noisy, which further makes the learning model wrong, regardless of whether they are based on the sophisticated and sound mathematical foundations. The author also claims that prediction of space data should not be the ultimate goal. Instead, the goal should be an understanding of physical laws, theoretical models, and scientific principles. He suggests that ML methods should be used to address different problems such as noise reduction, calibration, speeding up computations, etc. In other words, the author opposes the application of ML methods in the pure data-driven fashion, which just produces outputs without intermediary theoretical explanations.

A contemporary review of applications of ML methods in astronomy and astrophysics is made in (Fluke & Jacobs, 2020). The authors survey existing literature and categorize it into the following seven categories: 1) classification, 2) regression, 3) clustering, 4) forecasting, 5) generation and reconstruction, 6) discovery, and 7) insight. They systematically explore the cross-sections that these categories make with seven groups of astronomical/astrophysical data used in literature: 1) image, 2) spectroscopy, 3) photometry, 4) light curve, 5) time series, 6) catalogue, and 7) simulation.

In (Hocking et al., 2018), the authors present an unsupervised ML technique for segmentation and labelling of galaxies using raster images. The proposed technique combines the growing neural gas (GNG) algorithm proposed in (Fritzke, 1995), hierarchical clustering, and connected component labelling.

George and Huerta (2018) introduce the so-called deep filtering approach based on two deep convolutional neural networks. They further demonstrate its efficiency and accuracy in detection and estimation of parameters of gravitational waves from binary black hole mergers.

SUMMARIZATION OF THE PRESENTED STUDIES

Table 1 contains a brief overview of the previously reviewed studies. The columns respectively show: 1) reference, 2) task or a discipline to which the task belongs, 3) main finding(s) of the study, 4) advantage(s) of the study and 5) study disadvantage(s). Disadvantage(s) have a different meaning depending on the type of the study, whether it is a research paper or a survey. In surveys they mostly address issues like completeness and systematicity, while in research papers they are usually concerned with the proposed ML method quality or evaluation methodology.

SELECTED APPLICATIONS OF THE ARTIFICIAL NEURAL NETWORK

Image Classification

The convolutional neural network (CNN) has revolutionized many areas of ML applications, especially computer vision. One of the early and insightful views on the potential of CNN was made in the book of LeCun and Bengio (1995). Since that time, the research and applications of CNN have blossomed. The applications were especially boosted by the seminal paper of Krizhevsky, Sutskeve, and Hinton (Krizhevsky et al., 2012), in which a large CNN with many layers (deep) was trained by employing multiple GPUs.

For a deep CNN to work, it is important to feed it with a large amount of training data, which in the case of image classification consists of class-labeled images. The most notable benchmark in image classification is called The ImageNet Large Scale Visual Recognition Challenge (ILSVRC). Russakovsky

Table 1. Summarization of surveyed studies

Study	Task or Discipline	Main Findings	Main Advantage	Main Disadvantage
Janai et al. (2020)	Computer vision in general	Review of problems, data sets and methods for computer vision in autonomous vehicles.	Thorough review of state-of-the-art.	Hard to predict future of autonomous vehicles.
Zhao et al. (2019)	Object detection	Compares different neural network alternatives with focus on CNN.	Systematic review and future research analysis.	Missing comparison to non-ANN approaches.
Soleimanitaleb et al. (2019)	Object tracking	Reviews four method groups: feature, segmentation, estimation, learning (-based).	Provides interesting taxonomy of approaches.	Missing quantitative comparison of the reviewed approaches.
Luo et al. (2020)	Multiple object tracking (MOT)	The review and cross-comparison of evaluation metrics, data sets and methods.	Thorough and unified review.	MOT approaches are difficult to compare. Parameter tuning issues.
Yu et al. (2018)	Semantic segmentation	Three categories of methods: hand-engineered features, learned features and weakly supervised.	Thorough review with many quantitative comparisons.	Hard to understand why CNNs work so well and how to further improve them.
Garcia-Garcia et al. (2017)	Semantic segmentation	Deep learning for various applications.	Reviews many CNN approaches.	Missing comparison to non-ANN approaches.
Chicco (2017)	Computational biology	Provides brief and easy to understand overview of common tasks in ML.	Useful for ML beginners.	Relatively brief, but this is in line with the goal of the study.
Olson et al. (2018)	Biomedical classification	Analysis of performances of 13 classification algorithms.	Fairly unified.	Relatively brief and not mathematically rigorous.
Angermueller et al. (2016)	Regulatory genomics ad cellular imaging	Deriving biological insights using deep learning.	Overall review of deep learning challenges and methods.	Not too exhaustive.
Cuperlovic-Culf (2018)	Metabolic networks	Applications of ML for modelling metabolism.	Covers relevant aspects of (un)supervised learning.	Missing quantitative comparison of methods.
Camacho et al. (2018)	Biological networks in general	Focus on the trending applications: disease/synthetic biology, drug discovery, etc.	Trending applications in focus.	Missing quantitative comparison of methods.
Silva et al. (2019)	Plant molecular biology	Systematic guideline for applying ML methods in plant biology.	Systematic and easy to follow guidelines.	Missing quantitative comparison of methods.
Cote (2018)	Communication networks in general	Real-world problem examined: capacity exhaust, bandwidth congestion and device failures.	Interesting use-cases covered.	Does not cover too many methods and their comparisons.
Kibria et al. (2018)	Positioning wireless antennas.	Employing ML methods for automatic and dynamic wireless network management.	Top-level overview of problems in comm. networks.	A brief introduction of the existing ML approaches.
Chen et al. (2019)	Next-generation wireless networks	Artificial neural networks for a variety of trending applications such as IoT, unmanned aerial vehicles, etc.	Wide and in-depth analysis of ANN methods and applications.	Missing comparison to non-ANN approaches.
Sun et al. (2019)	Communication networks in general	Recent applications per network layer: MAC layer, IP layer, application layer, etc.	Systematic overview per layer combined with a variety of methods.	Not easy to cover all the aspects since the field of study is fast growing.
Kumar et al. (2019)	Wireless sensor networks	Various applications (anomaly, fault detection, routing, etc.) are solved with various methods.	In-depth and critical review with many comparisons.	Not easy to identify appropriate ML technique for a given task.
Wang et al. (2020)	Various communication networks	Thirty-year history of (un)supervised learning in communication networks.	In-depth evolution of ML methods with nice taxonomies.	Not easy to cover all the aspects since the field of study is fast growing.
Liang and Li (2018)	Vehicular networks	Using learned dynamics of vehicular networks to improve efficiency, avoid congestion, etc.	Covering emerging topics with high impact on autonomous vehicles.	A brief coverage without in-depth analysis of methods.
Ye et al. (2018)	Vehicular networks	Review of classification, regression, clustering, and dimension reduction methods.	Covers several interesting use-cases in vehicular networks.	Brief overview without many details on the applied methods.
Tang et al. (2019)	Vehicular networks	Challenges of the future 6G vehicular networks specially focusing on security.	Reviews relevant and diverse approaches.	Missing quantitative comparison of methods.

continued on following page

Table 1. Continued

Study	Task or Discipline	Main Findings	Main Advantage	Main Disadvantage
Kremer et al. (2017)	Astronomy and astrophysics	Overviews two complementary approaches: physical modelling and data-driven like ANN.	Deals with issues such as scalability in Big Data context.	Missing systematic comparison of state-of-the-art.
Hogg (2021)	Astronomy and astrophysics	Critical discussion on which tasks should be solved in data-driven manner.	Provides insights on how to use ML methods when modelling astronomical/ astrophysical phenomena.	ML methods still not able to solve complex modelling tasks by themselves.
Fluke and Jacobs (2020)	Astronomy and astrophysics	Systematic review of several ML methods applied to various problems.	Intersects relevant ML methods with relevant problems in astronomy/ astrophysics.	Brief review without ML technical insights.
Hocking et al. (2018)	Galaxy segmentation	Unsupervised ML technique for segmenting and labeling raster images.	Cleanly separates early and late type galaxies without any form of pre-directed training.	Choice of initial data matrix and efficiency can be improved.
George and Huerta (2018)	Gravitational waves	Deep neural network approach for detection and parameter estimation of gravitational waves.	Significantly outperforms traditional ML techniques while showing high efficiency.	Hyperparameter tuning is challenging.

et al. (2015) explain the way the large-scale collection of classified images is obtained. Besides that, this paper can also serve as a good review of state-of-the-art methods for the period since 2010, when the challenge was initiated, until 2015.

Back to the year 2012, deep CNN called SuperVision (Krizhevsky et al., 2012) beat the second-best method by an almost two times lower classification error. One of the ImageNet data sets consisted of over 15 million labeled, high-resolution images in over 22,000 categories. When compared to standard feedforward networks of similar size (width and depth), CNNs tend to have fewer connections and are therefore more efficient to train. Even with this design, they are still difficult to converge when the number of images and objects to be learned is as high as in the ImageNet benchmark. Luckily, the computational model for CNNs is compatible with the many-core paradigm as its simple but numerous cores are available inside graphical processing units (GPUs). The flow diagram that shows the essential steps in CNN for image classification is given in Figure 1.

The first activity performed on each input image is its conversion into a fixed size CNN-compatible format. Since original images have a variable and generally high resolution, they need to be rescaled and reduced to a 256x256 pixel matrix, where each pixel is based on the RGB color model. The normalization of each resized image is further performed by subtracting mean RGB components from each pixel.

A deep CNN contains a high number of hidden layers. For example, eight learning layers were considered in (Krizhevsky et al., 2012): five convolutional

Figure 1. CNN overall process

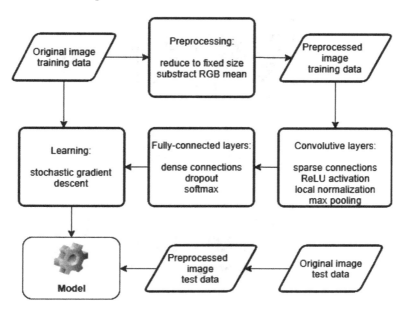

ones and three fully connected ones. The goal of the convolutional layer is to extract features, which is accomplished by defining a 3D-based filter and swiping with it through input data. The input data is: 1) the input pixel matrix in the case of the first layer or 2) the output of the previous layer in the case of later layers. The filter has three dimensions: width, height, and depth. The depth needs to be the same as in input data; for example, in the case of the starting input pixel matrix, three separate pixel matrices are provided for each RGB component. While swiping the filter over input data, the region over which the filter is positioned (receptive field) interacts with the filter and produces a single scalar as output. For example, this scalar can be obtained by using elementwise multiplication between the filter and the receptive field and further summing up those multiplication terms. The filter is swiped over input data from left to right, and further from top to bottom by steps of the given size called stride. The stride is usually smaller than feature width and height, so the successive receptive fields overlap.

Instead of using a single filter-per-pixel color component, the usual scenario is to use multiple filters and stack them along the depth axis. Different filters have different roles, and the intuition behind successive filters is that they progressively build more complex image features—those positioned deeper in the hidden layer structure relate to more complex filters, e.g., eyes and

Figure 2. An example of convolution: matrix-based filter

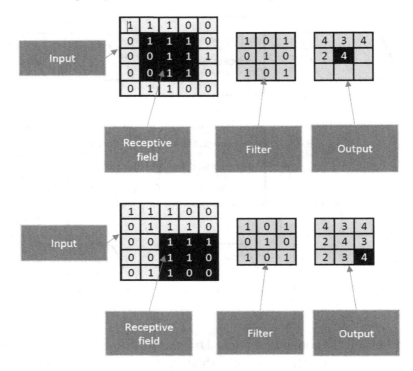

nose in the case of face recognition, while those positioned at the starting layers are usually related to some more general features, like lines, triangles, circles, and other types of contours or regions.

Figure 2 shows a convolution example where filter size is 3x3x1, stride is equal to 1, the size of input data is 5x5x1, and the size of convoluted feature matrix is 3x3x1. The intermediate step of forming the output matrix demonstrates the application of the filter positioned at the center of the input matrix. After the element-wise multiplication of the receptive field at that position (the black region in the input matrix) and the filter matrix, and further summation, value 4 is obtained and entered into the output matrix.

The standard way of modeling neuron output in CNNs is using rectified linear unit nonlinearity (ReLU) introduced by Nair & Hinton (2010). Unlike tangent or sigmoid functions often used in classical artificial neural networks, $ReLU(x)=max(0,x)$ enables much faster convergence of network coefficients. During communication between convolutional layers, data is sometimes normalized and/or pooled (max pooling). Normalization is done to improve the generalization of ReLU functions.

The purpose of max pooling is complexity reduction, i.e., down-sampling of neuron data output. It is similar to applying a filter, the difference being that, instead of the matrix-element-wise multiplication and later addition, the maximal value is simply pooled in the current receptive field and mapped to a given down-sampled output region. The stride, as with the filter, can be overlapping and non-overlapping. Figure 3 demonstrates the max-pool technique that is used in the SuperVision: it is based on the region sized 3x3, with the stride equal to 2, which makes it an overlapping max pooling.

As pointed out in Figure 1, after convolutional layers, the last few layers are fully connected. To avoid overfitting at the end and to improve performance, the dropout procedure is performed in the fully connected layers. This procedure sets zero at each hidden neuron output with probability 0.5, so the neurons that are dropped out do not further contribute to feed forward neither do they take part in back propagation. This dropout is changed during each feed step, i.e., for each new training record. The output of the last fully connected layer is input for the softmax function consisting of N inputs and N outputs, where N represents the number of image classes. The goal of using softmax is to normalize network output to a probability distribution consisting of N probabilities. The model is further trained by employing stochastic gradient descent and later tested on previously unseen images.

As previously mentioned, the results showed the superiority of the presented approach compared to other state-of-the-art results of that time. The standard way of reporting quality in ImageNet shows two types of error: 1) top-1 error is a standard classification error, which means that it accounts for all incorrectly labelled test input, while 2) top-5 error corresponds to a fraction of images whose correct label is not found in the set of the top-5 most probable labels produced by the model. Considering the results from ILSVRC-2010, presented in Table 2, CNN wins the competition by a high margin in both error-type categories.

SELECTED APPLICATION OF THE TREE ALGORITHM

Protein Structure Prediction

The next scientific-oriented application is based on a tree algorithm extension called random forests (RF). RF is an ensemble learning method that can be used for both classification and regression. It builds multiple decision trees

Figure 3. An example of max pooling with 3x3 region and stride 2

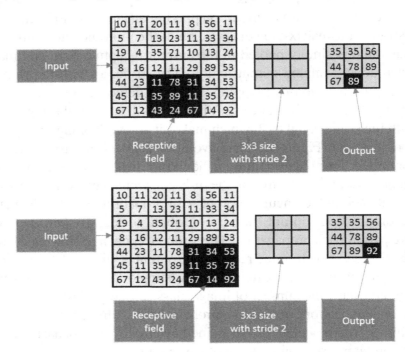

during its training and further uses aggregation over multiple produced outputs, e.g., mode class for classification or average/median value for regression.

Protein structure prediction deals with the problem of determination of three-dimensional protein structure (secondary and tertiary structure) based on the primary structure, which is simply the sequence of amino acids. Determining the structural class of proteins is important for further secondary and tertiary protein function analysis. According to the initial study of protein structure classes (Levitt & Chothia, 1976), there are four classes: $all\text{-}\alpha$, $all\text{-}\beta$, α / β, and $\alpha + \beta$. Later research identified some other structural classes, but

Table 2. ILSVRC-2010 test results

Model	Top-1	Top-5
Sparse coding (Berg et al., 2010)	47.1%	28.2%
SIFT + FVs (Sanchez & Perronnin, 2011)	45.7%	25.7%
CNN	**37.5%**	**17.0%**

(table data from Krizhevsky et al. (2012))

Figure 4. Random forest method for protein structural class prediction

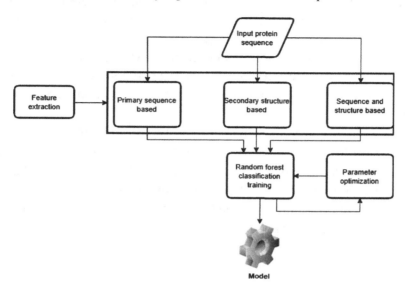

the aforementioned four make up about 90% of all observed structural classes. There are many computational methods for predicting structural classes but most of them are based on the ML approach. The following case-study example is based on the paper of Wei et al. (2014), which uses the RF approach along with three different feature extraction methods.

Table 3. Amino acids

Amino Acid	3 Letter Code	1 Letter Code	Amino Acid	3 Letter Code	1 Letter Code
Alanine	Ala	A	Leucine	Leu	L
Arginine	Arg	R	Lysine	Lys	K
Asparagine	Asn	N	Methionine	Met	M
Aspartate	Asp	D	Phenylalanine	Phe	F
Cysteine	Cys	C	Proline	Pro	P
Histidine	His	H	Serine	Ser	S
Isoleucine	Ile	I	Threonine	Thr	T
Glutamine	Gln	Q	Thryptophan	Trp	W
Glutamate	Glu	E	Tyrosine	Tyr	Y
Glycine	Gly	G	Valine	Val	V

Figure 4 depicts the overall method presented in (Wei et al., 2014). As it can be seen, feature extraction (FE) is an important part in the overall methodology. All features are extracted by looking at the composition of the input sequence, along with using certain external tools for prediction of the secondary structure. Since RF is a discriminatory-based method, the focus is on the selection of features that best reflect the differences among structural classes.

A query (input) protein sequence S is represented with L amino acid residues (peptide) $S_1 S_2 S_3 \ldots S_L$. An alphabet used in defining the sequences is formed of one letter capital characters and has the length of 20 characters, thus reflecting the usage of 20 different amino acids (Table 3).

Example. An exemplary peptide that will be used in further text is called Lysozyme. It can be found in chicken egg white and its sequence is as follows:

```
KVFGRCELAAAMKRHGLDNYRGYSLGNWVCAAKFESNFNTQATNRNTGSTDYGIL
QINSRWWCNDGRTPGSRNLCNIPCSALLSSDIT
ASVNCAKKIVSDGNGMNAWVAWRNRCKGTDVQAWIRGCRL.
```

The first group of features, sequence-based features, are calculated by employing n-gram counting. An n-gram represents a subsequence of consecutive elements from S with length n. For example, the 3-grams in the previous example would be: KVF, VFG, FGR, GRC, RCE, ..., RGC, GCR, CRL. The number of different possible n-grams for a 20-character alphabet is 20^n. Therefore, the length of n-gram frequency feature vector in uncompressed form is 20^n long.

Secondary structure features constitute the second group. In secondary structure prediction, every amino acid residue from the primary sequence (primary structure) is assigned one of the following classes: H (helix), E (strand), and C (coil). This prediction is done by using an external tool for secondary structure prediction, e.g., PSIPRED (Jones, 1999). The output of this prediction for a given primary sequence is the same-length sequence with values from {H, E, C}. Secondary structure features are further created in several ways, including the following procedures:

- by counting frequencies of all secondary structure classes,
- by analyzing the positions of these classes within the sequence,
- by analyzing segments consisting of the same consecutive secondary structure class.

Table 4. Random forests versus other algorithms for α/β and α+β class prediction

Data Set	Method	α/β	α=β
25PDB	SCPRED (Kurgan et al., 2008)	76.0	83.2
	RKS-PPSC (Yang et al., 2010)	86.4	82.8
	Ding et al. (2012)	85.0	88.2
	RF (proposed method)	**87.9**	**93.9**
640	SCPRED (Kurgan et al., 2008)	89.3	77.2
	RKS-PPSC (Yang et al., 2010)	88.1	83.6
	Ding et al. (2012)	89.3	83.6
	RF (proposed method)	**97.7**	**97.1**
1189	SCPRED (Kurgan et al., 2008)	88.6	63.1
	RKS-PPSC (Yang et al., 2010)	83.8	81.3
	Ding et al. (2012)	85.9	73.9
	RF (proposed method)	**92.8**	**86.7**

(table data from (Wei et al., 2014))

Finally, the last group of features uses a combination of the first two groups of features, obtained by interleaving information from the primary structure and its corresponding secondary structure.

Once all the features are created, the next step is to train the RF classifier on top of the constructed data set that consists of all abovementioned features (generated) as independent values and four structural classes $all-\alpha$, $all-\beta$, α/β, and $\alpha+\beta$ as dependent (given) ones. This is done by employing the bagging technique (Breiman, 1996), in which multiple decision tree classifiers are trained based on different random samples of records from the original input data (horizontal sampling). Unlike traditional bagging, RF in this case uses random feature sampling during tree construction. This means that when the node splitting criterion is to be determined, this is done in a random way, i.e., the random sample of available features is used as a splitting criterion.

The results showed that the performance of the presented RF method was superior to several alternative algorithms from literature. Table 4.4 demonstrates some of the presented algorithm comparisons.

SELECTED APPLICATION OF RULE INDUCTION

Intrusion Detection in Communication Networks

There are many ways to generate rules from data. In this section, we will focus on one specific type of rule generation that combines genetic algorithms and decision trees. The application that will be considered comes from the communication network field.

The aim of intrusion detection systems (IDS) is to protect systems from attacks by automatically detecting whether the requests to access the system are legitimate or dangerous. When speaking about automatic detection of attacks, the goal is to minimize the total prediction error which consists of two error types: 1) a false positive (FP) error, which corresponds to scenarios in which an attack is recognized but it is just a normal request—false alarm, and 2) a true negative (TN) error, which relates to a fraction of situations in which the attacker is not detected. A high FP error means that the IDS is too pessimistic, which translates to dissatisfied users being banned for no reason. On the other hand, a high TN error usually means that the system is too optimistic, so attacks can pass unnoticed.

The case study we analyze comes from paper (Papamartzivanos et al., 2018), which uses a hybrid approach with the genetic algorithm and decision trees to generate rules. The rule model is built on top of low-level network traffic data. Therefore, this application mostly belongs to the area of communication networks. The authors of the paper focus on three circumstances that make the problem difficult to solve:

1. There are many types of attacks, so the implied classification task is highly multi-classed.
2. There are many network traffic features, so the classification model is to be built on the multi-featured data set.
3. The problem is naturally very imbalanced since most requests are normal, and only a small fraction represent attacks.

The proposed approach is called *Dendron,* and it evolves the population of decision trees by using the genetic algorithm. The authors focused on two objectives:

Figure 5. Exemplary decision tree

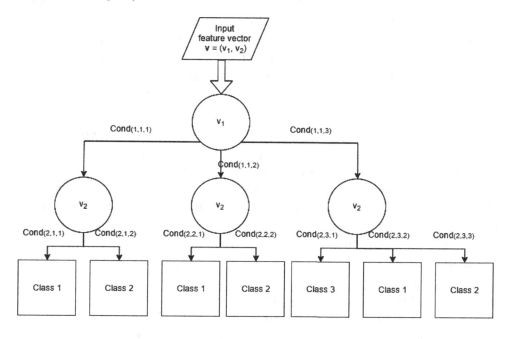

1. high coverage of as many different attacks as possible, even those that occur very rarely;
2. high interpretability of generated rule sets.

Having the decision tree (DT) at hand, the rule generation phase is straightforward. Every branch inside DT is simply transformed to the "IF *Conditions* THEN *Class*" rule where *Conditions* is a logical expression formed as a conjunction of separate conditions obtained by traversing DT from the root node toward leaves. For example, the tree shown in Figure 5 would produce the following seven rules:

1. IF $Cond_{(1,1,1)}(v_1) \wedge Cond_{(2,1,1)}(v_2)$ THEN Class = 1
2. IF $Cond_{(1,1,1)}(v_1) \wedge Cond_{(2,1,2)}(v_2)$ THEN Class = 2
3. IF $Cond_{(1,1,2)}(v_1) \wedge Cond_{(2,2,1)}(v_2)$ THEN Class = 1
4. IF $Cond_{(1,1,2)}(v_1) \wedge Cond_{(2,2,2)}(v_2)$ THEN Class = 2
5. IF $Cond_{(1,1,3)}(v_1) \wedge Cond_{(2,3,1)}(v_2)$ THEN Class = 3
6. IF $Cond_{(1,1,3)}(v_1) \wedge Cond_{(2,3,2)}(v_2)$ THEN Class = 1
7. IF $Cond_{(1,1,3)}(v_1) \wedge Cond_{(2,3,3)}(v_2)$ THEN Class = 2.

Here, $\text{Cond}_{(x,y,z)}$ corresponds to a condition on level x, the branching node on position y at that level, and branching condition numbered by z. There are several more considerations regarding DT-to-rules generation. For example, what if conditions at a certain level are not mutually exclusive? In this situation, condition priority might be defined. Another question arises regarding continuous attributes, which is usually solved by discretization to a fixed number of regions.

The genetic algorithm (GA) is a method used for discrete and combinatorial optimization. It is inspired by a biological mechanism of species evolution, and it belongs to a wider group of evolutionary optimization methods. GA was invented by John Holland in the 1960s and further improved by Holland and his students and colleagues during the 1960s and 1970s. In the following few paragraphs, we will briefly discuss the basic building blocks of GA, and for a deeper understanding of genetic algorithms, the reader is referred to one of the most influential books on this matter, by Mitchell (1998).

GA is inspired by two natural mechanisms that comprise the evolution in most organisms: natural selection and sexual reproduction. Obviously, evolution takes thousands or even millions of years. Computers allow us to emulate this process, whereby the time dimension is modeled by algorithm iterations, while groups of organisms (or populations) are modeled as appropriate data structures.

GA works on a population of individuals also called chromosomes. Each chromosome represents a solution to the problem. In the most simplistic scenario, a solution can be represented as a vector of bits, where each bit encodes the existence of certain characteristics in the corresponding problem. For example, if the problem is to find a minimum vertex cover on a graph, then bit 1 at position i means that vertex i is selected as a part of the cover; otherwise, vertex i is not in the cover. In the biologically inspired context of chromosomes, bits represent gene values. The second important element of GA is fitness function, i.e., the function that quantifies how well the proposed solution solves the corresponding problem. Again, in the context of biology, having a certain chromosome (or genotype) makes the individual better or worse suited to the environment. Being better suited to environment means having a better fitness function value and vice versa—individuals with worse adaptation to the environment have a worse fitness function value.

GA starts with the phase of population initialization. The most simplistic way of performing it is random generation. Following up on the previous example, this means producing M individuals as random binary vectors, where M represents population size (GA control parameter). After this phase, GA population is changed (evolved) through iterations, each of which consists of the following steps:

1. Selection—chromosomes are selected to form pairs, which reflects the idea of partner selection in the biological evolution.
2. Crossover—selected pairs of chromosomes (parents) are combined to produce children (offspring) chromosomes.
3. Mutation—on the children's chromosomes, random mutations are performed, which also exists in the biological evolution.
4. Population replacement—children solutions replace some or all parent solutions, depending on the population replacement policy.

There are multiple GA parameters that control the aforementioned steps and various ways of their implementation, but they will not be discussed in detail here.

Considering IDS, the population is formed of individuals each of which represents a single DT. The fitness of DT is calculated by imposing several different classification metrics, such as classification accuracy, mean F-measure, average accuracy per class, etc. The GA in which population consists of such nonlinear, usually graph-like structures is also known in literature as genetic programming (GP). The credits for this approach go to John Koza (Koza, 1990) who showed that it can be used to evolve computer programs, represented by abstract syntax trees, and solve targeted problems.

Initialization is done by producing DTs that are not branched at all. In other words, for each vector feature, there is only a single branching condition that is always true—it simply asks if the feature value is anything from the feature domain. This effectively creates a list of nodes, which is a degenerated type of tree. Classes are determined in the leaf nodes, and they are equally distributed across the whole population. The order of features is the same across all individuals and is determined by giving priority to the features that obtain higher information gain.

The selection of parents is based on the roulette wheel selection, which represents a standard implementation of fitness proportionate selection. However, instead of using solely the fitness function value, the authors use a linear combination of 1) fitness function value, 2) class-based selection function value and 3) missing classes function value. The class-based selection function awards DTs that have more minority classes leaves, while the missing classes function is conditionally called to award individuals that contain classes missing from the best DT in the population. Before entering linear

Figure 6. Decision tree after mutation

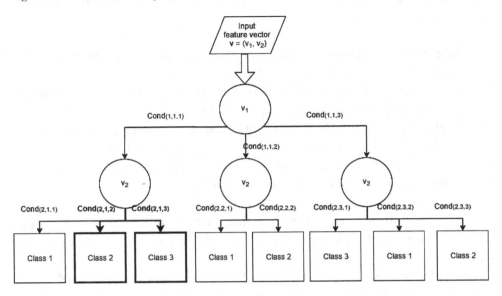

combination, all elements are scaled to interval [0, 1], while the corresponding linear combination coefficients are adjusted in the initialization phase.

Crossover among selected pairs of parents is done by swapping randomly chosen branches at the same level (same feature). Therefore, this does not introduce new tree sub-structures without mutation—it only recombines the existing ones. On the other hand, the mutation operator can introduce a new structural form inside DT by introducing a new branching condition inside a certain randomly selected DT branching (internal) node. Of course, other conditions exiting that node should be revised so as to be consistent with the newly introduced. For example, DT shown Figure 6 might be mutated so that condition $Cond_{(2,1,2)}$ is split into two conditions.

Population replacement is done by selecting individuals from the union of parents and children in a way that keeps the best individuals with respect to their fitness function value. Additional criterion that can potentially override this elitist replacement policy is keeping the new population normal—all classes are considered in the population of DTs.

The authors tested the method on three simulated data sets, namely:

1. KDDCup'99—a standard benchmark in building systems for intrusion detection based on simulated network traffic with 22 different types of intrusions.

2. NSL-KDD—an improvement of the first one which also introduces some additional types of attacks.
3. UNSW-NB15—modernized IDS data set with contemporary network traffic features and some new difficult-to-detect attacks.

Table 5. Remaining features for KDD data sets

Feature	Type	Feature	Type
Service	discrete	hot	discrete
Flag	discrete	num_compromised	continuous
src_bytes	continuous	wrong_fragment	continuous
Count	continuous	root_shell	discrete
dst_host_same_srv_rate	continuous	num_file_creations	continuous
dst_host_serror_rate	continuous	num_root	continuous
dst_host_srv_serror_rate	continuous	num_access_files	continuous
logged_in	discrete	num_failed_logins	continuous
dst_host_rerror_rate	continuous	num_shells	continuous
Duration	continuous	su_attempted	discrete
protocol_type	discrete		

Table 6. Remaining features for UNSW-NB15 data set

Feature	Type	Feature	Type
ct_state_ttl	continuous	ct_dst_sport_ltm	continuous
Sttl	continuous	sjit	continuous
Dttl	continuous	dloss	continuous
dload	continuous	sbytes	continuous
ct_srv_dst	continuous	smean	continuous
service	discrete	ct_src_dport_ltm	continuous
proto	discrete	ct_dst_src_ltm	continuous
dmean	continuous	dwin	continuous
dbytes	continuous	response_body_len	continuous
State	discrete	ct_flw_http_mthd	continuous
dpkts	continuous	trans_depth	continuous
ct_srv_src	continuous		

After performing feature selection on KDDCup'99 and NSL-KDD data sets, the authors were left with 21 features that further entered the proposed methodology (Table 5). In a similar way, feature selection was performed for the UNSW-NB15 data set, reducing the set of features to 23 (Table 6).

The proposed approach was compared with multiple methods from literature showing high-quality results across a range of different comparison metrics and all considered data sets. Having a base of induced rules is a comparative advantage in modern intrusion detection systems, since it increases the interpretability of automatically made decisions. This way, administrators and network security experts can more easily understand what the system does under the hood.

SELECTED APPLICATION OF THE NEIGHBORHOOD ALGORITHM

Large Scale Applications in Astronomy

The nearest neighbor (NN) algorithms are intuitive and interpretable. However, their biggest disadvantage is their computational and spatial complexity. There are many different extensions that reduce computational complexity by increasing spatial complexity or vice-versa (Bhatia, 2010). Considering the problems in large-scale data sets coming from astronomical observations, both matters pose a problem, but computational complexity still seems to be the bigger bottleneck.

One of the central issues in supervised machine learning is called sample selection bias. It happens when the distribution of data on which the supervised learning model is applied differs from the distribution of labeled data on which the model was trained. For addressing this issue, one might assign weight to training samples in a way that reflects its importance throughout model exploitation. Determination of future importance can be made based on the available unlabeled training data. When the collection of these unlabeled objects is relatively small, the nearest neighbor algorithm can easily cope with computational complexity and provide weight estimates. However, weight estimates tend to be better when larger samples are used, and the amount of data in astronomical observations is certainly more than sufficient. Kremer et al. (2015) exploit previously introduced extension of the nearest neighbor algorithm that uses internal *k-d* tree as a structure to resolve the sample selection bias and apply it further in the astronomical case study.

Sample selection bias in astronomy happens due to a bias in astronomy observation prioritization. Namely, the astronomical objects that are expected to show more interesting properties are often explored more heavily than some common or less interesting objects. Weights can be used to adjust the importance of labeled training samples so that the overall weighted distribution of labelled training samples corresponds to real probability distribution. However, since the true probability distribution is not known, it must be estimated from the known unlabeled training data. Unlabeled data is always easily gathered and its quantity is therefore expected to be much bigger than the quantity of labeled data. One of the issues in estimating real probability distribution is controlling its variance.

Let us denote with x a feature vector from domain X, while the corresponding labels are denoted by y and belonging to domain Y. The ML model is trained based on labeled data S (source) that is sampled from $p_S(x, y)$, while the generally larger unlabeled data set T (target) is sampled from $p_T(x, y)$. The goal is to determine the so-called probability density ratio between the T and S, denoted as $\beta(x) = \dfrac{p_T(x)}{p_S(x)}$, which can be later used to re-weight query samples.

To improve the efficiency of the nearest neighbor algorithm, the authors employ the data structure known as *k-d* tree. This data structure was introduced in (Bentley, 1975). It is a binary tree constructed from a set of *d*-dimensional data points $S \in R^d$. The inner nodes of the *k-d* tree represent hyperplanes which recursively partition the starting set of points into smaller subsets. Leaf nodes finally refer to the set of data points whose union is the whole set S. The criterion at level i is based on the dimension $(i+1) \bmod d$, which means that all dimensions get a uniform chance to partition the data set throughout tree construction. Partitioning according to a given dimension (feature) is done by first calculating the median across all values of that dimension, and then the hyperplane with respect to the obtained median value. This consequently divides the remaining number of points from the observed data set into two balanced subsets.

Example. Let us illustrate the *k-d* tree construction through a simple numerical data set consisting of 10 three-dimensional data points

$$S = \left\{ (2,1,2),(2,3,1),(3,2,1),(3,4,2),(5,3,2),(1,4,7),(6,8,2),(4,5,3),(9,2,5),(4,3,8) \right\}.$$

At the start of construction, the whole set is considered, and the first dimension is used to partition it. The median value is 3.5, so by convention we partition the current data set so that the left subset contains all elements less or equal to 3.5, while the right one contains all elements strictly bigger than 3.5. The left subtree is now recursively created from data points

$$S_L = \left\{ (2,1,2),(2,3,1),(3,2,1),(3,4,2),(1,4,7) \right\},$$

while the right subtree is constructed from data points

$$S_R = \{ (5,3,2),(6,8,2),(4,5,3),($$

In the next step, we divide the left subset with respect to the second dimension. The median value is 3, which creates the new partitioning to

$$S_{LL} = \left\{ (2,1,2),(2,3,1),(3,2,1) \right\} \text{ and } S_{LR} = \left\{ (3,4,2),(1,4,7) \right\}.$$

Similarly, the partitioning of S_R produces

$$S_{RL} = \left\{ (5,3,2),(9,2,5),(4,3,8) \right\} \text{ and } S_{RR} = \left\{ (6,8,2),(4,5,3) \right\}.$$

Proceeding in the similar manner will bring us to the final tree shown in Figure 7. Note that leaves contain sometimes two elements and sometimes a single element. The *k-d* tree creation can be parameterized so that the number of elements inside leaf nodes is bounded from the above. In this example, we decided to bound it with two, so neither leaf has more than two elements.

Searching for the nearest neighbor of a given input data point will also be demonstrated through an example. Let us suppose that input (query) data point is (4,1,3). The first step is to recursively move down the *k-d* tree the same way the insertion is done: going to the left subtree of the current node if the corresponding dimension is lower or equal to the median, otherwise, insertion goes to the right. Once in the leaf node, the nearest neighbor inside

Figure 7. k-d Tree example

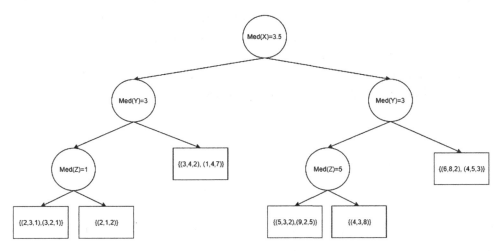

the collection of data points belonging to the leaf node is found and recorded as the current best nearest neighbor. The path followed for (4,1,3) goes right in the first level, then goes left, and finally goes left, reaching the leaf nodes $\left\{(5,3,2),(9,2,5)\right\}$ so the current nearest neighbor becomes (5,3,2) with Euclidean distance $\sqrt{6}$; other distances might be used as well. Now the search proceeds towards the top node, in which we ask if the sphere of radius $\sqrt{6}$ around the search point (4,1,3) intersects with the hyperplane that this interior node represents. This can be simplified to checking if the absolute difference of the corresponding coordinate of a search point and median at that level is greater than the current best distance. If it is, then there is a chance that the nearest neighbor exists on the other side of the hyperplane defined by the median value. In that case, search is recursively performed on the other side of the hyperplane, i.e., its corresponding subtree. In the present example, the distance between 3rd coordinate of (4,1,3) and median value 5 is 2, so there is an intersection of the hypersphere of radius $\sqrt{6}$ and a splitting hyperplane. This means searching the right subtree containing, in this case, only a leaf node with $\left\{(4,3,8)\right\}$. No nearest neighbor update is performed during this phase since the candidate point is farther from the query point than the current best (5,3,2). The search now proceeds towards the top, and similar steps are performed. Although (5,3,2) will remain the best nearest neighbor, note that the nearest neighbor of the same distance $\sqrt{6}$ also exists in the main left subtree—point (3,2,1). This means that a large part of this specific *k-d* tree will be traversed, which makes it as computationally intensive as the simple linear search. However, in the best case, the search might be logarithmic with respect to the number of tree elements.

Finally, having an efficient *k-d* tree at hand, the nearest neighbor density estimator for a query point $\mathbf{x}^q$ is calculated as:

$$\hat{\beta}\left(x^q\right) = \frac{\dfrac{N_S}{K}}{\dfrac{N_T}{L}} = \frac{L \cdot N_S}{K \cdot N_T}$$

where N_S and N_T represent the number of points in source and target data sets, K is the number of neighbors that are searched for in S, while the L is the number of neighbors inside T that have distance to a query point that is at most equal to the distance of the query point and the Kth nearest neighbor inside S.

The authors conducted two types of experiments: re-weighted regression on standard domain adaptation benchmarks and weight computation for photometric redshift estimation. Comparison to other relevant algorithms from literature showed that the proposed near neighbor density estimator is highly efficient, accurate and robust to hyperparameter choice.

REVIEW QUESTIONS

This section provides questions for better understanding of the key aspects of the chapter.

1. Present one application in computer vision suitable for dataflow paradigm.
2. Present one application in bioinformatics and computational biology suitable for dataflow paradigm.
3. Present one application in communication networks suitable for dataflow paradigm.
4. Present one application in astronomy and astrophysics suitable for dataflow paradigm.

REFERENCES

Angermueller, C., Pärnamaa, T., Parts, L., & Stegle, O. (2016). Deep learning for computational biology. *Molecular Systems Biology*, *12*(7), 878. doi:10.15252/msb.20156651 PMID:27474269

Bentley, J. L. (1975). Multidimensional binary search trees used for associative searching. *Communications of the ACM*, *18*(9), 509–517. doi:10.1145/361002.361007

Berg, A., Deng, J., & Fei-Fei, L. (2010). *Large scale visual recognition challenge 2010*. Academic Press.

Bhatia, N. (2010). *Survey of nearest neighbor techniques*. arXiv preprint arXiv:1007.0085.

Breiman, L. (1996). Bagging predictors. *Machine Learning*, *24*(2), 123–140. doi:10.1007/BF00058655

Camacho, D. M., Collins, K. M., Powers, R. K., Costello, J. C., & Collins, J. J. (2018). Next-generation machine learning for biological networks. *Cell*, *173*(7), 1581–1592. doi:10.1016/j.cell.2018.05.015 PMID:29887378

Chen, M., Challita, U., Saad, W., Yin, C., & Debbah, M. (2019). Artificial neural networks-based machine learning for wireless networks: A tutorial. *IEEE Communications Surveys and Tutorials*, *21*(4), 3039–3071. doi:10.1109/COMST.2019.2926625

Chicco, D. (2017). Ten quick tips for machine learning in computational biology. *BioData Mining*, *10*(1), 1–17. doi:10.118613040-017-0155-3 PMID:29234465

Côté, D. (2018). Using machine learning in communication networks. *Journal of Optical Communications and Networking*, *10*(10), D100–D109. doi:10.1364/JOCN.10.00D100

Cuperlovic-Culf, M. (2018). Machine learning methods for analysis of metabolic data and metabolic pathway modeling. *Metabolites*, *8*(1), 4. doi:10.3390/metabo8010004 PMID:29324649

Ding, S., Zhang, S., Li, Y., & Wang, T. (2012). A novel protein structural classes prediction method based on predicted secondary structure. *Biochimie*, *94*(5), 1166–1171. doi:10.1016/j.biochi.2012.01.022 PMID:22353242

Fluke, C. J., & Jacobs, C. (2020). Surveying the reach and maturity of machine learning and artificial intelligence in astronomy. *Wiley Interdisciplinary Reviews. Data Mining and Knowledge Discovery, 10*(2), e1349. doi:10.1002/widm.1349

Fritzke, B. (1994). A growing neural gas network learns topologies. *Advances in Neural Information Processing Systems, 7.*

Garcia-Garcia, A., Orts-Escolano, S., Oprea, S., Villena-Martinez, V., & Garcia-Rodriguez, J. (2017). *A review on deep learning techniques applied to semantic segmentation.* arXiv preprint arXiv:1704.06857.

George, D., & Huerta, E. A. (2018). Deep neural networks to enable real-time multimessenger astrophysics. *Physical Review. D, 97*(4), 044039. doi:10.1103/PhysRevD.97.044039

Hatwar, R. B., Kamble, S. D., Thakur, N. V., & Kakde, S. (2018). A review on moving object detection and tracking methods in video. *International Journal of Pure and Applied Mathematics, 118*(16), 511–526.

Hocking, A., Geach, J. E., Sun, Y., & Davey, N. (2018). An automatic taxonomy of galaxy morphology using unsupervised machine learning. *Monthly Notices of the Royal Astronomical Society, 473*(1), 1108–1129. doi:10.1093/mnrastx2351

Hogg, D. W. (2021, June). New Prospects for Machine Learning in Astrophysics. In *American Astronomical Society Meeting Abstracts* (*Vol. 53*, No. 6, pp. 301-01). Academic Press.

Janai, J., Güney, F., Behl, A., & Geiger, A. (2020). Computer vision for autonomous vehicles: Problems, datasets and state of the art. *Foundations and Trends® in Computer Graphics and Vision, 12*(1–3), 1-308.

Jones, D. T. (1999). Protein secondary structure prediction based on position-specific scoring matrices. *Journal of Molecular Biology, 292*(2), 195–202. doi:10.1006/jmbi.1999.3091 PMID:10493868

Kibria, M. G., Nguyen, K., Villardi, G. P., Zhao, O., Ishizu, K., & Kojima, F. (2018). Big data analytics, machine learning, and artificial intelligence in next-generation wireless networks. *IEEE Access: Practical Innovations, Open Solutions, 6*, 32328–32338. doi:10.1109/ACCESS.2018.2837692

Koza, J. R. (1990). A paradigm for genetically breeding populations of computer programs to solve problems. Computer Science Dept., Stanford Univ.

Kremer, J., Gieseke, F., Pedersen, K. S., & Igel, C. (2015). Nearest neighbor density ratio estimation for large-scale applications in astronomy. *Astronomy and Computing, 12*, 67–72. doi:10.1016/j.ascom.2015.06.005

Kremer, J., Stensbo-Smidt, K., Gieseke, F., Pedersen, K. S., & Igel, C. (2017). Big universe, big data: Machine learning and image analysis for astronomy. *IEEE Intelligent Systems, 32*(2), 16–22. doi:10.1109/MIS.2017.40

Krizhevsky, A., Sutskever, I., & Hinton, G. E. (2012). Imagenet classification with deep convolutional neural networks. *Advances in Neural Information Processing Systems, 25*.

Kumar, D. P., Amgoth, T., & Annavarapu, C. S. R. (2019). Machine learning algorithms for wireless sensor networks: A survey. *Information Fusion, 49*, 1–25. doi:10.1016/j.inffus.2018.09.013

Kurgan, L., Cios, K., & Chen, K. (2008). SCPRED: Accurate prediction of protein structural class for sequences of twilight-zone similarity with predicting sequences. *BMC Bioinformatics, 9*(1), 1–15. doi:10.1186/1471-2105-9-226 PMID:18452616

LeCun, Y., & Bengio, Y. (1995). Convolutional networks for images, speech, and time series. The handbook of brain theory and neural networks, 3361(10).

Levitt, M., & Chothia, C. (1976). Structural patterns in globular proteins. *Nature, 261*(5561), 552–558. doi:10.1038/261552a0 PMID:934293

Liang, L., Ye, H., & Li, G. Y. (2018). Toward intelligent vehicular networks: A machine learning framework. *IEEE Internet of Things Journal, 6*(1), 124–135. doi:10.1109/JIOT.2018.2872122

Luo, W., Xing, J., Milan, A., Zhang, X., Liu, W., & Kim, T. K. (2021). Multiple object tracking: A literature review. *Artificial Intelligence, 293*, 103448. doi:10.1016/j.artint.2020.103448

Mitchell, M. (1998). *An introduction to genetic algorithms*. MIT Press. doi:10.7551/mitpress/3927.001.0001

Nair, V., & Hinton, G. E. (2010, January). Rectified linear units improve restricted boltzmann machines. ICML.

Olson, R. S., Cava, W. L., Mustahsan, Z., Varik, A., & Moore, J. H. (2018). Data-driven advice for applying machine learning to bioinformatics problems. In *Pacific Symposium on Biocomputing 2018: Proceedings of the Pacific Symposium* (pp. 192-203). 10.1142/9789813235533_0018

Papamartzivanos, D., Mármol, F. G., & Kambourakis, G. (2018). Dendron: Genetic trees driven rule induction for network intrusion detection systems. *Future Generation Computer Systems*, *79*, 558–574. doi:10.1016/j.future.2017.09.056

Russakovsky, O., Deng, J., Su, H., Krause, J., Satheesh, S., Ma, S., Huang, Z., Karpathy, A., Khosla, A., Bernstein, M., Berg, A. C., & Fei-Fei, L. (2015). Imagenet large scale visual recognition challenge. *International Journal of Computer Vision*, *115*(3), 211–252. doi:10.100711263-015-0816-y

Sánchez, J., & Perronnin, F. (2011, June). High-dimensional signature compression for large-scale image classification. In *CVPR 2011* (pp. 1665–1672). IEEE. doi:10.1109/CVPR.2011.5995504

Silva, J. C. F., Teixeira, R. M., Silva, F. F., Brommonschenkel, S. H., & Fontes, E. P. (2019). Machine learning approaches and their current application in plant molecular biology: A systematic review. *Plant Science*, *284*, 37–47. doi:10.1016/j.plantsci.2019.03.020 PMID:31084877

Soleimanitaleb, Z., Keyvanrad, M. A., & Jafari, A. (2019, October). Object tracking methods: A review. In *2019 9th International Conference on Computer and Knowledge Engineering (ICCKE)* (pp. 282-288). IEEE.

Sun, Y., Peng, M., Zhou, Y., Huang, Y., & Mao, S. (2019). Application of machine learning in wireless networks: Key techniques and open issues. *IEEE Communications Surveys and Tutorials*, *21*(4), 3072–3108. doi:10.1109/COMST.2019.2924243

Tang, F., Kawamoto, Y., Kato, N., & Liu, J. (2019). Future intelligent and secure vehicular network toward 6G: Machine-learning approaches. *Proceedings of the IEEE*, *108*(2), 292–307. doi:10.1109/JPROC.2019.2954595

Wang, J., Jiang, C., Zhang, H., Ren, Y., Chen, K. C., & Hanzo, L. (2020). Thirty years of machine learning: The road to Pareto-optimal wireless networks. *IEEE Communications Surveys and Tutorials*, *22*(3), 1472–1514. doi:10.1109/COMST.2020.2965856

Wei, L., Liao, M., Gao, X., & Zou, Q. (2014). An improved protein structural classes prediction method by incorporating both sequence and structure information. *IEEE Transactions on Nanobioscience*, *14*(4), 339–349. doi:10.1109/TNB.2014.2352454 PMID:25248192

Yang, J. Y., Peng, Z. L., & Chen, X. (2010). Prediction of protein structural classes for low-homology sequences based on predicted secondary structure. *BMC Bioinformatics*, *11*(1), 1–10. doi:10.1186/1471-2105-11-S1-S9 PMID:20122246

Ye, H., Liang, L., Li, G. Y., Kim, J., Lu, L., & Wu, M. (2018). Machine learning for vehicular networks: Recent advances and application examples. *IEEE Vehicular Technology Magazine, 13*(2), 94-101.

Yu, H., Yang, Z., Tan, L., Wang, Y., Sun, W., Sun, M., & Tang, Y. (2018). Methods and datasets on semantic segmentation: A review. *Neurocomputing*, *304*, 82–103. doi:10.1016/j.neucom.2018.03.037

Zhao, Z. Q., Zheng, P., Xu, S. T., & Wu, X. (2019). Object detection with deep learning: A review. *IEEE Transactions on Neural Networks and Learning Systems*, *30*(11), 3212–3232. doi:10.1109/TNNLS.2018.2876865 PMID:30703038

KEY TERMS AND DEFINITIONS

CNN: Convolutional neural network used for image processing and classification.

Confusion Matrix: Machine learning technique for result evaluation using optimization metrics.

Feature Extraction: Step prior to model training that removes features that have minor impact on the outcome.

GA: Genetic algorithm for search inspired by natural evolution.

RELU: Activation function for neuron in neural network.

Chapter 5
Business and Industrial Applications of Machine Learning Algorithms

ABSTRACT

This chapter provides an overview of some popular business and industrial applications of machine learning/data mining algorithms. The survey-like introductory section provides a brief overview of some relevant historical and trending applications, while the other four sections present specific details on four selected business and industrial applications. Each section focuses on a different considered algorithm, namely neural networks, rule induction, tree algorithms, and neighborhood-based algorithms.

INTRODUCTION

Companies around the world are constantly searching for ways to increase their returns and reduce costs. Many business problems can be formalized and described in the language of mathematicians or computer scientists, i.e., by using concepts such as time-series, graphs, or matrices. Machine learning (ML) can be used in many business-related cases. For example, a retailing company can solve many issues by means of ML and optimization: assortment selection, physical organization of products, making suggested offers to known customers based on their purchase history, inventory organization, segmenting buyers, predicting shopping missions, etc. Similarly, industrial companies

DOI: 10.4018/978-1-7998-8350-0.ch005

might want to reduce their costs and increase their revenue. By using historical observations, and employing ML regression/classification, they can predict future expenditures and sales, which can enhance their decision-making potential. Moreover, robotic systems, which are now becoming standard for many industrial companies world-wide, use state-of-the-art ML methods, which further improves their efficiency and consequently produces more revenue with lower costs.

The presented overview is non-exhaustive and represents only a sample of all relevant applications of ML in business and industry, organized by categories. The following text will first give a more detailed insight of recent ML applications in the four selected business/industrial contexts:

1. e-commerce,
2. engineering,
3. healthcare and medical sensors,
4. school management.

After this, four specific business and industrial applications will be discussed in much more detail. More precisely, it will be presented how each of the following four selected ML algorithms is applied:

1. neural network algorithm for wind speed prediction,
2. tree-like algorithm for life insurance risk prediction,
3. rule-induction algorithm for business intelligence,
4. neighborhood algorithm for evaluating microstructure in metal alloy.

Applications in e-Commerce

Applications of ML in e-commerce were in their early years at the beginning of the 21st century. One of the first tasks that needed to be addressed was web merchandising. This task is related to the process of acquiring products and making them available over the Internet. In a special issue on this matter, Kohavi and Provost (2001) consider interesting early applications:

*   providing personalized recommendations for supermarket purchases,
*   creation of individual consumer profiles by using rule induction,

- analysis of clickstreams, i.e., the sequence of links followed by a customer on a website,
- measuring and improving website success by analyzing users' navigation patterns,
- building complex recommender systems by using collaborative filtering, statistics, etc.

Mobasher (2007) observes the solution to web personalization through three typical phases:

- data collection and preprocessing,
- pattern discovery and evaluation,
- real-time application of the knowledge to improve the interaction between the user and the web.

One of the essential problems in web personalization that is discussed by the authors is gathering and joining data from different sources as a technical step inside the business-motivated data enriching procedure. This work further reviews various data analysis methods, such as: clustering-based methods, rule induction, sequential pattern mining, Markov models and probabilistic mixture, and latent variable models.

Recent trends in e-commerce are increasingly oriented towards social networks. Predicting customer quality in an e-commerce social network (Ballestar et al., 2019) is one of the interesting problems with high monetization potential. The authors in the mentioned paper consider the case of so-called cashback websites, which are a centralized way of presenting the products of different, generally large retail brands. The most important asset these websites hold is information about user navigation habits, which can be further utilized in building prediction algorithms for the new or returning users. Besides the potential to build recommendation systems, this information is often used to predict user quality, i.e., their buying potential, which is of utmost importance to retailers.

Applications in e-commerce possess high financial gain potential. This potential is heavily correlated with an incentive to perform frauds on the Internet and is therefore particularly important to have a suitable fraud detection mechanism. A recent innovation in e-commerce were fraud detectors based on deep learning (Roy et al., 2018; Pumsirirat & Yan, 2018). It is interesting and promising that improvement of such systems is motivated not only by real fraud attacks but also by a purposely designed testing mechanism that performs attacks on these systems (Guo et al., 2019), similarly to the mechanism antivirus companies use to improve their software.

Applications in Engineering

Industry is an environment in which ML and optimization methods are of great interest due to their potential to improve quality, increase productivity, and reduce costs. In (Köksal et al., 2011), ML applications in the manufacturing industry are reviewed with respect to the several tasks:

- product/process quality description,
- predicting quality,
- classification of quality,
- and parameter optimization.

To achieve the abovementioned tasks, the authors observed that many different ML methods were used, both supervised and unsupervised. For example, the quality description task employs unsupervised methods such as the self-organizing map (SOM), k-means, and hierarchical clustering. Still, applications of some supervised methods such as decision trees, neural networks, and rule induction are also evident. Quality prediction and classification involve a wide variety of supervised methods for regression and classification, such as the general regression neural network, fuzzy regression, fuzzy adaptive network, nonparametric time series analysis, case-based reasoning, and many more. Finally, the process of parameter optimization, which is essential in the fine-tuning stages, was done with certain ML methods, such as various neural networks, but also by employing optimization techniques such as the genetic algorithm, simulated annealing, and mathematical programming techniques.

Xu et al. (2018) consider the quality management issues in automotive industry and offers a quality problem-solving ML method. The authors first build specific ontology based on the quality problem data. This ontology catches specific relations among car subsystems, parts, and properties. The ontology is built by using natural language processing (NLP) techniques on top of unprocessed original problem descriptions, which leads to structural description of the problem in terms of the vector space model. Based on the obtained ontology, the so-called knowledge transformation module constructs the quality problem-solving knowledge base of entities and relationships. This base defines relationships among problems, faults, their causes, and vehicle measurements. Furthermore, support vector machine (SVM) is used on top of the obtained knowledge database for the classification of cause texts into informative factors: man, machine, material, method, and environment.

(Yan et al., 2020) represents an exhaustive review of ML methods and applications in the construction industry. The authors reviewed 119 papers in the construction domain and classified them according to multiple criteria, such as data source type, ML function (prediction, classification, clustering, association, outlier detection), specific ML technique, used software tools, application areas, etc. There are several application areas in construction: energy, building occupancy and occupant behavior, cost estimation, material performance, safety management, textual knowledge discovery, framework establishment, building design, etc. For example, energy consumption prediction is of great interest for energy management in buildings. Various temporal regression-based techniques are employed in this domain, starting from recurrent neural networks over econometric models such as ARIMA, support vector regression, and others. Aside from looking at this problem from the long-run or medium-run perspective, establishing consumption patterns in the short-run is also important, which is why some non-temporal techniques such as k-means, DBSCAN, decision trees, and others are also used. Besides providing an in-depth insight into what has been done so far, the authors also provide opinion on future research directions such as knowledge discovery in unstructured data and learning methods for sustainable construction.

Xu et al. (2021) provide a recent review of ML methods in construction industry: from "shallow" to deep learning. The authors investigated the evolution of methods ranging from simple logistic regression to deep learning.

Applications in Healthcare and Medical Sensors

Healthcare transactions generate large amounts of data which, due to its additional complexity, poses a problem to be analyzed using traditional methods. By using ML methods, these data can be transformed to information later used for decision making.

In (Koh & Tan, 2011), some common applications in healthcare are discussed, such as: the evaluation of treatment effectiveness, healthcare management, patient relationship management and fraud and abuse. In addition, the authors also illustrate their view through an exemplary decision tree method for the identification of risk factors for chronic diabetes.

In a similar review (Durairaj & Ranjani, 2013), in addition to previously mentioned applications, the authors also point to applications in pharmaceutical industry, hospital management, and system biology. The last kind of application refers to huge and often heterogenous biological databases, which is an exciting playground for a scientist with various backgrounds. The authors also give examples of applications in the medical device industry, which includes mobile communications and low-cost wireless biosensors. These sensor devices are revolutionizing the way modern healthcare looks like by providing enormous amounts of potentially useful data. At the same time, they are making the usability of traditional methods increasingly difficult, which opens the space for the new era of big data methods.

In-home sensors are also popular healthcare sensing technology. Healthcare industries worldwide are currently making huge investments in the hardware and software development of this technology due to its potential of reducing healthcare costs. A piece of research on in-home sensing ML algorithms is presented in (Enshaeifar et al., 2018). The group of authors focused on developing ML algorithms for detection of high-level activities of patients with dementia. These activities, for example, include agitation, irritability, and aggression. The goal was to build a monitoring technology that will assist the patients and facilitate their well-being.

Ghazal et al. (2021) focus on the combining of Internet of Things (IoT), wireless sensor networks (WSN) and ML methods to improve the healthcare sector. They argue that these technologies offer a potential to relieve doctors and better identify diseases.

Applications in School Management

Education is, as everything else, becoming business-oriented: it strives towards profit maximization and cost reduction. The following issues in the context of higher education are discussed in (Luan, 2004):

- Which students will enroll in which course?
- Which students will have problems to graduate?
- What is the expected day of graduation for a given student?
- Which students are more likely to transfer?

Timely gained answers to these questions might enable decision-makers to better manage resources (mostly staff) and plan further expansions and costs. Authors conclude their point of view by three brief case studies. The first one discusses the usage of clustering algorithms to assess students' typologies. Further, authors consider the transfer prediction problem, which is essential for facilitating timely academic intervention. Finally, the problem of receiving donations from alumni is outlined. Here, ML algorithms are used to decide which alumni should be contacted to maximize total donations and reduce communication costs. Beside using information about alumni members, these kinds of models also use historical data about previous contacts with alumni.

Siguenza-Guzman et al. (2015) provide a comprehensive literature review of ML methods with applications in academic libraries. Many papers are categorized with respect to the ML task that is applied: clustering, association, classification, and regression. Another orthogonal categorization was with respect to library aspect: services, quality, collection, and usage behavior.

Recently, Bakhshinategh et al. (2018) made a systematic and thorough overview of data mining and ML applications in education. They organized the applications into the three major groups: student modeling, decision support systems, and other. Student modeling refers to modeling of cognitive aspects of student activities that are later used to perform predictions:

- predicting student performance, achievement of learning outcomes or characteristics,
- detecting undesirable student behaviors,
- profiling and grouping students,
- social network analysis.

In the second group, the authors consider decision-support systems that enable stakeholders (management) to receive feedback and alerts regarding students or group of students, which later enables them to plan further activities. These kinds of systems also generate automated recommendations for improving courseware or solving organizational issues. More precisely, according to the authors, the following tasks belong to this group:

- providing reports,
- creating alerts for stakeholders,
- planning and scheduling,
- creating courseware,
- developing concept maps,
- generating recommendation.

Finally, the authors also consider other various types of applications. Adaptive systems, for example, allow users (learners) of online course materials to have personalized content and learning dynamics. Further, the authors consider systems for knowledge evaluation and scientific inquiries.

Ho et al. (2021) predict student satisfaction with emergency remote learning (due to COVID-19 pandemic) by employing ML techniques. The study showed that students prefer face-to-face learning. ML techniques included: multiple linear regression, kNN, multilayer perceptron, and others. This was combined with a technique for recursive feature elimination based on random forest.

Summarization of the Presented Studies

Table 1 contains a brief overview of the previously reviewed studies. The columns respectively show: 1) reference, 2) task or a discipline to which the task belongs, 3) main finding(s) of the study, 4) advantage(s) of the study and 5) study disadvantage(s). Disadvantage(s) have a different meaning depending on the type of the study, whether it is a research paper or a survey. In surveys they mostly address issues like completeness and systematicity while in research papers they are usually concerned with the proposed ML method quality or evaluation methodology.

SELECTED APPLICATION OF THE ARTIFICIAL NEURAL NETWORK

Wind Speed Prediction

Recurrent neural networks (RNNs) are traditional ML learning methods with wide applications in science, industry, engineering, etc. Due to their capability of learning temporal and sequential relationships, the RNNs are usually used to solve time-series prediction and sequential learning problems. Nowadays, the variant of RNN called long short-term memory RNN (Hochreiter & Schmidhuber, 1997) is widely used for various tasks such as automated translation, activity prediction, voice recognition and synthesis, etc. However, due to its longevity and importance, this section will be dedicated to traditional RNNs and one of their applications in weather forecasting—wind speed prediction.

Table 1. Summarization of surveyed studies

Study	Task or Discipline	Main Findings	Main Advantage	Main Disadvantage
Kohavi and Provost (2001)	E-commerce optimization	Overview of early applications in e-commerce such as: personalized recommendations, consumer profile creation, website navigation patterns, etc.	Demonstrates how ML might improve profit and customer satisfaction.	Early work in the field. Since then, the e-commerce optimization has evolved significantly.
Mobasher (2007)	Web personalization	Solution to web personalization consisting of 3 phases: data collection and preprocessing, pattern discovery and evaluation, real-time application.	Various techniques employed and compared: clustering, association rules, Markov models, etc.	Modelling user context is challenging, and user interests change with time. Need for adaptive methods.
Ballestar et al. (2019)	Customer quality in social network	Predicting new or returning users based on the website navigation habits and ANN.	Provides predictive model for a company which later enables higher monetization.	Might benefit from the hybridization with expert-driven approaches.
Roy et al. (2018)	Credit card fraud detection	Evaluation of several deep learning topologies in solving the problem of fraud detection.	Compares several ANN alternatives.	Does not report test classification error. Insufficient number of benchmarks.
Pumsirirat and Yan (2018)	Credit card fraud detection	Focus on the fraud cases not detectable by using supervised approach (historical data).	Shows usage of unsupervised auto-encoder and restricted Boltzmann machine.	Missing quantitative comparison to methods other than AE and RBM.
Guo et al. (2019)	Fraud detection	Reveals potential risk of deploying deep learning-based fraud detection method by generating effective adversarial examples.	Bypasses tested detector with high probability and outperforms other state-of-the-art attack methods.	Not clear how difficult is the process of improving detector so that it becomes less prone to attacks.
Köksal et al. (2011)	Manufacturing industry	Reviews several manufacturing tasks (product/process quality description, predicting quality, etc.) and their solution methods.	Employs many different ML methods, both supervised and unsupervised.	Difficult to assess which method should be used for which task.
Xu et al. (2018)	Automotive industry quality management	By employing ontology that relates car subsystems and SVM, the system can predict causes of quality problems.	Approach successfully combines NLP and ML method and shows respectable accuracy.	Missing quantitative comparison to other methods.
Yan et al. (2020)	Construction industry	Reviews papers applying ML methods in construction domain and classifies them with respect to multiple criteria.	Useful top-level view of ML applications across the whole construction industry.	Brief when it comes to ML technical details.
Xu et al. (2021)	Construction industry	A review of ML methods in construction industry: from shallow to deep learning.	Exhaustive research of various methods.	Applications are briefly discussed.
Koh and Tan (2011)	Healthcare	Discusses common ML applications in healthcare: treatment effectiveness evaluation, healthcare management, etc.	Contains illustrative use-case of diabetes prediction via decision tree.	Lacks thoroughness and technical details regarding ML methods.
Durairaj and Ranjani (2013)	Healthcare, system biology	Reviews applications in healthcare, pharmaceutical industry, hospital management and system biology.	Touches a variety of important tasks.	Lacks technical details.
Ghazal et al. (2021)	Smart healthcare	Focuses on the combining of Internet of Things (IoT), wireless sensor networks (WSN) and ML methods to improve healthcare sector.	Top-down view of the current state and future perspectives in the smart healthcare.	Brief when it comes to ML, WSN and IoT technical details.
Enshaeifar et al. (2018)	Patient activity detection	Focuses on activity detection of patients with dementia. The goal is patient life quality improvement along with cost of care reduction.	Combines Internet of Things (IoT) solution with ML algorithm.	Missing quantitative comparison to other methods.
Luan (2004)	School management	Use ML algorithms to improve school management issues such as: predicting students' enrollment, transfer prediction, etc.	Addresses relevant issues in the school management using (un)supervised techniques.	Brief and without sufficient ML technical details.
Siguenza-Guzman et al. (2015)	Academic libraries	Comprehensive literature review of ML methods with applications in academic libraries.	Evaluates different ML techniques with respect to library services, quality, collection, etc.	Brief when it comes to ML technical details.
Bakhshinategh et al. (2018)	School management	ML methods for student modelling and decision-support systems for school management.	Reviews the overall school management pipeline: from problem detection to decision making.	Brief when it comes to ML technical details.
Ho et al. (2021)	Student satisfaction prediction	ML methods for predicting student satisfaction of emergency remote learning.	Compares various methods.	Representability of data collection. It is not clear if the obtained models can be applied world-wide.

120

Having accurate wind speed prediction is of strong interest for certain businesses and organizations such as construction building, electric power industry, offshore oil platforms, transportation, and financial markets. For the reader interested in methods and applications in the domain of forecasting, survey paper (Regnier, 2008) might be a relevant source. The literature review of previous methods and their success will not be further discussed here. The presented exemplary RNN model for wind speed prediction is based on the one introduced in (Cao et al., 2012).

The overall architecture of Jordan RNN (JRNN) is presented in Figure 1. To define recurrence relations, each successive training example that is fed to a network is denoted by an increasing sequence of numbers, usually referred as t (time step). The relative times required to define recurrence are further denoted as $t+1$, $t-1$, etc. The first (input) layer is fed by two types of inputs:

1. the standard external inputs denoted as vector $x(t)$,

2. the context inputs $c(t)$ are the outputs from the previous time step, so $c(t) = y(t-1)$.

Note that recurrent connections are not weighted, i.e., they are not updated. On the other hand, connections from the context layer towards the hidden layer are fully connected and weighted just as the usual connections between classical input and the first hidden layer. Learning is usually done by performing the backpropagation algorithm. There are certain extensions to the JRNN setting in which the context layer is also self-dependent, i.e., it depends on its previous value and on the newly arrived output value:

$$c(t) = \alpha y(t-1) + (1-\alpha)c(t-1).$$

Also, there are some considerations in which, instead of returning the produced output to a context layer, the actual target value can be returned.

The data benchmarks used in (Cao et al., 2012) were based on the measurements acquired from the Wind Engineering Research Field Laboratory (WERFL). The data were sampled with 10Hz frequency at different altitudes. For testing model performance, data were randomly divided, where around three-thirds were used for training while the rest was used for model testing. Further, the results were compared to those obtained by employing the standard econometric time series model called Autoregressive Integrated Moving

Figure 1. Jordan recurrent neural network architecture.

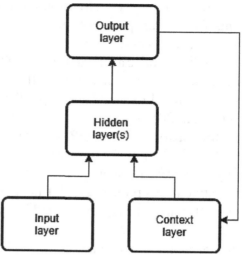

Average (ARIMA). The results showed that the RNN model provided better forecasts than linear ARIMA in both univariate and multivariate scenarios. This is mostly due to the nonlinear nature of RNN, which was able to catch subtle, nonlinear notion of wind speed dynamics. The authors also conclude that the multivariate setting produced better results than the univariate one in both RNN and ARIMA methods. Table 2 compares four algorithms (RNN and ARIMA in multivariate and univariate setting) for different heights above the ground, and under different regression quality metrics.

SELECTED APPLICATION OF THE TREE ALGORITHM

Life Insurance Risk Prediction

For life insurance companies, it is essential to make high-quality predictions on the life expectancy of their clients, which includes the analysis of health conditions, lifestyle, work information, and many other factors. Having optimistic predictions leads to unproportionate losses for these companies, while pessimism might lead to financially expensive offers for clients, resulting in low competitiveness on the life insurance market.

The standard approach in life insurance is highly theoretical, mostly based on actuarial (mathematical) methods for assessing mortality rates

Table 2. ARIMA versus RNN for univariate and multivariate setting and different heights.

Model	MSPE	MAE	MAPE%
Univariate ARIMA			
8 feet	8.637	16.686	40.6
13 feet	8.549	14.998	38.2
33 feet	8.014	12.203	36.1
70 feet	8.133	11.913	37.5
160 feet	8.042	10.683	35.7
Univariate RNN			
8 feet	6.411	14.778	28.3
13 feet	6.130	12.094	23.2
33 feet	6.265	9.416	25.6
70 feet	6.959	10.385	31.7
160 feet	7.873	7.796	33.1
Multivariate ARIMA			
8 feet	1.913	7.709	19.4
13 feet	1.493	6.053	15.3
33 feet	2.500	6.927	21.1
70 feet	3.806	7.904	23.6
160 feet	6.703	9.722	28.7
Multivariate RNN			
8 feet	1.728	6.935	15.7
13 feet	1.262	5.867	11.5
33 feet	2.241	6.312	17.9
70 feet	3.253	7.466	19.8
160 feet	6.088	8.234	15.7

(table data from (Cao et al., 2012))

based on demographics and other information. Besides this, the emerging area of scientific interest is in building ML prediction methods that can be used autonomously or as assistance for standard methods. The method from (Boodhun & Jayabalan, 2018) uses several different supervised learning algorithms along with certain preprocessing phases for life insurance risk assessment. As the decision tree approach named REPTree (Reduced Error Pruning Tree) showed the best results among the considered algorithms,

Figure 2. Life insurance risk assessment framework.

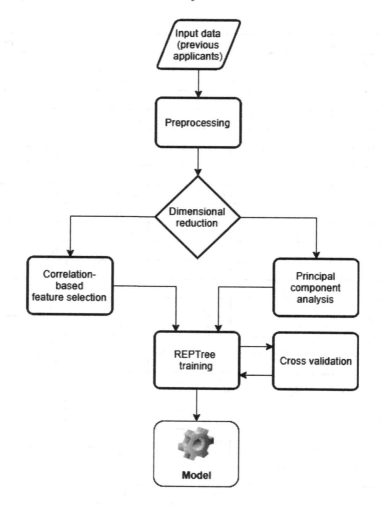

further text will focus on the REPTree method. Figure 2 depicts a part of the methodology from (Boodhun & Jayabalan, 2018).

The data set used in this research is composed of 59,381 life insurance applications, where each application is characterized by a set of 128 features. There are many different features that seem to be relevant for overall assessment. The feature groups are as follows:

- life insurance product information,
- demographic information,
- weight, height, and BMI,

- employment history,
- insurance history,
- family history,
- medical history.

The target (decision) variable indicates the risk, and it belongs to the ordinal type with 8 possible levels. During the preprocessing phase, standard data cleaning and improving techniques are performed. These include noise removal, data imputation, feature normalization, etc. Further, vertical dimensionality reduction is done in two ways: by correlation-based feature selection (CFS) and principal component analysis (PCA) feature extraction.

CFS focuses on the idea of feature subset selection in such a way that the correlation among the selected subset and the target value is maximized and the correlation among the subset elements is minimized. The first maximization is related to the determination of the feature set that is (as a whole) functionally relevant for the prediction goal. On the other hand, minimizing the within-subset correlation is related to the dimensionality reduction goal, which is later important for building an efficient prediction model. PCA operates differently: it creates new synthetic features called principal components that might not be logically observable in practice.

After the dimensional reduction, the last step is building a REPTree model that feeds on the newly created set of features and corresponding target values. REPTree resembles the previously mentioned Random forests algorithm, since it also builds several trees during its training. The difference is that here, instead of using all built trees and the voting mechanism across all produced predictions, REPTree evaluates all built trees independently and simply chooses the best one.

The comparison was made with three other ML methods: multiple linear regression, artificial neural network, and random tree by using two evaluation metrics, mean average error (MAE), and relative mean squared error (RMSE). The results presented in Table 3 clearly show that the REPTree with CFS produced the best overall MAE and RMSE.

Table 3. REPTree versus other algorithms for risk prediction in life insurance.

Algorithm	MAE		RMSE	
	CFS	PCA	CFS	PCA
Multiple linear regression	1.5872	1.6396	2.0309	2.0659
Artificial neural network	1.7859	1.7261	2.3690	2.3369
REPTree	**1.5285**	1.6973	**2.0270**	2.1607
Random tree	1.7892	2.0305	2.7475	2.9142

(table data from (Boodhun & Jayabalan, 2018))

SELECTED APPLICATION OF THE RULE INDUCTION ALGORITHM

Business Intelligence From Online Product Reviews

The amount of user-generated content on the Internet is growing intensively. Business intelligence (BI) applications tend to use this content and transform it into something useful. There is a variety of BI outputs based on this content; for example, manufacturers and service providers can get an insight into consumer opinions about their products/services which later translates into making decisions regarding products/services modifications and improvements. Retailers can reorganize their product assortment or improve various logistical aspects of distribution, inventory handling, etc.

E-commerce applications go beyond their initial purpose of buying or selling products/services online. They currently offer additional features such as user discussion groups and rating systems that increase the level of transparency about offered products/services. This is obviously useful for consumers since they can get additional information about product/service quality before purchasing it. Those who offer products/services therefore need to listen to what the crowd is satisfied/dissatisfied about and make changes to succeed on the market. The two most beneficial pieces of information obtained from a customer are their opinion, most often posted as textual content, and numerical rating. Of course, some other information, such as personal information, might also be collected depending on the legislation of the country/region, but since regulations go in the direction of forbidding those types of data recording, they will not be discussed in the further text. The numerical rating given by an individual consumer is not reliable, but when the number of ratings becomes larger, certain patterns start to appear.

Figure 3. Rule-based BI model.

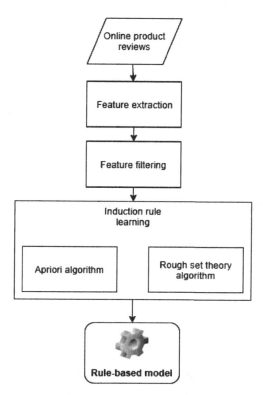

Further, by employing natural language processing (NLP) on top of the user textual content and combining it with numerical ratings, one can build supervised learning models such as regression or classification that can later generate implied numerical ratings based solely on users' textual comments. This enables data imputation and filling information gaps. Similarly, these techniques can be used to detect inconsistent ratings and content, therefore eliminating them from consideration or giving them lower importance.

Chung and Tseng (2012) provide a critical overview of different approaches used to process online product reviews made by consumers. Further, they develop a new hybrid rule-based BI system that can extract knowledge from textual content and corresponding numerical ratings. The proposed BI system is shown in Figure 3. The model is built on top of the reviews that contain two parts: 1) textual content and 2) numerical rating on a certain scale, e.g., from 1 to 5. The output is the model consisting of a set of inductive rules that take the form: "word 1, word 2, …, word n ⇒ rating". Additionally, each rule is assigned numerical confidence value that further reflects rule priority when various rules can be applied.

The first two phases—feature extraction and filtering—are preprocessing stages used to generate textual features and further eliminate those that do not have adequate informational power. The system uses the word-vector model in which each word corresponds to a single dimension in M-dimensional space, where M is the number of different words occurring in the training data (one of the problems with the word-vector model is its lack of sensitivity to word ordering).

The straightforward approach would be to simply count all occurrences of every word, and consequently map input texts to an M-dimensional space of natural numbers. This does not account for the total number of word occurrences inside a review, so the normalization must be performed, which brings us to a widely known measure of word (term) importance called term frequency or *tf*:

$$tf\left(t, d\right) = \frac{f_{t,d}}{\sum_{r \in d} f_{r,d}}$$

where $f_{t,d}$ represents the number of occurrences of word *t* inside a review *d*.

However, some words are too common to be accounted for the same relevance as some others. For example, words "and", "the", "a", etc. occur in almost every English sentence. Fortunately, this problem is appropriately solved by using the concept of the so-called inverse document frequency or just *idf*:

$$idf\left(t, D\right) = \log\log \frac{N}{|\{d \in D \mid t \in d\}|}$$

where *N* is the number of documents inside the corpus (or reviews in our case), and $|\{d \in D \mid t \in d\}|$ is the number of documents where word (term) *t* appears at least once. Obviously, words that are frequent in general will have smaller *idf*. By combining these two measures, we obtain the so-called term frequency—inverse document frequency or *tf-idf*.

Table 4. Example data set used for RST

Review	F1	F2	F3	F4	O
1	0	1	0	2	2
2	0	0	1	3	0
3	0	1	1	1	1
4	1	2	2	0	1
5	0	0	0	1	2

taken from (Chung & Tseng, 2012).

$$tfidf\left(t,d\right) = \frac{f_{t,d}}{\sum_{r \in d} f_{r,d}} \log\log \frac{N}{|\{d \in D \mid t \in d\}|}$$

Feature filtering is based on the imposed threshold for the *tfidf* value of each word in each review, so the words that are below this threshold are simply ignored.

Once the numerical feature vectors are constructed, the next phase is to perform rule-induction mechanisms to obtain rules. The proposed methodology relies on two rule-based mechanisms:

1. *apriori* algorithm that belongs to a wider group of association rule mining (ARM) algorithms,
2. rough set theory algorithm.

ARM is concerned with finding the rules that have support and confidence above certain user-imposed thresholds. Given the rule $X \Rightarrow Y$, where X is a subset of features (words) and Y is the rating, the rule support is the proportion of reviews containing both feature set X and rating Y. The confidence is the proportion of reviews that have rating Y inside the set of reviews that contain feature set X. The *apriori* algorithm implements ARM by performing the following steps:

- First, the feature sets whose support is higher or equal to the predefined threshold support are looked for; these subsets from the whole feature set are called *frequent sets*.
- Each *frequent set* is considered to generate rules that have at least minimal confidence and the threshold is also set by the user.

The second, more technically engaging part of this research, is related to the so-called Rough Set Theory (RST), which proves to be a helpful tool when there is ambiguity in data. RST was introduced by Pawlak (1982). A rough set is the approximation of the standard set bounded by its (set) lower and upper approximation. The purpose of the following example is the introduction of mathematical definitions required for RST without going into rigorous details.

Example. Given a set of feature vectors and its corresponding classes in Table 4, here representing textual features and rating of a review, respectively, the goal is to construct a rough set.

The given data set can be more formally described as ordered pair $I = (U, F)$ where U is a non-empty finite set of objects (or universe), while F is a non-empty finite set of features such that $I : U \rightarrow V_a$ for every $a \in A$ (V_a is a set of possible values for attribute a). Note that for a given feature subset $P \subseteq A$ there is a corresponding equivalence relation $IND(P)$:

$$IND(P) = \{(x, y) \in U^2 \mid \forall a \in P, a(x) = a(y)\}.$$

Note that this relation partitions an input set of objects U to a family of equivalence classes of *IND(P)* denoted as $[x]_P$. Therefore, if $(x, y) \in IND(P)$, there is no way to distinguish objects x and y solely based on the subset of attributes P. For example, when $P = \{F1\}$, we get two equivalence classes. The first one corresponds to objects $\{1, 2, 3, 5\}$ when $F1 = 0$, and the second one corresponds to $\{4\}$ when $F1 = 1$.

The next step is to approximate the target subset of objects $X \subseteq U$ via the rough set. In the review example, X will correspond to reviews corresponding to certain rating. For example, if $P = \{F1, F2\}$ and the target set is composed of objects $\{3, 4\}$ corresponding to rating 1, the P lower approximation of X is

$$\underline{P}X = \{[x]_P \subseteq X\} = \{4\}.$$

Note that $\{3\}$ cannot be distinguished from $\{1\}$ when $F1 = 0 \wedge F2 = 1$. Upper approximation P is

Table 5. Top-rated words (features) per product per rating.

Rating	Association Rule Maining	RST – Exhaustive	RST – LEM2
Acer Aspire One 8.9-inch Mini Laptop			
5	My (19.6), battery (14.5), great (10.4), acer (8.0), keyboard (7.9), laptop (7.3), aspire (5.7), small (5.6), computer (4.5), drive (4.4)	Acer (15.6), notebook (15.3), battery (12.79), great (10.9), computer (8.4), work (5.3)	N/A
4	None	Battery (9.5), work (6.7), long (4.7)	N/A
Sterling Silver M. & G. Glass Heart Pendant 18''			
5	Beautiful (1.69), my (1.68), chain (1.44), necklace (1.15), pendant (1.09), love (0.75)	Necklace (1.73), girlfriend (1.58), color (1.1), piece (0.82)	My (2.1), beautiful (1.87), necklace (1.76), picture (1.66), chain (1.63), pendant (1.56), wife (1.3), darker (0.92)
4	Bought (0.845), darker (0.63), my (0.285)	Piece (1.12)	My (1.72), picture (1.32), chain (0.91), bought (0.72)
2	None	Stone (1.32)	None
Razor Power Wing Caster Scooter			
5	My (26.6), great (14.3), scooter (13.7), year (11.8), fun (10.6), ride (9.7), kids (8.9), son (8.6), powerwing (7.2), bought (6.0)	My (23.4), great (16.12), year (12.22), scooter (11.2), fun (8.92), kids (5.61)	My (24.5), year (14.15), great (11.34), scooter (10.56), fun (9.6), easy (7.34), powerwing (6.4), product (4.32)
HP 2133-KR922UT 8.9-Inch Mini-Note PC			
5	Great (0.76), xp (0.26)	Great (1.83), note (0.96), xp (0.82)	None
4	Vista (2.4), my (0.9), machine (0.9), screen (0.8), battery (0.8), me (0.6), nice (0.5), keyboard (0.29), laptop (0.28), windows (0.25), hp (0.17)	My (0.87), xp (0.74)	Vista (3.2), my (2.4), screen (1.3), nice (1.24), battery (1,1), xp (0.92), system (0.7), keyboard (0.3)
1	None	None	Linux (0.88), slow (0.56)

(table data from (Chung & Tseng, 2012))

$$\underline{P}X = \left\{ [x]_P \cap X \neq \varnothing \right\} = \left\{ 1, 3 \right\} \cup \left\{ 4 \right\} = \left\{ 1, 3, 4 \right\}.$$

The intuition behind P approximations is that elements belonging to $\underline{P}X$ are certainly members of the target set, while the elements belonging $\underline{P}X$ are possible members of the target set.

The boundary regions given by $\underline{P}X - \underline{P}X = \left\{ 1, 3 \right\}$ contain objects that can be either ruled out or ruled in as members of the target set X.

The selection of P impacts the quality of the rough set approximation: the goal is to find the P that provides "tight" approximation, meaning that the lower and upper bound are close to each other, while the boundary region is ideally empty. Note that this analysis is done for a single target set only, i.e., the objects with rating 1. The same should be done for all relevant subset of objects. Here they are non-intersecting since each review has its distinctive rating. The authors applied two algorithms for generating rough sets: the first one is exhaustive (total search) while the other one is an LEM2 algorithm for decision rule induction.

The last phase was empirical evaluation, in which the authors compared the performances of the proposed models on real-world data sets. The collection of reviews was obtained by harvesting publicly available reviews about four products posted on the Amazon.com website. Each review includes a title, textual description, date, time, author name, location, ratings, and other ignored information. Rating 1 meant poor, while 5 meant excellent. The name of the product and its corresponding top-rated words (features) are shown in Table 5.

According to experimental results, the ARM algorithm achieved the best scalability, efficiency, and highest support and confidence for the products where a high number of reviews was recorded. On the other hand, RST algorithms provided the rules that are the most informative and interesting and have the highest overall confidence values.

SELECTED APPLICATION OF THE NEIGHBORHOOD ALGORITHM

Evaluating Microstructure in a Metal Alloy

Metal solidification is one of the most important processes in the metal production industry. It is responsible for microstructural metal formation, which later induces certain mechanical properties. Having in mind that metals are widely used in industry, construction, transportation, and other fields, paying enough attention to a phase of metal solidification is one of the primary concerns.

In this section, we will cover the application of a hybrid nearest neighbor algorithm in the monitoring of Nickle-based alloy after the weld solidification process, introduced in (Marinho et al., 2019). An especially complex scenario in welding is when it is performed between different materials, as this changes the chemical composition of the metal. There are many industrial branches that use welded materials, but one can hardly be confident that internal metal structure is appropriate. The preferred way of testing the metal microstructure is called non-destructive ultrasound testing (NDT), which is based on the correlations among ultrasonic attenuation and speed on one hand and different material properties on the other. There are few papers in literature that focus on improving NDT by additional analysis of NDT signals. According to Vejdannik et al. (2018), the building blocks of NDT signal processing are:

1. data generator (preprocessing),
2. feature extraction,
3. feature reduction,
4. and classification.

In the analyzed paper, the authors contribute to the last classification phase by combining two prominent ML techniques: one unsupervised, called Self-Organizing Maps (SOM), introduced by Kohonen (1982), and the other well-known supervised technique called k-Nearest neighbors (kNN).

SOM is a type of the artificial neural network (ANN) that unlike the majority of ANNs uses unsupervised learning. The learning goal is to produce a low-dimensional representation of input data, which, on the other hand, can have an arbitrary number of dimensions. Obviously, this characteristic also puts SOM into the group of dimensionality reduction methods, in addition to its learning capabilities. The important aspect of this space transition is that topological properties of input space are preserved. Less informally stated, the objects that were close in the original input space according to some closeness/distance metric, need to be close in the target space as well. An additional benefit of having low-dimensional space at hand is its visualization. Therefore, SOMs are often used to visualize data of high-dimensional origin. For example, Figure 4 is a cartographical representation of Wikipedia topics with respect to a word frequency distance metric. Input data is sampled from high-dimensional feature space with many different words inside Wikipedia articles. However, at the end, the output can be visualized in three dimensions by employing SOM and appropriate distance metric. The closeness (inversely proportional to distance) of articles regarding word frequencies is reflected in three-dimensional space, so these articles are spatially closer to each other.

Structurally, SOM is organized as a map of neurons. For example, in a two-dimensional case, this means that there is a matrix of neurons, where a

Figure 4. Wikipedia articles in a three-dimensional SOM.
(taken from Wikipedia under Creative Commons Attribution-Share Alike 3.0 Unported license)

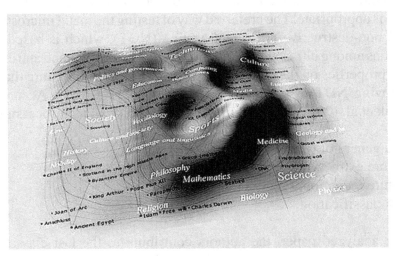

neuron in row i and column j is represented as a weight vector h_{ij} of size N (see Figure 5). The input object also has the size of N.

The previously mentioned concept of topological structure preservation means that close neurons will activate for two similar stimuli (input vectors) entering the SOM. This resembles the way visual, auditory, and other sensory inputs are handled in the cerebral cortex in the human brain. For example, when a human sees a shade of red color, certain neurons activate. The next time, when some other shade of red is presented, some close neurons will activate. This makes the human brain capable of handling totally new concepts that are similar but not the same as some previously seen ones. This is one of the human brain properties that differentiate it from a simple lookup-value memory. To train SOM to associate similar concepts (as human brain does), the following steps are done:

1. Neuron weights are initially randomly set.
2. SOM is fed with training vectors whose dimension is the same as the size of neuron weight vectors.
    a. For a given training vector, the closest neuron weight vector is found; this neuron is called the winning one.
    b. The winning neuron weight is adjusted in the direction of the training vector; the adjustment effect is controlled by the learning rate parameter.

Figure 5. SOM internal structure.

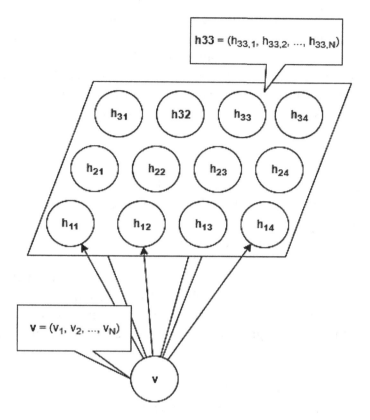

c. The neurons around the winning neuron are also adjusted, but with a smaller effect as the effect fades away as the neuron is more distant to the winning one.

Step 2c is what differentiates the lookup-value memory (classical scenario) from the associative memory. Gradually, as the training process progresses, SOM learns not only what was directly told, but also acquires some implicit knowledge.

The next step was to hybridize SOM with kNN into the method called SOM-kNN. The most problematic property of kNN is its computational complexity because the comparison of the input object that is to be classified needs to be compared to all training objects. SOM helps here, since it reduces the training data set to a fixed number of neurons.

In the training phase, SOM neurons are randomly initialized and the training set of objects is then fed into the SOM in a randomized order. Once all the training data are fed, the neurons are further considered as new training data prototypes, i.e., each neuron becomes labeled by a class. The class for an observed neuron is obtained by traversing the original set of labeled training objects and counting the number of votes per class. Finally, in the classification (application) phase, an object that is to be classified is compared to labeled neurons in the kNN manner.

The authors used three different steels, namely:

- Inconel 625 (AWS ERNiCrMo-3), which is a nickel-based superalloy,
- Hastelloy C276 (AWS ERNiCrMo-4), which is super duplex steel, as additional metal,
- Steel ASTM A516 Gr. 60 as the base metal.

To catch the heat deterioration characteristics of considered alloys, after welding, all three samples were subjected to a fast thermal treatment at temperatures of 650 °C and 950 °C for 10 h, 100 h, and 200 h. During NDT, 8 separate databases were gathered corresponding to a different combination of the following settings:

- temperature 650 °C or 950 °C,
- backscatter or echo signal measurement,
- frequency of 4 MHz or 5 MHz.

Each database consisted of 40 features and 4 classes. The classes simply referred to different heat exposure length: 0, 10, 100, and 200 hours. The authors further combine different SOM topologies (neuron maps of different dimensions) with three values of parameter k={1, 3, 5}. Tables 6 and 7 show the best topologies and their corresponding accuracies for both considered temperatures.

Table 6. Data usage and accuracy for 18 SOM-kNN topologies at temperature 650 °C.

Topology	%	Echo (Acc%)		Topology	%	Backscattered (Acc%)	
		4MHz	5MHz			4MHz	5Mhz
10×10, k = 1	0.3	54.34±0.01	54.78±0.26	10×10, k = 1	6.7	72.83±0.05	72.83±0.05
20×10, k = 1	0.7	72.83±0.05	77.37±0.03	14×10, k = 1	9.3	91.16±0.05	92.16±0.06
30×10, k = 1	1	85.76±0.01	86.76±0.01	18×10, k = 1	12	93.96±0.00	95.12±0.02
40×10, k = 1	1.3	90.08±0.00	91.44±0.00	14×14, k = 1	17.3	92.68±0.02	96.28±0.02
50×10, k = 1	1.7	93.12±0.00	95.48±0.00	18×14, k = 1	20	94.64±0.00	97.32±0.01
60×10, k = 1	2	95.50±0.00	97.42±0.00	26×10, k = 1	16.8	93.80±0.01	97.28±0.01
40×20, k = 1	2.7	96.82±0.01	98.84±0.00	22×14, k = 1	20.5	94.68±0.01	97.76±0.01
30×30, k = 1	3	96.71±0.00	99.11±0.00	18×18, k = 1	24.3	94.64±0.01	98.08±0.00
50×20, k = 1	3.3	97.95±0.00	99.50±0.00	26×14, k = 1	28	93.96±0.01	97.40±0.01
60×20, k = 1	4	99.04±0.00	99.82±0.00	22×18, k = 1	26.4	95.24±0.00	97.76±0.00
50×30, k = 1	**5**	99.65±0.00	**100.00±0.00**	26×18, k = 1	31.2	95.36±0.03	98.24±0.00
40×40, k = 1	5.3	99.30±0.00	99.86±0.00	22×22, k = 1	36	94.32±0.05	98.12±0.01
60×30, k = 1	6	99.80±0.00	99.91±0.00	30×18, k = 1	32.3	94.20±0.02	98.40±0.00
50×40, k = 1	6.7	99.72±0.00	99.96±0.00	26×22, k = 1	38.1	95.08±0.03	97.80±0.00
60×40, k = 1	8	99.98±0.00	100.00±0.00	30×22, k = 1	44	94.56±0.02	98.40±0.00
50×50, k = 1	8.3	99.92±0.00	99.98±0.00	26×26, k = 1	45.1	93.68±0.03	98.40±0.00
60×50, k = 1	10	99.95±0.00	100.00±0.00	30×26, k = 1	52	95.24±0.01	98.08±0.01
60×60, k = 1	12	99.99±0.00	100.00±0.00	30×30, k = 1	60	93.92±0.01	98.40±0.00

(table data from (Marinho et al., 2019))

Table 7. Data usage and accuracy for 18 SOM-kNN topologies at temperature 950 °C.

Topology	%	Echo (Acc%)		Topology	%	Backscattered (Acc%)	
		4MHz	5MHz			4MHz	5Mhz
10 × 10, k = 1	0.3	40.41±0.00	41.61±0.00	10 × 10, k = 1	6.7	78.84±0.20	86.36±0.02
20 × 10, k = 1	0.7	47.36±0.00	51.50±0.03	14 × 10, k = 1	9.3	87.44±0.02	94.04±0.03
30 × 10, k = 1	1	49.86±0.00	57.45±0.00	18 × 10, k = 1	12	92.68±0.01	96.20±0.00
40 × 10, k = 1	1.3	54.89±0.01	61.20±0.01	14 × 14, k = 1	17.3	92.64±0.01	95.72±0.01
50 × 10, k = 1	1.7	56.57±0.01	63.57±0.01	18 × 14, k = 1	20	94.20±0.02	97.16±0.01
60 × 10, k = 1	2	57.51±0.00	65.72±0.01	26 × 10, k = 1	16.8	94.12±0.01	97.92±0.00
40 × 20, k = 1	2.7	60.75±0.00	67.24±0.00	22 × 14, k = 1	20.5	94.40±0.00	97.80±0.01
30 × 30, k = 1	3	61.99±0.01	68.30±0.00	18 × 18, k = 1	24.3	95.04±0.01	97.56±0.01
50 × 20, k = 1	3.3	63.22±0.00	69.24±0.00	6 × 14, k = 1	28	94.80±0.01	97.96±0.00
60 × 20, k = 1	4	64.04±0.00	68.92±0.00	22 × 18, k = 1	26.4	96.60±0.00	97.52±0.01
50 × 30, k = 1	5	65.38±0.00	69.99±0.00	26 × 18, k = 1	31.2	95.16±0.02	97.88±0.00
40 × 40, k = 1	5.3	66.10±0.00	70.58±0.00	22 × 22, k = 1	36	95.76±0.02	97.92±0.00
60 × 30, k = 1	6	66.01±0.00	70.86±0.00	30 × 18, k = 1	32.3	95.44±0.01	97.84±0.01
50 × 40, k = 1	6.7	65.88±0.00	71.48±0.00	**26 × 22, k = 1**	**38.1**	94.80±0.01	**98.36±0.00**
60 × 40, k = 1	8	66.31±0.00	71.17±0.00	30 × 22, k = 1	44	95.64±0.02	97.68±0.00
50 × 50, k = 1	8.3	66.50±0.00	71.15±0.00	26 × 26, k = 1	45.1	95.52±0.03	97.76±0.01
60 × 50, k = 1	10	66.39±0.00	72.02±0.00	30 × 26, k = 1	52	95.20±0.02	97.96±0.01
60 × 60, k = 1	12	66.64±0.00	72.47±0.00	30 × 30, k = 1	60	94.60±0.02	97.76±0.00

(table data from (Marinho et al., 2019))

REVIEW QUESTIONS

This section provides questions for better understanding of the key aspects of the chapter.

1. Present one application in e-commerce suitable for dataflow paradigm.
2. Present one application in engineering suitable for dataflow paradigm.
3. Present one application in school management suitable for dataflow paradigm.
4. Present one application in healthcare and medical sensors suitable for dataflow paradigm.

REFERENCES

Bakhshinategh, B., Zaiane, O. R., ElAtia, S., & Ipperciel, D. (2018). Educational data mining applications and tasks: A survey of the last 10 years. *Education and Information Technologies*, *23*(1), 537–553. doi:10.100710639-017-9616-z

Ballestar, M. T., Grau-Carles, P., & Sainz, J. (2019). Predicting customer quality in e-commerce social networks: A machine learning approach. *Review of Managerial Science*, *13*(3), 589–603. doi:10.100711846-018-0316-x

Boodhun, N., & Jayabalan, M. (2018). Risk prediction in life insurance industry using supervised learning algorithms. *Complex & Intelligent Systems*, *4*(2), 145–154. doi:10.100740747-018-0072-1

Cao, Q., Ewing, B. T., & Thompson, M. A. (2012). Forecasting wind speed with recurrent neural networks. *European Journal of Operational Research*, *221*(1), 148–154. doi:10.1016/j.ejor.2012.02.042

Chung, W., & Tseng, T. L. B. (2012). Discovering business intelligence from online product reviews: A rule-induction framework. *Expert Systems with Applications*, *39*(15), 11870–11879. doi:10.1016/j.eswa.2012.02.059

Durairaj, M., & Ranjani, V. (2013). Data mining applications in healthcare sector: a study. *International Journal of Scientific & Technology Research*, *2*(10), 29-35.

Enshaeifar, S., Zoha, A., Markides, A., Skillman, S., Acton, S. T., Elsaleh, T., Hassanpour, M., Ahrabian, A., Kenny, M., Klein, S., Rostill, H., Nilforooshan, R., & Barnaghi, P. (2018). Health management and pattern analysis of daily living activities of people with dementia using in-home sensors and machine learning techniques. *PLoS One*, *13*(5), e0195605. doi:10.1371/journal.pone.0195605 PMID:29723236

Ghazal, T. M., Hasan, M. K., Alshurideh, M. T., Alzoubi, H. M., Ahmad, M., Akbar, S. S., Al Kurdi, B., & Akour, I. A. (2021). IoT for smart cities: Machine learning approaches in smart healthcare—A review. *Future Internet*, *13*(8), 218. doi:10.3390/fi13080218

Guo, Q., Li, Z., An, B., Hui, P., Huang, J., Zhang, L., & Zhao, M. (2019, May). Securing the deep fraud detector in large-scale e-commerce platform via adversarial machine learning approach. In *The World Wide Web Conference* (pp. 616-626). 10.1145/3308558.3313533

Ho, I. M. K., Cheong, K. Y., & Weldon, A. (2021). Predicting student satisfaction of emergency remote learning in higher education during COVID-19 using machine learning techniques. *PLoS One*, *16*(4), e0249423. doi:10.1371/journal.pone.0249423 PMID:33798204

Hochreiter, S., & Schmidhuber, J. (1997). Long short-term memory. *Neural Computation*, *9*(8), 1735–1780. doi:10.1162/neco.1997.9.8.1735 PMID:9377276

Koh, H. C., & Tan, G. (2011). Data mining applications in healthcare. *Journal of Healthcare Information Management*, *19*(2), 65. PMID:15869215

Kohavi, R., & Provost, F. (2001). Applications of data mining to electronic commerce. In *Applications of data mining to electronic commerce* (pp. 5–10). Springer. doi:10.1007/978-1-4615-1627-9_1

Kohonen, T. (1982). Self-organized formation of topologically correct feature maps. *Biological Cybernetics*, *43*(1), 59–69. doi:10.1007/BF00337288

Köksal, G., Batmaz, I., & Testik, M. C. (2011). A review of data mining applications for quality improvement in manufacturing industry. *Expert Systems with Applications*, *38*(10), 13448–13467. doi:10.1016/j.eswa.2011.04.063

Luan, J. (2004). Data mining applications in higher education. *SPSS Executive, 7.*

Marinho, L. B., Rebouças Filho, P. P., & de Albuquerque, V. H. C. (2019). Ultrasonic sensor signals and self organized mapping with nearest neighbors for the microstructural characterization of thermally-aged Inconel 625 alloy. *Computers in Industry*, *107*, 1–10. doi:10.1016/j.compind.2019.01.009

Mobasher, B. (2007). Data mining for web personalization. In *The adaptive web* (pp. 90–135). Springer. doi:10.1007/978-3-540-72079-9_3

Pawlak, Z. (1982). Rough sets. *International Journal of Computer & Information Sciences, 11*(5), 341-356.

Pumsirirat, A., & Yan, L. (2018). Credit card fraud detection using deep learning based on auto-encoder and restricted boltzmann machine. *International Journal of Advanced Computer Science and Applications*, *9*(1), 18–25. doi:10.14569/IJACSA.2018.090103

Regnier, E. (2008). Doing something about the weather. *Omega*, *36*(1), 22–32. doi:10.1016/j.omega.2005.07.011

Roy, A., Sun, J., Mahoney, R., Alonzi, L., Adams, S., & Beling, P. (2018, April). Deep learning detecting fraud in credit card transactions. In *2018 Systems and Information Engineering Design Symposium (SIEDS)* (pp. 129-134). IEEE. 10.1109/SIEDS.2018.8374722

Siguenza-Guzman, L., Saquicela, V., Avila-Ordóñez, E., Vandewalle, J., & Cattrysse, D. (2015). Literature review of data mining applications in academic libraries. *Journal of Academic Librarianship, 41*(4), 499–510. doi:10.1016/j. acalib.2015.06.007

Vejdannik, M., Sadr, A., de Albuquerque, V. H. C., & Tavares, J. M. R. (2018). Signal processing for NDE. Handbook of advanced non-destructive evaluation. doi:10.1007/978-3-319-30050-4_53-1

Xu, Y., Zhou, Y., Sekula, P., & Ding, L. (2021). Machine learning in construction: From shallow to deep learning. *Developments in the Built Environment, 6*, 100045. doi:10.1016/j.dibe.2021.100045

Xu, Z., Dang, Y., & Munro, P. (2018). Knowledge-driven intelligent quality problem-solving system in the automotive industry. *Advanced Engineering Informatics, 38*, 441–457. doi:10.1016/j.aei.2018.08.013

Yan, H., Yang, N., Peng, Y., & Ren, Y. (2020). Data mining in the construction industry: Present status, opportunities, and future trends. *Automation in Construction, 119*, 103331. doi:10.1016/j.autcon.2020.103331

KEY TERMS AND DEFINITIONS

BI: Business intelligence.

Cross Validation: Machine learning technique for evaluating performance of a model using labeled data.

NLP: Natural language processing.

PCA: Principal component analysis that transforms data in sub-dimensional space.

RNN: Recurrent neural networks suitable for NLP.

Chapter 6

Implementation Details of Neural Networks Using Dataflow

ABSTRACT

This chapter presents dataflow paradigm in general and loop unrolling and data pipelines as key points for acceleration and discusses implementation details of multilayer perceptron neural networks. The iterative nature of the algorithm makes it suitable for dataflow implementation using matrix multiplication as a basic operation. Also, it presents major differences in code execution between conventional controlflow paradigm and dataflow paradigm. It is shown how part of an algorithm (feed-forward phase) can be migrated to the accelerator while the rest remains the same.

INTRODUCTION

Rapid development of edge devices led to exponential growth in data. Machine learning algorithms are used for data analysis and thus presents an essential component in many applications. They are widely used in almost every industry today. In order to efficiently process data using machine learning algorithms in environments where resources are limited, i.e. on edge devices, it is important to use an architecture that will dissipate small amounts of electrical power and in the same time be efficient to process significant amounts of data. Requirements mentioned above puts the control-flow paradigm out

DOI: 10.4018/978-1-7998-8350-0.ch006

and brings the dataflow paradigm into the focus (Trifunovic, Milutinovic, Salom, & Kos, 2015).

The dataflow approach is based on the Feynman paradigm and relies on reconfigurable FPGA cards (Flynn, et al., 2013) (Milutinović, Salom, Trifunović, & Giorgi, 2015). The reconfigurable cards generate an execution graph that matches an algorithm, and thus could achieve significant performance improvements. The dataflow paradigm can achieve speedups over the conventional control-flow paradigm and consumes less power at the same time. The speedup depends on the number of loops, their characteristics and on the amount of time that the algorithm spends executing the loops. The power saving depends on the clock frequency and on characteristics of the underlying FPGA cards.

Iterative nature of neural networks makes them suitable for architectures that enable massive parallelization, like GPU, FPGA, and ASIC cards. All of these architectures contain nodes as working units where tasks are distributed on the nodes and executed simultaneously.

This chapter discusses key points of the dataflow paradigm, explains the compilation process and presents the pipelines and loop unrolling as a key challenge for implementation of neural networks on such architecture. It also presents important implementation details of neural networks.

DATAFLOW PARADIGM

In the controlflow paradigm, source code is transformed into a list of low level instructions and then loaded into memory, where the processor executes instructions and communicates with the memory, as shown in Figure 1. Memory access is slow operation and in order to optimize it there is a memory hierarchy that contains several levels of caching, where the closest level to the processor has the shortest access time.

In the dataflow paradigm, the data is retrieved from memory into the execution graph that consists of connected nodes called units, as shown in Figure 2. Each unit represents simple arithmetic or logic operation. Graph of such connected units is called an execution graph where data is streamed from the input of the graph to the output.

In the dataflow paradigm, execution goes to the lower code level where acceleration depends on the level of data reusability inside the moved loops,

Figure 1. Illustration of controlflow paradigm where the processor executes instructions and communicates with the memory.

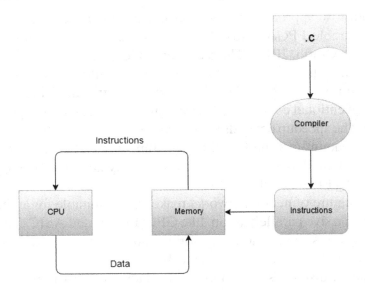

Figure 2. Illustration of dataflow paradigm where each unit represents simple arithmetic or logic operation.

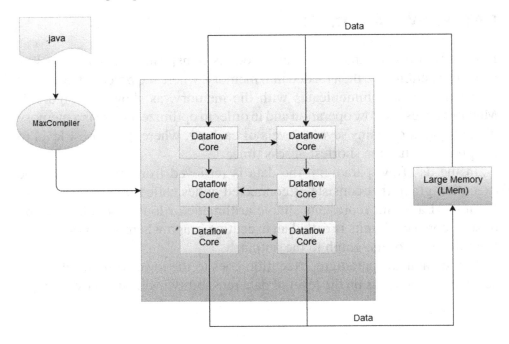

as well as on the number of loops and loop iterations. Dataflow accelerator used in this book is based on MaxJ programming language which is a superset of Java programming language, extended with classes for describing concepts of execution graphs. Dataflow accelerators rely on Intel FPGA cards where several accelerators are integrated and connected together. Files written in MaxJ compile first in execution graphs which contain pipelines of arithmetic and logic units. Then using third party tools provided by FPGA vendors, the compiler converts an execution graph into a file.

In order to create an execution graph, two types of files are necessary: kernel file and manager file. Kernel file describes an execution graph of the migrated loop that will be mapped to the FPGA card. Manager file controls data flow between the host machine, which is the CPU in this case, and the accelerator. At the beginning of the execution, execution of the manager code checks if the underlying FPGA card is configured. If it is not, the accelerator starts configuring based on the created file. When the configuration is done, data is streamed to the input of the mapped execution graph, and the algorithm begins. After that, each time when the same algorithm executes again, there is no need for FPGA card reconfiguration.

IMPLEMENTATION DETAILS

Neural networks depending on the configuration and activation functions differ (Walczak, 2019) (Gaikwad, Tiwari, Keskar, & Shivaprakash, 2019). Well known back-propagation algorithm used for training of multilayer neural networks is often applied in classification tasks and presents the basic algorithm for training that can be further extended to more complex use cases. Iterative nature of an algorithm makes it suitable for dataflow architecture that relies on FPGA cards. Algorithm consists of two phases, feed-forward phase where output is calculated based on weight values and feed-back phase where weight values are updated based on given error. Listing 1 presents a pseudo-code of feed-forward phase for one node in a multilayer neural network. In essence, the feed-forward phase is implemented as multiplication of two matrices where the first one represents data inputs and the second represents weights. Matrix multiplication is suitable for parallelization and thus will be migrated to the accelerator.

First, the training set is generated on the host machine and streamed to the accelerator. After that feed-forward phase is performed for each data instance from the training set. Listing 2 shows how training data is streamed

Listing 1. Pseudo-code of of feed-forward phase for one node in a multilayer network

```
for (int i = 1; i < length; i++){
        for (int j = 0; j < width; j++){
                double sum = out[i][width];
                for (int k = 0; k < width; k++){
                        sum += out[i - 1][k]*weight[i-1][k]
[j];
                }
                out[i][j] = (1.0 / (1.0 + exp(-sum)));
        }
}
```

to the accelerator. Accelerator and host machine communicate using interface (SLiC interface). First parameter presents the size of the training dataset, next one is bias for the nodes, the following parameters are training instances and initial weights. Training instances and initial weights are streamed as mapped ROM memory in order to enable context changes during and between the executions, without a need for recompilation.

The manager file is shown in Listing 3, and it describes types for each interface parameter. It could also control data streams as well as communication between accelerators.

Listing 4 illustrates the process of initializing mapped ROM memories and dataflow variables. The size of the mapped ROM memory is equal to the size of neurons in this case.

In order to implement the feed-forward phase on dataflow paradigm it is necessary to shift focus from conventional processing units to space-based processing units. It means that processing should be done on different units at the same time. Pipeline presents a set of connected acyclic processing units. In this implementation, each connection between two neurons is represented with a different pipeline that contains several processing nodes. It means that all calculations are performed in parallel using different pipelines. Kernel file that describes the execution graph contains a main loop that iterates through layers and creates input of pipelines. The inner loop iterates through neurons

Listing 2. Dataflow interface for streaming data to the accelerator

```
startTime = getTime();
FeedForwardDFE(size, bias, w_avg,mappedRom_points,mappedRom_w);
dfeDuration = getTime() - startTime;
```

Listing 3. Dataflow interface for streaming data to the accelerator

```
CPUTypes    intType = CPUTypes.INT;
CPUTypes    floatType = CPUTypes.FLOAT;
int         floatSize = floatType.sizeInBytes();
InterfaceParam size    = engine_interface.addParam("N",
intType);
InterfaceParam bias    = engine_interface.addParam("bias",
floatType);
engine_interface.setTicks(s_kernelName, size);
engine_interface.setScalar(s_kernelName, "bias", bias);
engine_interface.setStream("w_avg", floatType, size *
floatSize);
```

in each layer and creates appropriate arithmetic and logic units. The inner loop creates output units for each neuron in the corresponding layer. Such an approach is called loop unrolling where iterations are executed simultaneously and presents the significant level of parallelism, as shown in Figure 3.

Listing 5 presents implementation of feed-forward phase of multilayer neural network in MaxJ. At the beginning, weights and bias values are loaded from mapped ROM memory and converted to the vectors. In order to iterate through memory space it is necessary to create an address variable that has the same length as memory space in order to avoid violation accesses.

After computing the output values for all layers, the feed-forward phase is completed and the next phase is to calculate the global error of the network for the current training instance. The global error presents the difference between the obtained and the desired output. This difference is squared and the new value is calculated on the host machine in order to present a hybrid approach where only part of an algorithm is transferred to the accelerator.

Listing 4. Mapped ROM memories with dataflow variables

```
//Memory
Memory<DFEVar> ROM_points=mem.alloc(floatingType, width*size);
ROM_points.mapToCPU("mappedRom_1");
Memory<DFEVar> ROM_w=mem.alloc(floatingType, width*length);
ROM_w.mapToCPU("mappedRom_2");
DFEVar [] out=new DFEVar[length];
for (int k=0;k<width;k++){
        out[k]=constant.var(0);
}
```

Matrix multiplication presents common task suitable for parallelization used in a number of use cases. Source code is available at the following

Figure 3. Feed-forward phase on dataflow accelerator

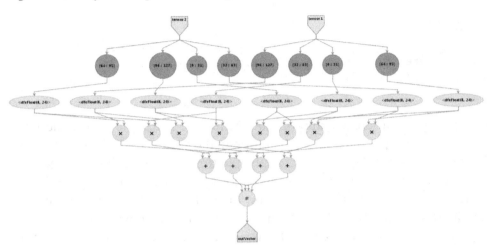

Listing 5. Implementation of feed-forward phase of multilayer neural network in MaxJ

```
DFEVar address=constant.var(i);
address=address.cast(dfeUInt(MathUtils.
bitsToAddress(width*length)));
DFEVar w=ROM_w.read(address);
w=w.cast(fixedType);
DFEVar sum=bias;
...
DFEVector<DFEVar> outVector = vectorType.newInstance(this);
for(int i = 0; i < Math.sqrt(vectorSize); i++){
        for(int j=0;j<Math.sqrt(vectorSize);j++){
                DFEVar temp = constant.var(0);
                for (int k=0;k<Math.sqrt(vectorSize);k++){
                        temp +=
inVector1[i*(int)Math.sqrt(vectorSize)+k]*inVector2[j*(int)
Math.sqrt(vectorSize)+k];
                }
                outVector[i*(int)Math.
sqrt(vectorSize)+j]<==temp;
        }
}
```

link: https://github.com/kotlarmilos/tensorcalculus/tree/master/composition/
Composition_A

DISCUSSION

Performance of the proposed solution can be affected with a large number of layers, where latency before the first result is computed could be high. Also, in some cases, with a large number of layers, it is not possible to map the execution graph onto one FPGA card. In order to overcome it, multiple cards can be connected together or a tailing approach could be used to allocate less resources by processing only a part of the network.

Another case where performance could be affected refers to the variable number of neurons per layer, while the number of layers are constant. With an increasing number of layers, execution time on the engine does not increase. In this case, only resource allocation could be a bottleneck, but still less than in the previous case.

In order to illustrate the size of an execution graph, Figure 4 presents an execution graph for a single neuron in the network for several loop iterations unrolled. The following image depicts an execution graph which is mapped to the FPGA card, where each pipeline is aimed for single path in neural network.

Neural networks based on matrix multiplications such as multilayer neural networks are suitable for accelerating using the dataflow accelerators based on FPGA cards, especially if the learning process is permanent. By using such an approach in cases where electrical power resources are limited it is possible to implement neural networks using dataflow accelerators.

Topics for further research in this field includes creating FPGA cards which could reconfigure without recompiling, executing multiple kernels in parallel on the same card, as well as any other innovation which contributes to improving FPGA cards.

REVIEW QUESTIONS

This section provides questions for better understanding of the key aspects of the chapter.

1. What are the main components of neural network?
2. What is an execution graph?

Figure 4. Feed-forward phase for single neuron in the network

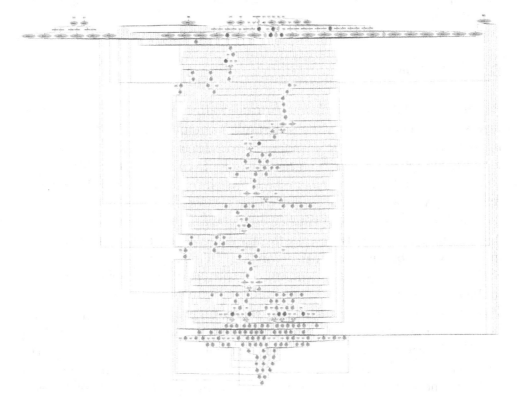

3. What are the key advantages of the dataflow paradigm?
4. What is mapped ROM memories in dataflow paradigm?

REFERENCES

Trifunovic, N., Milutinovic, V., Salom, J., & Kos, A. (2015). Paradigm shift in big data supercomputing: dataflow vs. controlflow. *Journal of Big Data*. Flynn, M. J., Mencer, O., Milutinovic, V., Rakocevic, G., Stenstrom, P., Trobec, R., & Valero, M. (2013). Moving from petaflops to petadata. *Communications of the ACM*, 39-42. Milutinović, V., Salom, J., Trifunović, N., & Giorgi, R. (2015). *Guide to dataflow supercomputing*. Springer.

Walczak, S. (2019). *Advanced Methodologies and Technologies in Artificial Intelligence. Computer Simulation, and Human-Computer Interaction.* IGI Global. Gaikwad, N. B., Tiwari, V., Keskar, A., & Shivaprakash, N. C. (2019). Efficient FPGA implementation of multilayer perceptron for real-time human activity classification. *IEEE Access.*

KEY TERMS AND DEFINITIONS

FPGA: Field programmable gate array.

Kernel: Dataflow program file that describes execution graph.

Loop Unrolling: Dataflow technique for implementing controlflow loops.

Manager: Dataflow program file describes data orchestration between kernel and the host machine.

Pipeline Utilization: Optimization technique for dataflow paradigm.

Chapter 7

Implementation Details of Decision Tree Algorithms Using Dataflow

ABSTRACT

This chapter presents dataflow paradigm in general and streams of data, offsets, different number representations as key points for acceleration and discusses implementation details of C4.5 on the dataflow accelerators. The limited number range of the algorithm makes it suitable for dataflow implementation using custom data types and its iterative nature enables utilization of data streams. It is shown how part of an algorithm (information gain entropy) can be migrated using advanced optimization constructs.

INTRODUCTION

Decision tree algorithms belong to the supervised machine learning algorithms and can be used for classification and regression. In decision tree algorithms, the target class can take a discrete set of values instead of numerical values. Algorithms for constructing decision trees can be intensive and thus it is beneficial to present implementation details which could be used for implementation on dataflow accelerators.

Architecture of dataflow accelerators based on Xilinx and Intel FPGA cards are discussed in the previous chapter. This chapter presents implementation details for the dataflow paradigm that could be utilized for algorithms that

DOI: 10.4018/978-1-7998-8350-0.ch007

Listing 1. implementation details of the C4.5 algorithm. Information gain ratio is the ratio of observations to the total number of observations.

```
•  Check for the above base cases.
•  For each attribute a, find the normalized information gain
ratio from splitting on a.
•  Let a_best be the attribute with the highest normalized
information gain.
•  Create a decision node that splits on a_best.
•  Recurse on the sublists obtained by splitting on a_best, and
add those nodes as children of node.
```

construct decision trees. First, it provides a brief overview of decision tree algorithms with a pseudocode example. Later, optimization constructs that exploit advantages of the dataflow paradigm and could be used for the decision tree algorithms are presented.

ALGORITHM

This section presents implementation details of the C4.5 algorithm (Hssina, Merbouha, Ezzikouri, & Erritali, 2014) (Dai & Ji, 2014) for decision tree construction. Listing 1 presents a pseudocode of the algorithm that utilizes information theory methods to choose the attribute of the training data that most effectively splits instances into subsets described with labels.

Figure 2 presents an example of a decision tree created by the C4.5 algorithm. According to the training data, attribute *outlook* has the best information gain ratio and thus is in the root of the tree. Leaves in the tree present the class or output of an algorithm which in this case predicts whether an action will be taken.

IMPLEMENTATION DETAILS

In order to implement such an algorithm on the dataflow accelerator, the first thing is to encode categorical values to numerical. Numerical values could be stored on the host machine either on card memory and streamed to the accelerator in order to compute information gain for each attribute.

Figure 1. An example of a decision tree which predicts whether an action will be taken according to the weather data.

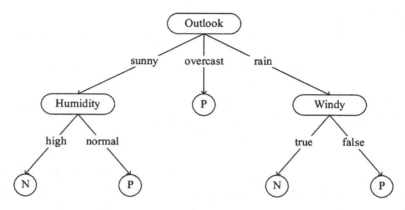

Data streams connect two endpoints and transfer data in ticks between them (Pell, Mencer, Tsoi, & Luk, 2013). Figure 2 illustrates data streams used in the accelerators for streaming variables to the accelerator and back to

Figure 2. An example of data streams in dataflow accelerators

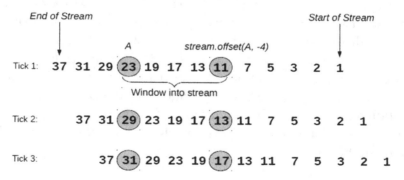

the host machine or on card memory. In the first tick, the start of the stream presents number 1 while in the second tick stream shifts and next element is 2.

Streams enable accessing neighbor elements relative to the head of the stream. It could be beneficial for calculating information gain to access neighbor elements in a stream in order to produce the result faster. They are used in use cases where neighbor elements are necessary for producing the result, as illustrated in Figure 3.

Figure 3. An example of stream offsets utilization in a matrix

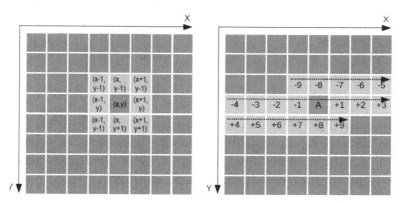

In order to use offsets it is important to determine what type of offsets is needed:

- **static** offsets have a size fixed at compile-time
- **variable** offsets have size set at run time before a stream is processed
- **dynamic** offsets have sizes set at run time during stream processing

Static and variable offsets require a variable which indicates the offset during the compilation time and thus doesn't allocate a significant amount of resources on the FPGA card. However, if it is not possible to determine offset during the compilation time, dynamic offsets can be determined during the

Table 1. Resource utilization for different offset types

	Static Offsets	Variable Offsets	Dynamic Offsets
Size configurable	At compile-time	Before a stream	tick-by-tick
On-chip resource cost	Low	Moderate	High
Compiler optimizes	Yes	Yes	No

runtime by specifying min and max possible values for the offset. Resource allocation is presented in Table 1 for different offset types (Milutinović, Salom, Trifunović, & Giorgi, 2015).

This approach allocates a significant amount of resources on the FPGA card and thus should be used only when it is necessary. Listing 2 presents different methods for offsets depending on the type.

Listing 2. Different offset types for streams

```
stream.offset(DFEVar in_stream, int constant)
stream.offset(KernelObject src, DFEVar offset, int min offset,
int max offset)
```

Decision tree algorithm is an iterative algorithm which means that it can't be fully parallelized by unrolling the loops because output of an iteration serves as an input for the next iteration. Thus to achieve significant performance alternative optimization constructs should be utilized.

The accelerator can work with custom number types and using different number representations. By reducing number precision and changing number representation acceleration can be achieved due to smaller resource allocation and better pipeline utilization. Figure 4 presents differences between floating number representation and fixed number representation. Floating point representation utilizes mantissa and exponent to represent numbers in

Figure 4. Illustrates different number representations in the accelerator. First figure represents floating point number representation. Second figure represents fixed point representation.

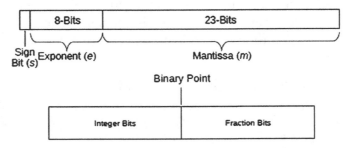

the system. Fixed point representation utilizes offsets for decimal places to indicate where the decimal point is.

Presented optimization constructs are important for achieving acceleration for such kind of algorithms. Detailed examples of machine learning algorithms including those mentioned in this chapter are available at the Maxeler Application gallery: https://appgallery.maxeler.com/

Figure 5. Resource allocation of FPGA card using different number precisions as well as number representations

```
Double
[java] Mon 08:27: Logic utilization:       28632 / 297600 (9.62%)
[java] Mon 08:27:   LUTs:                   19361 / 297600 (6.51%)
[java] Mon 08:27:   Primary FFs:            24961 / 297600 (8.39%)
[java] Mon 08:27:   Secondary FFs:           3756 / 297600 (1.26%)
[java] Mon 08:27: Multipliers (25x18):          0 / 2016   (0.00%)
[java] Mon 08:27:   DSP blocks:                 0 / 2016   (0.00%)
[java] Mon 08:27: Block memory (BRAM18):      112 / 2128   (5.26%)
```

```
Float
[java] Mon 09:57: Logic utilization:       17828 / 297600 (5.99%)
[java] Mon 09:57:   LUTs:                   12819 / 297600 (4.31%)
[java] Mon 09:57:   Primary FFs:            15154 / 297600 (5.09%)
[java] Mon 09:57:   Secondary FFs:           2761 / 297600 (0.93%)
[java] Mon 09:57: Multipliers (25x18):          0 / 2016   (0.00%)
[java] Mon 09:57:   DSP blocks:                 0 / 2016   (0.00%)
[java] Mon 09:57: Block memory (BRAM18):       70 / 2128   (3.29%)
```

```
Int_32
[java] Mon 10:31: Logic utilization:        9802 / 297600 (3.29%)
[java] Mon 10:31:   LUTs:                    6901 / 297600 (2.32%)
[java] Mon 10:31:   Primary FFs:             7921 / 297600 (2.66%)
[java] Mon 10:31:   Secondary FFs:           1842 / 297600 (0.62%)
[java] Mon 10:31: Multipliers (25x18):          0 / 2016   (0.00%)
[java] Mon 10:31:   DSP blocks:                 0 / 2016   (0.00%)
[java] Mon 10:31: Block memory (BRAM18):       70 / 2128   (3.29%)
```

```
Int_16
[java] Mon 12:40: Logic utilization:        7763 / 297600 (2.61%)
[java] Mon 12:40:   LUTs:                    6663 / 297600 (2.24%)
[java] Mon 12:40:   Primary FFs:             6088 / 297600 (2.05%)
[java] Mon 12:40:   Secondary FFs:           2081 / 297600 (0.70%)
[java] Mon 12:40: Multipliers (25x18):          0 / 2016   (0.00%)
[java] Mon 12:40:   DSP blocks:                 0 / 2016   (0.00%)
[java] Mon 12:40: Block memory (BRAM18):       49 / 2128   (2.30%)
```

DISCUSSION

Decision trees algorithms like C4.5 can effectively utilize optimization constructs such as streams, offsets and custom number representation to achieve acceleration and electrical power savings. Streams and offsets can be utilized for calculating information entropy by accessing neighbor elements in an array and thus creating pipelines for elements of an array. By using custom number representation which includes switching from floating point representation to the fixed point representation, additional speedup can be achieved. Figure 5 presents resource allocations for different number precisions as well as number representations.

It is shown that the same algorithm takes about five times more resources if it uses double precision floating point numbers compared to the fixed point 16 bit numbers. Algorithms for decision tree construction could determine numbers range before the execution and create custom number representation which will improve the performance of the algorithm.

REVIEW QUESTIONS

This section provides questions for better understanding of the key aspects of the chapter.

1. What are decision trees?
2. What are streams in the dataflow engine?
3. How numbers can be represented in the dataflow engine?

4. How is acceleration achieved by reducing number precision?

REFERENCES

Dai, W., & Ji, W. (2014). A mapreduce implementation of C4. 5 decision tree algorithm. *International Journal of Database Theory and Application*, 49-60.

Hssina, B., Merbouha, A., Ezzikouri, H., & Erritali, M. (2014). A comparative study of decision tree ID3 and C4. 5. *International Journal of Advanced Computer Science and Applications*, 13-19.

Milutinović, V., Salom, J., Trifunović, N., & Giorgi, R. (2015). *Guide to dataflow supercomputing*. Springer. doi:10.1007/978-3-319-16229-4

Pell, O., Mencer, O., Tsoi, K. H., & Luk, W. (2013). Maximum performance computing with dataflow engines. High-performance computing using FPGAs, 747-774.

KEY TERMS AND DEFINITIONS

C4.5: Decision tree algorithm.

Fixed-Point: Number representation frequently used in the dataflow paradigm.

Floating-Point: Number representation frequently used in the controlflow paradigm.

Offset: Dataflow technique for accessing neighbor elements in stream.

Stream: Dataflow technique for moving data between the host machine and the DFE.

Chapter 8
Implementation Details of Rule–Based Algorithms Using Dataflow

ABSTRACT

This chapter presents dataflow paradigm in general and cyclic execution graphs, auto-loop offsets, and counters as key points for acceleration and discusses implementation details of iterative rule based algorithms on the dataflow accelerators. Auto-loop offsets create buffers in cyclic execution graphs for streaming results from previous iteration to the next. Counters control input and outputs of the execution graph based on auto-loop offsets. It is shown how part of an algorithm (iterative steps) can be migrated using advanced optimization constructs.

INTRODUCTION

Rule-based algorithms are used in classification problems and presents an alternative to decision tree algorithms presented in the previous chapter. They belong to supervised machine learning algorithms and are well studied methods for extracting rules from training data. Rules are extracted in form IF-THEN directly from the training data using association rule learning or indirectly from decision trees (Ahmad & Khanum, 2008).

This chapter discusses implementation details of association rule learning for rule based algorithms on the dataflow paradigm. The idea is to utilize

DOI: 10.4018/978-1-7998-8350-0.ch008

Listing 1. Basic components of Apriori algorithm used as rule learning algorithm.

```
Use k-1 itemsets to generate k itemsets
Getting C[k] by joining L[k-1] and L[k-1]
Prune C[k] with subset testing
Generate L[k] by extracting the itemsets in C[k] that satisfy
minSup
```

dataflow accelerators to reduce electrical power consumption which is important in cases where resources are limited. Such an approach could be used in edge devices for classification tasks. Optimization constructs presented in this chapter are considered by evaluating structure of the association rule learning algorithms.

IMPLEMENTATION DETAILS

The main difference between rule based algorithms and decision trees is in representation, where rule based algorithms provide IF THEN statements that are executed sequentially in order provide classification results (Del Jesus, Hoffmann, Navascués, & & Sánchez, 2004). Decision tree algorithms contain vertices with attributes where decisions lead to a particular leaf, which represents an output for a given input. Listing 1 presents a pseudocode for association rule learning algorithm. The presented algorithm is Apriori which performs data pruning by identifying the frequent individual items and extending them to be larger item sets.

Iterative nature of the algorithm enables dataflow accelerators utilization by using concepts of streaming data between iterations and creating cyclic execution graphs. This problem can be considered as an aggregated sum, where input from the previous iteration is necessary in the present one. In general a cycle in the dataflow execution graphs arises from a dependence from one iteration to the next one. Figure 1 illustrates the problem of dependency between iterations where the result of one iteration is input for the next iteration.

One of the problems with cyclic graphs is that it is necessary to create pipeline buffers in order to meet deadlines for the frequency (Ali, Akesson, & Pinho, 2015). In essence, each arithmetic or logic unit in the graph takes a certain amount of time to produce the result. For example, multiplication of two floating point numbers on referent hardware could take n ticks to

Figure 1. An example of a cyclic execution graph where the red pipeline as output of an iteration is used as input for the next iteration.

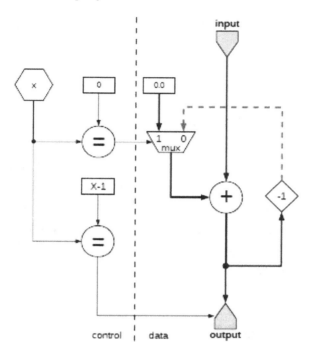

produce the result. Addition of two floating point numbers could take m ticks to produce the result on the same referent hardware, where $m < n$. If those two results present an input for the next unit it is necessary to create buffers on the output pipeline of the additional unit in order to have both results at the same time at the input of the next unit. Without buffers, one result will arrive before another one, and the result of the next unit will be invalid.

In order to meet deadlines in cyclic execution graphs, developers could create buffers for each unit. However, the compiler has a built-in feature called auto-loop offset that automatically detects offsets and creates buffers where necessary in order to achieve the lowest valid offset for the graph. Listing 2 presents method definitions for creating auto-loop offsets.

Association rule learning algorithms like Apriori are iterative algorithms that require results from previous iterations as inputs for the next iteration. In some cases, acceleration of such algorithms could be achieved by modifying input data choreograph. If association rule learning algorithms fully utilize pipelines, it leads to producing results in each iteration. An example of how data choreography can fully utilize pipelines is illustrated in Figure 2.

Listing 2. Method definitions for creating auto-loop offsets in cyclic execution graphs.

```
Stream.OffsetExpr makeOffsetAutoLoop(String name)
Stream.OffsetExpr makeOffsetAutoLoop(String name, int min size,
int max size)
DFEVar Stream.OffsetExpr.getDFEVar(KernelLib design)
```

Figure 2. An illustration of data pipeline utilization and input data choreography.

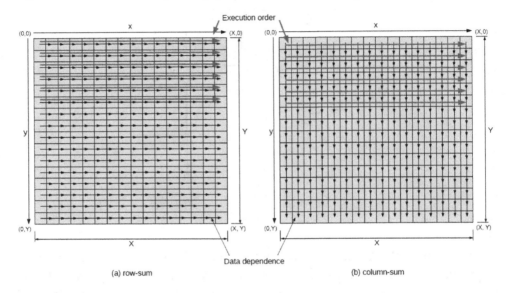

(a) row-sum   (b) column-sum

In the example, the task is to summarize rows of a matrix. If data elements are streamed in a row-wise order where each iteration takes n ticks to produce the result, the accelerator waits for n ticks to retrieve results from the iteration and stream the next element as an input. It means that the pipeline doesn't accept input data for a certain amount of time. However, if data elements are streamed in column-wise order where matrix is splitted to n dimensional matrices, in each tick the execution graph can accept input data. When the first result is computed after n ticks, input data for the next iteration will be a valid element from the matrix (Becker, Mencer, Weston, & Gaydadjiev, 2015) (Kotlar & Milutinovic, 2018). Described example is illustrated in Figure 3, where the pipeline state is presented for several ticks.

Another important optimization construct that can be used in iterative algorithms as Apriori is counters. Counties are used to track executing ticks

Figure 3. An example of a pipeline for the aggregated sum with different states.

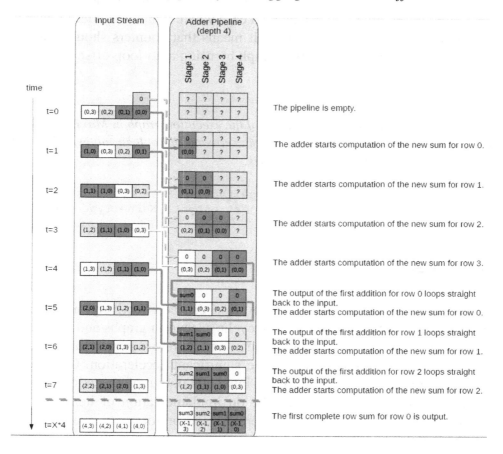

in the accelerator. It is important in boundary cases, where the result from the previous iteration doesn't exist. Listing 3 presents counter methods with advanced options.

Listing 3. Counters in dataflow accelerators with options

```
Count.Params control.count.makeParams(int bit_width)
Counter control.count.makeCounter(Count.Params params)
Options: bit width, initial value, increment, count mode,
maximum value, wrap mode, wrap value, enable
```

Counters are important constructs for controlling input and outputs. In the previous example was discussed a case where a pipeline doesn't accept inputs for a certain period of time. It means that counters should control input and output of the execution graph by using auto-loop offset value, as shown in Listing 4.

Listing 4. Controlled input and outputs of the execution graph in MaxJ. Dataflow inputs and outputs could be controlled using streams of Boolean values, telling the gate to be open or closed during each tick.

```
io. input(String name, KernelType type, DFEVar control)
io.output(String name, KernelObject output, KernelType type,
DFEVar control)
```

DISCUSSION

Iterative rule based algorithms like Apriori can be effectively migrated to the dataflow accelerator by utilizing cyclic execution graphs and auto-loop offsets. Data choreography presents an important role in performance where fully utilized pipelines could achieve significant acceleration. Constructs like counters are used for controlling input and output of execution graphs. Focus of further research should be on implementation of iterative rule based algorithms on dataflow accelerators and performance evaluation in environments where resources are limited.

Presented optimization constructs are important for achieving acceleration for such kind of algorithms. Detailed examples of machine learning algorithms including those mentioned in this chapter are available at the Maxeler Application gallery: https://appgallery.maxeler.com/

REVIEW QUESTIONS

This section provides questions for better understanding of the key aspects of the chapter.

1. What is a rule-based algorithm?
2. What is a cyclic execution graph in the dataflow engine?
3. What is matrix tiling?

4.   How can input data choreography achieve better performance on the dataflow engine?

REFERENCES

Ahmad, R., & Khanum, A. (2008). *Document topic generation in text mining by using cluster analysis with EROCK. International Journal of Computer Science & Security.*

Ali, H. I., Akesson, B., & Pinho, L. M. (2015). Generalized extraction of real-time parameters for homogeneous synchronous dataflow graphs. *2015 23rd Euromicro International Conference on Parallel, Distributed, and Network-Based Processing*, 701-710.

Becker, T., Mencer, O., Weston, S., & Gaydadjiev, G. (2015). Maxeler dataflow in computational finance. In *FPGA Based Accelerators for Financial Applications*. Springer. doi:10.1007/978-3-319-15407-7_11

Del Jesus, M. J., Hoffmann, F., Navascués, L. J., & Sánchez, L. (2004). Induction of fuzzy-rule-based classifiers with evolutionary boosting algorithms. *IEEE Transactions on Fuzzy Systems, 12*(3), 296–308. doi:10.1109/TFUZZ.2004.825972

Kotlar, M., & Milutinovic, V. (2018). Comparing controlflow and dataflow for tensor calculus: speed, power, complexity, and MTBF. In *Conference on High Performance Computing* (pp. 329-346). Springer. 10.1007/978-3-030-02465-9_22

KEY TERMS AND DEFINITIONS

Auto-Loop Offset: Dataflow technique calculating buffers size in cyclic graphs.

Counters: Dataflow technique for counting number of ticks in the graph.

Cyclyc Graph: Execution graph with looping branches.

Hardware Variable: Dataflow variable that existing only during runtime.

Software Variable: Dataflow variable that existing only during compile time, which describes the execution graph.

Chapter 9

Implementation Details of Density–Based Algorithms Using Dataflow

ABSTRACT

This chapter presents dataflow paradigm in general and different memory types and compiler's optimization constructs like tree reduction as key points for acceleration and discusses implementation details of KNN and k-means density based algorithms on the dataflow accelerators. On-chip and on-board memories allow data to be nearby computational units and thus can provide acceleration. Tree reduction enables higher acceleration by reducing resource allocation that could be used for memory management mechanisms. It is shown how part of an algorithm (calculating distances between neighbor elements or to cluster centers) can be migrated using advanced optimization constructs.

INTRODUCTION

Density-based algorithms belong to supervised machine learning algorithms and are often used in classification tasks. This chapter analyzes the k-nearest neighbor (KNN) algorithm as a representative algorithm from a density-based group. It is a simple algorithm that classifies an instance based on neighbor instances (Zhang, Li, Zong, Zhu, & Wang, 2017).

DOI: 10.4018/978-1-7998-8350-0.ch009

The algorithm iterates through dataset instances and labels them based on neighbor labels. Similar algorithm from the same group but used for clustering that belongs to unsupervised machine learning algorithms is k-means where the goal is to create clusters of data (Sinaga & Yang, 2020). Both algorithms utilize distance functions and in each iteration calculate distances to the neighbor elements or data clusters.

IMPLEMENTATION DETAILS

Iterative nature of algorithms and proximity based approach makes accelerator memories a suitable approach for storing neighbor elements or cluster centers. There are two types of memories: fast memory (FMem) placed on-chip and can store small amounts of data but has high bandwidth; and large memory (LMem) placed off-chip and can store large amounts of data in tensor structures but has lower bandwidth compared to FMem (Flynn, et al., 2013). Depending on a number of data instances required for iterations, FMem or LMem can be used. FMem is used for keeping small size data structures which have a high level of reusability. Both memories are placed nearby computation units and because of that, data can be efficiently saved in memory.

Figure 1. Illustration of LMem and FMem in the dataflow accelerator. Both memories have higher bandwidth compared to the host machine memory.

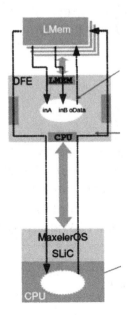

Density based algorithm on the dataflow accelerator can be divided into three phases. Fetch phase reads memory addresses and retrieves results from the memories to the input of the execution graph. Computation phase measures distances between data and retrieved values and provides the result on the output of the execution graph. Load phase sends data to the memories which will be used in the next iteration.

All inputs and outputs to kernel memories are represented as streams. Basic operations include streams of addresses that go in, streams of data that come out. Listing 1 presents basic methods for memory manipulation.

Listing 1. Basics methods for memory manipulation in dataflow accelerator

```
Memory<DFEVar> mem.alloc(DFEType type, int depth)
Memory.write(DFEVar address, DFEVar data, DFEVar enable)
Memory.read(DFEVar address)
```

Before writing or reading memory, it is necessary to allocate it by providing data type and depth of memory. Write operation requires address for writing, value, and control but that indicates whether memory address should be written or not, if data value is ready or not in particular tick. Read operation requires only address to retrieve value. Variables used for navigating through address space must have the same size as memory depth in order to avoid memory violation access (Milutinović, Salom, Trifunović, & Giorgi, 2015).

Special type of memory presents ROM memory that maps address space from the host machine memory to the accelerator's memory. For KNN algorithm it is an important optimization construct where training data could be mapped form the host machine and later used in the accelerator. It also enables context switching without need for hardware reconfiguration which allows frequent updates of training data. Listing 2 presents an interface for ROM memory mapped from the host machine.

Listing 2. ROM memory interface in the dataflow accelerator

```
Memory<DFEVar> mappedRom = mem.alloc(dfeFloat(8,24), dataSize);
mappedRom.mapToCPU("mappedRom")
```

Dataflow memories as optimization constructs could allocate a significant amount of resources on the chip and have some constraints. For example, if one writes to a memory address in a kernel tick, he can not call read with the same address in the same tick. Attempting to do so will return undefined data. As an optimization, it is possible to create a single memory port which both reads and writes in the same tick (Trifunovic, Milutinovic, Salom, & Kos, 2015), as shown in Listing 3.

Listing 3. Single memory port for both reads and writes in the same tick

```
DFEVar Memory.port(DFEVar address, DFEVar data in, DFEVar
enable, RamWriteMode portMode)
```

Another optimization construct that could be utilized for calculating distances between neighbor elements or cluster centers is called tree reduction. Distance functions are implemented in an execution graph as a set of arithmetic units inter-connected. Compiler automatically detects unoptimized sub-graphs and performs tree reduction methods, as shown in Figure 2.

Figure 2. Tree reduction example that is performed by dataflow compiler. On the left side is an unoptimized graph. On the right side is an optimized graph that produces the same result as the left one.

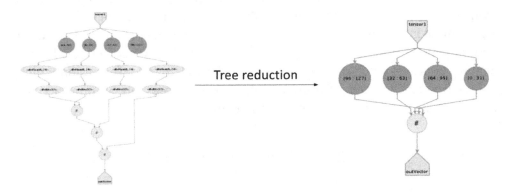

DISCUSSION

Density based algorithms like KNN and k-means are simple algorithms that are used for clustering and classification and can be effectively implemented on the dataflow accelerators using optimization constructs like on-chip and on-board memories for states between iterations. Additionally, resource allocation can be reduced by performing tree reduction optimizations by the compiler. This can result in allocating memory space for neighbor elements and optimizing the algorithm by keeping data nearby computational units.

Presented optimization constructs are important for achieving acceleration for such kind of algorithms. Detailed examples of machine learning algorithms including those mentioned in this chapter are available at the Maxeler Application gallery: https://appgallery.maxeler.com/

REVIEW QUESTIONS

This section provides questions for better understanding of the key aspects of the chapter.

1. What is a density-based algorithm?
2. What kind of memories exist in the accelerator?
3. What is a three reduction in the execution graphs?
4. What is the difference between on-chip and on-board memories?

REFERENCES

Flynn, M. J., Mencer, O., Milutinovic, V., Rakocevic, G., Stenstrom, P., Trobec, R., & Valero, M. (2013). Moving from petaflops to petadata. *Communications of the ACM*.

Milutinović, V., Salom, J., Trifunović, N., & Giorgi, R. (2015). *Guide to dataflow supercomputing*. Springer.

Sinaga, K. P., & Yang, M. S. (2020). Unsupervised K-means clustering algorithm. *IEEE Access : Practical Innovations, Open Solutions*.

Trifunovic, N., Milutinovic, V., Salom, J., & Kos, A. (2015). Paradigm shift in big data supercomputing: Dataflow vs. controlflow. Journal of Big Data.

Zhang, S., Li, X., Zong, M., Zhu, X., & Wang, R. (2017). Efficient kNN classification with different numbers of nearest neighbors. *IEEE Transactions on Neural Networks and Learning Systems*, 1774–1785.

KEY TERMS AND DEFINITIONS

FMEM: Dataflow fast memory with high bandwidth.

LMEM: Dataflow large memory with multidimensional addressing space.

On-Board Memory: Referred as LMEM with multidimensional addressing space.

On-Chip Memory: Referred as FMEM with high bandwidth.

Tree Reduction: Dataflow optimization technique provided by compiler to compress the execution graph.

Chapter 10
Issues Related to Acceleration of Algorithms

ABSTRACT

This chapter provides examples on acceleration of various algorithms using the dataflow paradigm. Implementation of algorithms demands input data changes, operation substitutions, and data tilling to achieve significant performance. The implementation becomes even more challenging if data are coming via a serial stream. This chapter presents acceleration mechanisms on three different use cases related to presented algorithms. This chapter consists of three parts: Acceleration of Algorithms Using Innovations in Suboptimal Calculus and Approximate Computing, Acceleration of Algorithms Using Innovations in Computer Architecture and Implementational Technologies, and Speeding up the Execution of Data Mining Algorithms.

ACCELERATION OF ALGORITHMS USING INNOVATIONS IN SUBOPTIMAL CALCULUS AND APPROXIMATE COMPUTING

In some cases, especially in Big Data applications and with complex datamining algorithms, demanding operations like multiplication could be substituted by less demanding operations like shift-and-add, or even increment/decrement. The implementation becomes even more challenging if data are coming via a serial stream.

DOI: 10.4018/978-1-7998-8350-0.ch010

If the computational complexity is somehow drastically reduced, so does not only the problem become treatable in real-time, but also the transistor count for the VLSI implementations gets reduced and the implementation is less complex. This also means that more data streams could be processed in parallel, for the same VLSI complexity. Also, in some cases, one could achieve robustness in noisy environments.

Here, one approach of this type (suboptimal) is described for the case of data signal detection. Data signals have to be properly received before they could be further processed by the chosen Data Mining algorithm. Or the selected Data Mining algorithm could be applied at the same time when the data detection is done.

In some other cases, however, simplifications are, in general case, multi-dimensional, and could be applied both in the space domain and in the time domain, or in any other logical domain. In this context, if some kind of multi-dimensionality is involved, we are talking about approximate computing.

One specific example of approximate computing is presented here. It includes some level of quantization noise in the space domain (amplitudes) and some level of processing delay in the time domain (latency from input till output). The presented example covers the transversal filter equalization, which is an essential element of data purification processes, prior to data acquisition by further processing stages, or concurrently with further processing stages (datamining).

Both suboptimal and approximate computing examples presented here are based on previous research of the author (Milutinovic, 1980). Notions from (McDonough & Magar, 1982) are utilized, too. The method of this presentation is based on (Milutinovic, A good method for presentation of research results, 1996) and (Milutinovic, The best method for presentation of research results, 1996).

AN EXAMPLE OD SUBOPTIMAL COMPUTING

The suboptimum detection procedure based on the weighting of partial decisions (WPD) was first introduced in ELECTRONICS LETTERS, 14th August 1980, Vol. 16 No. 17, p.681-2.

It was derived on the basis of two other suboptimum procedures formerly treated in the open literature, i.e. d.m.f. (digital matched filtering) and b.m.f. (binary matched filtering). Both are based on a finite number of received signal samples. In this chapter, the dependence of the error probability on the signal/noise power ratio is being analyzed for all three procedures. The process v(t) at the input of the detector is assumed to be band-limited and represents the sum of the binary communication signal and the additive Gaussian noise with zero mean. The set of samples upon which the detection is based (N) is assumed to be equal for all three procedures discussed here.

Certain conclusions could be derived on the basis of experimental results, which, naturally, are valid only for the values of N and SNR (Signal-to-Noise Ratio) lying in the range of the analysis. Basic conclusions could be derived through mathematical analysis alone. Both approaches have been applied in the cited references.

A hardware multiplier must be used in the case od d.m.f. With WPD and b.m.f. this is not the case. There is no essential difference in the implementation of WPD and b.m.f., as far as the hardware requirements. Ion the side of software, the differences in program duration could be neglected, if any. The only essential difference is that WPD needs a d/a convertor, while the b.m.f. needs a hard-limiter. This is because the d/a convertor generates quantized samples of the incoming analog signal, while the hard limiter generates only the sign of the sample.

The analysis has shown that WPD is not much worse than w.d.f. but is considerably easier to implement.

Formerly, the WPD was analysed only for binary transmission with an antipodal set of signalling waveforms. In this chapter, the concept of the WPD is generalized and analysed theoretically for M-ary transmission with an arbitrary set of equal-energy signaling waveforms. Here, WPD is treated as the generalized procedure with BMF as its special case.

The detection is assumed to be performed on the basis of a previously established correspondence between all possible sign patterns and all possible signaling symbols. Sensitivity to the phase distortions in the communications channel is minimized (and tolerable for the wide range of conditions met in the real environment), if the sampling is tightly coupled to the fluctuating boundaries of signaling elements.

The main advantage of this procedure is time-efficient and cost-effective implementation. The procedure is suitable for implementation on the simplest microprocessors found in space vehicles collecting remote signals (e.g., Intel 8085), or on extremely small VLSI cells that could be multiplied a huge amount of times, for inclusion into some complex VLSI chip.

The implementation involves no analogue-to-digital conversion (a/d), no multiplication, and no time-consuming processing. In addition, initial synchronization and continuous maintenance of synchronization could be realized simultaneously with detection.

The less processing power needed for demodulation and detection, the easier it will be to incorporate other relevant functions (e.g., equalization, scrambling, etc.) on the same microprocessor system or VLSI chip.

However, it has been noticed that the performance of this procedure could be improved, without any negative implications on the simplicity of practical implementation, if certain a priori knowledge of the signaling technique and noise is incorporated.

First, in data modem design, after the signaling technique has been specified, all possible signaling waveforms at the output of the transmitter could be made known to the receiver. The number of these waveforms could be made low if certain easy-to-establish conditions are met.

So, for example, in voice-band data modems with time-varying signaling waveforms, signs in the sign pattern (derived by the receiver) belong to signal samples of different amplitudes and, consequently, of different immunity to additive noise and phase distortions. This means that the additive noise can be suppressed more efficiently if, instead of only 'hard' knowledge of the sign pattern, 'soft' knowledge of the sign pattern is involved in the detection, too.

By 'soft' knowledge we mean the knowledge of both the elements of the sign pattern and the nominal values of samples corresponding to the sampling instants from which the elements of the sign pattern were derived. Hence, if a set of correctly chosen weighting coefficients is introduced for the weighting of sign information, a better performance could be expected.

Second, a priori knowledge of the characteristics of all possible signaling waveforms and noise could be used to establish a set of statistically independent sampling instants for the detection of a band-limited mixture of signal and noise, which minimizes the detection error probability.

Third, a priori knowledge of the characteristics of all possible signaling waveforms and noise could be used to establish a set of optimal detection thresholds that minimize the detection error probability. The incorporation of these three types of detection parameters into BMF, together with the introduction of multilevel transmission, leads to the generalized WPD, which is the subject of this chapter.

Performance comparison of BMF, WPD and DMF (optimum digital matched filtering) for binary transmission with an antipodal set of signaling waveforms and additive zero mean Gaussian noise was given in former studies.

As regards the signaling waveforms, only relatively mild constraints are assumed, which tells in favor of a relatively wide application field of the detection procedure treated here.

Bayesian analysis is applied independently to all statistically independent samples of the receiving signals. Weighting factors based on statistical distances could be used to combine the results corresponding to different samples.

The determination of the appropriate region R corresponding to the new incoming sample is called a partial decision. After each partial decision, the statistical distance for all M signaling waveforms from the region R is computed.

After each partial decision, the WPD detector (processor) waits for the next sampling instant and the whole process is repeated. After the last partial decision and the last updating of counters, final detection is done by comparison of contents in all counters.

The final detection is performed by the following two basic operations:

1. Search for the boundaries of the symbol Sd
2. Association of the bit sequence Ak; k = 0, 1, 2, ..., with the symbol Sd transmitted during the signaling interval k; k = 0, 1, 2, ...

It is evident from what has been exposed that the WPD is computationally relatively simple. As indicated before, neither multiplication nor analogue-to-digital conversion is involved.

The question arising now is: What are the optimum values of algorithmic parameters that ensure the best possible performance of the WPD. Another question is whether the WPD is the best possible procedure without multiplication and analogue-to-digital conversion?

The basic criterion for the optimization of sampling vector elements should be the minimization of detection error probability.

In the case of a signal corrupted by linear distortions and additive noise, the less the signal at the input of the detector differs from an ideal signal, the lower the detection error probability. In fact, what is important is that this difference be minimum just in sampling instants.

The mean quadratic error has been chosen since, under the conditions assumed in our analysis, signal power is the main factor in the suppression of noise.

The basic criterion for the optimization of threshold matrix elements is also the minimization of detection error probability. In order to minimize the overall error probability, it is necessary to minimize the error probability for each one of N partial decisions, separately. So every partial decision is to be optimum in the Bayes sense. If the influence of only the two nearest signaling waveforms corresponding to a given sampling instant is considered, the optimum value of each one of $N * (M - 1)$ possible thresholds is determined from a Bayes-type equation applied to each partial decision.

The optimization of thresholds is performed only after the optimization of sampling instants. A point to be stressed here is that the thresholds differ in significance, namely in their order e; $e = 0, 1, ..., (\log 2 M) - 1$.

Zero-order threshold ($e = 0$) serves for the elimination of $M/2$ signaling symbols. There is only one zero-order threshold. The thresholds of the e-th order serve for the elimination of additional $M/2e + 1$ signalling symbols. There are 2e such thresholds.

This point is stressed because it is possible to eliminate lower order thresholds, in order to simplify the implementation of the WPD detection procedure. Of course, this can be done only at a cost of some performance deterioration.

The basic criterion for the optimization of the weighting matrix elements is to enable the performance of the WPD (given processing resources available in the WPD algorithm) to have the lowest possible degradation in comparison with the performance of DMF, which is, theoretically, the best detection procedure when N is a finite number. With that purpose in mind, we start from the definition of DMF and we transform it into the equivalent form in which we have multiplicatively separated the term with a priori known signal parameters from the term with parameters to be measured by the processing resources not available in the WPD algorithm.

By discarding the second term, we discard the need for analogue-to-digital conversion and multiplication; however, without any loss of information, the processing of which can be completely realized by resources available in the WPD algorithm. In this way, we pass to a suboptimum realization of DMF, which we refer to as WPD.

Both DMF and BMF are convergent procedures (i.e., error probability PE decreases when SNR increases). So, it follows that WPD is also a convergent procedure. However, this convergence applies only to the case when the elements of t, p and W are chosen so as to be optimum for a given signaling structure.

However, WPD can easily be rearranged into $M/2$ additions after each partial decision. This can be accomplished by pre-calculating the weighting factors corresponding to the relative detection counters (one counter per pair of signaling elements) into the weighting factors corresponding to the absolute detection counters (one counter per signaling element).

In the case of off-the-shelf microprocessors, both incrementing and addition are the built-in functions and have about the same execution time.

In the case of the standard cell VLSI design, for both procedures only a few types of very simple cells have to be used. The WPD will require an adder which will not be the case with the BMF; however, this difference is of minor importance. Also, note that M^n various implementation techniques (e.g., look-up tables, etc.) could be efficiently used, in order to further simplify the implementation.

Suboptimal detection procedures are also of interest for technologies which are characterized with a low on-chip transistor count, such as GaAs. The highest reliable GaAs chip density for fabrications till the end of this decade is relatively low.

However, GaAs chips are characterized with a relatively high speed. For the same power consumption, GaAs technology is up to about half order of magnitude faster than silicon technology. Also, it is several orders of magnitude more radiation-hard, Because of these characteristics, signal detection is seen as one of the promising application areas for GaAs.

In the cases when only the Gaussian noise is present, or Gaussian noise is combined with amplitude deviations, WPD is shown to be typically better than SAS (Sample-and-Sum) or BMF. However, in the case of the relatively high-phase and/or frequency deviations, WPD is shown to be more sensitive than the other two suboptimal procedures.

The most important value of this study is that it provides numerical basis for comparison of selected suboptimal procedures, in conditions typical of real communications channels (noise, amplitude distortions, frequency distortions, etc.).

AN EXAMPLE OF APROXIMATE COMPUTING

The example to follow includes approximate computing in both special (amplitude) and time (latency) domains.

Adaptive equalization based on a transversal filter is extremely important for error free transmission and effective data mining of Big Data over communication channels of any type. Unfortunately, implementation of rapidly converging and small residual distortion algorithms on the standard microprocessors or standard-cell VLSI chips is difficult because of their mathematical complexity. In this chapter, an adaptive equalization algorithm is proposed which is suitable for cost-effective implementation on microprocessors and standard-cell VLSI chips. It is based on the same principle of delayed decision that was used successfully in delta modulation. It involves neither multiplication nor analog-to-digital conversion, but is relatively fast and provides a relatively low residual distortion. The proposed algorithm has been simulated in both noise-free and noisy environments and has been compared to two well-known classical algorithms.

Essential issues in adaptive equalization with transversal filters are fast tap gain setting and small residual distortion. Two basic types of algorithms for tap gain setting are mean-square (MS) and zero-forcing (ZF).

The mean-square algorithms are used for higher-speed data transmission. They are faster and are convergent even if the initial "eye" is closed. Unfortunately, they are computationally complex and consequently very difficult to implement.

The zero-forcing algorithms are slower and convergent only if the initial oscilloscope "eye" is open. However, they are less complex and easier to implement. Fortunately, they are quite satisfactory for medium-speed data transmission, which covers a high percentage of today's commercial requirements.

Recent advances in VLSI technology are now enabling the implementation of a medium-speed data modem on a single many-core microprocessor or on a single standard-cell VLSI chip. The processing power of a many-core microprocessor is limited, as well as the area of a small VLSI cell. So, after the implementation of other necessary functions is accomplished, only a limited amount of resources is still available for implementation of a transversal filter and the corresponding algorithm for tap gain setting. Consequently, finding simpler, but sufficiently powerful tap gain setting algorithms, has become an important research issue.

The problem is especially critical because of the fact, that the tap gain algorithm has to be repeated for each tap, and the number of taps needed for the medium-speed data transmission could be extremely high.

With all this in mind, an algorithm has been proposed which is based on the principle of delayed decision and will be referred to as the delayed decision algorithm (DD).

The implementation of the proposed algorithm is almost as simple as the implementation of the classical fixed-step algorithm by Lucky. Yet, it is almost as fast as the well-known amplitude-dependent algorithm by Gersho.

Both desirable features are achieved by simply postponing the decision about the tap-gain adjustment step, and not by increasing the computational complexity.

The proposed algorithm is also free of multiplication and of analog-to-digital conversion. Consequently, it is very suitable for implementation on many-core microprocessors and/or standard-cell VLSI structures.

In the rest of the chapter, the delayed decision algorithm will be discussed and compared to the fixed-step algorithm of Lucky and the amplitude-dependent algorithm of Gersho, respectively.

These two algorithms have been denoted as L and, G in the text to follow. The comparisons have been provided for both noise-free (interference only) and noisy (noise and interference) environments.

Next, we define the delayed-decision (DD) algorithm.

Research experience has shown that a problem in one field may often be solved successfully by employing methods from other fields. The principle of delayed decision (DD) was used successfully in adaptive delta modulation. Here, it has been employed to shorten the time for setting the adaptive transversal filter tap gain without increasing the computational complexity of the algorithm. The proposed algorithm has been introduced together with Lucky's and Gersho's algorithms, as already indicated.

The control function for all three algorithms treated in this chapter has been defined on the basis of the condition that tap interaction could be neglected.

The total number of transversal filter taps is equal to 2N + 1. This condition assumes a small initial distortion, which is true in medium-speed data transmission. Vector E of dimension 2N + 1 refers to the transversal filter output error given by $Z=x'-J$, where x' is a matrix with signal elements $\{x_i\}$; t is a vector of tap gains $\{t_i\}$; $i = -N, ..., +N$; $j = -N, ..., +N$.

The form of the above defined control function indicates that the new value of the adjustment step will not be assumed until after the effect of the existing adjustment step on the output error in the next iteration becomes evident. So, the control function reflects directly the principle of delayed decision.

In the case of Gersho's amplitude-dependent algorithm, the control function is defined by appropriate variable slope. Variable slope helps to achieve fast convergence in the low noise cases and small residual distortion in the high noise cases.

Both Lucky's and Gersho's algorithms satisfy the conditions of convergence for a tap gain setting algorithm. That condition requires that control function $g(e_i(k))$; $i = -N, .-, +N$, $k = 1, 2, ...,$ is monotonic non-decreasing and an odd-function bounded.

The DD algorithm is heuristic in nature and the above condition cannot be applied to it. However, as already said, empirical results have shown that DD is convergent for all "open eye" channels used in simulation, and for a wide range of values of the coefficient R.

Simulation results have also shown that, depending on the channel characteristics, the fastest convergence is ensured for R in the range of Rmax. Having in mind that $R = 2$ is within that range, and that it also ensures a relatively simple implementation, only the value $R = 2$ will be considered in the rest of the text.

Also, note that it may be more efficient if the minimal step value of the DD algorithm is position-dependent, i.e., of different value for different taps. However, this case was not considered as a part of this work.

The setting time is a basic performance parameter of each transversal filter. For the preset equalization, it is defined as the time interval from the beginning of equalization until the moment when all of the tap gains take their optimal value.

These bounds of optimal values are absolutely tight, i.e., the best case setting time is equal to the lower bound and the worst case setting time to the upper bound, for any numerical form of the vector E.

Both bounds were obtained by examining the time needed to arrive at the optimal setting of the value. Analysis has shown that the average value of Ts is very close to the arithmetic average of two bounds. For the same conditions, the setting time of Gersho's algorithm is upper bounded.

These theoretical values for the setting time have been later used to check the correctness of the setting time values obtained by simulation of three algorithms in the low-noise and noise-free cases.

Residual distorsion is an important issue for approximate algorithms. Residual distortion is defined by $DR = Dmin + Ds$.

The Dmin is distortion corresponding to the optimal setting of the transversal filter, and could be neglected if N is large enough.

The Ds component is due to noise and quantized tap gains, and is obtained from the difference equation that describes the action of noise. For the Lucky' algorithm, this difference equation reads:

$$U(m) = \text{Prob} (i- < 01) ; i = -N, ---, +N$$

Symbol U refers to the sample of the zero-mean Gaussian noise with variance sigma^2, which is existing at the tap "i" during the iteration step "k". This difference equation defines a probability distribution p(k)(m) and the final system distortion per tap for the Lucky's algorithm.

For the DD algorithm, the difference equation, pg, that describes the action of an error component reads as follows:

pg = p(k-l)(m - 1) * p(k)(m + I) * [I - u(m + I)] + p(k-l)(m - 2) * p(k)(m + 2) * [I - u(m + 2)]

A computer simulation has been conducted for noise-free and noisy environments. In both cases, the channel was assumed to be equal to an attenuated transversal function, as in the original research by Lucky and Gersho.

The effect of noise is included in the simulation by adding independent, normally distributed numbers with a prescribed variance to the sample values of the output pulse. The initial signal-to-noise ratio ISNR was chosen to be 10 and 30 dB.

The DD had been shown to be always much faster than the Lucky's algorithm. For all values of ISNR used here, it was 2-4 times faster. On the other side, from the implementation point of view, the only essential difference between the DD algorithm and the Lucky's algorithm is in the existence of a shifter. In the case of the standard-cell VLSI design, the shifter is almost trivial to implement. In the case of the many-core microprocessor-based design, shifting is a built-in function.

The proposed delay decision algorithm has been compared to the Lucky's classical fixed-step algorithm and the Gersho's amplitude-dependent algorithm. Comparison has been done for inter-symbol interference in the noiseless and the Gaussian noise cases. It has been shown that the delayed decision algorithm is considerably faster than the fixed-step algorithm and almost as fast as the amplitude-dependent algorithm. The delayed decision algorithm is free of multiplication and analog-to-digital conversion and is very suitable for implementation on standard microprocessors and/or standard-cell VLSI chips. Figure 1 describes the structure of a data signal detector and Figure 1 describes the structure of a transversal filter for data communications.

Figure 1.

1. AD = analog to data convertor 2. NE = noise elimination 3. IE = interference elimination 4. FE = fading elimination 5. DM = data multiplexer

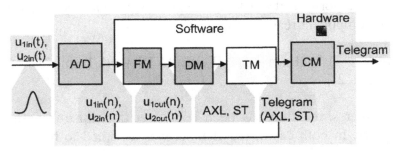

Figure 2.

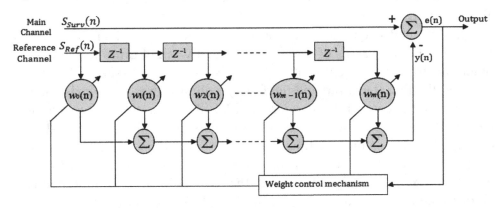

ACCELERATION OF ALGORITHMS USING INNOVATIONS IN COMPUTER ARCHITECTURE AND IMPLEMENTATIONAL TECHNOLOGIES

This chapter evaluates two different computing architectures: Pipelined MISD and Systolic SIMD. The first one is suitable for data coming like a serial stream, and the second one for parallel input data. Both approaches could be used for any type of algorithms found in on-line datamining. In the examples given here, the first one is better used for Fourier Calculus, while the second one is better used for Matrix Calculus. The first one, in our research, is meant for implementation in the GaAs technology, while the second one is meant for implementation in the Silicon technology. Therefore, the approach of this chapter leaves space for comparison of the two technologies: Silicon and GaAs. The presented approaches are based on earlier research of the author (Flynn, 1972). General reference used in this chapter is (Gajski & Abraham, 1984). The presentation is based on (Milutinovic, A good method for presentation of research results, 1996).

As already indicated, we first present here a multi-microprocessor system meant for a class of real-time processing applications in on-line datamining. The applications considered require the computation of a subset of an N-input Fourier Transform under the assumption of a serial data input. The two different algorithms and the corresponding parallel architecture are analyzed and compared.

More specifically, in our research we compared the computation of the FFT algorithms on an SIMD (single instruction multiple data) machine and the implementation of the DFT algorithm on an MISD (multiple instruction single data) machine. Our results indicate that the latter is better suited for a large plethora of applications. An actual operational MISD computer, implemented with off-the-shelf microprocessors intended for one of the targeted applications, is also described here.

The efficiency of any problem solving with parallel computers is determined by numerous factors: 1) the problem nature, 2) the algorithm used, 3) the computer architecture, and 4) the efficiency measure.

This chapter discusses a computer problem solving approach in which a careful study of the above factors results in a somewhat unconventional choice of the computer architectures. More specifically, it is shown that the MISD architecture is well suited for the computation of the discrete Fourier Transform (DFT), as required by a class of problems in signal, image, and speech processing.

According to the classification of Professor Michael J. Flynn of Stanford University, possible types of computers are denoted as: SISD (single instruction single data), SIMD (single instruction multiple data), MIMD (multiple instruction multiple data), and MISD (multiple instruction single data).

With the exception of MISD computers, extensive research and literature has been dedicated to the design, implementation, and use of these types of machines. Using multiplicity of streams as the basic identifier and without going into explanatory details, we consider dataflow and pipelined computers as special cases of MIMD computers.

Figure 3.

$$s(t) = \sum_{j=1}^{L=16} \sin [s\pi f_j(t - kT) + \phi_{j,k}];$$

$$kT \le t \le (k + 1)T$$

$$k = 0, 1, 2, \cdots$$

where

$$f_j = 55 * (15 + 2j) \text{ Hz}; \qquad j = 1, \cdots, 16,$$

$$\phi_{j,k} = \frac{a\pi}{4}; \qquad a = 0, \cdots, 7,$$

$$T = (1/75) \text{ Hz} \simeq 13,33 \text{ ms}.$$

A CLASS OF PROBLEMS REQUIRING FOURIER TRANSFORM

In this section, problems that may require the computation of a Fourier transform are described. All of them share some characteristics that make them well suited for the implementation using a computer architecture of the MISD type.

Data Transmission Over HF Radio Channels

The first algorithm is used in data transmission over HF radio channels. These channels are characterized by both the time-selective and the frequency-selective fading. One possible approach to data transmission in this environment is parallel transmission over the narrow-band sub-channels. If the frequency band of each sub-channel (Af) is narrow enough (e.g., Af < 200 Hz), then the effects of frequency-selective fading within a single sub-channel could be neglected. In these systems, typically the spectra of signals in neighboring channels overlap, in order to minimize the overall bandwidth. To enable the signal decomposition and detection in the receiver (which cannot be done by filtering in the frequency domain), the signals in sub-channels were chosen to be mutually orthogonal. In the transmitter, the signal is formed as:

On the receiving side, the signal is sampled with T = (1/7040) Hz = 142ps and the processing of the new sample is done before the next one becomes

Figure 4.

$$\Phi_{j,k} = \sum_{n=1}^{N=64} S(t_n) \cos (2\pi f_j t_n + \phi_{j,k-1})$$

$$j = 1, \cdots, 16 \qquad k = 0, 1, 2, \cdots$$

$$Q_{j,k} = \sum_{n=1}^{N=64} S(t_n) \sin (2\pi f_j t_n + \phi_{j,k-1})$$

$$j = 1, \cdots, 16 \qquad k = 0, 1, 2, \cdots .$$

Figure 5.

$$\hat{\phi}_{j,k} = \phi_{j,k-1} + \arctan (Q_{j,k}/\Phi_{j,k})$$

$$j = 1, \cdots, 16 \qquad k = 0, 1, 2 \cdots .$$

available. The in-phase (+) and quadrature (Q) component are computed in each sub-channel using the formula for orthogonal decomposition:

Note that this processing is done only during the middle portion To = 64T = (1 / 110) Hz. This is 9.09ms of the signaling interval T. The signal phase in each sub-channel is estimated by:

In some applications (diversity in the frequency domain), it can be helpful for channels to exchange the information on phase deviation. This information is given by:

Actually, values of D are the only data to be exchanged, and this exchange is done during the idle guard interval (TG) of duration Tx = T - To = 4.04 ms. Typically, only the four processors, corresponding to the same sub-channel

Figure 6.

$$D = \min_{j} [\arctan (Q_{j,k}/\Phi_{j,k}) - b\pi/4]$$

$$b = 0, \cdots, 7 \qquad k = 0, 1, 2, \cdots ,$$

$$j = 1, \cdots, 16.$$

Figure 7. The MISD architecture for DFT

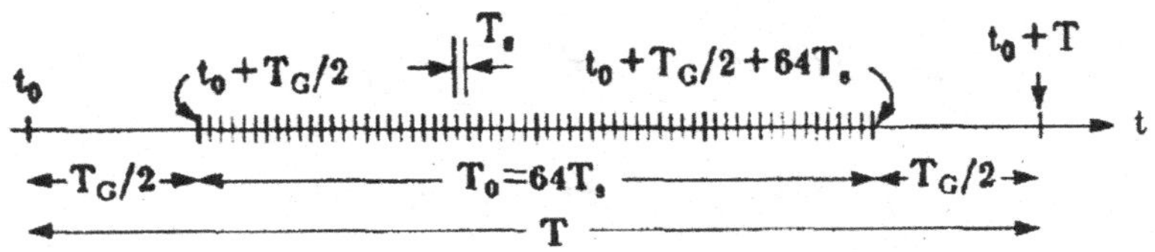

group, exchange data. This group of four processors will be referred to as the "sub-vector." The detection process described here is basically a DFT with N = 64 real inputs used to compute only a subset of L = 16 complex outputs.

Consequently, the DFT implementation requires only s = L/log N = 2.67 times more processing power than the straightforward FFT implementation. Figure 1 shows the architecture utilized, while Figure 2 shows the time organization of all the related computational activities.

```
BIG DATA INPUT -> 16 PARALLEL CHANNELS -> ARCUS.TANGENS
CALCULATOR -> OUTPUT
```

The number of re-sampled data points is typically N = 256 to N = 2098. The next step is the application of the Fourier Transform to the re-sampled image, in order to produce the Fourier descriptor (Figure 8), where R'(n) corresponds to the resampled image. After this, the normalization is done, which is based only on the L most significant complex coefficients in the Fourier descriptor. In other words, N - L complex coefficients are discarded and only L of them are used for further processing. Typically, in most applications, L = 32, which proves to be enough for frequency representation of the contour. Details of the normalization are not important in this context except that the same factor is used for all coefficients. Finally, a comparison to library representations is done and a decision on the type of the flying object is made.

The basic functions of the postprocessor are: 1) collecting the final results of processing in the processing array, 2) data post-processing of the SISD type, e.g., code conversion, logarithmic expansion, etc., 3) data output to the external environment, and 4) control functions dedicated to fault tolerance. Note that the preprocessor and post-processor could be integrated into the same unit, but it would reduce the uniformity of the VLSI layout.

The basic function of the broadcast sub-network is distribution of input data to all processors in the array. The serial broadcast bus is an appropriate

Figure 8.

$$A(j) = \sum_{n=0}^{N-1} R'(n) \cdot e^{-j(2\pi/N)nj}; \qquad j = 0, 1, \cdots, N - 1$$

solution due to the relatively low frequency of data transfer (e.g., in the case of the telephone quality voice-band signal processing, data transfer frequency is only about 8 kHz). Note that the analogous sub-network in the SIMD approach is used for transfer of instructions and typically is implemented as a parallel broadcast bus, due to higher frequency of instruction transfer.

The basic function of the interconnection sub-network is exchange of intermediate results. In principle, any of the interconnection sub-networks used in the SIMD approach could be used here as well. The choice depends on the application and structure of intermediate data transfers.

In the case of the SIMD approach, the interconnection sub-network can be one of the most complex system elements. Although in principle this may also be the case for an MISD approach, for the MISD architecture, it is one of the simplest system elements. Actually, it is not needed at all in the case of the straightforward implementation of the algorithms described.

Note that we are concerned here with the dedicated real-time processing for on-line datamining, and not with the general-purpose processing. We therefore assume that only one program is being run through the whole lifetime of the system. It will be shown later that the MISD architecture proposed here could be used efficiently for implementation of the Fourier Transform-based algorithms discussed and for many more algorithms.

In this chapter, we also underline that in some applications requiring the computation of a particular case of the Fourier Transform, it is more efficient to use an MISD architecture and a straightforward implementation of the DFT algorithm than the generally accepted SIMD computer for FFT computation.

These algorithms require only a subset of size $L = ZN$ of the DFT outputs. Very often it is cited that the DFT is better suited than the FFT only if the number of outputs L is less than log N, i.e., if the speedup ratio s = LN/log N = L/log N is less than one. This is true for SISD implementations, but not for multiprocessor implementations, where the cost of added processors and the related interconnection network may have a considerable influence on the overall implementation cost. For a multiprocessor architecture, it may also be necessary to take the time for the serial arrival of the input data into account. Consequently, the DFT may be better suited even for values of L higher than log N. The cutoff point is dependent on the problem, architecture, and technology under consideration.

In this chapter, it has been shown that the MISD architecture, in the case of a chosen microprocessor technology, offers a relatively high cut-off value. As an example, this chapter describes a microprocessor-based implementation in which DFT-on-MISD is better suited than the FFT-on-SIMD, although the value of $s = L/\log N$ is higher than one, and is equal to 2.67 - the cost of processors and the interconnection network, in the case of the SIMD implementation with a perfect shuffle-like interconnection network, is higher compared to the MISD implementation without interconnection network.

Analysis of Time-Varying Images

The second algorithm mentioned here is used for shape analysis in time-varying images. It is the algorithm for the Fourier descriptor based detection, recognition, identification, and tracking of objects. It has been proven to be well suited to identification and tracking of flying objects.

If the contour of an image is given in the form of a chain code, the number of chain code inputs is typically in the range of a few hundred to a few thousand, depending on the size and form of the object contour. The first step in the processing is the re-sampling of the image at equally spaced intervals. Systolic architectures could be well suited for such applications. The interconnection network could be of one of the 17 types elaborated in the classical taxonomy by Professor H. J. Siegel at Purdue University.

A CLASS OF PROBLEMS THAT REQUIRE THE UTILIZATION OF THE GALIUM-ARSENIDE TECHNOLOGY

This technology is needed in two cases: When a higher speedup is required and/ or when the equipment produced has to be radiation-hard. The first requirement is needed if big-data are to be processed with a limited computing power, while the second requirement is needed for space and defense applications.

A subset of the authors of this book were involved in two GaAs design projects – one related to the implementation of a DARPA microprocessor and the other one related to the implementation of a DARPA systolic array for Gram-Schmidt orthogonalization. Both efforts were described extensively in the cited open literature, to which the interested reader is referred to.

The bottom line of the first project is that the entire CPU design had to be re-considered. Solutions that worked for decades in Silicon technology were not applicable to GaAs technology. This was due to the fact that gate delays depend on their fan-out and the wire delays are not negligible any more. Consequently, the carry-look-ahead adder had to be substituted with the ripple-carry adder, etc…

The bottom line of the second project mentioned here was to create a systolic architecture that needs wiring of the minimal overall length. Consequently, a reduced hardware structure with minimal wiring lengths was used for data waves going into two opposing directions. An most effective implementation is best based on a systolic array.

SPEEDING UP THE EXECUTION OF DATA MINING ALGORITHMS

The speedup required by more demanding applications could be obtained via innovations in either computer architecture or implementation innovations, and best by combining these two options. Of course, there is a also the fourth possibility, which is to simplify the algorithm, using methods that will not degrade the performance in visible ways.

This is why this chapter includes four parts: One about the Systolic Array architectures, one about computing based on the GaAs technology, one about Systolic Array processing using GaAs technology, and one about Approximate Computing and for data processing in noisy environments with numerous other degradations of the medium that passes data from point A to point B.

The four parts are based on our former publications and summarize the essence of the four approaches. For details, the interested reader is referred to original texts. The major references of this chapter are (Milutinovic, Computer Architecture: Concepts and Systems, 1988) about Systolic Arrays, (Milutinovic, Surviving the Design of a 200 MHz RISC Microprocessor: Lessons Learned, 1997) about GaAs computing, (Fortes & Milutinovic, 1986) about Systolic Arrays for GaAs, and (Milutinovic, A Microprocessor-Oriented Algorithm for Adaptive Equalization, 1985) about Approximate Computing of data signals.

The viewpoint of this chapter is based on: Speed, Power, Size, and Precision. The goal is to shed light on solutions that could enhance not only the speed, but could also achieve a joint optimization of Speed, Power, Size, and Precision. The vision is to enable the most complex algorithms to be low-power in execution, small-size in implementation, and accurate in precision. The mission is human well being.

Systolic Arrays

One can get some acceleration if one moves the execution of an algorithm from a software-based Control Flow environment, like Multi Core or Many Core, to a reconfigurable and flexible hardware-based Data Flow environment, as explained previously in this book. However, one can get more performance for less power, smaller size, and a potentially higher precision, if one makes one step farther, which means moving the algorithm from a flexible hardware-based Data Flow environment to a fixed hardware-based Systolic Array environment. In this way, some flexibility is sacrificed in the domain of re-programmability, but the conditions are met for the most frequently encountered algorithms to execute extremely fast, while the many less frequently used algorithms would be executed in the environment offering more flexibility: Data Flow. This section sheds light on the essence of Systolic Arrays.

GaAs Computing

One could get a further acceleration if one changes the implementation technology. By changing the technology, one could get a better speed, but not necessarily a better power consumption, smaller implementation size, or a better precision. However, one could get other benefits that may be of importance for a given implementation. GaAs is a technology which brings speedup, and also radiation hardness, which is of interest for aerospace and defense applications. This section sheds light on GaAs technology and its differences compared to silicon technology. It reviews possible architectural choices that fit into the requirements of GaAs technology, especially those of interest for datamining algorithms.

GaAs Systolic Arrays

This section describes one possible implementation of a Systolic Array in GaAs, through a project financed by DARPA. It is tuned to the Gramm-Schmidt Orthogonalization algorithm. This section describes the hardware structure as well as the details of the implementation, using a radiation-hard technology, and also discusses the possible implementation of selected data mining algorithms, as well as the related trade-offs..

Approximate Computing

One could get a further acceleration if one changes the implementation precision and latency, to the level which does not have a negative impact on the overall performance. In such a way, the fight against noise and distortions in the communication medium could be a lot more effective. This section sheds light both on suboptimal detection and on methods that use increased system latency for a better performance with less hardware resources.

REVIEW QUESTIONS

This section provides questions for better understanding of the key aspects of the chapter.

1. What is a suboptimal computing?
2. What is an approximate computing?
3. List different types of parallelism according to the Flynn's taxonomy.
4. Provide an example of systolic array.

REFERENCES

Flynn, M. J. (1972). Some computer organizations and their effectiveness. *IEEE Transactions on Computers*, 948–960.

Fortes, J., & Milutinovic, V. (1986). A High-Level Systolic Architecture for GaAs. In *Nineteenth Hawaii International Conference on System Sciences*. IEEE.

Gajski, D., & Abraham, S. (1984). A communication algorithm for a wafer scale integrated multiprocessor. In *Int. Conf. Parallel Processing* (pp. 147-154). IEEE.

McDonough, K., & Magar, S. (1982). A single chip microcomputer architecture optimized for signal processing. In *IEEE Int. Conf. Acoust., Speech, Signal Processing* (pp. 1-17). IEEE.

Milutinovic, V. (1980). Sub-optimal detection procedure based on the weighting of partial decisions. *IEEE Electronic Letters*, 237-238.

Milutinovic, V. (1985). A Microprocessor-Oriented Algorithm for Adaptive Equalization. *IEEE Transactions on Communications*, *33*(6), 522–527. doi:10.1109/TCOM.1985.1096343

Milutinovic, V. (1988). Computer Architecture: Concepts and Systems. North-Holland.

Milutinovic, V. (1996). *A good method for presentation of research results*. IEEE TCCA Newsletter.

Milutinovic, V. (1996). The best method for presentation of research results. IEEE TCCA Newsletter, 1-6.

Milutinovic, V. (1997). *Surviving the Design of a 200 MHz RISC Microprocessor: Lessons Learned*. IEEE Computer Society Press.

KEY TERMS AND DEFINITIONS

MIMD: Multiple instruction multiple data approach for parallelization.
MISD: Multiple instruction single data approach for parallelization.
SIMD: Single instruction multiple data approach for parallelization.
SISD: Single instruction single data approach for parallelization.
Suboptimal Computing: Procedure based on the weighting of partial decisions.

Conclusion

The main purpose of this book is to shed light on the synergy of selected data mining and machine learning algorithms, on one side, and two important computing paradigms, control flow and data flow, on the other side.

After the general introductory that stresses aspects, of the mentioned algorithms and of the two paradigms, that are of importance for their synergy, we go into the details of importance for effective implementations of data mining algorithms on a dataflow architecture that proves to be successful for a number of different applications.

The elaboration of algorithms is given both through a rigorous mathematical treatment and through a set of examples that could be frequently found in numerous applications.

The elaboration of the two paradigms is given using formal mechanisms found in the common literature on computer architectures and the related programming models.

Finally, a discussion is presented which explains possible avenues for the further speedup of the algorithms, using faster technologies, as well as the principles of suboptimal computing. These two techniques, if combined properly, could bring not only the speedup related benefits, but also the benefits in the domain of complexity, power dissipation, or radiation hardness.

The interested readers are directed into the related literature, for further readings, and also to web sites with more programming examples. The interested readers are also welcome to contact the four co-authors directly.

Glossary

ALU: Arithmetic logic unit in processor.

ANN: Artificial neural network dominant in supervised machine learning.

Auto-Loop Offset: Dataflow technique calculating buffers size in cyclic graphs.

BI: Business intelligence.

C4.5: Decision tree algorithm.

CART: Algorithm for classification entitled Classification and Regression Trees.

CNN: Convolutional neural network used for image processing and classification.

Confusion Matrix: Machine learning technique for result evaluation using optimization metrics.

Control-flow: Convectional programming paradigm for general purpose.

Counters: Dataflow technique for counting number of ticks in the graph.

Cross Validation: Machine learning technique for evaluating performance of a model using labeled data.

Cyclyc Graph: Execution graph with looping branches.

Data Mining: Technique for extracting hidden knowledge from data.

Dataflow: Programming paradigm based on execution graphs.

DFE: Dataflow engine which reconfigures according to the execution graph.

Ensemble Learning: Machine learning technique that combines results of multiple algorithms for achieving better results.

Execution Graph: Execution graph of the dataflow paradigm which describes the program.

Feature Extraction: Step prior to model training that removes features that have minor impact on the outcome.

Fixed-Point: Number representation frequently used in the dataflow paradigm.

Floating-Point: Number representation frequently used in the controlflow paradigm.

FMEM: Dataflow fast memory with high bandwidth.

FPGA: Field programmable gate array.

Functional Programming: Programming model based on expressions and closures.

GA: Genetic algorithm for search inspired by natural evolution.

Hardware Variable: Dataflow variable that existing only during runtime.

Hidden Knowledge: Output of data mining techniques where valuable data are extracted from unstructured data.

Kernel: Dataflow program file that describes execution graph.

KNN: Algorithm for classification entitled K nearest neighbors.

Layer: One layer in neural network consisted of many neurons.

LMEM: Dataflow large memory with multidimensional addressing space.

Loop Unrolling: Dataflow technique for implementing controlflow loops.

Manager: Dataflow program file describes data orchestration between kernel and the host machine.

MIMD: Multiple instruction multiple data approach for parallelization.

MISD: Multiple instruction single data approach for parallelization.

Neuron: Neuron in one layer of neural network.

NLP: Natural language processing.

Offset: Dataflow technique for accessing neighbor elements in stream.

On-Board Memory: Referred as LMEM with multidimensional addressing space.

On-Chip Memory: Referred as FMEM with high bandwidth.

PCA: Principal component analysis that transforms data in sub-dimensional space.

Pipeline Utilization: Optimization technique for dataflow paradigm.

RELU: Activation function for neuron in neural network.

RNN: Recurrent neural networks suitable for NLP.

SIMD: Single instruction multiple data approach for parallelization.

SISD: Single instruction single data approach for parallelization.

Software Variable: Dataflow variable that existing only during compile time, which describes the execution graph.

Stream: Dataflow technique for moving data between the host machine and the DFE.

Suboptimal Computing: Procedure based on the weighting of partial decisions.

Tree Reduction: Dataflow optimization technique provided by compiler to compress the execution graph.

Von Neumann: Von Neumann paradigm as conventional programming paradigm.

Related Readings

To continue IGI Global's long-standing tradition of advancing innovation through emerging research, please find below a compiled list of recommended IGI Global book chapters and journal articles in the area of data-mining algorithms, mathematical treatment, and energy efficient implementations. These related readings will provide additional information and guidance to further enrich your knowledge and assist you with your own research.

Aamir, T. (2021). Transforming Digital Enterprises Towards Web Scale With Machine Learning. In K. Sandhu (Ed.), *Emerging Challenges, Solutions, and Best Practices for Digital Enterprise Transformation* (pp. 241–260). IGI Global., doi:10.4018/978-1-7998-8587-0.ch013

Abdollahi, H. (2020). An Adaptive Neuro-Based Fuzzy Inference System (ANFIS) for the Prediction of Option Price. [IJAMC]. *International Journal of Applied Metaheuristic Computing*, 11(2), 99–117. doi:10.4018/IJAMC.2020040105

Abouzid, H., & Chakkor, O. (2020). Autoencoders in Deep Neural Network Architecture for Real Work Applications. In J. Zbitou, C. I. Pruncu, & A. Errkik (Eds.), *Handbook of Research on Recent Developments in Electrical and Mechanical Engineering* (pp. 214–236). IGI Global., doi:10.4018/978-1-7998-0117-7.ch007

Acharya, A., Ghosh, M., & Jha, S. (2021). Automated Detection and Removal of Cycles in a Concept Map. In D. Chatham (Ed.), *Advancing Online Course Design and Pedagogy for the 21st Century Learning Environment* (pp. 305–321). IGI Global., doi:10.4018/978-1-7998-5598-9.ch016

Agarwal, I. Y., & Rana, D. P. (2021). Fake News and Imbalanced Data Perspective. In D. P. Rana & R. G. Mehta (Eds.), *Data Preprocessing, Active Learning, and Cost Perceptive Approaches for Resolving Data Imbalance* (pp. 195–210). IGI Global., doi:10.4018/978-1-7998-7371-6.ch011

Agarwal, I. Y., Rana, D. P., Bhatia, D., Rathod, J., Gandhi, K. J., & Sodagar, H. (2021). Detection of Bot Accounts on Social Media Considering Its Imbalanced Nature. In D. P. Rana & R. G. Mehta (Eds.), *Data Preprocessing, Active Learning, and Cost Perceptive Approaches for Resolving Data Imbalance* (pp. 162–176). IGI Global., doi:10.4018/978-1-7998-7371-6.ch009

Aggarwal, D., Mittal, S., & Bali, V. (2021). Identifying Non-Performing Students in Higher Educational Institutions Using Data Mining Techniques. [IJISMD]. *International Journal of Information System Modeling and Design*, *12*(1), 94–110. doi:10.4018/IJISMD.2021010105

Aggarwal, D., Mittal, S., & Bali, V. (2021). Significance of Non-Academic Parameters for Predicting Student Performance Using Ensemble Learning Techniques. [IJSDA]. *International Journal of System Dynamics Applications*, *10*(3), 38–49. doi:10.4018/IJSDA.2021070103

Ahamed, S. A., & Ravi, C. (2021). Study of Swarm Intelligence Algorithms for Optimizing Deep Neural Network for Bitcoin Prediction. [IJSIR]. *International Journal of Swarm Intelligence Research*, *12*(2), 22–38. doi:10.4018/IJSIR.2021040102

Ahlawat, K., Chug, A., & Singh, A. P. (2019). Empirical Evaluation of Map Reduce Based Hybrid Approach for Problem of Imbalanced Classification in Big Data. [IJGHPC]. *International Journal of Grid and High Performance Computing*, *11*(3), 23–45. doi:10.4018/IJGHPC.2019070102

Ahmed, H. I., Nasr, A. A., Abdel-Mageid, S. M., & Aslan, H. K. (2021). DADEM. [IJACI]. *International Journal of Ambient Computing and Intelligence*, *12*(1), 114–139. doi:10.4018/IJACI.2021010105

Ahuja, R., Jain, D., Sachdeva, D., Garg, A., & Rajput, C. (2019). Convolutional Neural Network Based American Sign Language Static Hand Gesture Recognition. [IJACI]. *International Journal of Ambient Computing and Intelligence*, *10*(3), 60–73. doi:10.4018/IJACI.2019070104

Ahuja, R., Vivek, V., Chandna, M., Virmani, S., & Banga, A. (2019). Comparative Study of Various Machine Learning Algorithms for Prediction of Insomnia. In C. Chakraborty (Ed.), *Advanced Classification Techniques for Healthcare Analysis* (pp. 234–257). IGI Global., doi:10.4018/978-1-5225-7796-6.ch011

Ajaypradeep, N., & Sasikala, R. (2021). Statistical Perspectives and Machine Learning Algorithms. In Y. Kats & F. Stasolla (Eds.), *Education and Technology Support for Children and Young Adults With ASD and Learning Disabilities* (pp. 315–338). IGI Global., doi:10.4018/978-1-7998-7053-1.ch016

Akgül, Y. (2018). A SEM-Neural Network Approach for Predicting Antecedents of Factors Influencing Consumers' Intent to Install Mobile Applications. In F. J. Mtenzi, G. Oreku, D. Lupiana, & J. J. Yonazi (Eds.), *Mobile Technologies and Socio-Economic Development in Emerging Nations* (pp. 262–308). IGI Global., doi:10.4018/978-1-5225-4029-8.ch012

Al Qasem, O., & Akour, M. (2019). Software Fault Prediction Using Deep Learning Algorithms. [IJOSSP]. *International Journal of Open Source Software and Processes*, 10(4), 1–19. doi:10.4018/IJOSSP.2019100101

Al-Ammal, H. M. (2020). A Review of Machine Learning Techniques for Anomaly Detection in Static Graphs. In Albastaki, Y. A., & Awad, W. (Eds.), Implementing Computational Intelligence Techniques for Security Systems Design (pp. 146-162). IGI Global. https://doi.org/ doi:10.4018/978-1-7998-2418-3.ch007

Alaoui, A., & Elberrichi, Z. (2020). Enhanced Ant Colony Algorithm for Best Features Selection for a Decision Tree Classification of Medical Data. In M. Sarfraz (Ed.), *Critical Approaches to Information Retrieval Research* (pp. 278–293). IGI Global., doi:10.4018/978-1-7998-1021-6.ch015

Albastaki, Y. A. (2020). Odor Sensing Techniques. In Albastaki, Y. A., & Awad, W. (Eds.), Implementing Computational Intelligence Techniques for Security Systems Design (pp. 73-96). IGI Global. https://doi.org/ doi:10.4018/978-1-7998-2418-3.ch004

Al-Dmour, A. H., & Al-Dmour, R. H. (2018). Applying Multiple Linear Regression and Neural Network to Predict Business Performance Using the Reliability of Accounting Information System. [IJCFA]. *International Journal of Corporate Finance and Accounting*, 5(2), 12–26. doi:10.4018/IJCFA.2018070102

Alharbi, O. (2020). Negation Handling in Machine Learning-Based Sentiment Classification for Colloquial Arabic. [IJORIS]. *International Journal of Operations Research and Information Systems*, *11*(4), 33–45. doi:10.4018/IJORIS.2020100102

Ali, M. N., Sarowar, M. G., Rahman, M. L., Chaki, J., Dey, N., & Tavares, J. M. (2019). Adam Deep Learning With SOM for Human Sentiment Classification. [IJACI]. *International Journal of Ambient Computing and Intelligence*, *10*(3), 92–116. doi:10.4018/IJACI.2019070106

Alkasassbeh, M. S., & Khairallah, M. Z. (2020). Network Attack Detection With SNMP-MIB Using Deep Neural Network. In B. B. Gupta & S. Srinivasagopalan (Eds.), *Handbook of Research on Intrusion Detection Systems* (pp. 66–76). IGI Global., doi:10.4018/978-1-7998-2242-4.ch004

Alkhalil, A., Abdallah, M. A., Alogali, A., & Aljaloud, A. (2021). Applying Big Data Analytics in Higher Education. [IJICTE]. *International Journal of Information and Communication Technology Education*, *17*(3), 29–51. doi:10.4018/IJICTE.20210701.oa3

Allam, M., Nandhini, M., & Thangadarshini, M. (2021). Optimization of Machine Learning Models for Early Diagnosis of Autism Spectrum Disorder. In S. Kautish & G. Dhiman (Eds.), *Artificial Intelligence for Accurate Analysis and Detection of Autism Spectrum Disorder* (pp. 138–166). IGI Global., doi:10.4018/978-1-7998-7460-7.ch009

AlMubarak, H. A., Stanley, J., Guo, P., Long, R., Antani, S., Thoma, G., Zuna, R., Frazier, S., & Stoecker, W. (2019). A Hybrid Deep Learning and Handcrafted Feature Approach for Cervical Cancer Digital Histology Image Classification. [IJHISI]. *International Journal of Healthcare Information Systems and Informatics*, *14*(2), 66–87. doi:10.4018/IJHISI.2019040105

Almubarak, H., Guo, P., Stanley, R. J., Long, R., Antani, S., Thoma, G., Zuna, R., Frazier, S. R., Moss, R. H., Stoecker, W. V., & Hagerty, J. (2018). Algorithm Enhancements for Improvement of Localized Classification of Uterine Cervical Cancer Digital Histology Images. In J. Tan (Ed.), *Handbook of Research on Emerging Perspectives on Healthcare Information Systems and Informatics* (pp. 234–250). IGI Global., doi:10.4018/978-1-5225-5460-8.ch010

Al-Nawasrah, A., Almomani, A. A., Atawneh, S., & Alauthman, M. (2020). A Survey of Fast Flux Botnet Detection With Fast Flux Cloud Computing. [IJCAC]. *International Journal of Cloud Applications and Computing, 10*(3), 17–53. doi:10.4018/IJCAC.2020070102

Al-Qerem, A., Abutahoun, B. M., Nashwan, S. I., Shakhatreh, S., Alauthman, M., & Almomani, A. (2020). Network-Based Detection of Mirai Botnet Using Machine Learning and Feature Selection Methods. In B. B. Gupta & D. Gupta (Eds.), *Handbook of Research on Multimedia Cyber Security* (pp. 308–318). IGI Global., doi:10.4018/978-1-7998-2701-6.ch016

Alrahhal, M., & Supreethi, K. P. (2020). Multimedia Image Retrieval System by Combining CNN With Handcraft Features in Three Different Similarity Measures. [IJCVIP]. *International Journal of Computer Vision and Image Processing, 10*(1), 1–23. doi:10.4018/IJCVIP.2020010101

Ameer, I., & Sidorov, G. (2021). Author Profiling Using Texts in Social Networks. In R. A. Pazos-Rangel, R. Florencia-Juarez, M. A. Paredes-Valverde, & G. Rivera (Eds.), *Handbook of Research on Natural Language Processing and Smart Service Systems* (pp. 245–265). IGI Global., doi:10.4018/978-1-7998-4730-4.ch011

Amudha, P., & Sivakumari, S. (2020). Hybridization of Machine Learning Algorithm in Intrusion Detection System. In P. Ganapathi & D. Shanmugapriya (Eds.), *Handbook of Research on Machine and Deep Learning Applications for Cyber Security* (pp. 150–175). IGI Global., doi:10.4018/978-1-5225-9611-0.ch008

Angadi, S., & Nandyal, S. (2020). Human Identification System Based on Spatial and Temporal Features in the Video Surveillance System. [IJACI]. *International Journal of Ambient Computing and Intelligence, 11*(3), 1–21. doi:10.4018/IJACI.2020070101

Anitha Elavarasi, S., & Jayanthi, J. (2020). Programming Language Support for Implementing Machine Learning Algorithms. In S. Velayutham (Ed.), *Handbook of Research on Applications and Implementations of Machine Learning Techniques* (pp. 402–421). IGI Global., doi:10.4018/978-1-5225-9902-9.ch021

Anitha, N., & Devi Priya, R. (2020). Prediction of High-Risk Factors in Surgical Operations Using Machine Learning Techniques. In S. Velayutham (Ed.), *Handbook of Research on Applications and Implementations of Machine Learning Techniques* (pp. 201–221). IGI Global., doi:10.4018/978-1-5225-9902-9.ch011

Ansari, G., Gupta, S., & Singhal, N. (2021). Natural Language Processing in Online Reviews. In F. Pinarbasi & M. Taskiran (Eds.), *Natural Language Processing for Global and Local Business* (pp. 40–64). IGI Global., doi:10.4018/978-1-7998-4240-8.ch003

Aridoss, M., Dhasarathan, C., Dumka, A., & Loganathan, J. (2020). DUICM Deep Underwater Image Classification Mobdel using Convolutional Neural Networks. [IJGHPC]. *International Journal of Grid and High Performance Computing*, *12*(3), 88–100. doi:10.4018/IJGHPC.2020070106

Arivudainambi, D., Varun Kumar, K. A., Vinoth Kumar, R., & Visu, P. (2020). Ransomware Traffic Classification Using Deep Learning Models. [IJWP]. *International Journal of Web Portals*, *12*(1), 1–11. doi:10.4018/IJWP.2020010101

Arjaria, S. K., & Rathore, A. S. (2019). Heart Disease Diagnosis. In C. Chakraborty (Ed.), *Advanced Classification Techniques for Healthcare Analysis* (pp. 161–181). IGI Global., doi:10.4018/978-1-5225-7796-6.ch008

Arora, A., Srivastava, A., & Bansal, S. (2019). Graph and Neural Network-Based Intelligent Conversation System. In H. Banati, S. Mehta, & P. Kaur (Eds.), *Nature-Inspired Algorithms for Big Data Frameworks* (pp. 339–357). IGI Global., doi:10.4018/978-1-5225-5852-1.ch014

Arul Murugan, R., & Sathiyamoorthi, V. (2020). Introduction to Machine Learning and Its Implementation Techniques. In S. Velayutham (Ed.), *Handbook of Research on Applications and Implementations of Machine Learning Techniques* (pp. 334–358). IGI Global., doi:10.4018/978-1-5225-9902-9.ch018

Arul, R., Moorthy, R. S., & Bashir, A. K. (2019). Ensemble Learning Mechanisms for Threat Detection. In M. S. Khan (Ed.), *Machine Learning and Cognitive Science Applications in Cyber Security* (pp. 240–281). IGI Global., doi:10.4018/978-1-5225-8100-0.ch010

Ashour, D. S., Abou Rayia, D. M., Dey, N., Ashour, A. S., Hawas, A. R., & Alotaibi, M. B. (2018). Schistosomal Hepatic Fibrosis Classification. [IJNCR]. *International Journal of Natural Computing Research*, 7(2), 1–17. doi:10.4018/IJNCR.2018040101

Ashraf, S., Kadery, I., Chowdhury, M. A., Mahbub, T. Z., & Rahman, R. M. (2019). Fruit Image Classification Using Convolutional Neural Networks. [IJSI]. *International Journal of Software Innovation*, 7(4), 51–70. doi:10.4018/IJSI.2019100103

Aswathy, M. A., & Mohan, J. (2020). Analysis of Machine Learning Algorithms for Breast Cancer Detection. In S. Velayutham (Ed.), *Handbook of Research on Applications and Implementations of Machine Learning Techniques* (pp. 1–20). IGI Global., doi:10.4018/978-1-5225-9902-9.ch001

Atsa'am, D. D. (2020). Feature Selection Algorithm Using Relative Odds for Data Mining Classification. In A. Haldorai & A. Ramu (Eds.), *Big Data Analytics for Sustainable Computing* (pp. 81–106). IGI Global., doi:10.4018/978-1-5225-9750-6.ch005

Awad, W. S., & Rafiq, W. M. (2020). Improving Spam Email Filtering Systems Using Data Mining Techniques. In Albastaki, Y. A., & Awad, W. (Ed.), Implementing Computational Intelligence Techniques for Security Systems Design (pp. 43-72). IGI Global. https://doi.org/ doi:10.4018/978-1-7998-2418-3.ch003

B. S. C., Neela Madheswari, A., K., S., & Arumugam, C. (2021). Crucial Role of Data Analytics in the Prevention and Detection of Cyber Security Attacks. In Misra, S., Arumugam, C., Jaganathan, S., & S., S. (Ed.), Confluence of AI, Machine, and Deep Learning in Cyber Forensics (pp. 67-80). IGI Global. https://doi.org/ doi:10.4018/978-1-7998-4900-1.ch004

B. V. R., N., S., & M., G. (2020). A Decision Tree on Data Mining Framework for Recognition of Chronic Kidney Disease. In Sriraam, N. (Ed.), Biomedical and Clinical Engineering for Healthcare Advancement (pp. 78-95). IGI Global. https://doi.org/ doi:10.4018/978-1-7998-0326-3.ch005

Baareh, A. K. (2018). Temperature Forecasting System Using Fuzzy Mathematical Model. [IJAEC]. *International Journal of Applied Evolutionary Computation*, 9(3), 48–57. doi:10.4018/IJAEC.2018070105

Babu, S. K., & Vasavi, S. (2018). Visualization of Feature Engineering Strategies for Predictive Analytics. [IJNCR]. *International Journal of Natural Computing Research*, *7*(4), 20–44. doi:10.4018/IJNCR.2018100102

Bagui, S., & Benson, D. (2021). Android Adware Detection Using Machine Learning. [IJCRE]. *International Journal of Cyber Research and Education*, *3*(2), 1–19. doi:10.4018/IJCRE.2021070101

Bagui, S., Shah, K. M., Hu, Y., & Bagui, S. (2021). Binary Classification of Network-Generated Flow Data Using a Machine Learning Algorithm. [IJISP]. *International Journal of Information Security and Privacy*, *15*(1), 26–43. doi:10.4018/IJISP.2021010102

Bajaj, A., Sharma, T., & Sangwan, O. P. (2020). Information Retrieval in Conjunction With Deep Learning. In A. Solanki, S. Kumar, & A. Nayyar (Eds.), *Handbook of Research on Emerging Trends and Applications of Machine Learning* (pp. 300–311). IGI Global., doi:10.4018/978-1-5225-9643-1.ch014

Baker, J. D. (2021). Introduction to Machine Learning as a New Methodological Framework for Performance Assessment. In M. C. Bocarnea, B. E. Winston, & D. Dean (Eds.), *Handbook of Research on Advancements in Organizational Data Collection and Measurements* (pp. 326–342). IGI Global., doi:10.4018/978-1-7998-7665-6.ch021

Bakri Hassan, M., Sayed Ali Ahmed, E., & Saeed, R. A. (2021). Machine Learning for Industrial IoT Systems. In J. Zhao & V. Kumar (Eds.), *Handbook of Research on Innovations and Applications of AI, IoT, and Cognitive Technologies* (pp. 336–358). IGI Global., doi:10.4018/978-1-7998-6870-5.ch023

Bala, K., Choubey, D. K., Paul, S., & Lala, M. G. (2018). Classification Techniques for Thunderstorms and Lightning Prediction. In U. P. Singh, A. Tiwari, & R. K. Singh (Eds.), *Soft-Computing-Based Nonlinear Control Systems Design* (pp. 1–17). IGI Global., doi:10.4018/978-1-5225-3531-7.ch001

Balakumar, A., & S., S. (2020). Machine Learning Is the Future for Lung Cancer Prognosis and Prediction. In Wason, R., Goyal, D., Jain, V., Balamurugan, S., & Baliyan, A. (Ed.), *Applications of Deep Learning and Big IoT on Personalized Healthcare Services* (pp. 176-196). IGI Global. https://doi.org/doi:10.4018/978-1-7998-2101-4.ch011

Balamurali, A., & Ananthanarayanan, B. (2020). Develop a Neural Model to Score Bigram of Words Using Bag-of-Words Model for Sentiment Analysis. In S., S., & M., J. (Ed.), Neural Networks for Natural Language Processing (pp. 122-142). IGI Global. https://doi.org/ doi:10.4018/978-1-7998-1159-6.ch008

Bali, V., Kumar, A., & Gangwar, S. (2020). A Novel Approach for Wind Speed Forecasting Using LSTM-ARIMA Deep Learning Models. [IJAEIS]. *International Journal of Agricultural and Environmental Information Systems, 11*(3), 13–30. doi:10.4018/IJAEIS.2020070102

Balogun, J. A., Asinobi, A. O., Olaniyi, O., Adegoke, S. A., Oladeji, F. A., & Idowu, P. A. (2019). Ensemble Model for the Risk of Anemia in Pediatric Patients With Sickle Cell Disorder. [IJCCP]. *International Journal of Computers in Clinical Practice, 4*(2), 33–59. doi:10.4018/IJCCP.2019070103

Banerjee, N., & Das, S. (2021). Machine Learning for Prediction of Lung Cancer. In S. Saxena & S. Paul (Eds.), *Deep Learning Applications in Medical Imaging* (pp. 114–139). IGI Global., doi:10.4018/978-1-7998-5071-7.ch005

Bangotra, D. K., Singh, Y., & Selwal, A. K. (2020). An Intelligent Opportunistic Routing Protocol for Big Data in WSNs. [IJMDEM]. *International Journal of Multimedia Data Engineering and Management, 11*(1), 15–29. doi:10.4018/ IJMDEM.2020010102

Banik, D., & Bhattacharjee, D. (2021). Mitigating Data Imbalance Issues in Medical Image Analysis. In D. P. Rana & R. G. Mehta (Eds.), *Data Preprocessing, Active Learning, and Cost Perceptive Approaches for Resolving Data Imbalance* (pp. 66–89). IGI Global., doi:10.4018/978-1-7998-7371-6. ch004

Bansal, A., Ahirwar, M. K., & Shukla, P. K. (2019). Assessment on Different Classification Algorithms Used in Internet of Things Applications. [IJOCI]. *International Journal of Organizational and Collective Intelligence, 9*(1), 1–11. doi:10.4018/IJOCI.2019010101

Bansal, A., Shukla, P. K., & Ahirwar, M. K. (2019). Opinion on Different Classification Algorithms Used in Internet of Things Environment for Large Data Set. [IJOCI]. *International Journal of Organizational and Collective Intelligence, 9*(1), 51–60. doi:10.4018/IJOCI.2019010104

Bansal, P., Kumar, S., Srivastava, R., & Agarwal, S. (2021). Using Transfer Learning and Hierarchical Classifier to Diagnose Melanoma From Dermoscopic Images. [IJHISI]. *International Journal of Healthcare Information Systems and Informatics*, *16*(2), 73–86. doi:10.4018/IJHISI.20210401.oa4

Baranwal, A., Bagwe, B. R., & M, V. (2020). Machine Learning in Python. In Velayutham, S. (Ed.), *Handbook of Research on Applications and Implementations of Machine Learning Techniques* (pp. 128-154). IGI Global. https://doi.org/ doi:10.4018/978-1-5225-9902-9.ch008

Barman, D., & Chowdhury, N. (2019). A Novel Approach for the Customer Segmentation Using Clustering Through Self-Organizing Map. [IJBAN]. *International Journal of Business Analytics*, *6*(2), 23–45. doi:10.4018/IJBAN.2019040102

Barrachina, M., & Valenzuela López, L. (2021). Machine Learning Techniques to Identify and Characterize Sleep Disorders Using Biosignals. In M. Kumar, R. Kumar, & D. Vaithiyanathan (Eds.), *Advancing the Investigation and Treatment of Sleep Disorders Using AI* (pp. 136–160). IGI Global., doi:10.4018/978-1-7998-8018-9.ch008

Barrera-Cámara, R. A., Canepa-Saenz, A., Ruiz-Vanoye, J. A., Fuentes-Penna, A., Ruiz-Jaimes, M. Á., & Bernábe-Loranca, M. B. (2021). Tools, Technologies, and Methodologies to Support Data Science. In B. Patil & M. Vohra (Eds.), *Handbook of Research on Engineering, Business, and Healthcare Applications of Data Science and Analytics* (pp. 50–72). IGI Global., doi:10.4018/978-1-7998-3053-5.ch004

Basheer, S., Gandhi, U. D., Priyan, M. K., & Parthasarathy, P. (2019). Network Support Data Analysis for Fault Identification Using Machine Learning. [IJSI]. *International Journal of Software Innovation*, *7*(2), 41–49. doi:10.4018/IJSI.2019040104

Bayır, A., Gülseçen, S., & Türkmen, G. (2021). Application of Data Mining Algorithms in Determination of Voting Tendencies in Turkey. In O. Yildiz (Ed.), *Recent Developments in Individual and Organizational Adoption of ICTs* (pp. 134–149). IGI Global., doi:10.4018/978-1-7998-3045-0.ch008

Bedi, P., Goyal, S. B., Kumar, J., & Kumar, S. (2021). Application of Image Processing for Autism Spectrum Disorder. In S. Kautish & G. Dhiman (Eds.), *Artificial Intelligence for Accurate Analysis and Detection of Autism Spectrum Disorder* (pp. 1–24). IGI Global., doi:10.4018/978-1-7998-7460-7.ch001

Beg, M. O., Awan, M. N., & Ali, S. S. (2019). Algorithmic Machine Learning for Prediction of Stock Prices. In A. Rafay (Ed.), *FinTech as a Disruptive Technology for Financial Institutions* (pp. 142–169). IGI Global., doi:10.4018/978-1-5225-7805-5.ch007

Behera, R. K., Sahoo, K. S., Naik, D., Rath, S. K., & Sahoo, B. (2021). Structural Mining for Link Prediction Using Various Machine Learning Algorithms. [IJSESD]. *International Journal of Social Ecology and Sustainable Development*, 12(3), 66–78. doi:10.4018/IJSESD.2021070105

Belaissaoui, M., & Jurassec, J. (2019). A Deep Convolutional Neural Network for Image Malware Classification. [IJSST]. *International Journal of Smart Security Technologies*, 6(1), 49–60. doi:10.4018/ijsst.2019010104

Bellamkonda, S., & Gopalan, N. P. (2020). An Enhanced Facial Expression Recognition Model Using Local Feature Fusion of Gabor Wavelets and Local Directionality Patterns. [IJACI]. *International Journal of Ambient Computing and Intelligence*, 11(1), 48–70. doi:10.4018/IJACI.2020010103

Bencherif, K., Malki, M., & Bensaber, D. A. (2018). An Unsupervised Approach for Determining Link Specifications. [IJITWE]. *International Journal of Information Technology and Web Engineering*, 13(4), 104–123. doi:10.4018/IJITWE.2018100106

Bera, A., Ghose, M. K., & Pal, D. K. (2020). Graph Classification Using Back Propagation Learning Algorithms. [IJSSSP]. *International Journal of Systems and Software Security and Protection*, 11(2), 1–12. doi:10.4018/ijsssp.2020070101

Berkane, M., Belhouchette, K., & Belhadef, H. (2019). Emotion Recognition Approach Using Multilayer Perceptron Network and Motion Estimation. [IJSE]. *International Journal of Synthetic Emotions*, 10(1), 38–53. doi:10.4018/IJSE.2019010102

Bezerra, L. N., & Silva, M. T. (2020). Educational Data Mining Applied to a Massive Course. [IJDET]. *International Journal of Distance Education Technologies*, 18(4), 17–30. doi:10.4018/IJDET.2020100102

Bezerra, L. N., & Terra da Silva, M. (2019). Application of EDM to Understand the Online Students' Behavioral Pattern. [JITR]. *Journal of Information Technology Research*, 12(3), 154–168. doi:10.4018/JITR.2019070109

Bhajantri, L. B., & Baluragi, P. M. (2020). Context Aware Data Perception in Cognitive Internet of Things - Cognitive Agent Approach. [IJHIoT]. *International Journal of Hyperconnectivity and the Internet of Things*, *4*(2), 1–24. doi:10.4018/IJHIoT.2020070101

Bhandari, G. P., & Gupta, R. (2020). Fault Prediction in SOA-Based Systems Using Deep Learning Techniques. [IJWSR]. *International Journal of Web Services Research*, *17*(3), 1–19. doi:10.4018/IJWSR.2020070101

Bhargavi, P., & Jyothi, S. (2020). Object Detection in Fog Computing Using Machine Learning Algorithms. In S. Goundar, S. B. Bhushan, & P. K. Rayani (Eds.), *Architecture and Security Issues in Fog Computing Applications* (pp. 90–107). IGI Global., doi:10.4018/978-1-7998-0194-8.ch006

Bhatia, A. S., & Wong, R. (2021). Recent Progress in Quantum Machine Learning. In N. Kumar, A. Agrawal, B. K. Chaurasia, & R. A. Khan (Eds.), *Limitations and Future Applications of Quantum Cryptography* (pp. 232–256). IGI Global., doi:10.4018/978-1-7998-6677-0.ch012

Bhattacharjee, A. K., Mukherjee, S., Mondal, A., & Majumdar, D. (2019). Metaheuristic-Based Feature Optimization for Portfolio Management. In J. Ray, A. Mukherjee, S. K. Dey, & G. Klepac (Eds.), *Metaheuristic Approaches to Portfolio Optimization* (pp. 109–125). IGI Global., doi:10.4018/978-1-5225-8103-1.ch005

Bhola, J., Dhiman, G., Singhal, T., & Sajja, G. S. (2021). A Novel Technique on Autism Spectrum Disorders Using Classification Techniques. In S. Kautish & G. Dhiman (Eds.), *Artificial Intelligence for Accurate Analysis and Detection of Autism Spectrum Disorder* (pp. 40–53). IGI Global., doi:10.4018/978-1-7998-7460-7.ch003

Biswas, S. K., Devi, D., & Chakraborty, M. (2018). A Hybrid Case Based Reasoning Model for Classification in Internet of Things (IoT) Environment. [JOEUC]. *Journal of Organizational and End User Computing*, *30*(4), 104–122. doi:10.4018/JOEUC.2018100107

Bogomolov, T., Korolkiewicz, M. W., & Bogomolova, S. (2020). Identifying Patterns in Fresh Produce Purchases. In F. P. Garcia Marquez (Ed.), *Handbook of Research on Big Data Clustering and Machine Learning* (pp. 378–408). IGI Global., doi:10.4018/978-1-7998-0106-1.ch018

Boldt, M., & Rekanar, K. (2019). Analysis and Text Classification of Privacy Policies From Rogue and Top-100 Fortune Global Companies. [IJISP]. *International Journal of Information Security and Privacy, 13*(2), 47–66. doi:10.4018/IJISP.2019040104

Bölükbaş, O., & Uğuz, H. (2018). Performance of Negative Selection Algorithms in Patient Detection and Classification. In U. Kose, G. E. Guraksin, & O. Deperlioglu (Eds.), *Nature-Inspired Intelligent Techniques for Solving Biomedical Engineering Problems* (pp. 78–102). IGI Global., doi:10.4018/978-1-5225-4769-3.ch004

Boobalan, M. P. (2019). Deep Clustering. In A. E. Hassanien, A. Darwish, & C. L. Chowdhary (Eds.), *Handbook of Research on Deep Learning Innovations and Trends* (pp. 164–179). IGI Global., doi:10.4018/978-1-5225-7862-8.ch010

Boopathy, P., & Deepa, N. (2021). Decision Analysis in Financial Marketing Using Multi-Criteria Decision-Making Methods. In I. Oncioiu, S. Căpusneanu, D. I. Topor, & D. M. Constantin (Eds.), *Sustainability Reporting, Ethics, and Strategic Management Strategies for Modern Organizations* (pp. 115–129). IGI Global., doi:10.4018/978-1-7998-4637-6.ch007

Borah, J., Sarma, K. K., & Gohain, P. J. (2019). All Pervasive Surveillance Techniques and AI-Based Applications. In J. J. Rodrigues, A. Gawanmeh, K. Saleem, & S. Parvin (Eds.), *Smart Devices, Applications, and Protocols for the IoT* (pp. 54–82). IGI Global., doi:10.4018/978-1-5225-7811-6.ch004

Borodkin, A., Eliseev, V., Filaretov, G., & Seyed, A. A. (2019). The Methodical Complex of Laboratory Works on the Study of Neural Network Technologies. In E. V. Smirnova & R. P. Clark (Eds.), *Handbook of Research on Engineering Education in a Global Context* (pp. 358–367). IGI Global., doi:10.4018/978-1-5225-3395-5.ch030

Bouarara, H. A. (2019). A Computer-Assisted Diagnostic (CAD) of Screening Mammography to Detect Breast Cancer Without a Surgical Biopsy. [IJSSCI]. *International Journal of Software Science and Computational Intelligence, 11*(4), 31–49. doi:10.4018/IJSSCI.2019100103

Boulaaba, A., & Faiz, S. (2018). Towards Big GeoData Mining and Processing. [IJOCI]. *International Journal of Organizational and Collective Intelligence, 8*(2), 60–73. doi:10.4018/IJOCI.2018040104

Related Readings

Bouras, C. J., Gkamas, A., Salgado, S. A., & Papachristos, N. (2021). A Comparative Study of Machine Learning Models for Spreading Factor Selection in LoRa Networks. [IJWNBT]. *International Journal of Wireless Networks and Broadband Technologies, 10*(2), 100–121. doi:10.4018/IJWNBT.2021070106

Breja, M., & Jain, S. K. (2021). Analyzing Linguistic Features for Classifying Why-Type Non-Factoid Questions. [IJITWE]. *International Journal of Information Technology and Web Engineering, 16*(3), 21–38. doi:10.4018/IJITWE.2021070102

Burch, M., Jalba, A., & van Dueren den Hollander, C. (2021). Convolutional Neural Networks for Real-Time Eye Tracking in Interactive Applications. In B. Christiansen & T. Škrinjarić (Eds.), *Handbook of Research on Applied AI for International Business and Marketing Applications* (pp. 455–473). IGI Global., doi:10.4018/978-1-7998-5077-9.ch022

Canbolat, M., Sohn, K., & Gardner, J. T. (2020). A Parsimonious Predictive Model of Movie Performance. [IJORIS]. *International Journal of Operations Research and Information Systems, 11*(4), 46–61. doi:10.4018/IJORIS.2020100103

Casañola-Martin, G. M., & Pham-The, H. (2019). Machine Learning Applications in Nanomedicine and Nanotoxicology. [IJANR]. *International Journal of Applied Nanotechnology Research, 4*(1), 1–7. doi:10.4018/IJANR.2019010101

Catak, F. O., Sahinbas, K., & Dörtkardeş, V. (2021). Malicious URL Detection Using Machine Learning. In A. K. Luhach & A. Elçi (Eds.), *Artificial Intelligence Paradigms for Smart Cyber-Physical Systems* (pp. 160–180). IGI Global., doi:10.4018/978-1-7998-5101-1.ch008

Çelik, S. (2020). They Know What You Will Do Next Click. In R. Luppicini (Ed.), *Interdisciplinary Approaches to Digital Transformation and Innovation* (pp. 100–122). IGI Global., doi:10.4018/978-1-7998-1879-3.ch005

Çetin, A., & Gökhan, T. (2018). Differential Diagnosis of Erythematous Squamous Diseases With Feature Selection and Classification Algorithms. In U. Kose, G. E. Guraksin, & O. Deperlioglu (Eds.), *Nature-Inspired Intelligent Techniques for Solving Biomedical Engineering Problems* (pp. 103–129). IGI Global., doi:10.4018/978-1-5225-4769-3.ch005

Chadha, A. (2018). Efficient Clustering Algorithms in Educational Data Mining. In Malheiro, A., Ribeiro, F., Leal Jamil, G., Rascao, J. P., & Mealha, O. (Eds.), Handbook of Research on Knowledge Management for Contemporary Business Environments (pp. 279-312). IGI Global. https://doi.org/ doi:10.4018/978-1-5225-3725-0.ch015

Chaganti, R., Gupta, D., & Vemprala, N. (2021). Intelligent Network Layer for Cyber-Physical Systems Security. [IJSST]. *International Journal of Smart Security Technologies*, 8(2), 42–58. doi:10.4018/IJSST.2021070103

Chaim, M. L., Santos, D. S., & Cruzes, D. S. (2018). What Do We Know About Buffer Overflow Detection? [IJSSSP]. *International Journal of Systems and Software Security and Protection*, 9(3), 1–33. doi:10.4018/IJSSSP.2018070101

Chakour, I., El Mourabit, Y., & Baslam, M. (2020). Multi-Agent System Based on Data Mining Algorithms to Detect Breast Cancer. In M. Sarfraz (Ed.), *Critical Approaches to Information Retrieval Research* (pp. 210–224). IGI Global., doi:10.4018/978-1-7998-1021-6.ch011

Chakraborty, S., & Mali, K. (2020). An Overview of Biomedical Image Analysis From the Deep Learning Perspective. In Chakraborty, S., & Mali, K. (Ed.), Applications of Advanced Machine Intelligence in Computer Vision and Object Recognition (pp. 197-218). IGI Global. https://doi.org/ doi:10.4018/978-1-7998-2736-8.ch008

Chakraborty, S., Aich, S., & Kim, H. (2021). A Novel Sleep Scoring Algorithm-Based Framework and Sleep Pattern Analysis Using Machine Learning Techniques. [IJSDA]. *International Journal of System Dynamics Applications*, 10(3), 1–20. doi:10.4018/IJSDA.2021070101

Chander, B. (2020). Deep Learning Network. In S., S., & M., J. (Eds.), Neural Networks for Natural Language Processing (pp. 1-30). IGI Global. https://doi.org/ doi:10.4018/978-1-7998-1159-6.ch001

Chandrakala, D., Sumathi, S., Saran Kumar, A., & Sathish, J. (2019). Text Clustering Using PSO Based Dynamic Adaptive SOM for Detecting Emergent Trends. [IJIIT]. *International Journal of Intelligent Information Technologies*, 15(3), 64–78. doi:10.4018/IJIIT.2019070104

Chathalingath, A., & Manoharan, A. (2019). Performance Optimization of Tridiagonal Matrix Algorithm [TDMA] on Multicore Architectures. [IJGHPC]. *International Journal of Grid and High Performance Computing*, 11(4), 1–12. doi:10.4018/IJGHPC.2019100101

Chatterjee, A., Roy, S., & Shrivastava, R. (2021). A Machine Learning Approach to Prevent Cancer. In G. Rani & P. K. Tiwari (Eds.), *Handbook of Research on Disease Prediction Through Data Analytics and Machine Learning* (pp. 112–141). IGI Global., doi:10.4018/978-1-7998-2742-9.ch007

Chaudhary, A., Chouhan, K. S., Gajrani, J., & Sharma, B. (2020). Deep Learning With PyTorch. In M. Mahrishi, K. K. Hiran, G. Meena, & P. Sharma (Eds.), *Machine Learning and Deep Learning in Real-Time Applications* (pp. 61–95). IGI Global., doi:10.4018/978-1-7998-3095-5.ch003

Chaurasia, P. K. (2020). Paradigms of Machine Learning and Data Analytics. In U. Shanker & S. Pandey (Eds.), *Handling Priority Inversion in Time-Constrained Distributed Databases* (pp. 156–174). IGI Global., doi:10.4018/978-1-7998-2491-6.ch009

Chellamuthu, G., Kannimuthu, S., & Premalatha, K. (2019). Data Mining and Machine Learning Approaches in Breast Cancer Biomedical Research. In D. S. Rajput, R. S. Thakur, & S. M. Basha (Eds.), *Sentiment Analysis and Knowledge Discovery in Contemporary Business* (pp. 175–204). IGI Global., doi:10.4018/978-1-5225-4999-4.ch011

Chemweno, P. K., & Pintelon, L. (2020). Towards E-Maintenance. In A. Martinetti, M. Demichela, & S. Singh (Eds.), *Applications and Challenges of Maintenance and Safety Engineering in Industry 4.0* (pp. 189–212). IGI Global., doi:10.4018/978-1-7998-3904-0.ch011

Chen, H., Meng, C., & Chen, J. (2021). DDoS Attack Simulation and Machine Learning-Based Detection Approach in Internet of Things Experimental Environment. [IJISP]. *International Journal of Information Security and Privacy*, 15(3), 1–18. doi:10.4018/IJISP.2021070101

Chen, Z., Tang, J., Gong, X., & Su, Q. (2020). Security of E-Health Systems Using Face Recognition Based on Convolutional Neural Network. [IJEACH]. *International Journal of Extreme Automation and Connectivity in Healthcare*, 2(2), 37–41. doi:10.4018/IJEACH.2020070104

Cheng, L., Hu, H., & Wu, C. (2021). Spammer Group Detection Using Machine Learning Technology for Observation of New Spammer Behavioral Features. [JGIM]. *Journal of Global Information Management*, 29(2), 61–76. doi:10.4018/JGIM.2021030104

Chitra, P., & Abirami, S. (2019). Smart Pollution Alert System Using Machine Learning. In D. J. Mala (Ed.), *Integrating the Internet of Things Into Software Engineering Practices* (pp. 219–235). IGI Global., doi:10.4018/978-1-5225-7790-4.ch011

Choubey, D. K., Paul, S., Bala, K., Kumar, M., & Singh, U. P. (2019). Implementation of a Hybrid Classification Method for Diabetes. In S. Bhattacharyya (Ed.), *Intelligent Innovations in Multimedia Data Engineering and Management* (pp. 201–240). IGI Global., doi:10.4018/978-1-5225-7107-0.ch009

Chouiekh, A., & El Haj, E. H. (2020). Deep Convolutional Neural Networks for Customer Churn Prediction Analysis. [IJCINI]. *International Journal of Cognitive Informatics and Natural Intelligence*, *14*(1), 1–16. doi:10.4018/IJCINI.2020010101

Chowdhury, M. M., & Amin, S. H. (2021). Forecasting Sales and Return Products for Retail Corporations and Bridging Among Them. In A. Taghipour (Ed.), *Demand Forecasting and Order Planning in Supply Chains and Humanitarian Logistics* (pp. 250–281). IGI Global., doi:10.4018/978-1-7998-3805-0.ch009

Cong, W. (2020). Study of Financial Warning Ensemble Model for Listed Companies Based on Unbalanced Classification Perspective. [IJIIT]. *International Journal of Intelligent Information Technologies*, *16*(1), 32–48. doi:10.4018/IJIIT.2020010103

Cruz-Reyes, L., Espin-Andrade, R. A., Irrarragorri, F. L., Medina-Trejo, C., Tristán, J. F., Martinez-Vega, D. A., & Peralta, C. E. (2019). Use of Compensatory Fuzzy Logic for Knowledge Discovery Applied to the Warehouse Order Picking Problem for Real-Time Order Batching. In A. Ochoa Ortiz-Zezzatti, G. Rivera, C. Gómez-Santillán, & B. Sánchez–Lara (Eds.), *Handbook of Research on Metaheuristics for Order Picking Optimization in Warehouses to Smart Cities* (pp. 62–88). IGI Global., doi:10.4018/978-1-5225-8131-4.ch004

Dabas, C., Agarwal, A., Gupta, N., Jain, V., & Pathak, S. (2020). Machine Learning Evaluation for Music Genre Classification of Audio Signals. [IJGHPC]. *International Journal of Grid and High Performance Computing*, *12*(3), 57–67. doi:10.4018/IJGHPC.2020070104

Dağ, Ö. H. (2019). Predicting the Success of Ensemble Algorithms in the Banking Sector. [IJBAN]. *International Journal of Business Analytics*, 6(4), 12–31. doi:10.4018/IJBAN.2019100102

Das, A., & Mohanty, M. N. (2020). Use of Deep Neural Network for Optical Character Recognition. In M. Sarfraz (Ed.), *Advancements in Computer Vision Applications in Intelligent Systems and Multimedia Technologies* (pp. 219–254). IGI Global., doi:10.4018/978-1-7998-4444-0.ch012

Das, S., Sanyal, M. K., & Datta, D. (2021). A Comprehensive Feature Selection Approach for Machine Learning. [IJDAI]. *International Journal of Distributed Artificial Intelligence*, 13(2), 13–26. doi:10.4018/IJDAI.2021070102

Dash, A. K., & Mohapatra, P. (2021). A Survey on Prematurity Detection of Diabetic Retinopathy Based on Fundus Images Using Deep Learning Techniques. In S. Saxena & S. Paul (Eds.), *Deep Learning Applications in Medical Imaging* (pp. 140–155). IGI Global., doi:10.4018/978-1-7998-5071-7.ch006

David, S. K., Saeb, A. T., Rafiullah, M., & Rubeaan, K. (2019). Classification Techniques and Data Mining Tools Used in Medical Bioinformatics. In S. K. Strydom & M. Strydom (Eds.), *Big Data Governance and Perspectives in Knowledge Management* (pp. 105–126). IGI Global., doi:10.4018/978-1-5225-7077-6.ch005

De Silva, S., Dayarathna, S. U., Ariyarathne, G., Meedeniya, D., & Jayarathna, S. (2021). fMRI Feature Extraction Model for ADHD Classification Using Convolutional Neural Network. [IJEHMC]. *International Journal of E-Health and Medical Communications*, 12(1), 81–105. doi:10.4018/IJEHMC.2021010106

De, P. (2019). Application of Neurogenetic Modeling in Optimization of Water Treatment Plant Based on the Temporal Monitoring of Water Input Quality. [IJEOE]. *International Journal of Energy Optimization and Engineering*, 8(3), 93–101. doi:10.4018/IJEOE.2019070105

Deivanathan, R. (2019). A Review of Artificial Intelligence Technologies to Achieve Machining Objectives. In A. Haldorai & A. Ramu (Eds.), *Cognitive Social Mining Applications in Data Analytics and Forensics* (pp. 138–159). IGI Global., doi:10.4018/978-1-5225-7522-1.ch008

Demirci, S., Şahin, D. Ö., & Toprak, I. H. (2021). Android-Based Skin Cancer Recognition System Using Convolutional Neural Network. In D. Yadav, A. Bansal, M. Bhatia, M. Hooda, & J. Morato (Eds.), *Diagnostic Applications of Health Intelligence and Surveillance Systems* (pp. 59–85). IGI Global., doi:10.4018/978-1-7998-6527-8.ch003

Desarkar, A., Sanyal, S., Baidya, A., Das, A., & Chaudhuri, C. (2019). Innovative Outlier Removal Techniques to Enhance Signature Authentication Accuracy for Smart Society. [IJDST]. *International Journal of Distributed Systems and Technologies*, *10*(2), 64–83. doi:10.4018/IJDST.2019040104

Dhanda, N., Datta, S. S., & Dhanda, M. (2019). Machine Learning Algorithms. In H. D. Purnomo (Ed.), *Computational Intelligence in the Internet of Things* (pp. 210–233). IGI Global., doi:10.4018/978-1-5225-7955-7.ch009

Dhankhar, A., Juneja, S., Juneja, A., & Bali, V. (2021). Kernel Parameter Tuning to Tweak the Performance of Classifiers for Identification of Heart Diseases. [IJEHMC]. *International Journal of E-Health and Medical Communications*, *12*(4), 1–16. doi:10.4018/IJEHMC.20210701.oa1

Ramachandran, Dharini., & Parvathi R. (2019). Enhanced Event Detection in Twitter Through Feature Analysis. [IJITWE]. *International Journal of Information Technology and Web Engineering*, *14*(3), 1–15. doi:10.4018/IJITWE.2019070101

Dif, N., & Elberrichi, Z. (2018). A Multi-Verse Optimizer Approach for Instance Selection and Optimizing 1-NN Algorithm. [IJSITA]. *International Journal of Strategic Information Technology and Applications*, *9*(2), 35–49. doi:10.4018/IJSITA.2018040103

Dif, N., & Elberrichi, Z. (2020). A New Intra Fine-Tuning Method Between Histopathological Datasets in Deep Learning. [IJSSMET]. *International Journal of Service Science, Management, Engineering, and Technology*, *11*(2), 16–40. doi:10.4018/IJSSMET.2020040102

Dif, N., & Elberrichi, Z. (2020). Efficient Regularization Framework for Histopathological Image Classification Using Convolutional Neural Networks. [IJCINI]. *International Journal of Cognitive Informatics and Natural Intelligence*, *14*(4), 62–81. doi:10.4018/IJCINI.2020100104

Do, P. (2019). A System for Natural Language Interaction With the Heterogeneous Information Network. In B. Gupta & D. P. Agrawal (Eds.), *Handbook of Research on Cloud Computing and Big Data Applications in IoT* (pp. 271–301). IGI Global., doi:10.4018/978-1-5225-8407-0.ch014

Donyanavard, B., Rahmani, A. M., Jantsch, A., Mutlu, O., & Dutt, N. (2021). Intelligent Management of Mobile Systems Through Computational Self-Awareness. In V. Milutinović & M. Kotlar (Eds.), *Handbook of Research on Methodologies and Applications of Supercomputing* (pp. 41–73). IGI Global., doi:10.4018/978-1-7998-7156-9.ch004

Doong, S. H. (2018). Autonomous Human Flow Counting Service With Deep Neural Network. [IJSSOE]. *International Journal of Systems and Service-Oriented Engineering*, *8*(3), 18–36. doi:10.4018/IJSSOE.2018070102

Doong, S. H. (2021). Automatic Reel Editing in Chip on Film Quality Control With Computer Vision. [IJSSOE]. *International Journal of Systems and Service-Oriented Engineering*, *11*(1), 1–14. doi:10.4018/IJSSOE.2021010101

Doshi, A. A., Sevugan, P., & Swarnalatha, P. (2018). Modified Support Vector Machine Algorithm to Reduce Misclassification and Optimizing Time Complexity. In P. Swarnalatha & P. Sevugan (Eds.), *Big Data Analytics for Satellite Image Processing and Remote Sensing* (pp. 34–56). IGI Global., doi:10.4018/978-1-5225-3643-7.ch003

Dubey, A. D., & Kumar, B. A. (2019). A Novel Cognitive Approach for Measuring the Trust in Robots. [JITR]. *Journal of Information Technology Research*, *12*(3), 60–73. doi:10.4018/JITR.2019070104

Dubey, D., Kushwah, D. S., & Dubey, D. (2018). Study of Feature Apprehension Using Soft Computing Approaches. In U. P. Singh, A. Tiwari, & R. K. Singh (Eds.), *Soft-Computing-Based Nonlinear Control Systems Design* (pp. 170–190). IGI Global., doi:10.4018/978-1-5225-3531-7.ch009

Dubey, R., Maurya, J. P., & Thakur, R. S. (2018). Detection Approaches for Categorization of Spam and Legitimate E-Mail. In V. Tiwari, R. S. Thakur, B. Tiwari, & S. Gupta (Eds.), *Handbook of Research on Pattern Engineering System Development for Big Data Analytics* (pp. 274–296). IGI Global., doi:10.4018/978-1-5225-3870-7.ch016

Dwivedi, R. K., Kumar, R., & Buyya, R. (2021). Gaussian Distribution-Based Machine Learning Scheme for Anomaly Detection in Healthcare Sensor Cloud. [IJCAC]. *International Journal of Cloud Applications and Computing*, *11*(1), 52–72. doi:10.4018/IJCAC.2021010103

Efeoglu, E., & Tuna, G. (2021). Traditional and Innovative Approaches for Detecting Hazardous Liquids. In J. Zhao & V. Kumar (Eds.), *Handbook of Research on Innovations and Applications of AI, IoT, and Cognitive Technologies* (pp. 290–309). IGI Global., doi:10.4018/978-1-7998-6870-5.ch020

Ekanayake, J. B. (2021). Predicting Bug Priority Using Topic Modelling in Imbalanced Learning Environments. [IJSSOE]. *International Journal of Systems and Service-Oriented Engineering*, *11*(1), 31–42. doi:10.4018/IJSSOE.2021010103

Eke, H., Petrovski, A., & Ahriz, H. (2020). Handling Minority Class Problem in Threats Detection Based on Heterogeneous Ensemble Learning Approach. [IJSSSP]. *International Journal of Systems and Software Security and Protection*, *11*(2), 13–37. doi:10.4018/IJSSSP.2020070102

Ekpezu, A. O., Umoh, E. E., Koranteng, F. N., & Abandoh-Sam, J. A. (2020). Biometric Authentication Schemes and Methods on Mobile Devices. In Yaokumah, W., Rajarajan, M., Abdulai, J., Wiafe, I., & Katsriku, F. A. (Ed.), Modern Theories and Practices for Cyber Ethics and Security Compliance (pp. 172-192). IGI Global. https://doi.org/ doi:10.4018/978-1-7998-3149-5.ch011

El-Alami, F., El Alaoui, S. O., & En-Nahnahi, N. (2020). Deep Neural Models and Retrofitting for Arabic Text Categorization. [IJIIT]. *International Journal of Intelligent Information Technologies*, *16*(2), 74–86. doi:10.4018/IJIIT.2020040104

Elleuch, M., & Kherallah, M. (2019). Boosting of Deep Convolutional Architectures for Arabic Handwriting Recognition. [IJMDEM]. *International Journal of Multimedia Data Engineering and Management*, *10*(4), 26–45. doi:10.4018/IJMDEM.2019100102

Elmurngi, E. I., & Gherbi, A. (2020). Building Sentiment Analysis Model and Compute Reputation Scores in E-Commerce Environment Using Machine Learning Techniques. [IJOCI]. *International Journal of Organizational and Collective Intelligence*, *10*(1), 32–62. doi:10.4018/IJOCI.2020010103

Eloy, S., Lopes, P. F., Pedro, T. M., Ourique, L., & Dias, L. S. (2018). Mobile Apps for Acting on the Physical Space. In S. Paiva (Ed.), *Mobile Applications and Solutions for Social Inclusion* (pp. 48–82). IGI Global., doi:10.4018/978-1-5225-5270-3.ch003

Falah Hassan Ali Al-akashi. (2019). Abstract Retrieval over Wikipedia Articles Using Neural Network. [IJSSCI]. *International Journal of Software Science and Computational Intelligence*, *11*(3), 26–43. doi:10.4018/IJSSCI.2019070102

Fan, G., Jin, X., & Peng, L. (2019). Application of GM (1,1) and Seasonal Cross-Trend Model in the Forecast of Tourist Population in Sanya. [IJAEC]. *International Journal of Applied Evolutionary Computation*, *10*(4), 51–64. doi:10.4018/IJAEC.2019100103

Fan, T., & Xu, J. (2020). Image Classification of Crop Diseases and Pests Based on Deep Learning and Fuzzy System. [IJDWM]. *International Journal of Data Warehousing and Mining*, *16*(2), 34–47. doi:10.4018/IJDWM.2020040103

Fantinato, M., Peres, S. M., Kafeza, E., Chiu, D. K., & Hung, P. C. (2021). A Review on the Integration of Deep Learning and Service-Oriented Architecture. [JDM]. *Journal of Database Management*, *32*(3), 95–119. doi:10.4018/JDM.2021070105

Fayoumi, A. G., & Hajjar, A. F. (2020). Advanced Learning Analytics in Academic Education. [IJSWIS]. *International Journal on Semantic Web and Information Systems*, *16*(3), 70–87. doi:10.4018/IJSWIS.2020070105

Fazlali, M., & Khodamoradi, P. (2018). Metamorphic Malware Detection Using Minimal Opcode Statistical Patterns. In Y. Maleh (Ed.), *Security and Privacy Management, Techniques, and Protocols* (pp. 337–359). IGI Global., doi:10.4018/978-1-5225-5583-4.ch014

Figueroa, C., Vagliano, I., Rocha, O. R., Torchiano, M., Zucker, C. F., Corrales, J. C., & Morisio, M. (2019). Executing, Comparing, and Reusing Linked-Data-Based Recommendation Algorithms With the Allied Framework. In M. D. Lytras, N. Aljohani, E. Damiani, & K. Chui (Eds.), *Semantic Web Science and Real-World Applications* (pp. 18–47). IGI Global., doi:10.4018/978-1-5225-7186-5.ch002

Fihavango, T., Mohsini, M. H., & Mselle, L. J. (2021). Using Data Mining Techniques to Predict Obstetric Fistula in Tanzania. In F. M. Nafukho & A. Boniface Makulilo (Eds.), *Handbook of Research on Nurturing Industrial Economy for Africa's Development* (pp. 169–191). IGI Global., doi:10.4018/978-1-7998-6471-4.ch009

Filiz, D., & Tanrıöver, Ö. Ö. (2020). An Exploration of Machine Learning Methods for Biometric Identification Based on Keystroke Dynamics. In G. Bekdaş, S. M. Nigdeli, & M. Yücel (Eds.), *Artificial Intelligence and Machine Learning Applications in Civil, Mechanical, and Industrial Engineering* (pp. 259–270). IGI Global., doi:10.4018/978-1-7998-0301-0.ch014

Firoze, A., Deb, T., & Rahman, R. M. (2018). Deep Learning and Data Balancing Approaches in Mining Hospital Surveillance Data. In J. Tan (Ed.), *Handbook of Research on Emerging Perspectives on Healthcare Information Systems and Informatics* (pp. 140–212). IGI Global., doi:10.4018/978-1-5225-5460-8.ch008

Fong, S. (2020). MEASURING SIMILARITY BETWEEN BIOMEDICAL DATA BY USING FURIA ENSEMBLES RULE-BASED CLASSIFICATION. [IJEACH]. *International Journal of Extreme Automation and Connectivity in Healthcare*, 2(1), 116–127. doi:10.4018/IJEACH.2020010107

Fouad, K. M., Elsheshtawy, T., & Dawood, M. F. (2021). Intelligent Approach for Enhancing Prediction Issues in Scalable Data Mining. [IJSKD]. *International Journal of Sociotechnology and Knowledge Development*, 13(2), 119–152. doi:10.4018/IJSKD.2021040108

Foung, D. (2019). Redesigning Prediction Algorithms for At-Risk Students in Higher Education. In A. Raman & M. Rathakrishnan (Eds.), *Redesigning Higher Education Initiatives for Industry 4.0* (pp. 232–250). IGI Global., doi:10.4018/978-1-5225-7832-1.ch014

Fujisawa, K., Nunome, A., Shibayama, K., & Hirata, H. (2018). Design Space Exploration for Implementing a Software-Based Speculative Memory System. [IJSI]. *International Journal of Software Innovation*, 6(2), 37–49. doi:10.4018/IJSI.2018040104

Funes, A., & Dasso, A. (2021). Methods and Techniques of Data Mining. In Khosrow-Pour D.B.A., M. (Ed.), Encyclopedia of Information Science and Technology, Fifth Edition (pp. 749-767). IGI Global. https://doi.org/doi:10.4018/978-1-7998-3479-3.ch051

G., M., Prabu, S., & B. C., L. (2021). Detecting DDoS Attack. In Swarnalatha, P., & Prabu, S. (Ed.), *Applications of Artificial Intelligence for Smart Technology* (pp. 55-66). IGI Global. https://doi.org/ doi:10.4018/978-1-7998-3335-2.ch004

G., S. S., L., M., & Patil, R. (2021). Real-Time Problems to Be Solved by the Combination of IoT, Big Data, and Cloud Technologies. In Velayutham, S. (Ed.), *Challenges and Opportunities for the Convergence of IoT, Big Data, and Cloud Computing* (pp. 265-276). IGI Global. https://doi.org/ doi:10.4018/978-1-7998-3111-2.ch015

Gadekallu, T., Kidwai, B., Sharma, S., Pareek, R., & Karnam, S. (2019). Application of Data Mining Techniques in Weather Forecasting. In D. S. Rajput, R. S. Thakur, & S. M. Basha (Eds.), *Sentiment Analysis and Knowledge Discovery in Contemporary Business* (pp. 162–174). IGI Global., doi:10.4018/978-1-5225-4999-4.ch010

Gadekallu, T., Soni, A., Sarkar, D., & Kuruva, L. (2019). Application of Sentiment Analysis in Movie reviews. In D. S. Rajput, R. S. Thakur, & S. M. Basha (Eds.), *Sentiment Analysis and Knowledge Discovery in Contemporary Business* (pp. 77–90). IGI Global., doi:10.4018/978-1-5225-4999-4.ch006

Galiautdinov, R., & Mkrttchian, V. (2020). Brain Machine Interface for Avatar Control and Estimation for Educational Purposes Based on Neural AI Plugs. In V. Mkrttchian, E. Aleshina, & L. Gamidullaeva (Eds.), *Avatar-Based Control, Estimation, Communications, and Development of Neuron Multi-Functional Technology Platforms* (pp. 294–316). IGI Global., doi:10.4018/978-1-7998-1581-5.ch016

Galli, B. J. (2020). Application of Statistical Analysis Tools and Concepts to Big Data and Predictive Analytics to New Product Development. [IJoSE]. *International Journal of Strategic Engineering, 3*(1), 17–35. doi:10.4018/IJoSE.2020010102

Ganapathy, J., & V., U. (2019). Reasoning Temporally Attributed Spatial Entity Knowledge Towards Qualitative Inference of Geographic Process. [IJIIT]. *International Journal of Intelligent Information Technologies, 15*(2), 32–53. doi:10.4018/IJIIT.2019040103

Gangadhar, P., Hota, A. K., Rao, M. V., & Rao, V. V. (2019). Performance of Memory Virtualization Using Global Memory Resource Balancing. [IJCAC]. *International Journal of Cloud Applications and Computing*, *9*(1), 16–32. doi:10.4018/IJCAC.2019010102

Gangal, A., Kumar, P., Kumari, S., & Saini, A. (2021). Prediction Models for Healthcare Using Machine Learning. In G. Rani & P. K. Tiwari (Eds.), *Handbook of Research on Disease Prediction Through Data Analytics and Machine Learning* (pp. 70–91). IGI Global., doi:10.4018/978-1-7998-2742-9.ch005

Gao, T., & Wang, G. Y. (2020). Brain Signal Classification Based on Deep CNN. [IJSPPC]. *International Journal of Security and Privacy in Pervasive Computing*, *12*(2), 17–29. doi:10.4018/IJSPPC.2020040102

Garanayak, M., Sahu, G., Mohanty, S. N., & Jagadev, A. K. (2021). Agricultural Recommendation System for Crops Using Different Machine Learning Regression Methods. [IJAEIS]. *International Journal of Agricultural and Environmental Information Systems*, *12*(1), 1–20. doi:10.4018/IJAEIS.20210101.oa1

Garg, N., & Sharma, K. (2020). Machine Learning in Text Analysis. In A. Solanki, S. Kumar, & A. Nayyar (Eds.), *Handbook of Research on Emerging Trends and Applications of Machine Learning* (pp. 383–402). IGI Global., doi:10.4018/978-1-5225-9643-1.ch018

Gasu, D. K. (2020). Threat Detection in Cyber Security Using Data Mining and Machine Learning Techniques. In Yaokumah, W., Rajarajan, M., Abdulai, J., Wiafe, I., & Katsriku, F. A. (Eds.), Modern Theories and Practices for Cyber Ethics and Security Compliance (pp. 234-253). IGI Global. https://doi.org/ doi:10.4018/978-1-7998-3149-5.ch015

Gavrilov, A. D., Jordache, A., Vasdani, M., & Deng, J. (2018). Preventing Model Overfitting and Underfitting in Convolutional Neural Networks. [IJSSCI]. *International Journal of Software Science and Computational Intelligence*, *10*(4), 19–28. doi:10.4018/IJSSCI.2018100102

Gazeloğlu, C., Toyganözü, Z. H., Toyganözü, C., & Keleş, M. K. (2019). Classification of the Usage of Wikipedia as a Tool of Teaching in Higher Education With Decision Tree Model. In K. Vatansever & Y. Akgül (Eds.), *Multi-Criteria Decision-Making Models for Website Evaluation* (pp. 44–63). IGI Global., doi:10.4018/978-1-5225-8238-0.ch003

Geetha, M. C. S., & Shanthi, I. E. (2020). Forecasting the Crop Yield Production in Trichy District Using Fuzzy C-Means Algorithm and Multilayer Perceptron (MLP). [IJKSS]. *International Journal of Knowledge and Systems Science, 11*(3), 83–98. doi:10.4018/IJKSS.2020070105

Geetha, N., & Sankar, A. (2020). An Intelligent IoT-Based Health Monitoring System for Tribal People. In P. Pankajavalli & G. Karthick (Eds.), *Incorporating the Internet of Things in Healthcare Applications and Wearable Devices* (pp. 137–149). IGI Global., doi:10.4018/978-1-7998-1090-2.ch008

Geethanjali, M., & Ramadoss, H. (2019). Fault Diagnosis of Induction Motors Using Motor Current Signature Analysis. In M. Irfan (Ed.), *Advanced Condition Monitoring and Fault Diagnosis of Electric Machines* (pp. 1–37). IGI Global., doi:10.4018/978-1-5225-6989-3.ch001

Ghosal, A., Dutta, S., & Banerjee, D. (2020). A Hierarchical Stratagem for Classification of String Instrument. [IJWLTT]. *International Journal of Web-Based Learning and Teaching Technologies, 15*(1), 1–23. doi:10.4018/IJWLTT.2020010101

Ghosal, S., & Jain, A. (2021). Research Journey of Hate Content Detection From Cyberspace. In F. Pinarbasi & M. Taskiran (Eds.), *Natural Language Processing for Global and Local Business* (pp. 200–225). IGI Global., doi:10.4018/978-1-7998-4240-8.ch009

Ghosh, A., Ho, C. C., & Bestak, R. (2020). Secured Energy-Efficient Routing in Wireless Sensor Networks Using Machine Learning Algorithm. In Sagayam, K., Bhushan, B., Andrushia, A., & Albuquerque, V. C. (Ed.), Deep Learning Strategies for Security Enhancement in Wireless Sensor Networks (pp. 23-41). IGI Global. https://doi.org/ doi:10.4018/978-1-7998-5068-7.ch002

Ghosh, R., Cingreddy, A. R., Melapu, V., Joginipelli, S., & Kar, S. (2021). Application of Artificial Intelligence and Machine Learning Techniques in Classifying Extent of Dementia Across Alzheimer's Image Data. [IJQSPR]. *International Journal of Quantitative Structure-Property Relationships, 6*(2), 29–46. doi:10.4018/IJQSPR.2021040103

Ghosh, S. K., Dey, S., & Ghosh, A. (2019). Knowledge Generation Using Sentiment Classification Involving Machine Learning on E-Commerce. [IJBAN]. *International Journal of Business Analytics, 6*(2), 74–90. doi:10.4018/IJBAN.2019040104

Giang, N. L., Son, L. H., Tuan, N. A., Ngan, T. T., Son, N. N., & Thang, N. T. (2021). Filter-Wrapper Incremental Algorithms for Finding Reduct in Incomplete Decision Systems When Adding and Deleting an Attribute Set. [IJDWM]. *International Journal of Data Warehousing and Mining*, *17*(2), 39–62. doi:10.4018/IJDWM.2021040103

Gite, S., & Agrawal, H. (2019). Early Prediction of Driver's Action Using Deep Neural Networks. [IJIRR]. *International Journal of Information Retrieval Research*, *9*(2), 11–27. doi:10.4018/IJIRR.2019040102

Glad Shiya, V. B., & K., S. (2021). Language Processing and Python. In Tanwar, P., Saxena, A., & Priya, C. (Ed.), Deep Natural Language Processing and AI Applications for Industry 5.0 (pp. 93-119). IGI Global. https://doi.org/ doi:10.4018/978-1-7998-7728-8.ch006

Godoy, P. D., Marianetti, O. L., & Garino, C. G. (2021). Experiences With Computer Architecture Remote Laboratories. In F. V. Cipolla-Ficarra (Ed.), *Handbook of Research on Software Quality Innovation in Interactive Systems* (pp. 133–153). IGI Global., doi:10.4018/978-1-7998-7010-4.ch005

Goel, N. (2021). Comparison of Performance of Various Machine Learning Classification Techniques With Ensemble Classifiers for Prediction of Chronic Kidney Disease. In S. Das & S. R. Mondal (Eds.), *Innovations in Digital Branding and Content Marketing* (pp. 245–270). IGI Global., doi:10.4018/978-1-7998-4420-4.ch011

Goel, N. (2021). Performance Analysis of Classification Techniques With Feature Selection Method for Prediction of Chronic Kidney Disease. In S. Das & S. R. Mondal (Eds.), *Innovations in Digital Branding and Content Marketing* (pp. 220–244). IGI Global., doi:10.4018/978-1-7998-4420-4.ch010

Gogi, V. J., & M. N., V. (2021). Characterization of Elevated Tumor Markers in Diagnosis of HCC Using Data Mining Methods. In Khosrow-Pour D.B.A., M. (Ed.), *Encyclopedia of Information Science and Technology, Fifth Edition* (pp. 847-855). IGI Global. https://doi.org/ doi:10.4018/978-1-7998-3479-3.ch058

Gond, S., & Singh, S. (2019). Dynamic Load Balancing Using Hybrid Approach. [IJCAC]. *International Journal of Cloud Applications and Computing*, *9*(3), 75–88. doi:10.4018/IJCAC.2019070105

Gooroochurn, M., Kerr, D., & Bouazza-Marouf, K. (2020). A Machine Learning Approach to Tracking and Characterizing Planar or Near Planar Fluid Flow. [IJNCR]. *International Journal of Natural Computing Research*, 9(3), 76–87. doi:10.4018/IJNCR.2020070105

Goosen, L. (2019). Technology-Supported Teaching and Research Methods for Educators. In L. N. Makewa, B. M. Ngussa, & J. M. Kuboja (Eds.), *Technology-Supported Teaching and Research Methods for Educators* (pp. 128–148). IGI Global., doi:10.4018/978-1-5225-5915-3.ch007

Gorbachenko, V. (2019). Digital Model for Diagnosis of Postoperative Complications in Medicine Using Bioinformatics. [IJARB]. *International Journal of Applied Research in Bioinformatics*, 9(2), 1–23. doi:10.4018/IJARB.2019070101

Gorbachev, S. V., & Abramova, T. V. (2018). Improving the Classification Accuracy of Multidimensional Overlapping Objects Based on Neuro-Fuzzy Analysis of Generalized Patterns. In S. De, S. Bhattacharyya, & P. Dutta (Eds.), *Intelligent Multidimensional Data and Image Processing* (pp. 320–358). IGI Global., doi:10.4018/978-1-5225-5246-8.ch013

Govindarajan, M. (2021). Big Data Mining Algorithms. In Khosrow-Pour D.B.A., M. (Eds.), Encyclopedia of Information Science and Technology, Fifth Edition (pp. 768-777). IGI Global. https://doi.org/ doi:10.4018/978-1-7998-3479-3.ch052

Govindarajan, M. (2021). Introduction to Data Science. In B. Patil & M. Vohra (Eds.), *Handbook of Research on Engineering, Business, and Healthcare Applications of Data Science and Analytics* (pp. 1–18). IGI Global., doi:10.4018/978-1-7998-3053-5.ch001

Goyal, S., & Saxena, A. (2021). Creditworthiness Assessment Using Natural Language Processing. In P. Tanwar, A. Saxena, & C. Priya (Eds.), *Deep Natural Language Processing and AI Applications for Industry 5.0* (pp. 120–141). IGI Global., doi:10.4018/978-1-7998-7728-8.ch007

Guggulothu, T., & Moiz, S. A. (2019). Detection of Shotgun Surgery and Message Chain Code Smells using Machine Learning Techniques. [IJRSDA]. *International Journal of Rough Sets and Data Analysis*, 6(2), 34–50. doi:10.4018/IJRSDA.2019040103

Güleç, N., Öztürk, C., & Efendioğlu, D. (2018). The Status of Foreign Trades Under Globalization in Developing and Developed Countries With Turkey. In A. C. Özer (Ed.), *Globalization and Trade Integration in Developing Countries* (pp. 167–201). IGI Global., doi:10.4018/978-1-5225-4032-8.ch008

Gulmez, H. (2020). Detection of Chronic Disease in Primary Care Using Artificial Intelligence Techniques. In M. Gul, E. Celik, S. Mete, & F. Serin (Eds.), *Computational Intelligence and Soft Computing Applications in Healthcare Management Science* (pp. 195–219). IGI Global., doi:10.4018/978-1-7998-2581-4.ch009

Gulyani, V., Dhiman, T., & Bhushan, B. (2020). Introducing Machine Learning to Wireless Sensor Networks. In Sagayam, K., Bhushan, B., Andrushia, A., & Albuquerque, V. C. (Ed.), Deep Learning Strategies for Security Enhancement in Wireless Sensor Networks (pp. 1-22). IGI Global. https:// doi.org/ doi:10.4018/978-1-7998-5068-7.ch001

Gumus, F., & Yiltas-Kaplan, D. (2020). Congestion Prediction System With Artificial Neural Networks. [IJITN]. *International Journal of Interdisciplinary Telecommunications and Networking*, *12*(3), 28–43. doi:10.4018/ IJITN.2020070103

Gunjan, V. K., Pathak, R., & Singh, O. (2019). Understanding Image Classification Using TensorFlow Deep Learning - Convolution Neural Network. [IJHIoT]. *International Journal of Hyperconnectivity and the Internet of Things*, *3*(2), 19–37. doi:10.4018/IJHIoT.2019070103

Guo, J., Shan, K., Wu, H., Bie, R., You, W., & Lu, D. (2018). Research on Facial Expression Recognition Technology Based on Convolutional-Neural-Network Structure. [IJSI]. *International Journal of Software Innovation*, *6*(4), 103–116. doi:10.4018/IJSI.2018100108

Gupta, A. (2021). Artificial Intelligence Approaches to Detect Neurodegenerative Disease From Medical Records. In G. Rani & P. K. Tiwari (Eds.), *Handbook of Research on Disease Prediction Through Data Analytics and Machine Learning* (pp. 254–267). IGI Global., doi:10.4018/978-1-7998-2742-9.ch013

Gupta, A. K., Agarwal, A., & Garg, R. R. (2019). Analysis of Back Propagation Neural Network Method for Heart Disease Recognition. [IJOCI]. *International Journal of Organizational and Collective Intelligence*, *9*(2), 45–54. doi:10.4018/IJOCI.2019040104

Gupta, S., & Singh, J. (2019). Review of Sentiment Detection. [IJDAI]. *International Journal of Distributed Artificial Intelligence*, *11*(1), 44–53. doi:10.4018/IJDAI.2019010105

Gupta, S., Goel, L., & Agarwal, A. K. (2020). Technologies in Health Care Domain. [IJeC]. *International Journal of e-Collaboration*, *16*(1), 33–44. doi:10.4018/IJeC.2020010103

Gupta, S., Goel, L., & Agarwal, A. K. (2021). A Novel Framework of Health Monitoring Systems. [IJBDAH]. *International Journal of Big Data and Analytics in Healthcare*, *6*(1), 1–14. doi:10.4018/IJBDAH.20210101.oa1

Gurbeta Pokvic, L., Spahic, L., & Badnjevic, A. (2020). Implementation of Industry 4.0 in Transformation of Medical Device Maintenance Systems. In I. Karabegović, A. Kovačević, L. Banjanović-Mehmedović, & P. Dašić (Eds.), *Handbook of Research on Integrating Industry 4.0 in Business and Manufacturing* (pp. 512–532). IGI Global., doi:10.4018/978-1-7998-2725-2.ch023

Gurle, A. S., Barathe, S. N., Gangule, R. S., Jagtap, S. D., & Patankar, T. (2019). Survey Paper on Tomato Crop Disease Detection and Pest Management. [IJAEC]. *International Journal of Applied Evolutionary Computation*, *10*(3), 10–18. doi:10.4018/IJAEC.2019070102

Hajiarbabi, M., & Agah, A. (2018). Novel Techniques in Skin and Face Detection in Color Images. In J. Garcia-Rodriguez (Ed.), *Advancements in Computer Vision and Image Processing* (pp. 190–220). IGI Global., doi:10.4018/978-1-5225-5628-2.ch008

Hakak, N., & Kirmani, M. (2018). Opinion Mining of Twitter Events using Supervised Learning. [IJSE]. *International Journal of Synthetic Emotions*, *9*(2), 23–36. doi:10.4018/IJSE.2018070102

Haldorai, A., & Ramu, A. (2018). An Intelligent-Based Wavelet Classifier for Accurate Prediction of Breast Cancer. In S. De, S. Bhattacharyya, & P. Dutta (Eds.), *Intelligent Multidimensional Data and Image Processing* (pp. 306–319). IGI Global., doi:10.4018/978-1-5225-5246-8.ch012

Hallur, V. C., Hegadi, R. S., & Hegadi, R. S. (2019). Handwritten Kannada Numerals Recognition by Using Zone Features and CNN Classifier. [IJTHI]. *International Journal of Technology and Human Interaction*, *15*(4), 63–79. doi:10.4018/IJTHI.2019100106

Hang, F. I., & Fong, S. (2020). AIR POLLUTANTS CONCENTRATION PREDICTION BASED ON TRANSFER LEARNING AND RECURRENT NEURAL NETWORK. [IJEACH]. *International Journal of Extreme Automation and Connectivity in Healthcare, 2*(1), 103–115. doi:10.4018/IJEACH.2020010106

Hannache, O., & Batouche, M. C. (2020). Neural Network-Based Approach for Detection and Mitigation of DDoS Attacks in SDN Environments. [IJISP]. *International Journal of Information Security and Privacy, 14*(3), 50–71. doi:10.4018/IJISP.2020070104

Hao, R., Yang, H., & Zhou, Z. (2019). Driving Behavior Evaluation Model Base on Big Data From Internet of Vehicles. [IJACI]. *International Journal of Ambient Computing and Intelligence, 10*(4), 78–95. doi:10.4018/IJACI.2019100105

Harikumar, S. (2020). Blended Models for Nearest Neighbour Algorithms for High Dimensional Smart Medical Data. In C. Chakraborty (Ed.), *Smart Medical Data Sensing and IoT Systems Design in Healthcare* (pp. 48–75). IGI Global., doi:10.4018/978-1-7998-0261-7.ch003

Hashmi, S. N., Kumar, K., Khandelwal, S., Lochan, D., & Mittal, S. (2019). Real Time License Plate Recognition from Video Streams using Deep Learning. [IJIRR]. *International Journal of Information Retrieval Research, 9*(1), 65–87. doi:10.4018/IJIRR.2019010105

Hegde, R. M., & Kenchannavar, H. H. (2019). A Survey on Predicting Resident Intentions Using Contextual Modalities in Smart Home. [IJAPUC]. *International Journal of Advanced Pervasive and Ubiquitous Computing, 11*(4), 44–59. doi:10.4018/IJAPUC.2019100104

Hernandez, M. K., Howard, C., Livingood, R., & Calongne, C. (2019). Applications of Decision Tree Analytics on Semi-Structured North Atlantic Tropical Cyclone Forecasts. [IJSKD]. *International Journal of Sociotechnology and Knowledge Development, 11*(2), 31–53. doi:10.4018/IJSKD.2019040103

Hirata, H., & Nunome, A. (2020). A Modified Parallel Heapsort Algorithm. [IJSI]. *International Journal of Software Innovation, 8*(3), 1–18. doi:10.4018/IJSI.2020070101

Hirata, H., & Nunome, A. (2020). Decoupling Computation and Result Write-Back for Thread-Level Parallelization. [IJSI]. *International Journal of Software Innovation, 8*(3), 19–34. doi:10.4018/IJSI.2020070102

Hiremath, S. R., C. P., & I., S. K. (2021). An Investigation Screen for Sleep Disorders Using AI/ML. In Kumar, M., Kumar, R., & Vaithiyanathan, D. (Ed.), Advancing the Investigation and Treatment of Sleep Disorders Using AI (pp. 161-183). IGI Global. https://doi.org/ doi:10.4018/978-1-7998-8018-9.ch009

Hlioui, F., Aloui, N., & Gargouri, F. (2020). Withdrawal Prediction Framework in Virtual Learning Environment. [IJSSMET]. *International Journal of Service Science, Management, Engineering, and Technology*, *11*(3), 47–64. doi:10.4018/IJSSMET.2020070104

Hlioui, F., Aloui, N., & Gargouri, F. (2021). A Withdrawal Prediction Model of At-Risk Learners Based on Behavioural Indicators. [IJWLTT]. *International Journal of Web-Based Learning and Teaching Technologies*, *16*(2), 32–53. doi:10.4018/IJWLTT.2021030103

Ho, S. C., Wong, K. C., Yau, Y. K., & Yip, C. K. (2019). A Machine Learning Approach for Predicting Bank Customer Behavior in the Banking Industry. In M. S. Khan (Ed.), *Machine Learning and Cognitive Science Applications in Cyber Security* (pp. 57–83). IGI Global., doi:10.4018/978-1-5225-8100-0.ch002

Hosny, K. M., Khashaba, M. M., Khedr, W. I., & Amer, F. A. (2020). An Efficient Neural Network-Based Prediction Scheme for Heterogeneous Networks. [IJSKD]. *International Journal of Sociotechnology and Knowledge Development*, *12*(2), 63–76. doi:10.4018/IJSKD.2020040104

Hsu, K., & Ko, Y. (2019). Analysis of Operation Performance of Blast Furnace With Machine Learning Methods. In J. Darmont & S. Loudcher (Eds.), *Utilizing Big Data Paradigms for Business Intelligence* (pp. 242–269). IGI Global., doi:10.4018/978-1-5225-4963-5.ch008

Huang, J., Yuan, Z., & Zhou, X. (2019). A Learning Framework for Target Detection and Human Face Recognition in Real Time. [IJTHI]. *International Journal of Technology and Human Interaction*, *15*(3), 63–76. doi:10.4018/ IJTHI.2019070105

Husna, A., Amin, S. H., & Shah, B. (2021). Demand Forecasting in Supply Chain Management Using Different Deep Learning Methods. In A. Taghipour (Ed.), *Demand Forecasting and Order Planning in Supply Chains and Humanitarian Logistics* (pp. 140–170). IGI Global., doi:10.4018/978-1-7998-3805-0.ch005

Hussain, A., Singh, J. K., Kumar, A. R., & Harne, K. R. (2019). Rainfall-Runoff Modeling of Sutlej River Basin (India) Using Soft Computing Techniques. [IJAEIS]. *International Journal of Agricultural and Environmental Information Systems, 10*(2), 1–20. doi:10.4018/IJAEIS.2019040101

Hussain, I., & Asif, M. (2020). Detection of Anomalous Transactions in Mobile Payment Systems. [IJDA]. *International Journal of Data Analytics, 1*(2), 58–66. doi:10.4018/IJDA.2020070105

Idowu, P. A., & Balogun, J. A. (2019). Development of a Classification Model for CD4 Count of HIV Patients Using Supervised Machine Learning Algorithms. In C. Chen & S. S. Cheung (Eds.), *Computational Models for Biomedical Reasoning and Problem Solving* (pp. 149–176). IGI Global., doi:10.4018/978-1-5225-7467-5.ch006

Idrees, A. M., Eldin, F. G., Mohsen, A. M., & Hassan, H. A. (2021). Tasks, Approaches, and Avenues of Opinion Mining, Sentiment Analysis, and Emotion Analysis. In J. Zhao & J. Richards (Eds.), *E-Collaboration Technologies and Strategies for Competitive Advantage Amid Challenging Times* (pp. 171–209). IGI Global., doi:10.4018/978-1-7998-7764-6.ch006

Ilic, M., Jaddivada, R., & Gebremedhin, A. (2021). Unified Modeling for Emulating Electric Energy Systems. In V. Milutinović & M. Kotlar (Eds.), *Handbook of Research on Methodologies and Applications of Supercomputing* (pp. 179–207). IGI Global., doi:10.4018/978-1-7998-7156-9.ch013

Imamura, N., Nomiya, H., & Hochin, T. (2020). Finding Useful Features for Facial Expression Recognition and Intensity Estimation by Neural Network. [IJSI]. *International Journal of Software Innovation, 8*(2), 68–84. doi:10.4018/IJSI.2020040105

Iqbal, S., Ahmad, S., Bano, B., Akkour, K., Alghamdi, M. A., & Alothri, A. M. (2021). A Systematic Review. [IJIIT]. *International Journal of Intelligent Information Technologies, 17*(1), 1–18. doi:10.4018/IJIIT.2021010101

Iyer, S. S., & Rajagopal, S. (2020). Applications of Machine Learning in Cyber Security Domain. In P. Ganapathi & D. Shanmugapriya (Eds.), *Handbook of Research on Machine and Deep Learning Applications for Cyber Security* (pp. 64–82). IGI Global., doi:10.4018/978-1-5225-9611-0.ch004

Iyyanki, M., Jayanthi, P., & Manickam, V. (2020). Machine Learning for Health Data Analytics. In R. Kashyap & A. Kumar (Eds.), *Challenges and Applications for Implementing Machine Learning in Computer Vision* (pp. 241–270). IGI Global., doi:10.4018/978-1-7998-0182-5.ch010

Wu, J., & Tien, C. (2020). *Deep Learning Theory and Software.* IGI Global., doi:10.4018/978-1-7998-1554-9.ch002

J. Wu, & C. Tien (2020). *iOS App and Architecture of Convolutional Neural Networks.* IGI Global. https://doi.org/ doi:10.4018/978-1-7998-1554-9.ch001

Jafari, R., Razvarz, S., Gegov, A., & Paul, S. (2021). Modeling of Uncertain Nonlinear System With Z-Numbers. In Khosrow-Pour D.B.A., M. (Ed.), Encyclopedia of Information Science and Technology, Fifth Edition (pp. 290-314). IGI Global. https://doi.org/ doi:10.4018/978-1-7998-3479-3.ch022

Jagtap, A. B., Hegadi, R. S., & Santosh, K. (2019). Feature Learning for Offline Handwritten Signature Verification Using Convolutional Neural Network. [IJTHI]. *International Journal of Technology and Human Interaction, 15*(4), 54–62. doi:10.4018/IJTHI.2019100105

Jain, A., Gairola, R., Jain, S., & Arora, A. (2018). Thwarting Spam on Facebook. In H. Bansal, G. Shrivastava, G. N. Nguyen, & L. Stanciu (Eds.), *Social Network Analytics for Contemporary Business Organizations* (pp. 51–70). IGI Global., doi:10.4018/978-1-5225-5097-6.ch004

Jain, R., Goel, V., Rekhi, J. K., & Alzubi, J. A. (2020). IoT-Based Green Building. In A. Solanki & A. Nayyar (Eds.), *Green Building Management and Smart Automation* (pp. 184–207). IGI Global., doi:10.4018/978-1-5225-9754-4.ch009

Jain, T., Garg, P., Tiwari, P. K., Kuncham, V. K., Sharma, M., & Verma, V. K. (2021). Performance Prediction for Crop Irrigation Using Different Machine Learning Approaches. In R. Raut & A. D. Mihovska (Eds.), *Examining the Impact of Deep Learning and IoT on Multi-Industry Applications* (pp. 61–79). IGI Global., doi:10.4018/978-1-7998-7511-6.ch005

Jaiswal, G., Sharma, A., & Sarup, R. (2020). Machine Learning in Higher Education. In A. Solanki, S. Kumar, & A. Nayyar (Eds.), *Handbook of Research on Emerging Trends and Applications of Machine Learning* (pp. 27–46). IGI Global., doi:10.4018/978-1-5225-9643-1.ch002

Jaiswal, G., Sharma, A., & Yadav, S. K. (2019). Analytical Approach for Predicting Dropouts in Higher Education. [IJICTE]. *International Journal of Information and Communication Technology Education*, *15*(3), 89–102. doi:10.4018/IJICTE.2019070107

Jalonen, H., & Helo, T. (2020). Co-Creation of Public Service Innovation Using Open Data and Social Media. [IJIDE]. *International Journal of Innovation in the Digital Economy*, *11*(3), 64–77. doi:10.4018/IJIDE.2020070105

Jan, M., & Ahmad, H. (2020). Image Features Based Intelligent Apple Disease Prediction System. [IJAEIS]. *International Journal of Agricultural and Environmental Information Systems*, *11*(3), 31–47. doi:10.4018/IJAEIS.2020070103

Janarish Saju, C., & Ravimaran, S. (2020). A Tool to Extract Name Entity Recognition From Big Data in Banking Sectors. [IJWSR]. *International Journal of Web Services Research*, *17*(2), 18–39. doi:10.4018/IJWSR.2020040102

Janghel, R. R., Rathore, Y. K., & Tatiparti, G. (2019). Epileptic Seizure Detection and Classification Using Machine Learning. In S. Paul, P. Bhattacharya, & A. Bit (Eds.), *Early Detection of Neurological Disorders Using Machine Learning Systems* (pp. 152–164). IGI Global., doi:10.4018/978-1-5225-8567-1.ch009

Janghel, R. R., Sahu, S. P., Rathore, Y. K., Singh, S., & Pawar, U. (2019). Application of Deep Learning in Speech Recognition. In A. E. Hassanien, A. Darwish, & C. L. Chowdhary (Eds.), *Handbook of Research on Deep Learning Innovations and Trends* (pp. 59–71). IGI Global., doi:10.4018/978-1-5225-7862-8.ch004

Jawale, A., & Magar, G. (2021). Study of Feature Extraction Techniques for Sensor Data Classification. [IJICTHD]. *International Journal of Information Communication Technologies and Human Development*, *13*(1), 33–46. doi:10.4018/IJICTHD.2021010103

Jayswal, A. K. (2020). Hybrid Load-Balanced Scheduling in Scalable Cloud Environment. [IJISMD]. *International Journal of Information System Modeling and Design*, *11*(3), 62–78. doi:10.4018/IJISMD.2020070104

Jena, B., Thakar, P., Nayak, V., Nayak, G. K., & Saxena, S. (2021). Malaria Parasites Detection Using Deep Neural Network. In S. Saxena & S. Paul (Eds.), *Deep Learning Applications in Medical Imaging* (pp. 209–222). IGI Global., doi:10.4018/978-1-7998-5071-7.ch009

Jeong, J. (2019). A Training Method of Convolution Neural Network for Illumination Robust Pedestrian Detection. [IJERTCS]. *International Journal of Embedded and Real-Time Communication Systems, 10*(2), 53–65. doi:10.4018/IJERTCS.2019040104

Jesu Vedha Nayahi, J., & Gokulakrishnan, K. (2019). Medical Image Classification. In A. Swarnambiga (Ed.), *Medical Image Processing for Improved Clinical Diagnosis* (pp. 59–80). IGI Global., doi:10.4018/978-1-5225-5876-7.ch003

Ji, M., Zhang, K., & Wu, Q. (2020). Introducing a Hybrid Model SAE-BP for Regression Analysis of Soil Temperature With Hyperspectral Data. [IJACI]. *International Journal of Ambient Computing and Intelligence, 11*(3), 66–79. doi:10.4018/IJACI.2020070104

Jiang, W., Yang, M., Xie, Y., & Li, Z. (2020). Machine Learning-Based Coding Decision Making in H.265/HEVC CTU Division and Intra Prediction. [IJMCMC]. *International Journal of Mobile Computing and Multimedia Communications, 11*(2), 41–60. doi:10.4018/IJMCMC.2020040103

Jiao, L., Wu, H., Bie, R., Umek, A., & Kos, A. (2018). Towards Real-Time Multi-Sensor Golf Swing Classification Using Deep CNNs. [JDM]. *Journal of Database Management, 29*(3), 17–42. doi:10.4018/JDM.2018070102

Jiménez, R., García, V., López, A., Mendoza Carreón, A., & Ponce, A. (2021). Opinion Mining for Instructor Evaluations at the Autonomous University of Ciudad Juarez. In R. A. Pazos-Rangel, R. Florencia-Juarez, M. A. Paredes-Valverde, & G. Rivera (Eds.), *Handbook of Research on Natural Language Processing and Smart Service Systems* (pp. 427–444). IGI Global., doi:10.4018/978-1-7998-4730-4.ch020

Johri, P., Saxena, V. S., & Kumar, A. (2021). Rummage of Machine Learning Algorithms in Cancer Diagnosis. [IJEHMC]. *International Journal of E-Health and Medical Communications, 12*(1), 1–15. doi:10.4018/IJEHMC.2021010101

Jones, G. M., & Winster, S. G. (2021). Analysis of Crime Report by Data Analytics Using Python. In V. Sathiyamoorthi & A. Elci (Eds.), *Challenges and Applications of Data Analytics in Social Perspectives* (pp. 54–79). IGI Global., doi:10.4018/978-1-7998-2566-1.ch003

Jorquera Valero, J. M., Gil Pérez, M., Huertas Celdrán, A., & Martínez Pérez, G. (2020). Identification and Classification of Cyber Threats Through SSH Honeypot Systems. In B. B. Gupta & S. Srinivasagopalan (Eds.), *Handbook of Research on Intrusion Detection Systems* (pp. 105–129). IGI Global., doi:10.4018/978-1-7998-2242-4.ch006

Joshi, A., Luu, P., Tucker, D. M., & Shofner, S. D. (2019). Leveraging Models of Human Reasoning to Identify EEG Electrodes in Images With Neural Networks. In Rivas-Lopez, M., Sergiyenko, O., Flores-Fuentes, W., & Rodríguez-Quiñonez, J. C. (Ed.), Optoelectronics in Machine Vision-Based Theories and Applications (pp. 106-133). IGI Global. https://doi.org/doi:10.4018/978-1-5225-5751-7.ch005

Joshi, D., Anwarul, S., & Mishra, V. (2020). Deep Leaning Using Keras. In M. Mahrishi, K. K. Hiran, G. Meena, & P. Sharma (Eds.), *Machine Learning and Deep Learning in Real-Time Applications* (pp. 33–60). IGI Global., doi:10.4018/978-1-7998-3095-5.ch002

Juneja, A., Juneja, S., Kaur, S., & Kumar, V. (2021). Predicting Diabetes Mellitus With Machine Learning Techniques Using Multi-Criteria Decision Making. [IJIRR]. *International Journal of Information Retrieval Research*, *11*(2), 38–52. doi:10.4018/IJIRR.2021040103

Kalash, M., Rochan, M., Mohammed, N., Bruce, N., Wang, Y., & Iqbal, F. (2020). A Deep Learning Framework for Malware Classification. [IJDCF]. *International Journal of Digital Crime and Forensics*, *12*(1), 90–108. doi:10.4018/IJDCF.2020010105

Kaliappan, J., & Sundararajan, K. (2020). Machine Learning in Video Games. In A. Solanki, S. Kumar, & A. Nayyar (Eds.), *Handbook of Research on Emerging Trends and Applications of Machine Learning* (pp. 425–443). IGI Global., doi:10.4018/978-1-5225-9643-1.ch020

Kalra, V., Kashyap, I., & Kaur, H. (2021). Machine Learning and Its Application in Monitoring Diabetes Mellitus. In B. Patil & M. Vohra (Eds.), *Handbook of Research on Engineering, Business, and Healthcare Applications of Data Science and Analytics* (pp. 228–288). IGI Global., doi:10.4018/978-1-7998-3053-5.ch012

Kamboj, V. K., Sandhu, K., & Chatterjee, S. (2020). Modelling Analysis and Simulation for Reliability Prediction for Thermal Power System. In C. Bhargava (Ed.), *AI Techniques for Reliability Prediction for Electronic Components* (pp. 136–163). IGI Global., doi:10.4018/978-1-7998-1464-1.ch008

Karegowda, A. G. G., D., & M., G. (2021). Deep Learning Solutions for Agricultural and Farming Activities. In Senthilnathan, K., Shanmugam, B., Goyal, D., Annapoorani, I., & Samikannu, R. (Ed.), Deep Learning Applications and Intelligent Decision Making in Engineering (pp. 256-287). IGI Global. https://doi.org/ doi:10.4018/978-1-7998-2108-3.ch011

Kari, V., & Amalanathan, G. M. (2019). Synthesis of Classification Models and Review in the Field of Machine Learning. In C. Chakraborty (Ed.), *Advanced Classification Techniques for Healthcare Analysis* (pp. 18–51). IGI Global., doi:10.4018/978-1-5225-7796-6.ch002

Kartal, B., & Sert, M. F. (2021). Review of the Studies Related to COVID-19 and Tourism Using Text Mining Techniques. In M. Demir, A. Dalgıç, & F. D. Ergen (Eds.), *Handbook of Research on the Impacts and Implications of COVID-19 on the Tourism Industry* (pp. 885–906). IGI Global., doi:10.4018/978-1-7998-8231-2.ch043

Karthick, G. S., & Pankajavalli, P. B. (2019). Healthcare IoT Architectures, Technologies, Applications, and Issues. In N. Bouchemal (Ed.), *Intelligent Systems for Healthcare Management and Delivery* (pp. 235–265). IGI Global., doi:10.4018/978-1-5225-7071-4.ch011

Karthick, G. S., & Pankajavalli, P. B. (2020). Architecting IoT based Healthcare Systems Using Machine Learning Algorithms. In P. Pankajavalli & G. Karthick (Eds.), *Incorporating the Internet of Things in Healthcare Applications and Wearable Devices* (pp. 40–66). IGI Global., doi:10.4018/978-1-7998-1090-2.ch003

Karthikeyan, T., Sekaran, K., Ranjith, D., Vinoth Kumar, V., & Balajee, J. M. (2019). Personalized Content Extraction and Text Classification Using Effective Web Scraping Techniques. [IJWP]. *International Journal of Web Portals, 11*(2), 41–52. doi:10.4018/IJWP.2019070103

Kashevnik, A., & Teslya, N. (2020). Ontology-Based Coalition Creation by Autonomous Agents in Smart Space. In S. Balandin & E. Balandina (Eds.), *Tools and Technologies for the Development of Cyber-Physical Systems* (pp. 28–50). IGI Global., doi:10.4018/978-1-7998-1974-5.ch002

Kateris, D., Gravalos, I., & Gialamas, T. (2019). Identification of Agricultural Crop Residues Using Non-Destructive Methods. In N. Razmjooy & V. V. Estrela (Eds.), *Applications of Image Processing and Soft Computing Systems in Agriculture* (pp. 114–144). IGI Global., doi:10.4018/978-1-5225-8027-0. ch005

Katsamakas, E., & Sun, H. (2020). Machine Learning Crowdfunding. [IJKBO]. *International Journal of Knowledge-Based Organizations*, *10*(2), 1–11. doi:10.4018/IJKBO.2020040101

Kaur, A., Sharma, S., & Saini, M. (2020). Code Clone Detection Using Machine Learning Techniques. [IJOSSP]. *International Journal of Open Source Software and Processes*, *11*(2), 49–75. doi:10.4018/IJOSSP.2020040104

Kaur, P., Kaur, P., & Singh, G. (2021). Diagnosis and Prognosis of Ultrasound Fetal Growth Analysis Using Neuro-Fuzzy Based on Genetic Algorithms. In G. Rani & P. K. Tiwari (Eds.), *Handbook of Research on Disease Prediction Through Data Analytics and Machine Learning* (pp. 281–342). IGI Global., doi:10.4018/978-1-7998-2742-9.ch015

Kaur, R., & Rani, R. (2020). Comparative Study on ASD Identification Using Machine and Deep Learning. In T. Wadhera & D. Kakkar (Eds.), *Interdisciplinary Approaches to Altering Neurodevelopmental Disorders* (pp. 250–270). IGI Global., doi:10.4018/978-1-7998-3069-6.ch015

Kaur, S., & Mann, K. S. (2020). Retinal Vessel Segmentation Using an Entropy-Based Optimization Algorithm. [IJHISI]. *International Journal of Healthcare Information Systems and Informatics*, *15*(2), 61–79. doi:10.4018/IJHISI.2020040105

Kavitha, G., & Elango, N. M. (2020). An Approach to Feature Selection in Intrusion Detection Systems Using Machine Learning Algorithms. [IJeC]. *International Journal of e-Collaboration*, *16*(4), 48–58. doi:10.4018/IJeC.2020100104

Kenekayoro, P. (2018). An Exploratory Study on the Use of Machine Learning to Predict Student Academic Performance. [IJKBO]. *International Journal of Knowledge-Based Organizations*, *8*(4), 67–79. doi:10.4018/IJKBO.2018100104

Kesavan, S. J., S., Y., S., & V., M. (2021). IoT Device Onboarding, Monitoring, and Management. In Velayutham, S. (Ed.), Challenges and Opportunities for the Convergence of IoT, Big Data, and Cloud Computing (pp. 196-224). IGI Global. https://doi.org/ doi:10.4018/978-1-7998-3111-2.ch012

Khadse, V. M., Mahalle, P. N., & Shinde, G. R. (2020). Statistical Study of Machine Learning Algorithms Using Parametric and Non-Parametric Tests. [IJACI]. *International Journal of Ambient Computing and Intelligence*, *11*(3), 80–105. doi:10.4018/IJACI.2020070105

Khamparia, A., & Pandey, B. (2018). SVM and PCA Based Learning Feature Classification Approaches for E-Learning System. [IJWLTT]. *International Journal of Web-Based Learning and Teaching Technologies*, *13*(2), 32–45. doi:10.4018/IJWLTT.2018040103

Khan, A. N., Cao, X., & Pitafi, A. H. (2019). Personality Traits as Predictor of M-Payment Systems. [JOEUC]. *Journal of Organizational and End User Computing*, *31*(4), 89–110. doi:10.4018/JOEUC.2019100105

Khan, A., & Madden, J. (2020). Long-Short Term Neural Network Analysis of Center of Pressure of Gait. [IJEACH]. *International Journal of Extreme Automation and Connectivity in Healthcare*, *2*(1), 15–34. doi:10.4018/IJEACH.2020010102

Khan, B., Shukla, P. K., Ahirwar, M. K., & Mishra, M. (2021). Strategic Analysis in Prediction of Liver Disease Using Different Classification Algorithms. In G. Rani & P. K. Tiwari (Eds.), *Handbook of Research on Disease Prediction Through Data Analytics and Machine Learning* (pp. 437–449). IGI Global., doi:10.4018/978-1-7998-2742-9.ch022

Khan, N. S., Muaz, M. H., Kabir, A., & Islam, M. N. (2019). A Machine Learning-Based Intelligent System for Predicting Diabetes. [IJBDAH]. *International Journal of Big Data and Analytics in Healthcare*, *4*(2), 1–20. doi:10.4018/IJBDAH.2019070101

Khan, S., Khan, A., Ullah, R., Ali, M., & Ullah, R. (2020). Insulin DNA Sequence Classification Using Levy Flight Bat With Back Propagation Algorithm. In S. Umair (Ed.), *Mobile Devices and Smart Gadgets in Medical Sciences* (pp. 232–252). IGI Global., doi:10.4018/978-1-7998-2521-0.ch011

Khatri, A., Garg, D., & Dangayach, G. S. (2019). Critical Success Factors of Sustainable Manufacturing and Procurement. [IJSESD]. *International Journal of Social Ecology and Sustainable Development*, *10*(3), 17–27. doi:10.4018/IJSESD.2019070102

Khatri, P., Agrawal, A. K., Sharma, A., Pannu, N., & Sinha, S. R. (2021). Vulnerability Assessment and Malware Analysis of Android Apps Using Machine Learning. In M. Dua & A. K. Jain (Eds.), *Handbook of Research on Machine Learning Techniques for Pattern Recognition and Information Security* (pp. 255–277). IGI Global., doi:10.4018/978-1-7998-3299-7.ch015

Khatter, K., & Malik, S. (2018). Ranking and Risk Factor Scheme for Malicious applications detection and Classifications. [IJISMD]. *International Journal of Information System Modeling and Design*, *9*(3), 67–84. doi:10.4018/IJISMD.2018070104

Khediri, A., Laouar, M. R., & Eom, S. B. (2021). Improving Intelligent Decision Making in Urban Planning. [IJBAN]. *International Journal of Business Analytics*, *8*(3), 40–58. doi:10.4018/IJBAN.2021070104

Khedr, A. E., Idrees, A. M., & Shaaban, E. (2020). Automated Ham-Spam Lexicon Generation Based on Semantic Relations Extraction. [IJeC]. *International Journal of e-Collaboration*, *16*(2), 45–64. doi:10.4018/IJeC.2020040104

Khieu, B. T., & Moh, M. (2020). Neural Network Applications in Hate Speech Detection. In S., S., & M., J. (Ed.), Neural Networks for Natural Language Processing (pp. 188-204). IGI Global. https://doi.org/ doi:10.4018/978-1-7998-1159-6.ch012

Kim, J., & Kim, H. (2018). Multidimensional Text Warehousing for Automated Text Classification. [JITR]. *Journal of Information Technology Research*, *11*(2), 168–183. doi:10.4018/JITR.2018040110

Klaine, P. V., Onireti, O., Souza, R. D., & Imran, M. A. (2019). The Role and Applications of Machine Learning in Future Self-Organizing Cellular Networks. In I. Comşa & R. Trestian (Eds.), *Next-Generation Wireless Networks Meet Advanced Machine Learning Applications* (pp. 1–23). IGI Global., doi:10.4018/978-1-5225-7458-3.ch001

Klepac, G. (2018). Using Particle Swarm Optimization Algorithm as an Optimization Tool Within Developed Neural Networks. In Y. Shi (Ed.), *Critical Developments and Applications of Swarm Intelligence* (pp. 215–244). IGI Global., doi:10.4018/978-1-5225-5134-8.ch009

Kodati, S., & Selvaraj, J. (2021). Analysis of Heart Disorder by Using Machine Learning Methods and Data Mining Techniques. In K. Senthilnathan, B. Shanmugam, D. Goyal, I. Annapoorani, & R. Samikannu (Eds.), *Deep Learning Applications and Intelligent Decision Making in Engineering* (pp. 212–221). IGI Global., doi:10.4018/978-1-7998-2108-3.ch009

Kompalli, P. L. (2018). Knowledge Discovery Using Data Stream Mining. In H. Bansal, G. Shrivastava, G. N. Nguyen, & L. Stanciu (Eds.), *Social Network Analytics for Contemporary Business Organizations* (pp. 231–258). IGI Global., doi:10.4018/978-1-5225-5097-6.ch012

Kompalli, P. L. (2019). Knowledge Discovery From Evolving Data Streams. In G., D. K. (Eds.), Machine Learning Techniques for Improved Business Analytics (pp. 19-39). IGI Global. https://doi.org/ doi:10.4018/978-1-5225-3534-8.ch002

Krishna, S., Ridha, S., & Vasant, P. (2020). Development of DNN Model for Predicting Surge Pressure Gradient During Tripping Operations. In J. J. Thomas, U. Fiore, G. P. Lechuga, V. Kharchenko, & P. Vasant (Eds.), *Handbook of Research on Smart Technology Models for Business and Industry* (pp. 294–315). IGI Global., doi:10.4018/978-1-7998-3645-2.ch012

Krishnamoorthy, M., Ahamed, B. B., Suresh, S., & Alagappan, S. (2020). Deep Learning Techniques and Optimization Strategies in Big Data Analytics. In J. J. Thomas, P. Karagoz, B. B. Ahamed, & P. Vasant (Eds.), *Deep Learning Techniques and Optimization Strategies in Big Data Analytics* (pp. 142–153). IGI Global., doi:10.4018/978-1-7998-1192-3.ch009

Kuchuk, H., Podorozhniak, A., Hlavcheva, D., & Yaloveha, V. (2020). Application of Deep Learning in the Processing of the Aerospace System's Multispectral Images. In T. Shmelova, Y. Sikirda, & A. Sterenharz (Eds.), *Handbook of Research on Artificial Intelligence Applications in the Aviation and Aerospace Industries* (pp. 134–147). IGI Global., doi:10.4018/978-1-7998-1415-3.ch005

Kuhaneswaran, B., Kumara, B. T., & Paik, I. (2020). Strengthening Post-Disaster Management Activities by Rating Social Media Corpus. [IJSSOE]. *International Journal of Systems and Service-Oriented Engineering*, *10*(1), 34–50. doi:10.4018/IJSSOE.2020010103

Kumar, A., Chauda, P., & Devrari, A. (2021). Machine Learning Approach for Brain Tumor Detection and Segmentation. [IJOCI]. *International Journal of Organizational and Collective Intelligence*, *11*(3), 68–84. doi:10.4018/IJOCI.2021070105

Kumar, A., Jaiswal, A., Garg, S., Verma, S., & Kumar, S. (2019). Sentiment Analysis Using Cuckoo Search for Optimized Feature Selection on Kaggle Tweets. [IJIRR]. *International Journal of Information Retrieval Research*, *9*(1), 1–15. doi:10.4018/IJIRR.2019010101

Kumar, A., Terang, P. P., & Bali, V. (2020). User-Based Load Visualization of Categorical Forecasted Smart Meter Data Using LSTM Network. [IJMDEM]. *International Journal of Multimedia Data Engineering and Management*, *11*(1), 30–50. doi:10.4018/IJMDEM.2020010103

Kumar, S. U., Azar, A. T., Inbarani, H. H., Liyaskar, O. J., & Almustafa, K. M. (2019). Weighted Rough Set Theory for Fetal Heart Rate Classification. [IJSKD]. *International Journal of Sociotechnology and Knowledge Development*, *11*(4), 1–19. doi:10.4018/IJSKD.2019100101

Kumar, S., & Acharya, S. (2020). Application of Machine Learning Algorithms in Stock Market Prediction. In J. J. Thomas, U. Fiore, G. P. Lechuga, V. Kharchenko, & P. Vasant (Eds.), *Handbook of Research on Smart Technology Models for Business and Industry* (pp. 153–180). IGI Global., doi:10.4018/978-1-7998-3645-2.ch007

Kumar, U., & Yadav, S. (2021). Application of Machine Learning to Analyse Biomedical Signals for Medical Diagnosis. In G. Rani & P. K. Tiwari (Eds.), *Handbook of Research on Disease Prediction Through Data Analytics and Machine Learning* (pp. 205–236). IGI Global., doi:10.4018/978-1-7998-2742-9.ch011

Labiod, Y., Korba, A. A., & Ghoualmi-Zine, N. (2021). Detecting DDoS Attacks in IoT Environment. [IJISP]. *International Journal of Information Security and Privacy*, *15*(2), 145–180. doi:10.4018/IJISP.2021040108

Related Readings

Lakkad, A. K., Bhadaniya, R. D., Shah, V. N., & Lavanya, K. (2021). Complex Events Processing on Live News Events Using Apache Kafka and Clustering Techniques. [IJIIT]. *International Journal of Intelligent Information Technologies*, *17*(1), 39–52. doi:10.4018/IJIIT.2021010103

Lakshmi, B., & Parthasarathy, S. (2019). Human Action Recognition Using Median Background and Max Pool Convolution with Nearest Neighbor. [IJACI]. *International Journal of Ambient Computing and Intelligence*, *10*(2), 34–47. doi:10.4018/IJACI.2019040103

Lal, A. M., Reddy, B. K., & D., A. (2020). Review on Various Machine Learning and Deep Learning Techniques for Prediction and Classification of Quotidian Datasets. In Voulodimos, A., & Doulamis, A. (Ed.), *Recent Advances in 3D Imaging, Modeling, and Reconstruction* (pp. 296-323). IGI Global. https://doi.org/ doi:10.4018/978-1-5225-5294-9.ch014

Lamsal, R., & Kumar, T. V. (2020). Classifying Emergency Tweets for Disaster Response. [IJDREM]. *International Journal of Disaster Response and Emergency Management*, *3*(1), 14–29. doi:10.4018/IJDREM.2020010102

Lamsal, R., & Kumar, T. V. (2021). Twitter-Based Disaster Response Using Recurrent Nets. [IJSKD]. *International Journal of Sociotechnology and Knowledge Development*, *13*(3), 133–150. doi:10.4018/IJSKD.2021070108

Lappas, P. Z., & Yannacopoulos, A. N. (2021). Credit Scoring. In B. Christiansen & T. Škrinjarić (Eds.), *Handbook of Research on Applied AI for International Business and Marketing Applications* (pp. 580–605). IGI Global., doi:10.4018/978-1-7998-5077-9.ch028

Lasisi, A., Tairan, N., Ghazali, R., Mashwani, W. K., Qasem, S. N., Harish Kumar, G. R., & Arora, A. (2019). Predicting Crude Oil Price Using Fuzzy Rough Set and Bio-Inspired Negative Selection Algorithm. [IJSIR]. *International Journal of Swarm Intelligence Research*, *10*(4), 25–37. doi:10.4018/IJSIR.2019100102

Latif, R. M., Ferzund, J., Farhan, M., Jhanjhi, N. Z., & Umer, M. (2021). A Case Study of Career Counseling for ICT. In N. Zaman, K. Rafique, & V. Ponnusamy (Eds.), *ICT Solutions for Improving Smart Communities in Asia* (pp. 162–184). IGI Global., doi:10.4018/978-1-7998-7114-9.ch008

Latifinavid, M., Elisevich, K., & Soltanian-Zadeh, H. (2019). Algorithmic Analysis of Clinical, Neuropsychological, and Imaging Data in Localization-Related Epilepsy. In K. Chui & M. D. Lytras (Eds.), *Computational Methods and Algorithms for Medicine and Optimized Clinical Practice* (pp. 46–79). IGI Global., doi:10.4018/978-1-5225-8244-1.ch004

Latreche, A., & Benyahia, K. (2021). A New Bio-Inspired Method for Spam Image-Based Emails Filtering. [IJOCI]. *International Journal of Organizational and Collective Intelligence*, *11*(2), 29–50. doi:10.4018/ IJOCI.2021040102

Laughlin, B., Sankaranarayanan, K., & El-Khatib, K. (2020). A Service Architecture Using Machine Learning to Contextualize Anomaly Detection. [JDM]. *Journal of Database Management*, *31*(1), 64–84. doi:10.4018/ JDM.2020010104

Lavanya, R., Chakkaravarthy, G. V., & Alli, P. (2020). An Integrated GIS and Knowledge-Based Automated Decision Support System for Precision Agriculture Using IoT. In P. Mukherjee, P. K. Pattnaik, & S. N. Panda (Eds.), *IoT and WSN Applications for Modern Agricultural Advancements* (pp. 86–98). IGI Global., doi:10.4018/978-1-5225-9004-0.ch006

Le Hung, T., & Sinh, M. D. (2019). Classification of Remote Sensing Imagery Based on Density and Fuzzy c-Means Algorithm. [IJFSA]. *International Journal of Fuzzy System Applications*, *8*(2), 1–15. doi:10.4018/ IJFSA.2019040101

Leal, E., Gruenwald, L., & Zhang, J. (2019). A Survey of Parallel Indexing Techniques for Large-Scale Moving Object Databases. In J. Darmont & S. Loudcher (Eds.), *Utilizing Big Data Paradigms for Business Intelligence* (pp. 72–105). IGI Global., doi:10.4018/978-1-5225-4963-5.ch003

Lederer, M., & Riedl, J. (2020). Data Science Techniques in Knowledge-Intensive Business Processes. [IJDA]. *International Journal of Data Analytics*, *1*(1), 52–67. doi:10.4018/IJDA.2020010104

Leon-Medina, J. X., Vejar, M. A., & Tibaduiza, D. A. (2020). Signal Processing and Pattern Recognition in Electronic Tongues. In D. A. Burgos, M. A. Vejar, & F. Pozo (Eds.), *Pattern Recognition Applications in Engineering* (pp. 84–108). IGI Global., doi:10.4018/978-1-7998-1839-7.ch004

Li, L., Chu, Y., Liu, G., & Wu, X. (2019). Multi-Objective Optimization-Based Networked Multi-Label Active Learning. [JDM]. *Journal of Database Management, 30*(2), 1–26. doi:10.4018/JDM.2019040101

Li, T., & Fong, S. (2019). A Fast Feature Selection Method Based on Coefficient of Variation for Diabetics Prediction Using Machine Learning. [IJEACH]. *International Journal of Extreme Automation and Connectivity in Healthcare, 1*(1), 55–65. doi:10.4018/IJEACH.2019010106

Li, T., & Fong, S. (2019). Similarity Measure of Breast Cancer Datasets Using Fuzzy Rule-Based Classification by Attribute. [IJEACH]. *International Journal of Extreme Automation and Connectivity in Healthcare, 1*(1), 12–28. doi:10.4018/IJEACH.2019010103

Li, T., Marques, J. A., & Fong, S. (2020). Health and Well-Being Education. [IJEACH]. *International Journal of Extreme Automation and Connectivity in Healthcare, 2*(2), 42–53. doi:10.4018/IJEACH.2020070105

Li, Y. Z., Zhang, S. P., Li, Y., & Wang, S. (2020). Research on Intrusion Detection Algorithm Based on Deep Learning and Semi-Supervised Clustering. [IJCRE]. *International Journal of Cyber Research and Education, 2*(2), 38–60. doi:10.4018/IJCRE.2020070105

Li, Y., Shi, H., Chen, L., & Jiang, F. (2019). Convolutional Approach Also Benefits Traditional Face Pattern Recognition Algorithm [208!] [IJSSCI]. *International Journal of Software Science and Computational Intelligence, 11*(4), 1–16. doi:10.4018/IJSSCI.2019100101

Lin, H., Garza, J., Schreiber, G., Yang, M., & Cui, Y. (2021). Brain State Intelligence and Cognitive Health Through EEG Date Modeling. [IJEHMC]. *International Journal of E-Health and Medical Communications, 12*(1), 46–61. doi:10.4018/IJEHMC.2021010104

Liu, R., Wang, Z., & Xu, X. (2019). Parameter Tuning for S-ABCPK. [IJWSR]. *International Journal of Web Services Research, 16*(2), 88–109. doi:10.4018/IJWSR.2019040105

Liu, X., Zhang, X., Wang, T., Cheng, K., Jiao, S., Liu, D., Su, J., & Wang, X. (2020). Analysis of Social Value of TV Dramas Based on Audience Comments. In P. Ordoñez de Pablos, X. Zhang, & K. Chui (Eds.), *Handbook of Research on Managerial Practices and Disruptive Innovation in Asia* (pp. 69–88). IGI Global., doi:10.4018/978-1-7998-0357-7.ch004

Liu, Y., Yan, L., & Xu, J. (2018). Application of Neural Network With New Hybrid Algorithm in Volcanic Rocks Seismic Prediction. [IJCINI]. *International Journal of Cognitive Informatics and Natural Intelligence, 12*(4), 55–68. doi:10.4018/IJCINI.2018100103

Liyanage, S. R., & Kasthuriarachchi, K. T. (2020). Predicting the Academic Performance of Students Using Utility-Based Data Mining. In C. Bhatt, P. S. Sajja, & S. Liyanage (Eds.), *Utilizing Educational Data Mining Techniques for Improved Learning* (pp. 56–85). IGI Global., doi:10.4018/978-1-7998-0010-1.ch004

Loey, M., ElSawy, A., & Afify, M. (2020). Deep Learning in Plant Diseases Detection for Agricultural Crops. [IJSSMET]. *International Journal of Service Science, Management, Engineering, and Technology, 11*(2), 41–58. doi:10.4018/IJSSMET.2020040103

Lu, W., & Xing, R. (2019). Research on Movie Box Office Prediction Model With Conjoint Analysis. [IJISSCM]. *International Journal of Information Systems and Supply Chain Management, 12*(3), 72–84. doi:10.4018/IJISSCM.2019070104

Lukyamuzi, A., Ngubiri, J., & Okori, W. (2020). Towards Ensemble Learning for Tracking Food Insecurity From News Articles. [IJSDA]. *International Journal of System Dynamics Applications, 9*(4), 129–142. doi:10.4018/IJSDA.2020100107

Lv, X., Hou, H., You, X., Zhang, X., & Han, J. (2020). Distant Supervised Relation Extraction via DiSAN-2CNN on a Feature Level. [IJSWIS]. *International Journal on Semantic Web and Information Systems, 16*(2), 1–17. doi:10.4018/IJSWIS.2020040101

Kudari, M. J. (2021). Data Analytics to Predict, Detect, and Monitor Chronic Autoimmune Diseases Using Machine Learning Algorithms. In Roy, M., & Gupta, L. R. (Eds.), Machine Learning and Data Analytics for Predicting, Managing, and Monitoring Disease (pp. 150-182). IGI Global. https://doi.org/ doi:10.4018/978-1-7998-7188-0.ch012

M. S., S., & Sasidaran, K. (2021). Machine Learning for Big Data. In Goundar, S., & Rayani, P. K. (Ed.), *Applications of Big Data in Large- and Small-Scale Systems* (pp. 56-76). IGI Global. https://doi.org/ doi:10.4018/978-1-7998-6673-2.ch004

M., D. N., Kousalya, G., P., B., & Raj, P. (2018). Fuzzy-Logic-Based Decision Engine for Offloading IoT Application Using Fog Computing. In Raj, P., & Raman, A. (Ed.), *Handbook of Research on Cloud and Fog Computing Infrastructures for Data Science* (pp. 175-194). IGI Global. https://doi.org/ doi:10.4018/978-1-5225-5972-6.ch009

M., M., Kesavan, S., & K., P. (2021). Segmentation of Spine Tumour Using K-Means and Active Contour and Feature Extraction Using GLCM. In Anbarasan, K. (Ed.), *AI Innovation in Medical Imaging Diagnostics* (pp. 194-207). IGI Global. https://doi.org/ doi:10.4018/978-1-7998-3092-4.ch011

Maake, B. M., Ojo, S. O., & Zuva, T. (2019). A Survey on Data Mining Techniques in Research Paper Recommender Systems. In R. K. Bhardwaj & P. Banks (Eds.), *Research Data Access and Management in Modern Libraries* (pp. 119–143). IGI Global., doi:10.4018/978-1-5225-8437-7.ch006

Machado, C. J., Maciel, A. M., Rodrigues, R. L., & Menezes, R. (2019). An Approach for Thematic Relevance Analysis Applied to Textual Contributions in Discussion Forums. [IJDET]. *International Journal of Distance Education Technologies*, *17*(3), 37–51. doi:10.4018/IJDET.2019070103

Madadi, S., Nazari-Heris, M., Mohammadi-Ivatloo, B., & Tohidi, S. (2018). Implementation of Genetic-Algorithm-Based Forecasting Model to Power System Problems. In D. Kim, S. Sekhar Roy, T. Länsivaara, R. Deo, & P. Samui (Eds.), *Handbook of Research on Predictive Modeling and Optimization Methods in Science and Engineering* (pp. 140–155). IGI Global., doi:10.4018/978-1-5225-4766-2.ch007

Madaleno, M., Marques, J. L., & Tufail, M. (2021). Data Science in Economics and Business. In V. Chkoniya (Ed.), *Handbook of Research on Applied Data Science and Artificial Intelligence in Business and Industry* (pp. 544–568). IGI Global., doi:10.4018/978-1-7998-6985-6.ch026

Mahmoud, A., & Zrigui, M. (2020). Distributional Semantic Model Based on Convolutional Neural Network for Arabic Textual Similarity. [IJCINI]. *International Journal of Cognitive Informatics and Natural Intelligence*, *14*(1), 35–50. doi:10.4018/IJCINI.2020010103

Mahoto, N. A., & Babar, A. H. (2019). Developing an Effective Classification Model for Medical Data Analysis. In C. Chakraborty (Ed.), *Advanced Classification Techniques for Healthcare Analysis* (pp. 1–17). IGI Global., doi:10.4018/978-1-5225-7796-6.ch001

Mahyoub, F. H., & Abdullah, R. (2020). Protein Secondary Structure Prediction Approaches. In J. J. Thomas, P. Karagoz, B. B. Ahamed, & P. Vasant (Eds.), *Deep Learning Techniques and Optimization Strategies in Big Data Analytics* (pp. 251–273). IGI Global., doi:10.4018/978-1-7998-1192-3.ch015

Majhi, S. K. (2018). An Efficient Feed Foreword Network Model with Sine Cosine Algorithm for Breast Cancer Classification. [IJSDA]. *International Journal of System Dynamics Applications*, 7(2), 1–14. doi:10.4018/IJSDA.2018040101

Majhi, V., Saikia, A., Datta, A., Sinha, A., & Paul, S. (2020). Comprehensive Review on Deep Learning for Neuronal Disorders. [IJNCR]. *International Journal of Natural Computing Research*, 9(1), 27–44. doi:10.4018/IJNCR.2020010103

Majumder, A., Roy Sarkar, M., & Lal Sarakar, J. (2020). An Architectural Layer Classification of Energy Conservation Techniques in Internet of Things. In E. Koç (Ed.), *Internet of Things (IoT) Applications for Enterprise Productivity* (pp. 270–307). IGI Global., doi:10.4018/978-1-7998-3175-4.ch011

Malan, N. S., & Sharma, S. (2020). Introduction to Motor Imagery-Based Brain-Computer Interface. In N. Sriraam (Ed.), *Biomedical and Clinical Engineering for Healthcare Advancement* (pp. 168–197). IGI Global., doi:10.4018/978-1-7998-0326-3.ch009

Maldonado, M., & Barsoum, A. (2019). Machine Learning for Web Proxy Analytics. [IJCRE]. *International Journal of Cyber Research and Education*, 1(2), 30–41. doi:10.4018/IJCRE.2019070103

Maleh, Y. (2019). Malware Classification and Analysis Using Convolutional and Recurrent Neural Network. In A. E. Hassanien, A. Darwish, & C. L. Chowdhary (Eds.), *Handbook of Research on Deep Learning Innovations and Trends* (pp. 233–255). IGI Global., doi:10.4018/978-1-5225-7862-8.ch014

Mallikarjuna, B., Addanke, S., & D. J., A. (2022). An Improved Deep Learning Algorithm for Diabetes Prediction. In Krishna, P. (Ed.), *Handbook of Research on Advances in Data Analytics and Complex Communication Networks* (pp. 103-119). IGI Global. https://doi.org/ doi:10.4018/978-1-7998-7685-4.ch007

Related Readings

Mallikarjuna, B. M., S. R., Addanke, S., & Sabharwal, M. (2022). An Improved Model for House Price/Land Price Prediction using Deep Learning. In Krishna, P. (Ed.), Handbook of Research on Advances in Data Analytics and Complex Communication Networks (pp. 76-87). IGI Global. https://doi.org/ doi:10.4018/978-1-7998-7685-4.ch005

Manian, V., & P., V. (2021). Challenges and Applications of Data Analytics in Social Perspectives. In Bouarara, H. A. (Ed.), *Advanced Deep Learning Applications in Big Data Analytics* (pp. 51-67). IGI Global. https://doi.org/ doi:10.4018/978-1-7998-2791-7.ch003

Manu, C., Vijaya Kumar, B. P., & Naresh, E. (2019). Anomaly Detection Using Deep Learning With Modular Networks. In A. E. Hassanien, A. Darwish, & C. L. Chowdhary (Eds.), *Handbook of Research on Deep Learning Innovations and Trends* (pp. 256–290). IGI Global., doi:10.4018/978-1-5225-7862-8.ch015

Manukumar, S. T., & Muthuswamy, V. (2020). A Novel Resource Management Framework for Fog Computing by Using Machine Learning Algorithm. In S. Goundar, S. B. Bhushan, & P. K. Rayani (Eds.), *Architecture and Security Issues in Fog Computing Applications* (pp. 42–52). IGI Global., doi:10.4018/978-1-7998-0194-8.ch002

Mardi, V., Naresh, E., & Vijaya Kumar, B. P. (2019). A Survey on Deep Learning Techniques Used for Quality Process. In A. E. Hassanien, A. Darwish, & C. L. Chowdhary (Eds.), *Handbook of Research on Deep Learning Innovations and Trends* (pp. 131–152). IGI Global., doi:10.4018/978-1-5225-7862-8.ch008

Marimuthu, P., Perumal, V., & Vijayakumar, V. (2020). Intelligent Personalized Abnormality Detection for Remote Health Monitoring. [IJIIT]. *International Journal of Intelligent Information Technologies, 16*(2), 87–109. doi:10.4018/ IJIIT.2020040105

Masih, N., & Ahuja, S. (2018). Prediction of Heart Diseases Using Data Mining Techniques. [IJBDAH]. *International Journal of Big Data and Analytics in Healthcare, 3*(2), 1–9. doi:10.4018/IJBDAH.2018070101

Massaro, A., & Galiano, A. (2020). Image Processing and Post-Data Mining Processing for Security in Industrial Applications. In S. M. Bilan & S. I. Al-Zoubi (Eds.), *Handbook of Research on Intelligent Data Processing and Information Security Systems* (pp. 117–146). IGI Global., doi:10.4018/978-1-7998-1290-6.ch006

Massaro, A., & Galiano, A. (2020). Infrared Thermography for Intelligent Robotic Systems in Research Industry Inspections. In M. K. Habib (Ed.), *Handbook of Research on Advanced Mechatronic Systems and Intelligent Robotics* (pp. 98–125). IGI Global., doi:10.4018/978-1-7998-0137-5.ch005

Master, L. (2020). Ranking with Genetics. [IJIRR]. *International Journal of Information Retrieval Research, 10*(3), 20–34. doi:10.4018/IJIRR.2020070102

Mazumdar, S., Chaudhary, R., Suruchi, S., Mohanty, S., Kumari, D., & Swetapadma, A. (2019). Motor Imagery Classification Using EEG Signals for Brain-Computer Interface Applications. In S. Paul, P. Bhattacharya, & A. Bit (Eds.), *Early Detection of Neurological Disorders Using Machine Learning Systems* (pp. 241–251). IGI Global., doi:10.4018/978-1-5225-8567-1.ch013

Mehra, R., & Iyer, M. (2020). AI-Driven Prognosis and Diagnosis for Personalized Healthcare Services. In D. S. Sisodia, R. Pachori, & L. Garg (Eds.), *Handbook of Research on Advancements of Artificial Intelligence in Healthcare Engineering* (pp. 124–162). IGI Global., doi:10.4018/978-1-7998-2120-5.ch008

Mekonnen, A. A., Seid, H. W., Mohapatra, S. K., & Prasad, S. (2021). Developing Brain Tumor Detection Model Using Deep Feature Extraction via Transfer Learning. In M. Panda & H. Misra (Eds.), *Handbook of Research on Automated Feature Engineering and Advanced Applications in Data Science* (pp. 119–137). IGI Global., doi:10.4018/978-1-7998-6659-6.ch007

Memon, M. S., Kumar, P., Mirani, A. A., Qabulio, M., & Sodhar, I. N. (2020). Deep Learning and IoT. In P. Kumar, V. Ponnusamy, & V. Jain (Eds.), *Industrial Internet of Things and Cyber-Physical Systems* (pp. 47–60). IGI Global., doi:10.4018/978-1-7998-2803-7.ch003

Menad, H., Ben-Naoum, F., & Amine, A. (2019). A Thresholding Approach for Pollen Detection in Images Based on Simulated Annealing Algorithm. [IJAEIS]. *International Journal of Agricultural and Environmental Information Systems, 10*(4), 18–36. doi:10.4018/IJAEIS.2019100102

Menad, H., Farah Ben-naoum, & Amine, A. (2020). A Hybrid Grey Wolves Optimizer and Convolutional Neural Network for Pollen Grain Recognition. [IJSIR]. *International Journal of Swarm Intelligence Research, 11*(3), 49–71. doi:10.4018/IJSIR.2020070104

Meng, X., Liu, M., & Wu, Q. (2020). Prediction of Rice Yield via Stacked LSTM. [IJAEIS]. *International Journal of Agricultural and Environmental Information Systems*, *11*(1), 86–95. doi:10.4018/IJAEIS.2020010105

Menon, S. P. (2020). A Survey on Algorithms in Deep Learning. In P. Kumar, V. Ponnusamy, & V. Jain (Eds.), *Industrial Internet of Things and Cyber-Physical Systems* (pp. 339–350). IGI Global., doi:10.4018/978-1-7998-2803-7.ch017

Michalek, A. M., Jayawardena, G., & Jayarathna, S. (2019). Predicting ADHD Using Eye Gaze Metrics Indexing Working Memory Capacity. In C. Chen & S. S. Cheung (Eds.), *Computational Models for Biomedical Reasoning and Problem Solving* (pp. 66–88). IGI Global., doi:10.4018/978-1-5225-7467-5.ch003

Mihret, E. T. (2020). Robotics and Artificial Intelligence. [IJAIML]. *International Journal of Artificial Intelligence and Machine Learning*, *10*(2), 57–78. doi:10.4018/IJAIML.2020070104

Miller, S., Curran, K., & Lunney, T. (2020). Detection of Virtual Private Network Traffic Using Machine Learning. [IJWNBT]. *International Journal of Wireless Networks and Broadband Technologies*, *9*(2), 60–80. doi:10.4018/IJWNBT.2020070104

Milutinović, V., Kotlar, M., Ratković, I., Korolija, N., Djordjevic, M., Yoshimoto, K., & Valero, M. (2021). The Ultimate Data Flow for Ultimate Super Computers-on-a-Chip. In V. Milutinović & M. Kotlar (Eds.), *Handbook of Research on Methodologies and Applications of Supercomputing* (pp. 312–318). IGI Global., doi:10.4018/978-1-7998-7156-9.ch021

Mimouni, M., Zoungrana, L. E., Ben Khatra, N., & Faiz, S. (2021). Machine Learning for Winter Crop Mapping Using High Spatiotemporal Time Series Satellite Imagery. In S. Faiz & S. Elhosni (Eds.), *Interdisciplinary Approaches to Spatial Optimization Issues* (pp. 123–147). IGI Global., doi:10.4018/978-1-7998-1954-7.ch008

Mishra, N. (2021). Emerging Technology Amendment Study in Smart Agro Farming to Diagnose the Agro Product Diseases. In T. H. Musiolik & A. D. Cheok (Eds.), *Analyzing Future Applications of AI, Sensors, and Robotics in Society* (pp. 273–283). IGI Global., doi:10.4018/978-1-7998-3499-1.ch016

Mishra, N., & Samuel, J. M. (2021). Towards Integrating Data Mining With Knowledge-Based System for Diagnosis of Human Eye Diseases. In G. Rani & P. K. Tiwari (Eds.), *Handbook of Research on Disease Prediction Through Data Analytics and Machine Learning* (pp. 470–485). IGI Global., doi:10.4018/978-1-7998-2742-9.ch024

Mishra, P. S., & Nandi, D. (2021). Deep Learning for Feature Engineering-Based Improved Weather Prediction. In M. Panda & H. Misra (Eds.), *Handbook of Research on Automated Feature Engineering and Advanced Applications in Data Science* (pp. 195–217). IGI Global., doi:10.4018/978-1-7998-6659-6.ch011

Misra, P., & Chaurasia, S. (2020). Data-Driven Trend Forecasting in Stock Market Using Machine Learning Techniques. [JITR]. *Journal of Information Technology Research*, *13*(1), 130–149. doi:10.4018/JITR.2020010109

Mittal, R., & Bhatia, M. (2019). Classifying the Influential Individuals in Multi-Layer Social Networks. [IJECME]. *International Journal of Electronics, Communications, and Measurement Engineering*, *8*(1), 21–32. doi:10.4018/IJECME.2019010102

Mittal, R., & Bhatia, M. P. (2021). Detection of Suspicious or Un-Trusted Users in Crypto-Currency Financial Trading Applications. [IJDCF]. *International Journal of Digital Crime and Forensics*, *13*(1), 79–93. doi:10.4018/IJDCF.2021010105

Mohapatra, S. K., & Mohanty, M. N. (2020). Arrhythmia Detection Using a Radial Basis Function Network With Wavelet Features. [IJKBO]. *International Journal of Knowledge-Based Organizations*, *10*(2), 48–56. doi:10.4018/IJKBO.2020040104

Money, W. H., & Cohen, S. J. (2020). Recognizing Threats From Unknown Real-Time Big Data System Faults. In M. E. Jennex (Ed.), *Current Issues and Trends in Knowledge Management, Discovery, and Transfer* (pp. 331–366). IGI Global., doi:10.4018/978-1-7998-2189-2.ch014

Montasari, R., Hosseinian-Far, A., Hill, R., Montaseri, F., Sharma, M., & Shabbir, S. (2018). Are Timing-Based Side-Channel Attacks Feasible in Shared, Modern Computing Hardware? [IJOCI]. *International Journal of Organizational and Collective Intelligence*, *8*(2), 32–59. doi:10.4018/IJOCI.2018040103

More, A. S., & Rana, D. P. (2021). Review of Imbalanced Data Classification and Approaches Relating to Real-Time Applications. In D. P. Rana & R. G. Mehta (Eds.), *Data Preprocessing, Active Learning, and Cost Perceptive Approaches for Resolving Data Imbalance* (pp. 1–22). IGI Global., doi:10.4018/978-1-7998-7371-6.ch001

Mousa, A., El-Sayed, A., Khalifa, A., El-Nashar, M., Mancy, Y. M., Younan, M., & Younis, E. (2020). A Blood Bank Management System-Based Internet of Things and Machine Learning Technologies. In Z. Altan (Ed.), *Applications and Approaches to Object-Oriented Software Design* (pp. 184–222). IGI Global., doi:10.4018/978-1-7998-2142-7.ch008

Mullaivanan, D., & R., K. (2021). A Comprehensive Survey of Data Mining Techniques in Disease Prediction. In Sathiyamoorthi, V., & Elci, A. (Ed.), *Challenges and Applications of Data Analytics in Social Perspectives* (pp. 27-53). IGI Global. https://doi.org/ doi:10.4018/978-1-7998-2566-1.ch002

Muniasamy, A. (2020). Applications of Data Mining Techniques in Smart Farming for Sustainable Agriculture. In N. Pradeep, S. Kautish, C. Nirmala, V. Goyal, & S. Abdellatif (Eds.), *Modern Techniques for Agricultural Disease Management and Crop Yield Prediction* (pp. 142–178). IGI Global., doi:10.4018/978-1-5225-9632-5.ch007

Munonye, K., & Martinek, P. (2021). Microservices Data Mining for Analytics Feedback and Optimization. [IJEIS]. *International Journal of Enterprise Information Systems*, *17*(1), 22–43. doi:10.4018/IJEIS.2021010102

Muraleedharan, N., & Janet, B. (2021). SCAFFY. [IJISP]. *International Journal of Information Security and Privacy*, *15*(3), 106–128. doi:10.4018/ IJISP.2021070107

Murugan, S., & Sumithra, M. G. (2020). Big Data-Based Spectrum Sensing for Cognitive Radio Networks Using Artificial Intelligence. In A. Haldorai & A. Ramu (Eds.), *Big Data Analytics for Sustainable Computing* (pp. 146–159). IGI Global., doi:10.4018/978-1-5225-9750-6.ch009

Musiolik, G. (2021). Predictability of AI Decisions. In T. H. Musiolik & A. D. Cheok (Eds.), *Analyzing Future Applications of AI, Sensors, and Robotics in Society* (pp. 17–28). IGI Global., doi:10.4018/978-1-7998-3499-1.ch002

Naaz, S. (2021). Detection of Phishing in Internet of Things Using Machine Learning Approach. [IJDCF]. *International Journal of Digital Crime and Forensics*, *13*(2), 1–15. doi:10.4018/IJDCF.2021030101

Nagata, F., Habib, M. K., & Watanabe, K. (2020). An Efficient Learning of Neural Networks to Acquire Inverse Kinematics Model. In M. K. Habib (Ed.), *Advanced Robotics and Intelligent Automation in Manufacturing* (pp. 203–232). IGI Global., doi:10.4018/978-1-7998-1382-8.ch008

Nagpal, A., & Singh, V. (2019). Coupling Multivariate Adaptive Regression Spline (MARS) and Random Forest (RF). [IJHISI]. *International Journal of Healthcare Information Systems and Informatics*, *14*(1), 1–18. doi:10.4018/IJHISI.2019010101

Naik, K. J., & Soni, A. (2021). Video Classification Using 3D Convolutional Neural Network. In A. Kumar & S. S. Reddy (Eds.), *Advancements in Security and Privacy Initiatives for Multimedia Images* (pp. 1–18). IGI Global., doi:10.4018/978-1-7998-2795-5.ch001

Nami, N., & Moh, M. (2019). Adversarial Attacks and Defense on Deep Learning Models for Big Data and IoT. In B. Gupta & D. P. Agrawal (Eds.), *Handbook of Research on Cloud Computing and Big Data Applications in IoT* (pp. 39–66). IGI Global., doi:10.4018/978-1-5225-8407-0.ch003

Narayan, V., & Shaju, B. (2020). Malware and Anomaly Detection Using Machine Learning and Deep Learning Methods. In P. Ganapathi & D. Shanmugapriya (Eds.), *Handbook of Research on Machine and Deep Learning Applications for Cyber Security* (pp. 104–131). IGI Global., doi:10.4018/978-1-5225-9611-0.ch006

Narayana Rao, T. V., Thumukunta, M., Kurni, M., & K., S. (2021). Computational Statistics-Based Prediction Algorithms Using Machine Learning. In Samanta, D., Rao Althar, R., Pramanik, S., & Dutta, S. (Ed.), *Methodologies and Applications of Computational Statistics for Machine Intelligence* (pp. 64-80). IGI Global. https://doi.org/ doi:10.4018/978-1-7998-7701-1.ch004

Narayanasamy, S. K., & Elçi, A. (2020). An Effective Prediction Model for Online Course Dropout Rate. [IJDET]. *International Journal of Distance Education Technologies*, *18*(4), 94–110. doi:10.4018/IJDET.2020100106

Narwane, S. V., & Sawarkar, S. D. (2021). Effects of Class Imbalance Using Machine Learning Algorithms. [IJAEC]. *International Journal of Applied Evolutionary Computation*, *12*(1), 1–17. doi:10.4018/IJAEC.2021010101

Nastenko, I. A., Konoval, O. O., Nosovets, O. K., & Pavlov, V. A. (2019). Set Classification. In A. Troussov & S. Maruev (Eds.), *Techno-Social Systems for Modern Economical and Governmental Infrastructures* (pp. 44–83). IGI Global., doi:10.4018/978-1-5225-5586-5.ch003

Natarajan, J. (2020). Cyber Secure Man-in-the-Middle Attack Intrusion Detection Using Machine Learning Algorithms. In M. Strydom & S. Buckley (Eds.), *AI and Big Data's Potential for Disruptive Innovation* (pp. 291–316). IGI Global., doi:10.4018/978-1-5225-9687-5.ch011

Nazeer, I., Rashid, M., Gupta, S. K., & Kumar, A. (2021). Use of Novel Ensemble Machine Learning Approach for Social Media Sentiment Analysis. In P. K. Wamuyu (Ed.), *Analyzing Global Social Media Consumption* (pp. 16–28). IGI Global., doi:10.4018/978-1-7998-4718-2.ch002

Nazir, S., Patel, S., & Patel, D. (2020). Assessing Hyper Parameter Optimization and Speedup for Convolutional Neural Networks. [IJAIML]. *International Journal of Artificial Intelligence and Machine Learning*, *10*(2), 1–17. doi:10.4018/IJAIML.2020070101

Nguyen, C., Kieu, C. T., & Nguyen, K. (2020). Improved Compact Routing Schemes for Random Interconnects. [IJDST]. *International Journal of Distributed Systems and Technologies*, *11*(3), 89–109. doi:10.4018/IJDST.2020070105

Nguyen, S., & Park, A. (2020). A Comparison of Machine Learning Algorithms of Big Data for Time Series Forecasting Using Python. In R. S. Segall & G. Niu (Eds.), *Open Source Software for Statistical Analysis of Big Data* (pp. 197–218). IGI Global., doi:10.4018/978-1-7998-2768-9.ch007

Ni, P., Li, Y., & Chang, V. (2020). Recommendation and Sentiment Analysis Based on Consumer Review and Rating. [IJBIR]. *International Journal of Business Intelligence Research*, *11*(2), 11–27. doi:10.4018/IJBIR.2020070102

Ni, P., Li, Y., & Chang, V. (2020). Research on Text Classification Based on Automatically Extracted Keywords. [IJEIS]. *International Journal of Enterprise Information Systems*, *16*(4), 1–16. doi:10.4018/IJEIS.2020100101

Nithin Prabhu, G., Nagavi, T. C., & Mahesha, P. (2019). Medical Image Lossy Compression With LSTM Networks. In N. Dey, A. S. Ashour, H. Kalia, R. Goswami, & H. Das (Eds.), *Histopathological Image Analysis in Medical Decision Making* (pp. 47–68). IGI Global., doi:10.4018/978-1-5225-6316-7.ch003

Niu, G., & Olinsky, A. (2020). Generalized Linear Model for Automobile Fatality Rate Prediction in R. In R. S. Segall & G. Niu (Eds.), *Open Source Software for Statistical Analysis of Big Data* (pp. 137–161). IGI Global., doi:10.4018/978-1-7998-2768-9.ch005

Niu, L., Saiki, S., & Nakamura, M. (2018). Using Non-Intrusive Environmental Sensing for ADLS Recognition in One-Person Household. [IJSI]. *International Journal of Software Innovation*, *6*(4), 16–29. doi:10.4018/IJSI.2018100102

Norah Abdullah Al-johani, & Elrefaei, L. A. (2020). Palmprint And Dorsal Hand Vein Multi-Modal Biometric Fusion Using Deep Learning. [IJAIML]. *International Journal of Artificial Intelligence and Machine Learning*, *10*(2), 18–42. doi:10.4018/IJAIML.2020070102

Obeidat, R., & Alzoubi, H. (2021). Why Are Hardware Description Languages Important for Hardware Design Courses? [IJICTE]. *International Journal of Information and Communication Technology Education*, *17*(2), 1–16. doi:10.4018/IJICTE.2021040101

Okatan, K. (2021). Machine Learning for Business Analytics. In V. Sathiyamoorthi & A. Elci (Eds.), *Challenges and Applications of Data Analytics in Social Perspectives* (pp. 232–256). IGI Global., doi:10.4018/978-1-7998-2566-1.ch013

P. Z. S., & Mohan, M. (2021). Detection and Prediction of Spam Emails Using Machine Learning Models. In Cruz-Cunha, M., & Mateus-Coelho, N. R. (Ed.), Handbook of Research on Cyber Crime and Information Privacy (pp. 201-218). IGI Global. https://doi.org/ doi:10.4018/978-1-7998-5728-0.ch011

P., A. (2018). Data Mining Algorithms and Techniques. In Raj, P., & Raman, A. (Eds.), *Handbook of Research on Cloud and Fog Computing Infrastructures for Data Science* (pp. 195-208). IGI Global. https://doi.org/ doi:10.4018/978-1-5225-5972-6.ch010

Pabreja, K., & Bhasin, A. (2021). A Predictive Analytics Framework for Blood Donor Classification. [IJBDAH]. *International Journal of Big Data and Analytics in Healthcare*, *6*(2), 1–14. doi:10.4018/IJBDAH.20210701.oa1

Pal, P., & Bhattacharyya, S. (2018). True Color Image Segmentation by MUSIG Activation Function Using Self-Supervised QMLSONN Architecture With Context-Sensitive Thresholding. In S. Bhattacharyya (Ed.), *Quantum-Inspired Intelligent Systems for Multimedia Data Analysis* (pp. 213–261). IGI Global., doi:10.4018/978-1-5225-5219-2.ch007

Pal, S. S. (2018). Grey Wolf Optimization Trained Feed Foreword Neural Network for Breast Cancer Classification. [IJAIE]. *International Journal of Applied Industrial Engineering*, 5(2), 21–29. doi:10.4018/IJAIE.2018070102

Paladhi, S., Chatterjee, S., Goto, T., & Sen, S. (2019). AFARTICA. [JDM]. *Journal of Database Management*, 30(3), 71–93. doi:10.4018/JDM.2019070104

Palo, H. K., & Sarangi, L. (2020). Overview of Machine Learners in Classifying of Speech Signals. In A. Solanki, S. Kumar, & A. Nayyar (Eds.), *Handbook of Research on Emerging Trends and Applications of Machine Learning* (pp. 461–489). IGI Global., doi:10.4018/978-1-5225-9643-1.ch022

Panda, M. (2019). Software Defect Prediction Using Hybrid Distribution Base Balance Instance Selection and Radial Basis Function Classifier. [IJSDA]. *International Journal of System Dynamics Applications*, 8(3), 53–75. doi:10.4018/IJSDA.2019070103

Pandey, K., Narula, A., Pandey, D., & Raw, R. S. (2021). An Approach Towards Intelligent Traffic Environment Using Machine Learning Algorithms. In R. S. Rao, N. Singh, O. Kaiwartya, & S. Das (Eds.), *Cloud-Based Big Data Analytics in Vehicular Ad-Hoc Networks* (pp. 1–22). IGI Global., doi:10.4018/978-1-7998-2764-1.ch001

Pandey, S., & Agarwal, A. K. (2021). Comparison of Machine Learning Algorithms for Cardiovascular Disease Prediction. In R. Singh, A. K. Singh, A. K. Dwivedi, & P. Nagabhushan (Eds.), *Computational Methodologies for Electrical and Electronics Engineers* (pp. 111–126). IGI Global., doi:10.4018/978-1-7998-3327-7.ch009

Pandey, S., & Agarwal, A. K. (2021). Machine Learning Approaches for Cardiovascular Disease Prediction. In R. Singh, A. K. Singh, A. K. Dwivedi, & P. Nagabhushan (Eds.), *Computational Methodologies for Electrical and Electronics Engineers* (pp. 75–84). IGI Global., doi:10.4018/978-1-7998-3327-7.ch006

Pang, S., Zou, G., Gan, Y., Niu, S., & Zhang, B. (2019). Augmenting Labeled Probabilistic Topic Model for Web Service Classification. [IJWSR]. *International Journal of Web Services Research*, 16(1), 93–113. doi:10.4018/IJWSR.2019010105

Panigrahi, R., Padhy, N., & Satapathy, S. C. (2019). Software Reusability Metrics Estimation From the Social Media by Using Evolutionary Algorithms. [IJOSSP]. *International Journal of Open Source Software and Processes*, *10*(2), 21–36. doi:10.4018/IJOSSP.2019040102

Pantano, E., Giglio, S., & Dennis, C. (2020). Integrating Big Data Analytics Into Retail Services Marketing Management. In S. S. Dadwal (Ed.), *Handbook of Research on Innovations in Technology and Marketing for the Connected Consumer* (pp. 205–222). IGI Global., doi:10.4018/978-1-7998-0131-3.ch010

Passi, K., Patel, P., & Jain, C. K. (2021). Prediction of Heart Cancer Data Using Hybrid Optimization and Machine Learning Techniques. [IJEACH]. *International Journal of Extreme Automation and Connectivity in Healthcare*, *3*(1), 1–17. doi:10.4018/IJEACH.2021010101

Patel, L., & Gaurav, K. A. (2020). Introduction to Machine Learning and Its Application. In S. Khalid (Ed.), *Applications of Artificial Intelligence in Electrical Engineering* (pp. 262–290). IGI Global., doi:10.4018/978-1-7998-2718-4.ch014

Patel, N. V., & Chhinkaniwala, H. (2019). Investigating Machine Learning Techniques for User Sentiment Analysis. [IJDSST]. *International Journal of Decision Support System Technology*, *11*(3), 1–12. doi:10.4018/IJDSST.2019070101

Pathak, L. K., & Jha, P. (2021). Application of Machine Learning in Chronic Kidney Disease Risk Prediction Using Electronic Health Records (EHR). In S. Goundar & P. K. Rayani (Eds.), *Applications of Big Data in Large- and Small-Scale Systems* (pp. 213–233). IGI Global., doi:10.4018/978-1-7998-6673-2.ch014

Patil, B., & Vohra, M. (2020). Contribution of Neural Networks in Different Applications. In S. Velayutham (Ed.), *Handbook of Research on Applications and Implementations of Machine Learning Techniques* (pp. 305–316). IGI Global., doi:10.4018/978-1-5225-9902-9.ch016

Patnaik, A., & Padhy, N. (2021). A Hybrid Approach to Identify Code Smell Using Machine Learning Algorithms. [IJOSSP]. *International Journal of Open Source Software and Processes*, *12*(2), 21–35. doi:10.4018/IJOSSP.2021040102

Patole, R. K., & Rege, P. P. (2020). Machine Learning in Authentication of Digital Audio Recordings. In M. Mahrishi, K. K. Hiran, G. Meena, & P. Sharma (Eds.), *Machine Learning and Deep Learning in Real-Time Applications* (pp. 145–167). IGI Global., doi:10.4018/978-1-7998-3095-5.ch007

Paul, P. V., Krishna, H., & L., J. (2020). Evolution of Data Analytics in Healthcare. In Solanki, A., Kumar, S., & Nayyar, A. (Ed.), *Handbook of Research on Emerging Trends and Applications of Machine Learning* (pp. 250-275). IGI Global. https://doi.org/ doi:10.4018/978-1-5225-9643-1.ch012

Pekel, E., & Özmen, E. P. (2020). Computational Intelligence Approach for Classification of Diabetes Mellitus Using Decision Tree. In M. Gul, E. Celik, S. Mete, & F. Serin (Eds.), *Computational Intelligence and Soft Computing Applications in Healthcare Management Science* (pp. 87–103). IGI Global., doi:10.4018/978-1-7998-2581-4.ch005

Peker, M., Özkaraca, O., & Şaşar, A. (2018). Use of Orange Data Mining Toolbox for Data Analysis in Clinical Decision Making. In P. K. Pattnaik, A. Swetapadma, & J. Sarraf (Eds.), *Expert System Techniques in Biomedical Science Practice* (pp. 143–167). IGI Global., doi:10.4018/978-1-5225-5149-2.ch007

Penmatsa, R. K., Kalidindi, A., & Mallidi, S. K. (2020). Feature Reduction and Optimization of Malware Detection System Using Ant Colony Optimization and Rough Sets. [IJISP]. *International Journal of Information Security and Privacy*, *14*(3), 95–114. doi:10.4018/IJISP.2020070106

Phong, P. H., & Hue, V. T. (2019). On Integration Linguistic Factors to Fuzzy Similarity Measures and Intuitionistic Fuzzy Similarity Measures. [IJSE]. *International Journal of Synthetic Emotions*, *10*(1), 1–37. doi:10.4018/IJSE.2019010101

Piconi, J., Maruatona, O., Ng, A., Kayes, A. S., & Watters, P. A. (2021). A Machine Learning-Based Cyber Defence System for an Intelligent City. In Z. Mahmood (Ed.), *Developing and Monitoring Smart Environments for Intelligent Cities* (pp. 271–299). IGI Global., doi:10.4018/978-1-7998-5062-5.ch011

Ponce, P., Polasko, K., & Molina, A. (2018). Neuro-Model for Improving the University-Industry Collaboration and Intellectual Property. In G. L. Jamil, J. Pinto Ferreira, M. M. Pinto, C. R. Magalhães Pessoa, & A. Xavier (Eds.), *Handbook of Research on Strategic Innovation Management for Improved Competitive Advantage* (pp. 163–191). IGI Global., doi:10.4018/978-1-5225-3012-1.ch010

Portegys, T. E. (2019). Generating an Artificial Nest Building Pufferfish in a Cellular Automaton Through Behavior Decomposition. [IJAIML]. *International Journal of Artificial Intelligence and Machine Learning*, *9*(1), 1–12. doi:10.4018/IJAIML.2019010101

Pramanik, P. K., Pal, S., & Mukhopadhyay, M. (2020). Big Data and Big Data Analytics for Improved Healthcare Service and Management. [IJPHIM]. *International Journal of Privacy and Health Information Management*, *8*(1), 13–51. doi:10.4018/IJPHIM.2020010102

Prayaga, L., Devulapalli, K., & Prayaga, C. (2019). Wearable Devices Data for Activity Prediction Using Machine Learning Algorithms. [IJBDAH]. *International Journal of Big Data and Analytics in Healthcare*, *4*(1), 32–46. doi:10.4018/IJBDAH.2019010103

Prayaga, L., Devulapalli, K., & Prayaga, C. (2020). Combining Clustering and Factor Analysis as Complementary Techniques. [IJDA]. *International Journal of Data Analytics*, *1*(2), 48–57. doi:10.4018/IJDA.2020070104

Preethi, D., & Khare, N. (2020). EFS-LSTM (Ensemble-Based Feature Selection With LSTM) Classifier for Intrusion Detection System. [IJeC]. *International Journal of e-Collaboration*, *16*(4), 72–86. doi:10.4018/IJeC.2020100106

Prins, A. J., & van Niekerk, A. (2020). Regional Mapping of Vineyards Using Machine Learning and LiDAR Data. [IJAGR]. *International Journal of Applied Geospatial Research*, *11*(4), 1–22. doi:10.4018/IJAGR.2020100101

Priya, G. B. K., Sultana, J., & M., U. R. (2022). Telugu News Data Classification Using Machine Learning Approach. In Krishna, P. (Ed.), Handbook of Research on Advances in Data Analytics and Complex Communication Networks (pp. 181-194). IGI Global. https://doi.org/ doi:10.4018/978-1-7998-7685-4.ch014

Priya, A., & Sahana, S. K. (2020). Processor Scheduling in High-Performance Computing (HPC) Environment. In B. Holland (Ed.), *Emerging Trends and Impacts of the Internet of Things in Libraries* (pp. 151–179). IGI Global., doi:10.4018/978-1-7998-4742-7.ch009

Priya, B. K., & Ramasubramanian, N. (2021). Improving the Lifetime of Phase Change Memory by Shadow Dynamic Random Access Memory. [IJSSMET]. *International Journal of Service Science, Management, Engineering, and Technology, 12*(2), 154–168. doi:10.4018/IJSSMET.2021030109

Priyadarshini, R., Barik, R. K., Dubey, H. C., & Mishra, B. K. (2021). A Survey of Fog Computing-Based Healthcare Big Data Analytics and Its Security. [IJACI]. *International Journal of Ambient Computing and Intelligence, 12*(2), 53–72. doi:10.4018/IJACI.2021040104

Protopapadakis, E., Rallis, I., Bakalos, N., & Kaselimi, M. (2020). Digitizing the Intangible. In A. Voulodimos & A. Doulamis (Eds.), *Recent Advances in 3D Imaging, Modeling, and Reconstruction* (pp. 79–107). IGI Global., doi:10.4018/978-1-5225-5294-9.ch004

Pudumalar, S., Suriya, K. S., & Rohini, K. (2018). Data Classification and Prediction. In Karthikeyan, P., & Thangavel, M. (Ed.), Applications of Security, Mobile, Analytic, and Cloud (SMAC) Technologies for Effective Information Processing and Management (pp. 149-173). IGI Global. https://doi.org/ doi:10.4018/978-1-5225-4044-1.ch008

Pujari, P., & Majhi, B. (2019). Recognition of Odia Handwritten Digits using Gradient based Feature Extraction Method and Clonal Selection Algorithm. [IJRSDA]. *International Journal of Rough Sets and Data Analysis, 6*(2), 19–33. doi:10.4018/IJRSDA.2019040102

Punia, S. K., Kumar, M., Stephan, T., Deverajan, G. G., & Patan, R. (2021). Performance Analysis of Machine Learning Algorithms for Big Data Classification. [IJEHMC]. *International Journal of E-Health and Medical Communications, 12*(4), 60–75. doi:10.4018/IJEHMC.20210701.oa4

Puri, S., & Singh, S. P. (2018). Hindi Text Document Classification System Using SVM and Fuzzy. [IJRSDA]. *International Journal of Rough Sets and Data Analysis, 5*(4), 1–31. doi:10.4018/IJRSDA.2018100101

Quiñonez, Y. (2021). An Overview of Applications of Artificial Intelligence Using Different Techniques, Algorithms, and Tools. In A. P. Negrón & M. Muñoz (Eds.), *Latin American Women and Research Contributions to the IT Field* (pp. 325–347). IGI Global., doi:10.4018/978-1-7998-7552-9.ch015

Qusef, A., Ayasrah, A., & Shaout, A. (2021). Comprehensive Approach to Implement E-Government Backend in Jordan Using Service-Oriented Architecture. [IJSI]. *International Journal of Software Innovation, 9*(2), 122–135. doi:10.4018/IJSI.2021040107

R. L. P., & Jinny, S. V. (2021). Comparison Analysis of Prediction Model for Respiratory Diseases. In Tyagi, A. K. (Ed.), Multimedia and Sensory Input for Augmented, Mixed, and Virtual Reality (pp. 86-98). IGI Global. https://doi.org/ doi:10.4018/978-1-7998-4703-8.ch004

R., H., & Devi, A. (2021). Chemical Named Entity Recognition Using Deep Learning Techniques. In Tanwar, P., Saxena, A., & Priya, C. (Ed.), *Deep Natural Language Processing and AI Applications for Industry 5.0* (pp. 59-73). IGI Global. https://doi.org/ doi:10.4018/978-1-7998-7728-8.ch004

R., R., Tiwari, H., Patel, J., R., R., & R., K. (2020). Bidirectional GRU-Based Attention Model for Kid-Specific URL Classification. In Thomas, J. J., Karagoz, P., Ahamed, B. B., & Vasant, P. (Ed.), *Deep Learning Techniques and Optimization Strategies in Big Data Analytics* (pp. 78-90). IGI Global. https://doi.org/ doi:10.4018/978-1-7998-1192-3.ch005

Radhakrishnan, S., & Vijayarajan, V. (2020). Optimized Deep Learning System for Crop Health Classification Strategically Using Spatial and Temporal Data. In J. J. Thomas, P. Karagoz, B. B. Ahamed, & P. Vasant (Eds.), *Deep Learning Techniques and Optimization Strategies in Big Data Analytics* (pp. 233–250). IGI Global., doi:10.4018/978-1-7998-1192-3.ch014

Rahaman, M. S., & Vasant, P. (2020). Artificial Intelligence Approach for Predicting TOC From Well Logs in Shale Reservoirs. In J. J. Thomas, P. Karagoz, B. B. Ahamed, & P. Vasant (Eds.), *Deep Learning Techniques and Optimization Strategies in Big Data Analytics* (pp. 46–77). IGI Global., doi:10.4018/978-1-7998-1192-3.ch004

Rahmani, M. E., & Amine, A. (2019). Ecological Data Exploration. In H. A. Bouarara, R. M. Hamou, & A. Rahmani (Eds.), *Advanced Metaheuristic Methods in Big Data Retrieval and Analytics* (pp. 27–62). IGI Global., doi:10.4018/978-1-5225-7338-8.ch002

Rahmani, M. E., Amine, A., & Hamou, R. M. (2018). Bagging Approach for Medical Plants Recognition Based on Their DNA Sequences. [IJSESD]. *International Journal of Social Ecology and Sustainable Development*, 9(4), 45–60. doi:10.4018/IJSESD.2018100103

Rahmani, M. E., Amine, A., & Hamou, R. M. (2018). Sonar Data Classification Using a New Algorithm Inspired from Black Holes Phenomenon. [IJIRR]. *International Journal of Information Retrieval Research*, 8(2), 25–39. doi:10.4018/IJIRR.2018040102

Raj, A., & Minz, S. (2021). A Scalable Unsupervised Classification Method Using Rough Set for Remote Sensing Imagery. [IJSSCI]. *International Journal of Software Science and Computational Intelligence*, 13(2), 65–88. doi:10.4018/IJSSCI.2021040104

Rajabalee, Y. B., Santally, M. I., & Rennie, F. (2020). Modeling Students' Performances in Activity-Based E-Learning From a Learning Analytics Perspective. [IJDET]. *International Journal of Distance Education Technologies*, 18(4), 71–93. doi:10.4018/IJDET.2020100105

Rajalingam, B., Priya, R., Bhavani, R., & Santhoshkumar, R. (2020). Image Fusion Techniques for Different Multimodality Medical Images Based on Various Conventional and Hybrid Algorithms for Disease Analysis. In Chakraborty, S., & Mali, K. (Ed.), Applications of Advanced Machine Intelligence in Computer Vision and Object Recognition (pp. 159-196). IGI Global. https://doi.org/ doi:10.4018/978-1-7998-2736-8.ch007

Rajamohana, S. P., Dharani, A., Anushree, P., Santhiya, B., & Umamaheswari, K. (2019). Machine Learning Techniques for Healthcare Applications. In A. Haldorai & A. Ramu (Eds.), *Cognitive Social Mining Applications in Data Analytics and Forensics* (pp. 236–251). IGI Global., doi:10.4018/978-1-5225-7522-1.ch012

Rajendran, G., & Vijayasundaram, U. (2020). Artificial Intelligence for Extended Software Robots, Applications, Algorithms, and Simulators. In M. Strydom & S. Buckley (Eds.), *AI and Big Data's Potential for Disruptive Innovation* (pp. 71–92). IGI Global., doi:10.4018/978-1-5225-9687-5.ch003

Rajendran, R., Kalidasan, A., & B., C. R. (2021). Convergence of AI, ML, and DL for Enabling Smart Intelligence. In Velayutham, S. (Ed.), *Challenges and Opportunities for the Convergence of IoT, Big Data, and Cloud Computing* (pp. 180-195). IGI Global. https://doi.org/ doi:10.4018/978-1-7998-3111-2. ch011

Raju, P. S., Rajendran, R. A., & Mahalingam, M. (2021). Perspectives of Machine Learning and Deep Learning in Internet of Things and Cloud. In S. Velayutham (Ed.), *Challenges and Opportunities for the Convergence of IoT, Big Data, and Cloud Computing* (pp. 248–264). IGI Global., doi:10.4018/978-1-7998-3111-2.ch014

Ram, B., Rashid, M., Lakhwani, K., & Kumar, S. S. (2020). Health Detection of Wheat Crop Using Pattern Recognition and Image Processing. [IJHISI]. *International Journal of Healthcare Information Systems and Informatics*, *15*(2), 50–60. doi:10.4018/IJHISI.2020040104

Rama, A., Kumaravel, A., & Nalini, C. (2019). Construction of Deep Convolutional Neural Networks For Medical Image Classification. [IJCVIP]. *International Journal of Computer Vision and Image Processing*, *9*(2), 1–15. doi:10.4018/IJCVIP.2019040101

Ramanathan, K., & Thangavel, B. (2021). Early Detection of Poor Academic Performers Using Machine Learning Predictive Modeling. [IJICTHD]. *International Journal of Information Communication Technologies and Human Development*, *13*(3), 56–69. doi:10.4018/IJICTHD.2021070104

Ramanujam, E., Rasikannan, L., Viswa, S., & Deepan Prashanth, B. (2021). Predictive Strength of Ensemble Machine Learning Algorithms for the Diagnosis of Large Scale Medical Datasets. In S. Goundar & P. K. Rayani (Eds.), *Applications of Big Data in Large- and Small-Scale Systems* (pp. 260–281). IGI Global., doi:10.4018/978-1-7998-6673-2.ch016

Ramchoun, H., Idrissi, M. A., Ghanou, Y., & Ettaouil, M. (2019). Multilayer Perceptron New Method for Selecting the Architecture Based on the Choice of Different Activation Functions. [IJISSS]. *International Journal of Information Systems in the Service Sector*, *11*(4), 21–34. doi:10.4018/IJISSS.2019100102

Ramesh Dhanaseelan, F., & Jeyasutha, M. (2021). A Novel Fuzzy Frequent Itemsets Mining Approach for the Detection of Breast Cancer. [IJIRR]. *International Journal of Information Retrieval Research*, *11*(1), 36–53. doi:10.4018/IJIRR.2021010102

Rani, D., Sangwan, A., Sangwan, A., & Singh, T. (2021). Machine Learning Techniques for Underwater Wireless Sensor Networks. In N. Goyal, L. Sapra, & J. K. Sandhu (Eds.), *Energy-Efficient Underwater Wireless Communications and Networking* (pp. 194–211). IGI Global., doi:10.4018/978-1-7998-3640-7.ch013

Rani, P., Kumar, R., Jain, A., & Chawla, S. K. (2021). A Hybrid Approach for Feature Selection Based on Genetic Algorithm and Recursive Feature Elimination. [IJISMD]. *International Journal of Information System Modeling and Design, 12*(2), 17–38. doi:10.4018/IJISMD.2021040102

Rani, S. (2021). A Study on COVID-19 Prediction and Detection With Artificial Intelligence-Based Real-Time Healthcare Monitoring Systems. In M. Roy & L. R. Gupta (Eds.), *Machine Learning and Data Analytics for Predicting, Managing, and Monitoring Disease* (pp. 52–63). IGI Global., doi:10.4018/978-1-7998-7188-0.ch004

Rao, N. R. (2021). Artificial Intelligence as an Enabler for Developing Business Systems. In Khosrow-Pour D.B.A., M. (Eds.), Encyclopedia of Organizational Knowledge, Administration, and Technology (pp. 421-432). IGI Global. https://doi.org/ doi:10.4018/978-1-7998-3473-1.ch032

Rashid, M., Goyal, V., Parah, S. A., & Singh, H. (2019). Drug Prediction in Healthcare Using Big Data and Machine Learning. In B. Pandey & A. Khamparia (Eds.), *Hidden Link Prediction in Stochastic Social Networks* (pp. 79–92). IGI Global., doi:10.4018/978-1-5225-9096-5.ch005

Rastogi, R., Chaturvedi, D. K., & Gupta, M. (2020). Computational Approach for Personality Detection on Attributes. In D. S. Sisodia, R. Pachori, & L. Garg (Eds.), *Handbook of Research on Advancements of Artificial Intelligence in Healthcare Engineering* (pp. 287–317). IGI Global., doi:10.4018/978-1-7998-2120-5.ch016

Rastogi, R., Chaturvedi, D. K., & Gupta, M. (2020). Exhibiting App and Analysis for Biofeedback-Based Mental Health Analyzer. In D. S. Sisodia, R. Pachori, & L. Garg (Eds.), *Handbook of Research on Advancements of Artificial Intelligence in Healthcare Engineering* (pp. 265–286). IGI Global., doi:10.4018/978-1-7998-2120-5.ch015

Rastogi, R., Chaturvedi, D. K., & Gupta, M. (2021). Mental Health Through Biofeedback Is Important to Analyze. In G. Rani & P. K. Tiwari (Eds.), *Handbook of Research on Disease Prediction Through Data Analytics and Machine Learning* (pp. 402–423). IGI Global., doi:10.4018/978-1-7998-2742-9.ch020

Rastogi, R., & Chaturvedi, D. K. (2021). Biofeedback-Based Mental Health Software and Its Statistical Analysis. In V. Sathiyamoorthi & A. Elci (Eds.), *Challenges and Applications of Data Analytics in Social Perspectives* (Vol. S, pp. 136–155). IGI Global., doi:10.4018/978-1-7998-2566-1.ch008

Rastogi, R., Chaturvedi, D. K., Gupta, M., & Singhal, P. (2020). Intelligent Mental Health Analyzer by Biofeedback. In N. Wickramasinghe (Ed.), *Handbook of Research on Optimizing Healthcare Management Techniques* (pp. 127–153). IGI Global., doi:10.4018/978-1-7998-1371-2.ch009

Rastogi, R., Chaturvedi, D. K., Gupta, M., & Singhal, P. (2021). Automated App for Mental Health Analysis. In T. H. Musiolik & A. D. Cheok (Eds.), *Analyzing Future Applications of AI, Sensors, and Robotics in Society* (pp. 104–131). IGI Global., doi:10.4018/978-1-7998-3499-1.ch007

Rather, S. A., & Bala, P. S. (2020). Analysis of Gravitation-Based Optimization Algorithms for Clustering and Classification. In F. P. Garcia Marquez (Ed.), *Handbook of Research on Big Data Clustering and Machine Learning* (pp. 74–99). IGI Global., doi:10.4018/978-1-7998-0106-1.ch005

Rathod, S. R., & Patil, C. Y. (2021). Performance Assessment of Ensemble Learning Model for Prediction of Cardiac Disease Among Smokers Based on HRV Features. [IJBCE]. *International Journal of Biomedical and Clinical Engineering*, 10(1), 19–34. doi:10.4018/IJBCE.2021010102

Ravi, N., Vimala Rani, P., Rajesh Alias Harinarayan, R., Mercy Shalinie, S., Seshadri, K., & Pariventhan, P. (2019). Deep Learning-based Framework for Smart Sustainable Cities. [IJIIT]. *International Journal of Intelligent Information Technologies*, 15(4), 76–107. doi:10.4018/IJIIT.2019100105

Rawat, B., & Dwivedi, S. K. (2019). Discovering Learners' Characteristics Through Cluster Analysis for Recommendation of Courses in E-Learning Environment. [IJICTE]. *International Journal of Information and Communication Technology Education*, 15(1), 42–66. doi:10.4018/IJICTE.2019010104

Revathi, T., Saroja, S., Haseena, S., & Blessa Binolin Pepsi, M. (2019). Multi-Criteria Decision-Making Techniques for Histopathological Image Classification. In N. Dey, A. S. Ashour, H. Kalia, R. Goswami, & H. Das (Eds.), *Histopathological Image Analysis in Medical Decision Making* (pp. 103–138). IGI Global., doi:10.4018/978-1-5225-6316-7.ch005

Rhmann, W. (2021). An Ensemble of Hybrid Search-Based Algorithms for Software Effort Prediction. [IJSSCI]. *International Journal of Software Science and Computational Intelligence*, *13*(3), 28–37. doi:10.4018/IJSSCI.2021070103

Rhmann, W. (2021). Quantitative Software Change Prediction in Open Source Web Projects Using Time Series Forecasting. [IJOSSP]. *International Journal of Open Source Software and Processes*, *12*(2), 36–51. doi:10.4018/IJOSSP.2021040103

Rodge, J., & Jaiswal, S. (2019). Comprehensive Overview of Neural Networks and Its Applications in Autonomous Vehicles. In H. D. Purnomo (Ed.), *Computational Intelligence in the Internet of Things* (pp. 159–173). IGI Global., doi:10.4018/978-1-5225-7955-7.ch007

Rodrigues, P. J., Igrejas, G. P., & Beato, R. F. (2020). Obtaining Deep Learning Models for Automatic Classification of Leukocytes. In M. Mahrishi, K. K. Hiran, G. Meena, & P. Sharma (Eds.), *Machine Learning and Deep Learning in Real-Time Applications* (pp. 1–32). IGI Global., doi:10.4018/978-1-7998-3095-5.ch001

Rodríguez, J. P., Corrales, D. C., & Corrales, J. C. (2018). A Process for Increasing the Samples of Coffee Rust Through Machine Learning Methods. [IJAEIS]. *International Journal of Agricultural and Environmental Information Systems*, *9*(2), 32–52. doi:10.4018/IJAEIS.2018040103

Rodríguez-Pardo, C., Patricio, M. A., Berlanga, A., & Molina, J. M. (2020). Machine Learning for Smart Tourism and Retail. In F. P. Garcia Marquez (Ed.), *Handbook of Research on Big Data Clustering and Machine Learning* (pp. 311–333). IGI Global., doi:10.4018/978-1-7998-0106-1.ch014

Roman, M., Khan, S., Khan, A., & Ali, M. (2020). Optimizing Learning Weights of Back Propagation Using Flower Pollination Algorithm for Diabetes and Thyroid Data Classification. In S. Umair (Ed.), *Mobile Devices and Smart Gadgets in Medical Sciences* (pp. 270–296). IGI Global., doi:10.4018/978-1-7998-2521-0.ch013

Rosa, L., Freitas, M. B., Henriques, J., Quitério, P., Caldeira, F., Cruz, T., & Simões, P. (2020). Evolving the Security Paradigm for Industrial IoT Environments. In M. D. Stojanović & S. V. Boštjančič Rakas (Eds.), *Cyber Security of Industrial Control Systems in the Future Internet Environment* (pp. 69–90). IGI Global., doi:10.4018/978-1-7998-2910-2.ch004

Rose Bindu Joseph, P., & Devarasan, E. (2018). Fuzzy Techniques for Content-Based Image Retrieval. In R. Das, S. De, & S. Bhattacharyya (Eds.), *Feature Dimension Reduction for Content-Based Image Identification* (pp. 41–64). IGI Global., doi:10.4018/978-1-5225-5775-3.ch003

Rowe, E., Asbell-Clarke, J., Bardar, E., Almeda, M. V., Baker, R. S., Scruggs, R., & Gasca, S. (2020). Advancing Research in Game-Based Learning Assessment. In E. Kennedy & Y. Qian (Eds.), *Advancing Educational Research With Emerging Technology* (pp. 99–123). IGI Global., doi:10.4018/978-1-7998-1173-2.ch006

Roy, M. (2020). A Generalized Overview of the Biomedical Image Processing From the Big Data Perspective. In Chakraborty, S., & Mali, K. (Eds.), Applications of Advanced Machine Intelligence in Computer Vision and Object Recognition (pp. 133-158). IGI Global. https://doi.org/ doi:10.4018/978-1-7998-2736-8.ch006

Fazzin, S. (2020). *Artificial Intelligence in Practice*. IGI Global., doi:10.4018/978-1-7998-2036-9.ch005

Hai-Jew, S. (2019). *Creating and Analyzing Induced Decision Trees From Online Learning Data*. IGI Global., doi:10.4018/978-1-5225-7528-3.ch006

S. P. A., G., K., & P., B. (2020). Activity Recognition System Through Deep Learning Analysis as an Early Biomarker of ASD Characteristics. In Wadhera, T., & Kakkar, D. (Ed.), Interdisciplinary Approaches to Altering Neurodevelopmental Disorders (pp. 228-249). IGI Global. https://doi.org/ doi:10.4018/978-1-7998-3069-6.ch014

Sedkaoui, S. (2019). *First of All, Understand Data Analytics Context and Changes*. IGI Global., doi:10.4018/978-1-5225-7609-9.ch004

Sedkaoui, S. (2019). *Plan and Rules for Data Analysis Success*. IGI Global., doi:10.4018/978-1-5225-7609-9.ch008

Sedkaoui, S. (2019). *Techniques and Methods That Help to Make Big Data the Simplest Recipe for Success.* IGI Global., doi:10.4018/978-1-5225-7609-9.ch006

S., G. K., & Thomas, T. (2020). Intrusion Detection Systems for Internet of Things. In Gupta, B. B., & Srinivasagopalan, S. (Ed.), *Handbook of Research on Intrusion Detection Systems* (pp. 148-171). IGI Global. https://doi.org/ doi:10.4018/978-1-7998-2242-4.ch008

S., J., & M., L. (2021). An Analysis of Pattern Recognition and Machine Learning Approaches on Medical Images. In Swarnalatha, P., & Prabu, S. (Ed.), *Applications of Artificial Intelligence for Smart Technology* (pp. 35-54). IGI Global. https://doi.org/ doi:10.4018/978-1-7998-3335-2.ch003

S., K., & D., T. (2020). Deep Learning Approach for Extracting Catch Phrases from Legal Documents. In S., S., & M., J. (Ed.), *Neural Networks for Natural Language Processing* (pp. 143-158). IGI Global. https://doi.org/ doi:10.4018/978-1-7998-1159-6.ch009

S., S., S., R., & S., I. (2020). Natural Language Processing-Based Information Extraction and Abstraction for Lease Documents. In S., S., & M., J. (Ed.), *Neural Networks for Natural Language Processing* (pp. 170-187). IGI Global. https://doi.org/ doi:10.4018/978-1-7998-1159-6.ch011

S., U., D., S., Mouliganth, C., & M., V. E. (2021). KidNet. In Senthilnathan, K., Shanmugam, B., Goyal, D., Annapoorani, I., & Samikannu, R. (Ed.), *Deep Learning Applications and Intelligent Decision Making in Engineering* (pp. 114-129). IGI Global. https://doi.org/ doi:10.4018/978-1-7998-2108-3.ch004

Safdari, R., & Rezaei-Hachesu, P., Marjan GhaziSaeedi, Samad-Soltani, T., & Zolnoori, M. (2018). Evaluation of Classification Algorithms vs Knowledge-Based Methods for Differential Diagnosis of Asthma in Iranian Patients. [IJISSS]. *International Journal of Information Systems in the Service Sector, 10*(2), 22–35. doi:10.4018/IJISSS.2018040102

Şahin, D. Ö., & Kılıç, E. (2021). An Extensive Text Mining Study for the Turkish Language. In F. Pinarbasi & M. Taskiran (Eds.), *Natural Language Processing for Global and Local Business* (pp. 272–306). IGI Global., doi:10.4018/978-1-7998-4240-8.ch012

Sahu, S. K., Katiyar, A., Kumari, K. M., Kumar, G., & Mohapatra, D. P. (2019). An SVM-Based Ensemble Approach for Intrusion Detection. [IJITWE]. *International Journal of Information Technology and Web Engineering, 14*(1), 66–84. doi:10.4018/IJITWE.2019010104

Sahu, T. P., & Khandekar, S. (2020). A Machine Learning-Based Lexicon Approach for Sentiment Analysis. [IJTHI]. *International Journal of Technology and Human Interaction, 16*(2), 8–22. doi:10.4018/IJTHI.2020040102

Said, H., Manyilizu, M. C., & Mohsini, M. H. (2021). Developing Dropout Predictive System for Secondary Schools Using Classification Algorithm. In F. M. Nafukho & A. Boniface Makulilo (Eds.), *Handbook of Research on Nurturing Industrial Economy for Africa's Development* (pp. 411–427). IGI Global., doi:10.4018/978-1-7998-6471-4.ch022

Saikia, A., & Paul, S. (2020). Application of Deep Learning for EEG. In D. S. Sisodia, R. Pachori, & L. Garg (Eds.), *Handbook of Research on Advancements of Artificial Intelligence in Healthcare Engineering* (pp. 106–123). IGI Global., doi:10.4018/978-1-7998-2120-5.ch007

Saito, T., & Watanobe, Y. (2020). Learning Path Recommendation System for Programming Education Based on Neural Networks. [IJDET]. *International Journal of Distance Education Technologies, 18*(1), 36–64. doi:10.4018/IJDET.2020010103

Sajja, P. S., & Akerkar, R. (2019). Deep Learning for Big Data Analytics. In H. Banati, S. Mehta, & P. Kaur (Eds.), *Nature-Inspired Algorithms for Big Data Frameworks* (pp. 1–21). IGI Global., doi:10.4018/978-1-5225-5852-1.ch001

Sakpere, W., & Gallerani, V. (2021). An Intelligent Machine-Driven Perspective to Archaeological Pottery Reassembly. In Khosrow-Pour D.B.A., M. (Ed.), Encyclopedia of Information Science and Technology, Fifth Edition (pp. 127-137). IGI Global. https://doi.org/ doi:10.4018/978-1-7998-3479-3.ch010

Saldana-Perez, M., Torres-Ruiz, M., & Moreno-Ibarra, M. (2019). Classification of Traffic Events in Mexico City Using Machine Learning and Volunteered Geographic Information. In M. D. Lytras, L. Daniela, & A. Visvizi (Eds.), *Knowledge-Intensive Economies and Opportunities for Social, Organizational, and Technological Growth* (pp. 141–162). IGI Global., doi:10.4018/978-1-5225-7347-0.ch008

Salhi, D. E., Tari, A., & Kechadi, M. T. (2021). Using E-Reputation for Sentiment Analysis. [IJCAC]. *International Journal of Cloud Applications and Computing*, *11*(2), 32–47. doi:10.4018/IJCAC.2021040103

Salih Ahmed, R., Sayed Ali Ahmed, E., & Saeed, R. A. (2021). Machine Learning in Cyber-Physical Systems in Industry 4.0. In A. K. Luhach & A. Elçi (Eds.), *Artificial Intelligence Paradigms for Smart Cyber-Physical Systems* (pp. 20–41). IGI Global., doi:10.4018/978-1-7998-5101-1.ch002

Sánchez Sánchez, P. M., Jorquera Valero, J. M., Huertas Celdran, A., & Martínez Pérez, G. (2020). Intelligent User Profiling Based on Sensors and Location Data to Detect Intrusions on Mobile Devices. In B. B. Gupta & S. Srinivasagopalan (Eds.), *Handbook of Research on Intrusion Detection Systems* (pp. 1–25). IGI Global., doi:10.4018/978-1-7998-2242-4.ch001

Sanchéz, P. A., González, J. R., Fajardo-Toro, C. H., & Sánchez, P. M. (2020). Designing a Neural Network Model for Time Series Forecasting. In B. Christiansen & F. Shuwaikh (Eds.), *Theoretical and Applied Mathematics in International Business* (pp. 259–284). IGI Global., doi:10.4018/978-1-5225-8458-2.ch012

Sánchez-Holgado, P., & Arcila-Calderón, C. (2020). Supervised Sentiment Analysis of Science Topics. [JITR]. *Journal of Information Technology Research*, *13*(3), 80–94. doi:10.4018/JITR.2020070105

Sandeep, V., Kondappan, S., Jone, A. A., & Raj Barath, S. (2021). Anomaly Intrusion Detection Using SVM and C4.5 Classification With an Improved Particle Swarm Optimization (I-PSO). [IJISP]. *International Journal of Information Security and Privacy*, *15*(2), 113–130. doi:10.4018/IJISP.2021040106

Sandosh, S., Govindasamy, V., & Akila, G. (2020). Enhanced Learning Vector Quantization for Detecting Intrusions In IDS. [IJWP]. *International Journal of Web Portals*, *12*(1), 57–72. doi:10.4018/IJWP.2020010105

Sandur, P., Naveena, C., Aradhya, V. M., & Nagasundara, K. B. (2018). Segmentation of Brain Tumor Tissues in HGG and LGG MR Images Using 3D U-net Convolutional Neural Network. [IJNCR]. *International Journal of Natural Computing Research*, *7*(2), 18–30. doi:10.4018/IJNCR.2018040102

Sangaiya, I., & Kumar, A. V. (2019). A Hybrid Feature Selection Method for Effective Data Classification in Data Mining Applications. [IJGHPC]. *International Journal of Grid and High Performance Computing*, *11*(1), 1–16. doi:10.4018/IJGHPC.2019010101

Sangwan, N., & Bhatnagar, V. (2020). Comprehensive Contemplation of Probabilistic Aspects in Intelligent Analytics. [IJSSMET]. *International Journal of Service Science, Management, Engineering, and Technology*, *11*(1), 116–141. doi:10.4018/IJSSMET.2020010108

Sankisa, A., Punjabi, A., & Katsaggelos, A. K. (2019). Optical Flow Prediction for Blind and Non-Blind Video Error Concealment Using Deep Neural Networks. [IJMDEM]. *International Journal of Multimedia Data Engineering and Management*, *10*(3), 27–46. doi:10.4018/IJMDEM.2019070102

Sanyal, M. K., Ghosh, I., & Jana, R. K. (2021). Characterization and Predictive Analysis of Volatile Financial Markets Using Detrended Fluctuation Analysis, Wavelet Decomposition, and Machine Learning. [IJDA]. *International Journal of Data Analytics*, *2*(1), 1–31. doi:10.4018/IJDA.2021010101

Saranya, N., & Selvam, S. (2020). A Detailed Study on Classification Algorithms in Big Data. In A. Haldorai & A. Ramu (Eds.), *Big Data Analytics for Sustainable Computing* (pp. 30–46). IGI Global., doi:10.4018/978-1-5225-9750-6.ch002

Sarfo-Manu, P., Siaw, G., & Appiahene, P. (2019). Intelligent System for Credit Risk Management in Financial Institutions. [IJAIML]. *International Journal of Artificial Intelligence and Machine Learning*, *9*(2), 57–67. doi:10.4018/IJAIML.2019070104

Sarhan, A., & Ramadan, A. (2020). Continuous User Authentication on Touchscreen Using Behavioral Biometrics Utilizing Machine Learning Approaches. In B. B. Gupta & D. Gupta (Eds.), *Handbook of Research on Multimedia Cyber Security* (pp. 243–281). IGI Global., doi:10.4018/978-1-7998-2701-6.ch013

Sathya, D., Sudha, V., & Jagadeesan, D. (2020). Application of Machine Learning Techniques in Healthcare. In S. Velayutham (Ed.), *Handbook of Research on Applications and Implementations of Machine Learning Techniques* (pp. 289–304). IGI Global., doi:10.4018/978-1-5225-9902-9.ch015

Savin, S., & Ivakhnenko, A. (2019). Enhanced Footsteps Generation Method for Walking Robots Based on Convolutional Neural Networks. In A. E. Hassanien, A. Darwish, & C. L. Chowdhary (Eds.), *Handbook of Research on Deep Learning Innovations and Trends* (pp. 16–39). IGI Global., doi:10.4018/978-1-5225-7862-8.ch002

Saxena, R., Adate, A. S., & Sasikumar, D. (2020). A Comparative Study on Adversarial Noise Generation for Single Image Classification. [IJIIT]. *International Journal of Intelligent Information Technologies*, *16*(1), 75–87. doi:10.4018/IJIIT.2020010105

Saxena, S., Paul, S., Garg, A., Saikia, A., & Datta, A. (2020). Deep Learning in Computational Neuroscience. In R. Kashyap & A. Kumar (Eds.), *Challenges and Applications for Implementing Machine Learning in Computer Vision* (pp. 43–63). IGI Global., doi:10.4018/978-1-7998-0182-5.ch002

Selvanambi, R., & Jaisankar, N. (2019). Healthcare. [IJEHMC]. *International Journal of E-Health and Medical Communications*, *10*(2), 63–85. doi:10.4018/IJEHMC.2019040104

Senbagavalli, M., Sathiyamoorthi, V., & Vijayakumar, D. S. (2020). Relative Analysis on Algorithms and Applications of Deep Learning. In S. Velayutham (Ed.), *Handbook of Research on Applications and Implementations of Machine Learning Techniques* (pp. 263–288). IGI Global., doi:10.4018/978-1-5225-9902-9.ch014

Shah, H. D., Bhatt, C. M., Patel, S. M., Khajanchi, J. B., & Makwana, J. N. (2021). Churn Prediction and Fraud Detection in Dairy Sector Using Machine Learning. In C. T. Chisita, R. T. Enakrire, O. O. Durodolu, V. W. Tsabedze, & J. M. Ngoaketsi (Eds.), *Handbook of Research on Records and Information Management Strategies for Enhanced Knowledge Coordination* (pp. 391–406). IGI Global., doi:10.4018/978-1-7998-6618-3.ch023

Shaila, S. G., Rajkumari, S., & Ayyasamy, V. (2020). Introducing the Deep Learning for Digital Age. In S. Velayutham (Ed.), *Handbook of Research on Applications and Implementations of Machine Learning Techniques* (pp. 317–333). IGI Global., doi:10.4018/978-1-5225-9902-9.ch017

Shanmugarajeshwari, V., & Ilayaraja, M. (2021). Intelligent Prediction Techniques for Chronic Kidney Disease Data Analysis. [IJAIML]. *International Journal of Artificial Intelligence and Machine Learning*, *11*(2), 19–37. doi:10.4018/IJAIML.20210701.oa2

Shanmugasundaram, S., & M., P. (2021). Liver Disease Detection Using Grey Wolf Optimization and Random Forest Classification. In Senthilnathan, K., Shanmugam, B., Goyal, D., Annapoorani, I., & Samikannu, R. (Ed.), *Deep Learning Applications and Intelligent Decision Making in Engineering* (pp. 130-160). IGI Global. https://doi.org/ doi:10.4018/978-1-7998-2108-3.ch005

Sharma, A., & Rani, R. (2021). Machine Learning Perspective in Cancer Research. In G. Rani & P. K. Tiwari (Eds.), *Handbook of Research on Disease Prediction Through Data Analytics and Machine Learning* (pp. 142–163). IGI Global., doi:10.4018/978-1-7998-2742-9.ch008

Sharma, A., Bhatnagar, V., & Bansal, A. (2018). SENSEX Price Fluctuation Forecasting Comparison Between Global Indices and Companies Making It. [JGIM]. *Journal of Global Information Management, 26*(3), 90–104. doi:10.4018/JGIM.2018070107

Sharma, P. K., & Bhargava, C. (2020). Nanocomposite-Based Humidity Sensor. In C. Bhargava (Ed.), *AI Techniques for Reliability Prediction for Electronic Components* (pp. 97–123). IGI Global., doi:10.4018/978-1-7998-1464-1.ch006

Sharma, P., Sengupta, J., & Suri, P. K. (2019). WLI Fuzzy Clustering and Adaptive Lion Neural Network (ALNN) for Cloud Intrusion Detection. [IJDAI]. *International Journal of Distributed Artificial Intelligence, 11*(1), 1–17. doi:10.4018/IJDAI.2019010101

Sharma, R., & Gundraniya, V. (2020). Artificial Intelligence Towards Water Conservation. In G. Bekdaş, S. M. Nigdeli, & M. Yücel (Eds.), *Artificial Intelligence and Machine Learning Applications in Civil, Mechanical, and Industrial Engineering* (pp. 141–151). IGI Global., doi:10.4018/978-1-7998-0301-0.ch008

Sharma, R., Sircar, P., & Pachori, R. B. (2020). Automated Seizure Classification Using Deep Neural Network Based on Autoencoder. In D. S. Sisodia, R. Pachori, & L. Garg (Eds.), *Handbook of Research on Advancements of Artificial Intelligence in Healthcare Engineering* (pp. 1–19). IGI Global., doi:10.4018/978-1-7998-2120-5.ch001

Sharma, S., & Jain, A. (2020). Hybrid Ensemble Learning With Feature Selection for Sentiment Classification in Social Media. [IJIRR]. *International Journal of Information Retrieval Research, 10*(2), 40–58. doi:10.4018/IJIRR.2020040103

Related Readings

Sharma, T., Bajaj, A., & Sangwan, O. P. (2020). Deep Learning Approaches for Textual Sentiment Analysis. In A. Solanki, S. Kumar, & A. Nayyar (Eds.), *Handbook of Research on Emerging Trends and Applications of Machine Learning* (pp. 171–182). IGI Global., doi:10.4018/978-1-5225-9643-1.ch009

Sheik Abdullah, A., Akash, K., Bhubesh, K. R. A., & Selvakumar, S. (2021). Development of a Predictive Model for Textual Data Using Support Vector Machine Based on Diverse Kernel Functions Upon Sentiment Score Analysis. [IJNCR]. *International Journal of Natural Computing Research, 10*(2), 1–20. doi:10.4018/IJNCR.2021040101

Sheykhkanloo, N. M., & Hall, A. (2020). Insider Threat Detection Using Supervised Machine Learning Algorithms on an Extremely Imbalanced Dataset. [IJCWT]. *International Journal of Cyber Warfare & Terrorism, 10*(2), 1–26. doi:10.4018/IJCWT.2020040101

Shirazi, Z. A., de Souza, C. P., Kashef, R., & Rodrigues, F. F. (2020). Deep Learning in the Healthcare Industry. In M. Gul, E. Celik, S. Mete, & F. Serin (Eds.), *Computational Intelligence and Soft Computing Applications in Healthcare Management Science* (pp. 220–245). IGI Global., doi:10.4018/978-1-7998-2581-4.ch010

Shrivastava, R., & Pandey, M. (2021). Human Fall Detection Using Efficient Kernel and Eccentric Approach. [IJEHMC]. *International Journal of E-Health and Medical Communications, 12*(1), 62–80. doi:10.4018/IJEHMC.2021010105

Shukla, R., Yadav, A. K., & Singh, T. R. (2021). Application of Deep Learning in Biological Big Data Analysis. In H. Saini, G. Rathee, & D. K. Saini (Eds.), *Large-Scale Data Streaming, Processing, and Blockchain Security* (pp. 117–148). IGI Global., doi:10.4018/978-1-7998-3444-1.ch006

Shyla, S. I., & Sujatha, S. (2020). An Efficient Automatic Intrusion Detection in Cloud Using Optimized Fuzzy Inference System. [IJISP]. *International Journal of Information Security and Privacy, 14*(4), 22–41. doi:10.4018/IJISP.2020100102

Siebra, C. A., Santos, R. N., & Lino, N. C. (2020). A Self-Adjusting Approach for Temporal Dropout Prediction of E-Learning Students. [IJDET]. *International Journal of Distance Education Technologies, 18*(2), 19–33. doi:10.4018/IJDET.2020040102

Sigamani, R. M. (2020). Adoption of Machine Learning With Adaptive Approach for Securing CPS. In P. Ganapathi & D. Shanmugapriya (Eds.), *Handbook of Research on Machine and Deep Learning Applications for Cyber Security* (pp. 388–415). IGI Global., doi:10.4018/978-1-5225-9611-0.ch018

Singh, A. K., & Gandhi, G. C. (2020). Computer Architecture. [IJSST]. *International Journal of Smart Security Technologies*, 7(1), 41–48. doi:10.4018/IJSST.2020010103

Singh, A. P., Gupta, C., Singh, R., & Singh, N. (2021). A Comparative Analysis of Evolutionary Algorithms for Data Classification Using KEEL Tool. [IJSIR]. *International Journal of Swarm Intelligence Research*, 12(1), 17–28. doi:10.4018/IJSIR.2021010102

Singh, A., & Tiwari, A. (2021). A Study of Feature Selection and Dimensionality Reduction Methods for Classification-Based Phishing Detection System. [IJIRR]. *International Journal of Information Retrieval Research*, 11(1), 1–35. doi:10.4018/IJIRR.2021010101

Singh, H. R., Biswas, S. K., & Bordoloi, M. (2019). Recent Neuro-Fuzzy Approaches for Feature Selection and Classification. In M. Sarfraz (Ed.), *Exploring Critical Approaches of Evolutionary Computation* (pp. 1–19). IGI Global., doi:10.4018/978-1-5225-5832-3.ch001

Singh, L. K., Pooja, Garg, H., & Khanna, M. (2021). An Artificial Intelligence-Based Smart System for Early Glaucoma Recognition Using OCT Images. [IJEHMC]. *International Journal of E-Health and Medical Communications*, 12(4), 32–59. doi:10.4018/IJEHMC.20210701.oa3

Singh, L. K. Pooja, Garg, H., Khanna, M., & Bhadoria, R. S. (2021). An Analytical Study on Machine Learning Techniques. In Chowdhury, N., & Chandra Deka, G. (Ed.), Multidisciplinary Functions of Blockchain Technology in AI and IoT Applications (pp. 137-157). IGI Global. https:// doi.org/ doi:10.4018/978-1-7998-5876-8.ch007

Singh, M. P., Chaturvedi, S., & Shudhalwar, D. D. (2019). Multilayer Neural Network Technique for Parsing the Natural Language Sentences. [IJAIML]. *International Journal of Artificial Intelligence and Machine Learning*, 9(2), 22–38. doi:10.4018/IJAIML.2019070102

Singh, N., & Mohanty, S. R. (2018). Short Term Price Forecasting Using Adaptive Generalized Neuron Model. [IJACI]. *International Journal of Ambient Computing and Intelligence*, 9(3), 44–56. doi:10.4018/IJACI.2018070104

Singh, P. (2021). Vehicle Monitoring and Surveillance Through Vehicular Sensor Network. In R. S. Rao, N. Singh, O. Kaiwartya, & S. Das (Eds.), *Cloud-Based Big Data Analytics in Vehicular Ad-Hoc Networks* (pp. 165–190). IGI Global., doi:10.4018/978-1-7998-2764-1.ch008

Singh, S. K., & Goyal, A. (2020). Performance Analysis of Machine Learning Algorithms for Cervical Cancer Detection. [IJHISI]. *International Journal of Healthcare Information Systems and Informatics*, *15*(2), 1–21. doi:10.4018/IJHISI.2020040101

Singh, S., Gautam, K., Singhal, P., Jangir, S. K., & Kumar, M. (2021). A Survey on Intelligence Tools for Data Analytics. In B. Patil & M. Vohra (Eds.), *Handbook of Research on Engineering, Business, and Healthcare Applications of Data Science and Analytics* (pp. 73–95). IGI Global., doi:10.4018/978-1-7998-3053-5.ch005

Singhania, S., Arju, N. A., & Singh, R. (2019). Image Tampering Detection Using Convolutional Neural Network. [IJSE]. *International Journal of Synthetic Emotions*, *10*(1), 54–63. doi:10.4018/IJSE.2019010103

Singla, J. (2019). A Fuzzy Expert System for Car Evaluation. [IJDAI]. *International Journal of Distributed Artificial Intelligence*, *11*(2), 11–19. doi:10.4018/IJDAI.2019070102

Sinha, K. (2021). A Study on Supervised Machine Learning Technique to Detect Anomalies in Networks. In B. Holland (Ed.), *Handbook of Research on Library Response to the COVID-19 Pandemic* (pp. 209–230). IGI Global., doi:10.4018/978-1-7998-6449-3.ch011

Sinha, U., Singh, A., & Sharma, D. K. (2020). Machine Learning in the Medical Industry. In A. Solanki, S. Kumar, & A. Nayyar (Eds.), *Handbook of Research on Emerging Trends and Applications of Machine Learning* (pp. 403–424). IGI Global., doi:10.4018/978-1-5225-9643-1.ch019

Sivaganesan, S., Maria Antony, S., & Udayakumar, E. (2020). An Event-Based Neural Network Architecture with Content Addressable Memory. [IJERTCS]. *International Journal of Embedded and Real-Time Communication Systems*, *11*(1), 23–40. doi:10.4018/IJERTCS.2020010102

Solanki, A., & Saxena, R. (2020). Text Classification Using Self-Structure Extended Multinomial Naive Bayes. In A. Solanki, S. Kumar, & A. Nayyar (Eds.), *Handbook of Research on Emerging Trends and Applications of Machine Learning* (pp. 107–129). IGI Global., doi:10.4018/978-1-5225-9643-1.ch006

Souprayen, B., Ayyanar, A., & Suresh Joseph, K. (2020). Optimization of C5.0 Classifier With Bayesian Theory for Food Traceability Management Using Internet of Things. [IJSSTA]. *International Journal of Smart Sensor Technologies and Applications*, *1*(1), 1–21. doi:10.4018/IJSSTA.2020010101

Sowmya, B. J., Krishna Chaitanya, S., Seema, S., & Srinivasa, K. (2020). Data Analytic Techniques for Developing Decision Support System on Agrometeorological Parameters for Farmers. [IJCINI]. *International Journal of Cognitive Informatics and Natural Intelligence*, *14*(2), 92–107. doi:10.4018/ IJCINI.2020040106

Sowmya, B. J., Shetty, C., Seema, S., & Srinivasa, K. G. (2019). An Image Processing and Machine Learning Approach for Early Detection of Diseased Leaves. [IJCPS]. *International Journal of Cyber-Physical Systems*, *1*(2), 56–73. doi:10.4018/IJCPS.2019070104

Srinivasan, N., & Lakshmi, C. (2019). Stock Price Prediction Using Fuzzy Time-Series Population Based Gravity Search Algorithm. [IJSI]. *International Journal of Software Innovation*, *7*(2), 50–64. doi:10.4018/IJSI.2019040105

Srinivasan, S., & Dhinesh Babu, L. D. (2019). A Parallel Neural Network Approach for Faster Rumor Identification in Online Social Networks. [IJSWIS]. *International Journal on Semantic Web and Information Systems*, *15*(4), 69–89. doi:10.4018/IJSWIS.2019100105

Srinivasan, S., & Dhinesh Babu, L. D. (2020). A Neuro-Fuzzy Approach to Detect Rumors in Online Social Networks. [IJWSR]. *International Journal of Web Services Research*, *17*(1), 64–82. doi:10.4018/IJWSR.2020010104

Srivastav, A., Khan, H., & Mishra, A. K. (2020). Advances in Computational Linguistics and Text Processing Frameworks. In L. Gaur, A. Solanki, V. Jain, & D. Khazanchi (Eds.), *Handbook of Research on Engineering Innovations and Technology Management in Organizations* (pp. 217–244). IGI Global., doi:10.4018/978-1-7998-2772-6.ch012

Srivastav, M. K., Bhadoria, R. S., & Pramanik, T. (2020). Integration of Multiple Cache Server Scheme for User-Based Fuzzy Logic in Content Delivery Networks. In M. Pal, S. Samanta, & A. Pal (Eds.), *Handbook of Research on Advanced Applications of Graph Theory in Modern Society* (pp. 386–396). IGI Global., doi:10.4018/978-1-5225-9380-5.ch016

Srivastava, A. K., Kumar, Y., & Singh, P. K. (2020). A Rule-Based Monitoring System for Accurate Prediction of Diabetes. [IJEHMC]. *International Journal of E-Health and Medical Communications*, *11*(3), 32–53. doi:10.4018/IJEHMC.2020070103

Srivastava, A., Singh, V., & Drall, G. S. (2019). Sentiment Analysis of Twitter Data. [IJHISI]. *International Journal of Healthcare Information Systems and Informatics*, *14*(2), 1–16. doi:10.4018/IJHISI.2019040101

Srivastava, D. K., & Tiwari, P. K. (2021). Chronic Kidney Disease Prediction Using Data Mining Algorithms. In G. Rani & P. K. Tiwari (Eds.), *Handbook of Research on Disease Prediction Through Data Analytics and Machine Learning* (pp. 92–111). IGI Global., doi:10.4018/978-1-7998-2742-9.ch006

Srivastava, M. (2020). A Surrogate Data-Based Approach for Validating Deep Learning Model Used in Healthcare. In R. Wason, D. Goyal, V. Jain, S. Balamurugan, & A. Baliyan (Eds.), *Applications of Deep Learning and Big IoT on Personalized Healthcare Services* (pp. 132–146). IGI Global., doi:10.4018/978-1-7998-2101-4.ch009

Subashini, P., Krishnaveni, M., Dhivyaprabha, T. T., & Shanmugavalli, R. (2020). Review on Intelligent Algorithms for Cyber Security. In P. Ganapathi & D. Shanmugapriya (Eds.), *Handbook of Research on Machine and Deep Learning Applications for Cyber Security* (pp. 1–22). IGI Global., doi:10.4018/978-1-5225-9611-0.ch001

Subramanian, K., Swathypriyadharsini, P., Gunavathi, C., & Premalatha, K. (2020). Trend and Predictive Analytics of Dengue Prevalence in Administrative Region. In S. Velayutham (Ed.), *Handbook of Research on Applications and Implementations of Machine Learning Techniques* (pp. 236–262). IGI Global., doi:10.4018/978-1-5225-9902-9.ch013

Suganya, R., Rajaram, S., & Kameswari, M. (2021). A Literature Review on Thyroid Hormonal Problems in Women Using Data Science and Analytics. In B. Patil & M. Vohra (Eds.), *Handbook of Research on Engineering, Business, and Healthcare Applications of Data Science and Analytics* (pp. 416–428). IGI Global., doi:10.4018/978-1-7998-3053-5.ch021

Sumana, B. V., & Punithavalli, M. (2020). Optimising Prediction in Overlapping and Non-Overlapping Regions. [IJNCR]. *International Journal of Natural Computing Research*, *9*(1), 45–63. doi:10.4018/IJNCR.2020010104

Sumathi, S., Indumathi, S., & Rajkumar, S. (2020). Medical Reports Analysis Using Natural Language Processing for Disease Classification. In S. Velayutham (Ed.), *Handbook of Research on Applications and Implementations of Machine Learning Techniques* (pp. 155–172). IGI Global., doi:10.4018/978-1-5225-9902-9.ch009

Sundara Kumar, M. R., Sankar, S., Nassa, V. K., Pandey, D., Pandey, B. K., & Enbeyle, W. (2021). Innovation and Creativity for Data Mining Using Computational Statistics. In D. Samanta, R. Rao Althar, S. Pramanik, & S. Dutta (Eds.), *Methodologies and Applications of Computational Statistics for Machine Intelligence* (pp. 223–240). IGI Global., doi:10.4018/978-1-7998-7701-1.ch012

Sundararaman, A. T. (2021). Big Data Quality for Data Mining in Business Intelligence Applications. In Azevedo, A., & Santos, M. F. (Eds.), Integration Challenges for Analytics, Business Intelligence, and Data Mining (pp. 64-91). IGI Global. https://doi.org/ doi:10.4018/978-1-7998-5781-5.ch004

Sundareswaran, A., & Lavanya, K. (2020). Real-Time Vehicle Traffic Prediction in Apache Spark Using Ensemble Learning for Deep Neural Networks. [IJIIT]. *International Journal of Intelligent Information Technologies*, 16(4), 19–36. doi:10.4018/IJIIT.2020100102

Suragala, A., & PapaRao A. V.,. (2020). Demystifying Disease Identification and Diagnosis Using Machine Learning Classification Algorithms. In Solanki, A., Kumar, S., & Nayyar, A. (Ed.), *Handbook of Research on Emerging Trends and Applications of Machine Learning* (pp. 200-249). IGI Global. https://doi.org/ doi:10.4018/978-1-5225-9643-1.ch011

Suresh, P. (2021). Macro and Micro Architectures for Network on Chip. In P. Suresh, G. Vairavel, & U. Saravanakumar (Eds.), *Design Methodologies and Tools for 5G Network Development and Application* (pp. 44–74). IGI Global., doi:10.4018/978-1-7998-4610-9.ch003

Swathy Akshaya, M., & Ganapathi, P. (2020). A Review of Machine Learning Methods Applied for Handling Zero-Day Attacks in the Cloud Environment. In P. Ganapathi & D. Shanmugapriya (Eds.), *Handbook of Research on Machine and Deep Learning Applications for Cyber Security* (pp. 364–387). IGI Global., doi:10.4018/978-1-5225-9611-0.ch017

T. Ganesan (2020). *Computational Intelligence in Energy Generation*. IGI Global. https://doi.org/ doi:10.4018/978-1-7998-1710-9.ch001

Related Readings

T. MuthamilSelvan, & Balamurugan, B. (2019). Comparative Performance Analysis of Various Classifiers for Cloud E-Health Users. [IJEHMC]. *International Journal of E-Health and Medical Communications*, *10*(2), 86–101. doi:10.4018/IJEHMC.2019040105

Tabar, S., Sharma, S., & Volkman, D. (2021). Stock Market Prediction Using Elliot Wave Theory and Classification. [IJBAN]. *International Journal of Business Analytics*, *8*(1), 1–20. doi:10.4018/IJBAN.2021010101

Tadepalli, S. K., & Lakshmi, P. (2019). Application of Machine Learning and Artificial Intelligence Techniques for IVF Analysis and Prediction. [IJBDAH]. *International Journal of Big Data and Analytics in Healthcare*, *4*(2), 21–33. doi:10.4018/IJBDAH.2019070102

Tali, R. V., Borra, S., & Mahmud, M. (2021). Detection and Classification of Leukocytes in Blood Smear Images. [IJACI]. *International Journal of Ambient Computing and Intelligence*, *12*(2), 111–139. doi:10.4018/IJACI.2021040107

Tandon, A. (2018). Mining Smart Meter Data. In Z. H. Gontar (Ed.), *Smart Grid Analytics for Sustainability and Urbanization* (pp. 196–214). IGI Global., doi:10.4018/978-1-5225-3996-4.ch007

Tezcan, O., Akcay, C., & Gazioglu, B. (2019). A Review on BIM and Information Technologies Research in the Construction Industry. [IJDIBE]. *International Journal of Digital Innovation in the Built Environment*, *8*(2), 1–19. doi:10.4018/IJDIBE.2019070101

Thang, N. T., Nguyen, G. L., Long, H. V., Tuan, N. A., Tran, T. M., & Tan, N. D. (2021). Efficient Algorithms for Dynamic Incomplete Decision Systems. [IJDWM]. *International Journal of Data Warehousing and Mining*, *17*(3), 44–67. doi:10.4018/IJDWM.2021070103

Thangavel, M., Abiramie Shree, T. G. R., Priyadharshini, P., & Saranya, T. (2020). Review on Machine and Deep Learning Applications for Cyber Security. In P. Ganapathi & D. Shanmugapriya (Eds.), *Handbook of Research on Machine and Deep Learning Applications for Cyber Security* (pp. 42–63). IGI Global., doi:10.4018/978-1-5225-9611-0.ch003

Thendiyath, R., & Prakash, V. (2020). Role of Regression Models in Bridge Pier Scour Prediction. [IJAMC]. *International Journal of Applied Metaheuristic Computing*, *11*(2), 156–170. doi:10.4018/IJAMC.2020040108

Thilagamani, S., Jayanthiladevi, A., & Arunkumar, N. (2018). Data Mining Algorithms, Fog Computing. In P. Raj & A. Raman (Eds.), *Handbook of Research on Cloud and Fog Computing Infrastructures for Data Science* (pp. 231–264). IGI Global., doi:10.4018/978-1-5225-5972-6.ch012

Thiyagarajan, P. (2020). A Review on Cyber Security Mechanisms Using Machine and Deep Learning Algorithms. In P. Ganapathi & D. Shanmugapriya (Eds.), *Handbook of Research on Machine and Deep Learning Applications for Cyber Security* (pp. 23–41). IGI Global., doi:10.4018/978-1-5225-9611-0.ch002

Thomas, J. J., Wei, L. T., Jinila, Y. B., & Subhashini, R. (2020). Smart Computerized Essay Scoring Using Deep Neural Networks for Universities and Institutions. In J. J. Thomas, U. Fiore, G. P. Lechuga, V. Kharchenko, & P. Vasant (Eds.), *Handbook of Research on Smart Technology Models for Business and Industry* (pp. 125–152). IGI Global., doi:10.4018/978-1-7998-3645-2.ch006

Tian, G., & Liu, Y. (2019). Simple Convolutional Neural Network for Left-Right Hands Motor Imagery EEG Signals Classification. [IJCINI]. *International Journal of Cognitive Informatics and Natural Intelligence*, *13*(3), 36–49. doi:10.4018/IJCINI.2019070103

Tianxing, M., Baimuratov, I. R., & Zhukova, N. A. (2019). A Knowledge-Oriented Recommendation System for Machine Learning Algorithm Finding and Data Processing. [IJERTCS]. *International Journal of Embedded and Real-Time Communication Systems*, *10*(4), 20–38. doi:10.4018/IJERTCS.2019100102

Tianxing, M., Osipov, V., Vodyaho, A. I., Lebedev, S., & Zhukova, N. (2019). Distributed Technical Object Model Synthesis Based on Monitoring Data. [IJKSS]. *International Journal of Knowledge and Systems Science*, *10*(3), 27–43. doi:10.4018/IJKSS.2019070103

Tikhomirova, O. (2020). Entrepreneurial innovative network and the design of socio-economic neural system. [IJSDA]. *International Journal of System Dynamics Applications*, *9*(2), 80–102. doi:10.4018/IJSDA.2020040105

Tikhomirova, O. (2020). Entrepreneurial Innovative Network and the Design of Socio-Economic Neural Systems. [IJSKD]. *International Journal of Sociotechnology and Knowledge Development*, *12*(4), 1–23. doi:10.4018/IJSKD.2020100101

Tiwari, P., & Shukla, P. K. (2019). A Review on Various Features and Techniques of Crop Yield Prediction Using Geo-Spatial Data. [IJOCI]. *International Journal of Organizational and Collective Intelligence*, *9*(1), 37–50. doi:10.4018/IJOCI.2019010103

Tiwari, S. (2020). A Blur Classification Approach Using Deep Convolution Neural Network. [IJISMD]. *International Journal of Information System Modeling and Design*, *11*(1), 93–111. doi:10.4018/IJISMD.2020010106

Tiwari, S. (2020). A Comparative Study of Deep Learning Models With Handcraft Features and Non-Handcraft Features for Automatic Plant Species Identification. [IJAEIS]. *International Journal of Agricultural and Environmental Information Systems*, *11*(2), 44–57. doi:10.4018/IJAEIS.2020040104

Touati, H. C., & Boutekkouk, F. (2020). Reliable Weighted Globally Congestion Aware Routing for Network on Chip. [IJERTCS]. *International Journal of Embedded and Real-Time Communication Systems*, *11*(3), 48–66. doi:10.4018/IJERTCS.2020070103

Tripathi, A., Kaur, S., Sankaranarayanan, S., Narayanan, L. K., & Tom, R. J. (2019). Water Demand Prediction for Housing Apartments Using Time Series Analysis. [IJIIT]. *International Journal of Intelligent Information Technologies*, *15*(4), 57–75. doi:10.4018/IJIIT.2019100104

Tuzova, L. N., Tuzoff, D. V., Nikolenko, S. I., & Krasnov, A. S. (2019). Teeth and Landmarks Detection and Classification Based on Deep Neural Networks. In K. Kamalanand, B. Thayumanavan, & P. Jawahar (Eds.), *Computational Techniques for Dental Image Analysis* (pp. 129–150). IGI Global., doi:10.4018/978-1-5225-6243-6.ch006

Tyagi, A. K., & Chahal, P. (2020). Artificial Intelligence and Machine Learning Algorithms. In R. Kashyap & A. Kumar (Eds.), *Challenges and Applications for Implementing Machine Learning in Computer Vision* (pp. 188–219). IGI Global., doi:10.4018/978-1-7998-0182-5.ch008

Tyagi, A. K., & Rekha, G. (2020). Challenges of Applying Deep Learning in Real-World Applications. In R. Kashyap & A. Kumar (Eds.), *Challenges and Applications for Implementing Machine Learning in Computer Vision* (pp. 92–118). IGI Global., doi:10.4018/978-1-7998-0182-5.ch004

Uddin, M. R., Amin, S. H., & Zhang, G. (2021). Demands and Sales Forecasting for Retailers by Analyzing Google Trends and Historical Data. In A. Taghipour (Ed.), *Demand Forecasting and Order Planning in Supply Chains and Humanitarian Logistics* (pp. 89–110). IGI Global., doi:10.4018/978-1-7998-3805-0.ch003

Ulku, I., Yuksektepe, F. U., Yilmaz, O., Aktas, M. U., & Akbalik, N. (2021). Churn Prediction in a Pay-TV Company via Data Classification. [IJAIML]. *International Journal of Artificial Intelligence and Machine Learning, 11*(1), 39–53. doi:10.4018/IJAIML.2021010104

Ullah, R., Khan, A., Shah Abid, S. B., Khan, S., Shah, S. K., & Ali, M. (2020). Crow-ENN. In S. Umair (Ed.), *Mobile Devices and Smart Gadgets in Medical Sciences* (pp. 173–213). IGI Global., doi:10.4018/978-1-7998-2521-0.ch009

Vaidyanathan, S., Sivakumar, M., & Kaliamourthy, B. (2021). Challenges of Developing AI Applications in the Evolving Digital World and Recommendations to Mitigate Such Challenges. In Misra, S., Arumugam, C., Jaganathan, S., & S., S. (Ed.), Confluence of AI, Machine, and Deep Learning in Cyber Forensics (pp. 177-198). IGI Global. https://doi.org/ doi:10.4018/978-1-7998-4900-1.ch011

Vaissnave, V., & Deepalakshmi, P. (2020). Data Transcription for India's Supreme Court Documents Using Deep Learning Algorithms. [IJEGR]. *International Journal of Electronic Government Research, 16*(4), 21–41. doi:10.4018/IJEGR.2020100102

Vanani, I. R., & Amirhosseini, M. (2019). Deep Learning for Opinion Mining. In R. Agrawal & N. Gupta (Eds.), *Extracting Knowledge From Opinion Mining* (pp. 40–65). IGI Global., doi:10.4018/978-1-5225-6117-0.ch003

Vanani, I. R., & Emamat, M. S. (2019). Analytical Review of the Applications of Multi-Criteria Decision Making in Data Mining. In Öner, S. C., & Yüregir, O. H. (Ed.), Optimizing Big Data Management and Industrial Systems With Intelligent Techniques (pp. 53-79). IGI Global. https://doi. org/ doi:10.4018/978-1-5225-5137-9.ch003

Vanitha, N., & Ganapathi, P. (2020). Traffic Analysis of UAV Networks Using Enhanced Deep Feed Forward Neural Networks (EDFFNN). In P. Ganapathi & D. Shanmugapriya (Eds.), *Handbook of Research on Machine and Deep Learning Applications for Cyber Security* (pp. 219–244). IGI Global., doi:10.4018/978-1-5225-9611-0.ch011

Vashisht, R., & Rizvi, S. A. (2021). Estimation of Target Defect Prediction Coverage in Heterogeneous Cross Software Projects. [IJISMD]. *International Journal of Information System Modeling and Design*, *12*(1), 73–93. doi:10.4018/IJISMD.2021010104

Velammal, B. L., & Aarthy, N. (2021). Improvised Spam Detection in Twitter Data Using Lightweight Detectors and Classifiers. [IJWLTT]. *International Journal of Web-Based Learning and Teaching Technologies*, *16*(4), 12–32. doi:10.4018/IJWLTT.20210701.oa2

Veloso, B., Gama, J., & Malheiro, B. (2021). Classification and Recommendation With Data Streams. In Khosrow-Pour D.B.A., M. (Ed.), Encyclopedia of Information Science and Technology, Fifth Edition (pp. 675-684). IGI Global. https://doi.org/ doi:10.4018/978-1-7998-3479-3.ch047

Venkatesan, M., & Prabhavathy, P. (2018). Big Data Computation Model for Landslide Risk Analysis Using Remote Sensing Data. In P. Swarnalatha & P. Sevugan (Eds.), *Big Data Analytics for Satellite Image Processing and Remote Sensing* (pp. 22–33). IGI Global., doi:10.4018/978-1-5225-3643-7.ch002

Venu, K., Palanisamy, N., Krishnakumar, B., & Sasipriyaa, N. (2020). Disease Identification in Plant Leaf Using Deep Convolutional Neural Networks. In S. Velayutham (Ed.), *Handbook of Research on Applications and Implementations of Machine Learning Techniques* (pp. 46–62). IGI Global., doi:10.4018/978-1-5225-9902-9.ch003

Veretekhina, S., & Gorbachenko, V. (2020). Avatar-Based Natural Neural Network as a Dynamic Virtual Model. [IJARB]. *International Journal of Applied Research in Bioinformatics*, *10*(1), 1–25. doi:10.4018/IJARB.2020010101

Verma, D. K., Kush, A., & Jain, R. (2020). Identifying Intruders in MANET. [IJITPM]. *International Journal of Information Technology Project Management*, *11*(4), 42–55. doi:10.4018/IJITPM.2020100104

Verma, J. P., Tanwar, S., Garg, S., Gandhi, I., & Bachani, N. H. (2019). Evaluation of Pattern Based Customized Approach for Stock Market Trend Prediction With Big Data and Machine Learning Techniques. [IJBAN]. *International Journal of Business Analytics*, *6*(3), 1–15. doi:10.4018/IJBAN.2019070101

Verma, M., & Kumar, D. (2021). A Correlation-Based Feature Selection and Classification Approach for Autism Spectrum Disorder. [IJISMD]. *International Journal of Information System Modeling and Design*, *12*(2), 51–66. doi:10.4018/IJISMD.2021040104

Véstias, M. P. (2020). Deep Learning on Edge. In J. M. Rodrigues, P. J. Cardoso, J. Monteiro, & C. M. Ramos (Eds.), *Smart Systems Design, Applications, and Challenges* (pp. 23–42). IGI Global., doi:10.4018/978-1-7998-2112-0.ch002

Victor, N., & Lopez, D. (2020). sl-LSTM. [IJGHPC]. *International Journal of Grid and High Performance Computing*, *12*(3), 1–16. doi:10.4018/IJGHPC.2020070101

Vidushi, A. M., Khamparia, A., & Khatoon, N. (2020). Wireless Environment Security. In Sagayam, K., Bhushan, B., Andrushia, A., & Albuquerque, V. C. (Ed.), Deep Learning Strategies for Security Enhancement in Wireless Sensor Networks (pp. 65-83). IGI Global. https://doi.org/ doi:10.4018/978-1-7998-5068-7.ch004

Vijayakumar, D. S. M., S., Thangaraju, J., & V., S. (2021). Social Media Content Analysis. In Sathiyamoorthi, V., & Elci, A. (Ed.), Challenges and Applications of Data Analytics in Social Perspectives (pp. 156-174). IGI Global. https://doi.org/ doi:10.4018/978-1-7998-2566-1.ch009

Vijayaprabakaran, K., Sathiyamurthy, K., & Ponniamma, M. (2020). Video-Based Human Activity Recognition for Elderly Using Convolutional Neural Network. [IJSPPC]. *International Journal of Security and Privacy in Pervasive Computing*, *12*(1), 36–48. doi:10.4018/IJSPPC.2020010104

Vinayakumar, R., Soman, K. P., & Poornachandran, P. (2019). A Comparative Analysis of Deep Learning Approaches for Network Intrusion Detection Systems (N-IDSs). [IJDCF]. *International Journal of Digital Crime and Forensics*, *11*(3), 65–89. doi:10.4018/IJDCF.2019070104

Vinodhini, V., Sathiyabhama, B., Sankar, S., & Somula, R. (2020). A Deep Structured Model for Video Captioning. [IJGCMS]. *International Journal of Gaming and Computer-Mediated Simulations*, *12*(2), 44–56. doi:10.4018/IJGCMS.2020040103

Virmani, C., Choudhary, T., Pillai, A., & Rani, M. (2020). Applications of Machine Learning in Cyber Security. In P. Ganapathi & D. Shanmugapriya (Eds.), *Handbook of Research on Machine and Deep Learning Applications for Cyber Security* (pp. 83–103). IGI Global., doi:10.4018/978-1-5225-9611-0.ch005

Vlah Jerić, S. (2021). Evaluation of Alternative Approaches in Classification Algorithms for Prediction of Stock Market Index. In T. Škrinjarić, M. Čižmešija, & B. Christiansen (Eds.), *Recent Applications of Financial Risk Modelling and Portfolio Management* (pp. 204–221). IGI Global., doi:10.4018/978-1-7998-5083-0.ch010

Vocaturo, E. (2021). Image Classification Techniques. In G. Rani & P. K. Tiwari (Eds.), *Handbook of Research on Disease Prediction Through Data Analytics and Machine Learning* (pp. 22–49). IGI Global., doi:10.4018/978-1-7998-2742-9.ch003

Vora, S. V., Mehta, R. G., & Patel, S. K. (2021). Impact of Balancing Techniques for Imbalanced Class Distribution on Twitter Data for Emotion Analysis. In D. P. Rana & R. G. Mehta (Eds.), *Data Preprocessing, Active Learning, and Cost Perceptive Approaches for Resolving Data Imbalance* (pp. 211–231). IGI Global., doi:10.4018/978-1-7998-7371-6.ch012

Voronin, A. (2019). Multicriteria Synthesis of Neural Network Architecture. In A. Troussov & S. Maruev (Eds.), *Techno-Social Systems for Modern Economical and Governmental Infrastructures* (pp. 84–99). IGI Global., doi:10.4018/978-1-5225-5586-5.ch004

Galus, W., & Starzyk, J. (2021). *Natural Brains and Motivated, Emotional Mind*. IGI Global., doi:10.4018/978-1-7998-5653-5.ch004

Waheed, A., & Shafi, J. (2022). Comparing Machine Learning Models for the Predictions of Speed in Smart Transportation Systems. In P. Krishna (Ed.), *Handbook of Research on Advances in Data Analytics and Complex Communication Networks* (Vol. S, pp. 34–46). IGI Global., doi:10.4018/978-1-7998-7685-4.ch002

Wang, P., Wang, J., & Zhang, J. (2018). Methodological Research for Modular Neural Networks Based on "an Expert With Other Capabilities". [JGIM]. *Journal of Global Information Management*, 26(2), 104–126. doi:10.4018/JGIM.2018040105

Wang, P., Zuo, Y., Wang, J., & Zhang, J. (2020). A Novel Cooperative Divide-and-Conquer Neural Networks Algorithm. In Z. Zhang (Ed.), *Novel Theories and Applications of Global Information Resource Management* (pp. 286–317). IGI Global., doi:10.4018/978-1-7998-1786-4.ch011

Wang, S. (2020). Research on Data Mining and Investment Recommendation of Individual Users Based on Financial Time Series Analysis. [IJDWM]. *International Journal of Data Warehousing and Mining, 16*(2), 64–80. doi:10.4018/IJDWM.2020040105

Wang, W., & Siau, K. (2019). Artificial Intelligence, Machine Learning, Automation, Robotics, Future of Work and Future of Humanity. [JDM]. *Journal of Database Management, 30*(1), 61–79. doi:10.4018/JDM.2019010104

Wang, Z., Yang, J., Guo, B., & Cheng, X. (2019). Security Model of Internet of Things Based on Binary Wavelet and Sparse Neural Network. [IJMCMC]. *International Journal of Mobile Computing and Multimedia Communications, 10*(1), 1–17. doi:10.4018/IJMCMC.2019010101

Wasif, M., Waheed, H., Aljohani, N. R., & Hassan, S. (2019). Understanding Student Learning Behavior and Predicting Their Performance. In M. D. Lytras, N. Aljohani, L. Daniela, & A. Visvizi (Eds.), *Cognitive Computing in Technology-Enhanced Learning* (pp. 1–28). IGI Global., doi:10.4018/978-1-5225-9031-6.ch001

Weiand, A., Manssour, I. H., & Silveira, M. S. (2019). Visual Analysis for Monitoring Students in Distance Courses. [IJDET]. *International Journal of Distance Education Technologies, 17*(2), 18–44. doi:10.4018/IJDET.2019040102

Wickramasinghe, N. (2020). Trying to Predict in Real Time the Risk of Unplanned Hospital Readmissions. In N. Wickramasinghe (Ed.), *Handbook of Research on Optimizing Healthcare Management Techniques* (pp. 299–310). IGI Global., doi:10.4018/978-1-7998-1371-2.ch022

Wong, M. L., & S., S. (2020). Development of Accurate and Timely Students' Performance Prediction Model Utilizing Heart Rate Data. In Gaur, L., Solanki, A., Jain, V., & Khazanchi, D. (Ed.), *Handbook of Research on Engineering Innovations and Technology Management in Organizations* (pp. 123-144). IGI Global. https://doi.org/ doi:10.4018/978-1-7998-2772-6.ch007

Related Readings

Wu, M., Lv, S., Zeng, C., Wang, Z., Zhao, N., Zhu, L., Wang, J., & Wu, M. (2020). A Hybrid Recommender Method Based on Multiple Dimension Attention Analysis. [IJMCMC]. *International Journal of Mobile Computing and Multimedia Communications*, *11*(1), 42–57. doi:10.4018/IJMCMC.2020010103

Xiang, M. (2020). Research on Quality Evaluation of Online Reservation Hotel APP Based on a RBF Neural Network and Support Vector Machine. [IJISSS]. *International Journal of Information Systems in the Service Sector*, *12*(2), 50–64. doi:10.4018/IJISSS.2020040104

Xu, C., Hu, X., Yang, A., Zhang, Y., Zhang, C., Xia, Y., & Cao, Y. (2020). Crime Hotspot Prediction Using Big Data in China. In P. Ordoñez de Pablos, X. Zhang, & K. Chui (Eds.), *Handbook of Research on Managerial Practices and Disruptive Innovation in Asia* (pp. 351–371). IGI Global., doi:10.4018/978-1-7998-0357-7.ch019

Yadav, D. C., & Pal, S. (2021). Analysis of Heart Disease Using Parallel and Sequential Ensemble Methods With Feature Selection Techniques. [IJBDAH]. *International Journal of Big Data and Analytics in Healthcare*, *6*(1), 40–56. doi:10.4018/IJBDAH.20210101.oa4

Yadav, N. S., Srinivasa, K. G., & Reddy, B. E. (2019). An IoT-Based Framework for Health Monitoring Systems. [IJFC]. *International Journal of Fog Computing*, *2*(1), 43–60. doi:10.4018/IJFC.2019010102

Yahya, M. R., Wu, N., & Ali, Z. A. (2020). Reliability and Security Challenges in Electrical/Optical On-Chip Interconnects for IoT Applications. In B. S. Chowdhry, F. K. Shaikh, & N. A. Mahoto (Eds.), *IoT Architectures, Models, and Platforms for Smart City Applications* (pp. 218–246). IGI Global., doi:10.4018/978-1-7998-1253-1.ch011

Yan, L., & Xiong, D. (2020). A Cloud Framework Design for A Disease Symptom Self-inspection Service. [IRMJ]. *Information Resources Management Journal*, *33*(2), 1–18. doi:10.4018/IRMJ.2020040101

Yan, Y. (2020). Software Aging Forecast Using Recurrent SOM with Local Model. [JITR]. *Journal of Information Technology Research*, *13*(1), 30–43. doi:10.4018/JITR.2020010103

Yang, J., Li, J., & Xu, Q. (2018). A Highly Efficient Big Data Mining Algorithm Based on Stock Market. [IJGHPC]. *International Journal of Grid and High Performance Computing*, *10*(2), 14–33. doi:10.4018/IJGHPC.2018040102

Yaokumah, W., & Wiafe, I. (2020). Analysis of Machine Learning Techniques for Anomaly-Based Intrusion Detection. [IJDAI]. *International Journal of Distributed Artificial Intelligence*, *12*(1), 20–38. doi:10.4018/IJDAI.2020010102

Yaokumah, W., Clottey, R. N., & Appati, J. K. (2021). Network Intrusion Detection in Internet of Things (IoT). [IJSST]. *International Journal of Smart Security Technologies*, *8*(1), 49–65. doi:10.4018/IJSST.2021010104

Yi, S., Mochitomi, K., Suzuki, I., Wang, X., & Yamasaki, T. (2020). Attention-Based Multimodal Neural Network for Automatic Evaluation of Press Conferences. [IJMDEM]. *International Journal of Multimedia Data Engineering and Management*, *11*(3), 1–19. doi:10.4018/IJMDEM.2020070101

Yu, C., Wang, S., & Guo, J. (2019). Learning Chinese Word Segmentation Based on Bidirectional GRU-CRF and CNN Network Model. [IJTHI]. *International Journal of Technology and Human Interaction*, *15*(3), 47–62. doi:10.4018/IJTHI.2019070104

Yucel, M., & Namlı, E. (2020). High Performance Concrete (HPC) Compressive Strength Prediction With Advanced Machine Learning Methods. In G. Bekdaş, S. M. Nigdeli, & M. Yücel (Eds.), *Artificial Intelligence and Machine Learning Applications in Civil, Mechanical, and Industrial Engineering* (pp. 118–140). IGI Global., doi:10.4018/978-1-7998-0301-0.ch007

Yue, T., & Zou, Y. (2019). Online Teaching System of Sports Training Based on Mobile Multimedia Communication Platform. [IJMCMC]. *International Journal of Mobile Computing and Multimedia Communications*, *10*(1), 32–48. doi:10.4018/IJMCMC.2019010103

Yumurtaci Aydogmus, H., & Turkan, Y. S. (2020). Application of Machine Learning Methods for Passenger Demand Prediction in Transfer Stations of Istanbul's Public Transportation System. In G. Bekdaş, S. M. Nigdeli, & M. Yücel (Eds.), *Artificial Intelligence and Machine Learning Applications in Civil, Mechanical, and Industrial Engineering* (pp. 196–216). IGI Global., doi:10.4018/978-1-7998-0301-0.ch011

Lu, Z., Xu, Q., Al-Rajab, M., & Chiazor, L. (2021). *An Overview on Bioinformatics*. IGI Global., doi:10.4018/978-1-7998-7316-7.ch002

Lu, Z., Xu, Q., Al-Rajab, M., & Chiazor, L. (2021). *Analysis, Discussion, and Evaluations for the Case Studies.* IGI Global., doi:10.4018/978-1-7998-7316-7.ch006

Lu, Z., Xu, Q., Al-Rajab, M., & Chiazor, L. (2021). *Design and Procedures for the Investigation Conducted.* IGI Global., doi:10.4018/978-1-7998-7316-7.ch004

Lu, Z., Xu, Q., Al-Rajab, M., & Chiazor, L. (2021). *Final Remarks for the Research With Advanced Machine Learning Methods in Colon Cancer Analysis.* IGI Global., doi:10.4018/978-1-7998-7316-7.ch007

Lu, Z., Xu, Q., Al-Rajab, M., & Chiazor, L. (2021). *Findings for the Conducted Investigations.* IGI Global., doi:10.4018/978-1-7998-7316-7.ch005

Lu, Z., Xu, Q., Al-Rajab, M., & Chiazor, L. (2021). *Importance of Information Working With Colon Cancer Research.* IGI Global., doi:10.4018/978-1-7998-7316-7.ch001

Lu, Z., Xu, Q., Al-Rajab, M., & Chiazor, L. (2021). *Methodology for the Research Conducted.* IGI Global., doi:10.4018/978-1-7998-7316-7.ch010

Lu, Z., Xu, Q., Al-Rajab, M., & Chiazor, L. (2021). *Overview of Big Data With Machine Learning Approach.* IGI Global., doi:10.4018/978-1-7998-7316-7.ch009

Lu, Z., Xu, Q., Al-Rajab, M., & Chiazor, L. (2021). *Research Approach With Machine Learning Underpinned.* IGI Global., doi:10.4018/978-1-7998-7316-7.ch003

Zafar, R., Zaib, S., & Asif, M. (2020). False Fire Alarm Detection Using Data Mining Techniques. [IJDSST]. *International Journal of Decision Support System Technology, 12*(4), 21–35. doi:10.4018/IJDSST.2020100102

Zagane, M., Abdi, M. K., & Alenezi, M. (2020). A New Approach to Locate Software Vulnerabilities Using Code Metrics. [IJSI]. *International Journal of Software Innovation, 8*(3), 82–95. doi:10.4018/IJSI.2020070106

Zermane, H., & Kasmi, R. (2020). Intelligent Industrial Process Control Based on Fuzzy Logic and Machine Learning. [IJFSA]. *International Journal of Fuzzy System Applications, 9*(1), 92–111. doi:10.4018/IJFSA.2020010104

Zerrouki, K., Hamou, R. M., & Rahmoun, A. (2020). Sentiment Analysis of Tweets Using Naïve Bayes, KNN, and Decision Tree. [IJOCI]. *International Journal of Organizational and Collective Intelligence*, *10*(4), 35–49. doi:10.4018/IJOCI.2020100103

Zgank, A., & Vlaj, D. (2021). Acoustic Presence Detection in a Smart Home Environment. In Khosrow-Pour D.B.A., M. (Ed.), Encyclopedia of Information Science and Technology, Fifth Edition (pp. 138-153). IGI Global. https://doi.org/ doi:10.4018/978-1-7998-3479-3.ch011

Zhai, W., Jiang, Y., & Ji, S. (2019). Research on the Application of Data Mining Algorithms in Intelligent Transportation. [IJAPUC]. *International Journal of Advanced Pervasive and Ubiquitous Computing*, *11*(2), 1–10. doi:10.4018/IJAPUC.2019040101

Zhang, K., Zhang, L., & Wu, Q. (2019). Identification of Cherry Leaf Disease Infected by Podosphaera Pannosa via Convolutional Neural Network. [IJAEIS]. *International Journal of Agricultural and Environmental Information Systems*, *10*(2), 98–110. doi:10.4018/IJAEIS.2019040105

Zhang, Y. (2020). Construction and Application of Regional Medical Information Sharing System Based on Big Data. [IJISMD]. *International Journal of Information System Modeling and Design*, *11*(3), 40–61. doi:10.4018/IJISMD.2020070103

Zhao, X., Jiang, Z., & Gray, J. (2020). Text Classification and Topic Modeling for Online Discussion Forums. In A. Fiori (Ed.), *Trends and Applications of Text Summarization Techniques* (pp. 151–186). IGI Global., doi:10.4018/978-1-5225-9373-7.ch006

About the Authors

Veljko Milutinović (1951) received his PhD from the University of Belgrade in Serbia, spent about a decade on various faculty positions in the USA (mostly at Purdue University and more recently at the University of Indiana in Bloomington), and was a co-designer of the DARPAs pioneering GaAs RISC microprocessor on 200MHz (about a decade before the first commercial effort on that same speed) and was a co-designer also of the related GaAs Systolic Array (with 4096 GaAs microprocessors). Later, for almost three decades, he taught and conducted research at the University of Belgrade in Serbia, for departments of EE, MATH, BA, and PHYS/CHEM. His research is mostly in data mining algorithms and dataflow computing, with the emphasis on mapping of data analytics algorithms onto fast energy efficient architectures. Most of his research was done in cooperation with industry (Intel, Fairchild, Honeywell, Maxeler, HP, IBM, NCR, RCA, etc.). For 20 of his edited books, publication forewords or other contributions were written by 20 different Nobel Laureates with whom he cooperated on his past industry sponsored projects. He published 40 books (mostly in the USA), he has over 100 papers in SCI journals (mostly in IEEE and ACM journals), and he presented invited talks at over 400 destinations worldwide. He has well over 1000 Thomson-Reuters WoS citations, well over 1000 Elsevier SCOPUS citations, and well over 5000 Google Scholar citations. His Google Scholar h index is equal to 40. He is a Life Fellow of the IEEE since 2003 and a Member of The Academy of Europe since 2011. He is a member of the Serbian National Academy of Engineering and a Foreign Member of the Montenegrin National Academy of Sciences and Arts.

Nenad Mitić is a full Professor at the Department of Computer Science, Faculty of Mathematics, University of Belgrade. He received his BSc, MSc and PhD from the University of Belgrade, Faculty of Mathematics. From 1983 to 1991 he was the system analyst on an IBM mainframe in Statistical Office of the Republic of Serbia, Belgrade. From 1991 till now he is with Faculty of Mathematics, Belgrade. His research interests cover areas of bioinformatics, data mining, big data, and functional programming.

Aleksandar Kartelj completed his PhD in Computer Science at Faculty of Mathematics in the year 2014. His research interests cover the areas of optimization, mathematical programming, and data mining. His publications are mostly related to metaheuristic optimization methods, data classification, and dimensionality reduction.

Miloš Kotlar received his B.Sc. (2016) and M.Sc. (2017) degrees in Electrical and Computer Engineering from the University of Belgrade, School of Electrical Engineering, Serbia. He is a Ph.D. candidate at the School of Electrical Engineering, University of Belgrade. His general research interests include implementation of energy efficient tensor implementations using the dataflow paradigm (FPGA and ASIC accelerators) and meta learning approaches for anomaly detection tasks.

Index

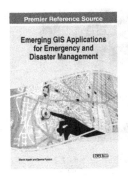

IGI Global Author Services

Providing a high-quality, affordable, and expeditious service, IGI Global's Author Services enable authors to streamline their publishing process, increase chance of acceptance, and adhere to IGI Global's publication standards.

Benefits of Author Services:

- **Professional Service:** All our editors, designers, and translators are experts in their field with years of experience and professional certifications.
- **Quality Guarantee & Certificate:** Each order is returned with a quality guarantee and certificate of professional completion.
- **Timeliness:** All editorial orders have a guaranteed return timeframe of 3-5 business days and translation orders are guaranteed in 7-10 business days.
- **Affordable Pricing:** IGI Global Author Services are competitively priced compared to other industry service providers.
- **APC Reimbursement:** IGI Global authors publishing Open Access (OA) will be able to deduct the cost of editing and other IGI Global author services from their OA APC publishing fee.

Author Services Offered:

English Language Copy Editing
Professional, native English language copy editors improve your manuscript's grammar, spelling, punctuation, terminology, semantics, consistency, flow, formatting, and more.

Scientific & Scholarly Editing
A Ph.D. level review for qualities such as originality and significance, interest to researchers, level of methodology and analysis, coverage of literature, organization, quality of writing, and strengths and weaknesses.

Figure, Table, Chart & Equation Conversions
Work with IGI Global's graphic designers before submission to enhance and design all figures and charts to IGI Global's specific standards for clarity.

Translation
Providing 70 language options, including Simplified and Traditional Chinese, Spanish, Arabic, German, French, and more.

Hear What the Experts Are Saying About IGI Global's Author Services

"Publishing with IGI Global has been *an amazing experience* for me for sharing my research. The *strong academic production* support ensures quality and timely completion." – **Prof. Margaret Niess, Oregon State University, USA**

"The service was *very fast, very thorough, and very helpful* in ensuring our chapter meets the criteria and requirements of the book's editors. I was *quite impressed and happy* with your service." – **Prof. Tom Brinthaupt, Middle Tennessee State University, USA**

Learn More or Get Started Here:

For Questions, Contact IGI Global's Customer Service Team at cust@igi-global.com or 717-533-8845

Celebrating **Over 30 Years** of Scholarly
Knowledge Creation & Dissemination

www.igi-global.com

InfoSci®-Books

A Database of Nearly 6,000 Reference Books Containing Over 105,000+ Chapters Focusing on Emerging Research

GAIN ACCESS TO **THOUSANDS** OF
REFERENCE BOOKS AT **A FRACTION**
OF THEIR INDIVIDUAL LIST **PRICE**.

InfoSci®-Books Database

The **InfoSci®-Books** is a database of
nearly 6,000 IGI Global single and multi-volume
reference books, handbooks of research, and
encyclopedias, encompassing groundbreaking
research from prominent experts worldwide that
spans over 350+ topics in 11 core subject areas
including business, computer science, education,
science and engineering, social sciences, and more.

Open Access Fee Waiver (Read & Publish) Initiative

For any library that invests in IGI Global's InfoSci-Books and/or
InfoSci-Journals (175+ scholarly journals) databases, IGI Global
will match the library's investment with a fund of equal value to
go toward **subsidizing the OA article processing charges
(APCs) for their students, faculty, and staff** at that institution
when their work is submitted and accepted under OA into an
IGI Global journal.*

INFOSCI® PLATFORM FEATURES

- Unlimited Simultaneous Access
- No DRM
- No Set-Up or Maintenance Fees
- A Guarantee of No More Than a 5%
  Annual Increase for Subscriptions
- Full-Text HTML and PDF
  Viewing Options
- Downloadable MARC Records
- COUNTER 5 Compliant Reports
- Formatted Citations With Ability to
  Export to RefWorks and EasyBib
- No Embargo of Content (Research is
  Available Months in Advance of the
  Print Release)

*The fund will be offered on an annual basis and expire at the end of
the subscription period. The fund would renew as the subscription is
renewed for each year thereafter. The open access fees will be waived
after the student, faculty, or staff's paper has been vetted and accepted
into an IGI Global journal and the fund can only be used toward
publishing OA in an IGI Global journal. Libraries in developing countries
will have the match on their investment doubled.

To Recommend or Request a Free Trial:
www.igi-global.com/infosci-books

eresources@igi-global.com • Toll Free: 1-866-342-6657 ext. 100 • Phone: 717-533-8845 x100

www.igi-global.com

Printed in the United States
by Baker & Taylor Publisher Services